The
Secret
YEARS

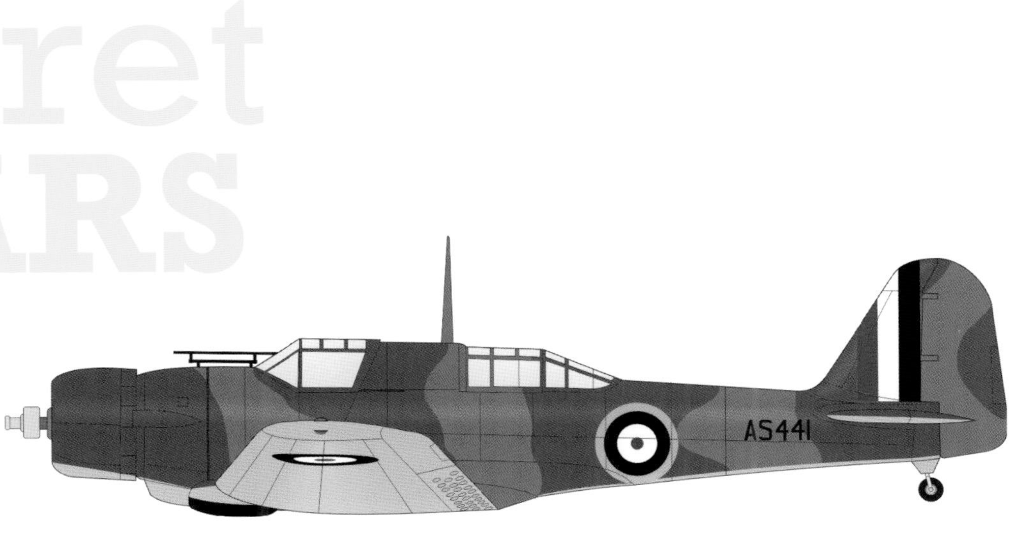

AS441

The Secret YEARS

Flight Testing at Boscombe Down 1935-1945

MX991

Tim Mason

First published in Great Britain in 1998 by
Hikoki Publications Ltd

Published in 2010 by Crécy Publishing Ltd

ISBN 9 781902 109145

Printed by Craft Print, Singapore

Crécy Publishing Limited
1a Ringway Trading Estate, Shadowmoss Rd,
Manchester M22 5LH
www.crecy.co.uk

Contents

This is a book about aeroplanes and their armament as tested at the Aeroplane & Armament Experimental Establishment at Boscombe Down, Wiltshire, during the Second World War. All land- and carrier-based aeroplanes intended for use by the Royal Navy, the Army and the Royal Air Force, plus a few experimental types, were flown. Had the Establishment not existed at the outbreak of war, it would have been necessary, sooner rather than later, to have created it to answer the question, 'Does this aeroplane and its armament meet Service requirements?' The Services, fully occupied in fighting the enemy, possessed neither the capacity nor the expertise to answer the question. That the Establishment already existed was of great benefit to the country's war effort from the early days of hostilities. That it was able to expand in size and scope as the demands on it grew is testament to the soundness of the concept of concentrating this vital testing in one place.

It is, perhaps, difficult in the 21st century, when every military aeroplane movement, modification and colour scheme is minutely observed and widely reported, to appreciate the completely different attitude held in 1939-45 by officials, servicemen and the public alike. Anything seen, heard or connected with work (and almost every activity contributed directly or indirectly to the country's war effort) was not discussed casually, and certainly not publicised. The catchphrase of 'Keeping Mum' was, at places working on the latest and most advanced weapons, very rigidly observed. The wartime period 1939-45 at Boscombe Down can, indeed, be described as 'The Secret Years'.

In the more than sixty years since the end of the war, the wartime work of the A&AEE has been frequently mentioned, usually in a limited and fragmentary way. In particular, some of the photographs taken there, both on the ground and in the air, have appeared in print, usually without attribution. The aim in this book has been to describe as comprehensively as space permits its function and achievements, and to use the Establishment's photographs for illustration. The sources used are documents at Boscombe Down, the Public Record Office and some at Farnborough. I have also drawn on the research of Rod Smith, Derek Collier Webb and the archive created by Terry Heffernan. Photographs have come from many sources, notably Boscombe Down, including outstanding prints from the small number of surviving original glass negatives. That other prints have survived is due to the efforts of a few knowledgeable individuals who have, without exception, made their invaluable collections freely available to me.

I therefore gratefully acknowledge the help of the following individuals: Chris Ashworth, Mike Bowyer, Derek Collier Webb, Sharon Evans, Peter Green, Jim Halley, Terry Heffernan, Philip Jarrett, David Langhurst, Maureen Lever, Frank Mason, Dudley O'Niell, Norman Parker, Bruce Robertson, John Sharp, Rod Smith, Ray Sturtivant, Gordon Swanborough and Wason Turner.

I would also like to offer special thanks to Sherri Carnson and her staff at the Information Centre, Boscombe Down, and the many people with wartime experience of Boscombe Down who have supplied anecdotes, and more significant background information, without which this book would have been the poorer. I am particularly grateful to Sir John Allison for the generous Foreword, and to Clare Wood, who valiantly overcame my inability to master a PC.

by Air Chief Marshal Sir John Allison
KCB CBE FRAeS

The achievements over many decades of the Royal Air Force, the Fleet Air Arm and the Army Air Corps have been due not least to the capabilities of the aircraft flown in many roles, in all parts of the world, in peace and in war. That the aircraft, some outstanding, others less successful, were in a fit state for their intended use by the Services was largely a result of the searching tests and evaluation of their capabilities by the Aeroplane & Armament Experimental Establishment, to which all land- and carrier-borne aircraft were sent. The Establishment, moving to Boscombe Down at the outbreak of war in September 1939, experienced the most intense and active six years of its existence, growing to a total of more than 2,400 servicemen, servicewomen and civilians, with frequently more than 140 aeroplanes. This book tells the story of those stirring times, and of the contribution made to the war effort of this country.

Looking back over more than half a century, the author gives us a clear insight into events at Boscombe Down in the period 1939-45. While contrasting the scale and pace of wartime activities with those of today, I am nevertheless struck by some of the similarities. Aircraft testing for the British armed forces continues there with a capable and enthusiastic team of scientific, technical, administrative and flying people, while today's air staffs continue to experience frustrations when trials seem to take an undue time – just as our predecessors did in wartime days. In choosing to describe in the first part of the book the organisation, flight and armament testing methods and personalities, the author has been able to devote the considerably longer second part to the aeroplanes and the tests made on them. Every one of 1,500 aeroplanes is covered in varying detail – some inevitably only briefly mentioned. The hundreds of photographs and colour drawings, however, are an enthusiast's delight, and add immensely to the value of the text. The illustrations and their captions contain a wealth of additional information, including matters as diverse as gun turrets, static vents and flame damping.

The Royal Navy, the Army and the Royal Air Force were well served by the A&AEE during the Second World War – the Establishment is now well served by this work. It is a fascinating story and I have no doubt that readers will appreciate the fruits of the author's research – his interpretation of events enhanced by considerable personal experience of test flying. I am delighted to write this Foreword, and to commend the book to all with an interest in the subject, whether student of aeronautical history, enthusiast or modeller.

Foreword to second edition

I am very pleased to add these few words as a Foreword to the second edition of The Secret Years. The book and particularly its photographs continue to be a delight both to me and to those who possess a copy of the first edition. Its success is reflected in the high prices that second hand copies command, and also in the publisher's decision for another edition. With several new photographs and enhancement of many of the originals in a new layout, I commend this new work.

Sir John Allison

Part I

The place, tests and people

This first part comprises four chapters, and sets the scene for the tests on individual aircraft in the second part. The physical characteristics of Royal Air Force Boscombe Down, and changes made to accommodate the Aeroplane and Armament Experimental Establishment are described.

The pre-war role remained that of testing aircraft for Service use and some armament development work was later added. The external and internal organisations are noted, together with outlines of the procedures for testing the myriad of new aircraft, modifications and armament and many of the people involved, their roles and achievements, receive mention.

Flying, frequently to the limits of performance, was the stock-in-trade of the Establishment. Great efforts were made to minimise the inherent risks – always present by the very nature of the tasks. Nevertheless, accidents occurred and lives lost (see Appendix 2), but the sacrifices were made in the cause of ensuring that the Services received aircraft that were fit for their intended roles.

Performance encompassed all non-armament testing, and thus included handling, performance and, at first, equipment such as radios, navigation aids and photography. Later, separate divisions were created as the work grew.

Armament in the Establishment's title involved initially guns, both fixed and free, and bombs – each having its own section; a rocket projectile section was added later, together with another for research. Many of the problems, including loading, fusing, sighting, dropping and firing were identified and subsequently remedied by the Establishment's armament staff who became acknowledged experts from their extensive experience.

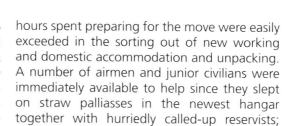

1 The Establishment

The move to Wiltshire

With the outbreak of war, the Aeroplane & Armament Experimental Establishment moved from its peacetime home in Suffolk and returned very near to its birthplace at Upavon on the Wiltshire Downs. Writing in 1912 (just two years before the testing Flight was formed) on a visit by gentlemen of the press to Upavon, C. G. Grey of *The Aeroplane* said, 'It has been located on the top of a mountain, where it is open to every wind that blows.'

Had he written about Boscombe Down, the Establishment's new home, in 1939, he may well have used very similar language. To those officers, airmen and civilians struggling from Martlesham Heath, the early description of Upavon well summarised their 1939 impressions of their new home. In spite of the proximity of the fleshpots of Amesbury (population 2,488) and a few substantial hangars and mess buildings, Boscombe Down had an ample grass airfield but just sufficient domestic and working accommodation; there was no shortage of fresh air. For the early arrivals, the situation was aggravated by the presence of the previous residents, two Fairey Battle Squadrons, which finally left for France on 11 September 1939.

The main group of fifty-one A&AEE aircraft arrived on 3 September, a second group (nineteen) the following day, and the remainder on 7 September; aircraft totals are quoted from the Operations Record Book, but include a number that made return flights. The exact total of individual aircraft has not been determined, but was about fifty-two. This number could well have been lower, had the local Army units been more accurate when they opened fire as the first 'gaggle' approached Boscombe Down. The main groups of people, service and civilian, together with all the movable paraphernalia of an aircraft testing establishment, came by road and rail on 8 and 14 September. The long

hours spent preparing for the move were easily exceeded in the sorting out of new working and domestic accommodation and unpacking. A number of airmen and junior civilians were immediately available to help since they slept on straw palliasses in the newest hangar together with hurriedly called-up reservists; there was no better facility available.

Group Captain B. McEntegart, the Commanding Officer (see Appendix 1), declared the Establishment open at Boscombe Down on 20 September 1939. E. T. Jones was the Chief Technical Officer – an appointment he held throughout the war, although its title changed – while F. Rowarth continued as Chief Engineer.

Wing Commander C. L. N. Bilney deputised for the Commanding Officer and led the armament side, with gunnery and bombing flights each with its specialist RAF officers, aircrew, groundcrew and aeroplanes. Squadron Leader J. F. X. McKenna combined the duties of Officer Commanding Performance Testing Squadron with those of commanding A Flight (fighters). B Flight (large aircraft) and C Flight (twins) completed Performance Squadron, whose trials were managed by the civilian staff in the Technical Office. Thus the pre-war organisation of the A&AEE was recreated at Boscombe Down in September 1939, while the close and harmonious working relations with the aircraft industry continued and, indeed, intensified. Of particular benefit was the presence throughout the war of companies' representatives from engine and airframe makers. For example, Messrs Geoff Mould and 'Dicky' Bird from Rolls Royce are remembered, as is Mr Roy Barratt of Bristol engines.

The Establishment also continued initially to report to, and make recommendations to, the same pre-war Directorates in the Air Ministry – Technical Development (DTD), Armament Development (D Arm D) and, to a lesser extent, Scientific Research (DSR), all under the Air

Member for Development and Production (AMDP). Service administration, at first continuing the pre-war association with No 24 Group in Training Command, was transferred in July 1940 to No 23 Group in the recently formed Flying Training Command.

Even when order and routine were established at Boscombe Down, business was not, for some months, as usual, due largely to the lack of ranges for weapons. In addition, the impetus of war led inexorably to organisation changes and additional burdens, particularly on accommodation and domestic arrangements.

Airfield and buildings

The pre-war airfield sloped down from 420 feet above sea level in the north-west corner to 360 feet in the south-east. It was downland, ie short grass on chalk with some rough and uneven patches. It remained virtually unchanged until 1944. Take-offs and landings could be made in any direction, with the longest run of 1,800 yards in a NW/SE direction. A light south-easterly wind could prove a bit embarrassing on landing if the speed was just a little high, as floating down the hill resulted in touch-down about halfway along the available run. Of more concern to a testing establishment was the effect on take-off, and to a lesser extent on landing, and the means of allowing for the slope on distance calculations. Partially for this reason, take-offs and landings were measured whenever possible by taking the more level run in a

Boscombe Down, looking from just south of east in 1943, showing the C Per T and (bottom right) B Arm T dispersals. The neat rows of 1918-vintage hangars are spoiled by the crop of haphazardly placed Second World War temporary buildings. More than thirty aeroplanes are visible including, apparently, a visiting Hamilcar glider.

south-westerly (or north-easterly) direction: the recording camera was mounted at a convenient point on the airfield. The aerodrome surface became rutted and uneven, and was responsible for several broken aeroplanes. The prototype Halifax lost its tail wheel in December 1940; two months later the aft fuselage of the first Mosquito broke when its tail wheel jammed in a rut, and the nose wheel structure of the first Liberator collapsed following a shimmy in May 1941. Another prototype, of the Typhoon, was extensively damaged on swinging into the concrete compass swinging base the following July. 1941's catalogue of damage continued in October when a Spitfire's undercarriage was carried away after hitting an airfield lighting post. Other breakages continued, and attempts were made to smooth out the ruts, but increasingly heavy aeroplanes took their toll of the surface, particularly in wet weather. The CO, Air Commodore Mansell, commenting on damage to one prototype, said, a trifle facetiously, that an uneven surface posed a further test of new aircraft, and was thus not entirely to be deprecated. Even OC Performance Testing Squadron, Wing Commander Purvis, was not immune; in July 1942 a ridge broke the tail wheel bolts on a Blenheim he was flying when landing in darkness. Renewed efforts swiftly followed to remove major ruts. The new concrete runway (see below) was a mixed blessing after its completion in early 1945. Access was only possible at one point via steel mesh, and this area became worn, rough and boggy in wet weather – aggravated by the extra water draining off the concrete.

The unimproved state of the grass airfield throughout the war is a puzzle in view of the nature and intensity of flying there, particularly considering the effort that went into constructing hard runways at hundreds of other sites throughout the country. One practical but inconvenient effect was the need to make take-off and landing measurements of heavy and/or large aircraft from nearby Thruxton or Ibsley, or distant Hartfordbridge Flats (Blackbushe) and later Farnborough. The need to lug the bulky camera to a new site each time measurements were to be made was unwelcome.

In one respect at least, Boscombe's airfield led the way – it was the first of eight Regional Control Centres (or Flying Control) set up in 1938 by Bomber Command. The first officer was Flight Lieutenant F. T. K. Bullimore (a CC class reservist and soon promoted to Squadron Leader), who spent three years at Boscombe. He was joined by three 'controllers' who maintained continuous watch from early in the war, together with a few assistants (known as recorders). Early equipment included a single HF radio with manual direction-finding equipment, a large map and details of weather from around the country. The airfield was equipped with night landing lights (Mk II layout) and a Lorenz equipment for airfield approaches through cloud. The exact date of installation has not been determined, but was probably in late 1939 (and thus the first in the country), as it is improbable that the Blind Approach Training & Development Unit (formed at Boscombe in September 1939) would have been based at an airfield without the necessary equipment. These new aids, designed for bomber operations, were of marginal use to the A&AEE, whose work was very largely conducted in daylight and good weather, frequently without the benefit of radio throughout the wartime period. The facilities were not wasted, however, as 850 bombers returning from night operations made a safe landing at Boscombe, often in marginal weather. No doubt surrounds the date of installation of Lorenz's development, the Standard Beam Approach (SBA) equipment; it was complete and ready for test in June 1945.

In 1940, two developments instigated by Bullimore (nicknamed 'Death' from his pale appearance) were the installation of a tie-line from the Observer Corps at Winchester and the excavation of an underground operations room, equipped with duplicate telephone exchange and airfield lighting controls. Bullimore was apparently fond of his underground creation, and was often to be found there whether or not an air raid was in prospect. At the end of 1940 work started above ground, at the western end of the line of hangars, on a new Flying Control building with extensive views over the airfield and extending to Salisbury Cathedral.

At the outbreak of war there was a line of five hangars (four dating from 1917/18 and the fifth from 1929/30), and, behind the easternmost of these, a recently completed sixth. The only hardstandings for aircraft were between and immediately in front of the hangars. Other permanent structures were several technical buildings, three messes (officers', sergeants' and airmen's), some barrack blocks and married quarters, and an extensive series of bomb stores; most were completed in 1929/30. At the end of the war in 1945, the only permanent additions were the Flying Control building, the large stop butts, the blower tunnel and the new runway; a civilian canteen was nearly complete. There were by the latter date some aircraft blister hangars, and a myriad of wooden and prefabricated huts on both the domestic and airfield sites. In addition, minor improvements were made to roads and other surfaces, in particular two spectacle-type dispersals (BRC surface) for fourteen aircraft on the southern side of the airfield. The extent of capital expenditure at Boscombe Down may he gauged from the sum of £43,160 approved by the Treasury for the two years to September 1943; this amount would have been spent largely on the control building and the stop butts. By comparison, the RAE (Farnborough and outstations) had approval for £1,147,000 over the same period. Once the case for a blower tunnel for flame-damping tests (see below) had been agreed in early 1943, the sum of £26,000 was earmarked. By the time the first trials began in June 1944 the cost had risen to more than £44,000; Messrs Sir William Arroll was the prime contractor. Four Merlin engines were used initially and repaired after a fire in September 1944, and the tunnel has continued in use to the present day. A 'one-off' trial of the V-1 rocket motor in the tunnel in 1944/5 rendered speech inaudible in nearby dispersals.

The most striking change to the physical appearance of Boscombe Down airfield by the end of the war was the completion of the main runway. By 1942 the continued operation of the latest aeroplanes from grass surfaces was becoming intolerable – not only on account of the damage being caused to aircraft, but

Boscombe Down in May 1943, looking just west of north with the hangars and other buildings on the far side and the railway to Amesbury curving out of sight.

because take-offs were becoming hazardous as weights of the larger machines increased. Verbal representations to the Ministry were followed by a formal approach in February 1943 for approval of an extension to the airfield and the provision of runways. In his letter of May 1943 the new CO, Air Commodore D. D'A. A. Greig, reiterated the case made by his predecessor, Air Commodore Mansell. He said that the A&AEE needed an airfield of adequate size capable of extension, near the 'centre of gravity' of the aircraft industry, should have grass (and concrete) runways, near weapons ranges, and have good weather. Boscombe Down met these considerations, except that it was too small. The letter then suggested where extensions to the airfield could be made, based on his recent investigation.

Prior to putting pen to paper, Air Commodore Greig with E. T. Jones had flown several times together around the local area with large-scale maps looking for a suitable line to lay a runway, but to no avail. D'Arcy Greig then decided to reconnoitre on foot; by striding through a wood (Porton Firs) and crossing a public road, he found a line (SW/NE) about 4,000 yards long and reasonably level. With the question of alignment of a long runway resolved, wartime procedures soon

had contractors on site, and in January 1944 work started on cutting down part of the wood, closing the road and laying the runway. The length was initially 2,500 yards, starting just inside the existing airfield, but in such a way that flying could continue uninterrupted during construction. A railway spur from the Amesbury branch line was laid for bringing in materials and plant. In June a USAAF Liberator landed from operations at night on the incomplete runway, with ensuing damage but without injury to the crew. The runway 24/06, in solitary splendour without taxiways, was first used in early 1945.

The need for a proper civilian mess (only the few civilians of 'officer status' used the RAF Officers' Mess) was a long-standing requirement for those requiring feeding, particularly at midday. By the end of 1943 the inadequate facilities and increasing numbers led to agreement being reached for a new properly equipped building; completion, however, was delayed from the intended date of November 1944 until April 1945, due largely to the difficulty of the contractor in recruiting manpower. The new mess was a first step in alleviating conditions, described as a slum, in the lower camp where junior staff were accommodated.

Wooden huts, probably tucked away on the south side of the airfield, illustrate the improvised nature of much wartime accommodation.

Accommodation

Working and domestic accommodation was at a premium from the first days of the Establishment at Boscombe Down; the total number of people working there grew from under 700 in 1939 to well over 2,000 in 1944/45. For domestic accommodation, civilian staff were expected to make their own arrangements, and the publicans and hotel-owners in Amesbury and Salisbury enjoyed good business at first. Billeting with local landladies and resident families gradually expanded, and two houses were requisitioned in Salisbury in 1943 for the growing number of young technical staff. Not until after the war was Ministry permanent housing for married staff built at Pauls Dene in Salisbury. The temporary huts built for offices, workshops and flight huts to supplement the permanent buildings were always crowded, muddy in wet weather, and alternatively freezing or boiling depending on the state of the inevitable coal-burning, smoking stove. Living conditions were equally unappealing for those not fortunate enough to occupy pre-war buildings; huts sprouted up as annexes to all three Service messes.

The compensations included the relative security of being 'away from the war', with decreasing risk of enemy bombing and, above all, the satisfaction of challenging, interesting and worthwhile work on the newest aircraft and weapons.

The impression gained some fifty years after the event is that the sense of common purpose coupled with the importance of individuals' contributions led to a well-defined but intangible esprit de corps; poor living and working conditions were a small price to pay, and shared by all. Cramped accommodation (both domestic and working) could, however, when added to wartime shortages of such desiderata as paper, furniture and scientific equipment, adversely affect working performance. Commenting in 1945 after visiting the extensive facilities in Germany, Wing Commander Garland (the senior Gunnery Technical Officer), who had shared his room in the Officers' Mess with two others, said, 'Even at the end of the war, in shared offices and in their own rooms, trials officers had to provide their own instruments and equipment. CRT [Cathode Ray Tubes] were few and used only in dry weather...'

If living conditions in the Officers' Mess were cramped, lunch times could be extremely cosy, the small bar was totally inadequate, and the corridor became the de facto watering hole – known as the 'wind tunnel' from the continual opening of doors. A link with more formal times was provided by the Mess Manager, Mr Noble, who was always immaculate in tails and ginger wig.

The Ranges

In September 1939 Wing Commander C. L. N. Bilney set about the task of finding areas suitable for air firing and bombing. Initially, the only bombing facilities were at nearby Porton and Larkhill; neither was under the control of the A&AEE and could be used only when available, and then with the agreement of the Chemical Defence Experimental Station or Army respectively. Even then, their usefulness for bombing development was minimal as only practice bombs could be dropped. These tribulations were somewhat eased when it was agreed that larger, but inert, bombs could be dropped at Porton from less than 14,000 feet, and much trials work was then done on the functioning of fuses and pistols and the penetration of larger bombs against the 300-foot-diameter and 18-inch-thick concrete apron, and two 12-inch-thick walls on the apron also proved useful. Apart from minor improvements such as telephone tie-lines, Porton range, and its restrictions, remained unchanged throughout the war.

Before the end of 1939 the A&AEE had its own bombing range at Crichel Down, 5 miles north-east of Blandford; about 1,800 yards in diameter, it eventually had two bombing targets (high and low level) and a gunnery target. The former were limited to bombs up to 1,000lb in weight from heights up to 14,000 feet (6,000 feet for live weapons), and the latter to a run-in on a southerly heading, and firing over the main Salisbury road. Also by the end of 1939, the Establishment started using Lyme Bay off the south coast for air firing trials, some live bombing and, later, rocket firing in an area approximately 12 miles long extending to 6 miles from the coast. The main limitation was its distance from Boscombe, involving more than half-an-hour's flying by slower aircraft; otherwise, provided firing took place at a distance greater than 1 mile from the coast, there were no limitations once the sea had been observed to be clear of ships.

Thus by early 1940 the weapons facilities so fundamental to an armament testing organisation were, at least partially, functioning, and another was in the process of opening at Ashley Walk in the New Forest. The achievement of the use of the new ranges was in very large measure due to the drive and initiative of Wing Commander Bilney, who, in addition, had to maintain an effective armament testing section in trying circumstances. He was also responsible for the start of the aircraft stop butts when he acquired a bulldozer, scooped out chalk and started what later became formidable earthworks. He chose a site to suit the conditions of 1940; seventy years later the butts remain in use. The hectic work had its lighter moments. The first live 1,000lb high-explosive bombs were tested shortly after Crichel Down was opened, and an unknown underground stream ran from the target to a boys' school. Halfway through the trial a perspiring and panting schoolmaster arrived on a bicycle, beseeching Bilney to stop at once, as shock waves were travelling along the stream and shaking the chandeliers over the boys' heads. The schoolmaster was advised to move the boys' desks. A few months later a test was to be made of a device (using magnesium) for setting fire to forests, and a suitable wood was found on Larkhill range.

The local General was horrified, saying, 'You can't do that, my boy – known that wood all my life – full of hares.' The trial nevertheless took place, although the wood remained intact and the hares undisturbed when the incendiary devices failed to perform.

Wing Commander Bilney was awarded the OBE in July 1940 and left the following December, but not before the opening of the large range at Ashley Walk near Fordingbridge in the New Forest following the patriotic agreement of the Verderers. Controlled by the A&AEE, it occupied an area 3½ miles by 1½ miles and ultimately contained ten targets plus other facilities; it was soon completely enclosed in a 6-foot-high fence, 10 miles long. Heather throughout the range led to a ban on incendiary weapons, and the maximum dropping height was 20,000 feet. Inevitably, with live bombs, fires occurred – that on 21 June 1942 caused serious injuries to two airmen, and burned out a lorry, while 100 acres burned out in March 1945 before the blaze was under control. With the advent of rocket projectiles, a further range was dedicated to this weapon at Enford on Salisbury Plain; the Army authorised its use daily. Crichel Down and Ashley Walk had a small party of servicemen under a senior NCO, Sgt Percy Hockey, a local man, who ran Ashley Walk for a lengthy period, and, no doubt, was able to forestall complaints about noise.

By early 1940 there was a marine craft section at Lyme Bay based at Lyme Regis for warning fishermen and the Royal Navy of impending lethal precipitation; sea rescue was also the boat's responsibility. By 1945, the land ranges had extensive instrumentation, including theodolites, high-speed cameras, and electronic radio and photo-electric recorders, the last three in a mobile laboratory. From these, the bomb trajectory, height of burst, operation of fuses, arming time and other parameters could be determined. Sometimes the most telling analysis followed painstaking recovery of the weapon from its point of impact, frequently buried deep in soil. Perhaps more important, and even more tedious, was the removal of remaining debris from previous trials to obviate possible confusion. Debris removal was particularly important at the two downland ranges at Porton and Crichel. A caterpillar tractor was developed with magnetic arms to assist in this task, and similar tractors later proved useful on the continent.

Ashley Walk bombing range in early 1945 provides a scene reminiscent of the Western Front in 1918. The crater in the centre was made by a live 22,000lb 'Grand Slam' bomb. The concrete structure was one of many reproductions of potential targets, in this case submarine pens. In 1997 the pens were covered with soil and undergrowth.

The comprehensive armament facilities at the end of the war underline the difficulties the Establishment experienced at first by their absence near Boscombe Down. Indeed, early in 1940 such was the concern at the limitations imposed by inadequacy of ranges that serious consideration was given to the removal of both gunnery and bombing trials to Exeter and West Freugh respectively. In the event, part of A Flight of the Armament Testing Squadron (gunnery) completed the move in June 1940. B Flight (bombing) did not move, although an RAE target building and airfield at West Freugh were used for some A&AEE bombing trials until August 1941; the Bombing Development Unit of the RAE was established there in mid-1942. The growth of gun testing at the A&AEE led to the examination of a firing area nearer to base than Lyme Bay and less prone to bad weather and interference by ships. On 22 September 1941 the Secretary for State for Air approved firing in an area just to the West of Boscombe Down, some 126 square miles in area and bounded by Wilton, Gillingham and Warminster. The population living there, some 14,400 souls, was considered to be at very slight risk, provided that

The somewhat modified caterpillar tractor with electro-magnets for picking up metal (mostly bomb fragments). Electric power was supplied by the second engine seen at the rear.

firing below 10,000 feet was made upwards; there were no restrictions above that height. Use of this area for turret firing appears to have been infrequent – possibly as the result of a spent bullet hitting a Lieutenant and causing a wound in his backside, the highest part of his anatomy as befitted an army officer face down in the weeds. Flying Officer A. J. (Al) Smitz had been testing a Stirling turret at the time.

Role

So much for the physical attributes of Boscombe Down in 1939-45. Although the work of the Establishment expanded in both scope and volume during the period, its role remained that of testing aeroplanes and their armament intended for use by the Services. The A&AEE was one of an increasing number of establishments concerned with aeronautical development and acceptance.[1] Among tasks not strictly within the A&AEE's terms of reference were the flying of some experimental aeroplanes for opinions on flying qualities, and the development of armaments. The distinction between testing for Service on the one hand, and research and development on the other, was usually reasonably clear, with the A&AEE involved at first only in the former. An example of the need to separate the two functions occurred in 1940 with the decision to form a unit for gun mounting work; originally intended for the A&AEE, the Unit was formed at Duxford, as its task was of a development nature. Later, this decision was reversed when the Aircraft Gun Mounting Establishment (AGME) was absorbed into the A&AEE. In January 1942, when the AGME arrived, the armament side of the Establishment possessed unique facilities, experience and expertise, well suited to the identification of problems and their resolution. Thus air armament development became an additional but intimately related role.

[1] In 1941 the others in MAP were the Marine Aircraft Experimental Establishment, Torpedo Development Unit, Royal Aircraft Establishment, Balloon Development Establishment, Aircraft Gun Mounting Establishment, Special Duty Flight (at Christchurch) and the Gunnery Research Unit. Later the Telecommunications Research Establishment and the Airborne Forces Experimental Establishment were added.

Higher Formation

The creation of the Ministry of Aircraft Production (MAP) by an Order-in-Council of 20 May 1940 gave the A&AEE a new master, but little changed as the directing departments and their staff remained, initially, the same on transfer from the Air Ministry. Thereafter during the war, MAP directed the activities at Boscombe Down, and by 1944 the principal agencies were the Director of Technical Development and the Director of Armament Development, together accounting equally for 75% of the effort; the Controller of Navigation and Radio, Deputy Director of Instruments (R&D), the Director of Scientific Research, and the Director of Communications Development together accounted for 20%, with the remaining 5% for communications and the Director of Equipment Development. This remarkably stable management structure paid dividends for the A&AEE in the close working relationships with 'Headquarters', as MAP became known, and the understanding there of the strengths and limitations of the Establishment.

Two surviving letters throw interesting light on the relationship between Headquarters (ie MAP) and the A&AEE. The first concerns stalling. Before the war, a series of Aircraft Design Memoranda (ADM) were produced for the guidance of the 'trade' and the Establishments. Although AMDs were subsumed in one document, AP970 (under the aegis of the Joint Airworthiness Committee set up in February 1940), stalling was frequently referred to as 'ADM293 Tests'. In discussion with the MAP, the Establishment said that it was obliged to include stalling tests precisely as laid down in 'ADM293'. The MAP replied that this was not so, and that the Establishment could make any tests it required. This was a significant departure from pre-war practice. The second example concerned the need for a Halifax to undertake urgent performance trials. The Headquarters Directorate involved suggested a particular airframe, which happened to be at the A&AEE but undergoing armament trials. Mr R. K. Cushing (the Senior Performance Technical Officer) wrote, '…arrangements will need to be made with D Arm D [of MAP] for the aircraft to be transferred to our Performance Squadron for this work.' While deferring to its master in the matter of the aircraft used, the A&AEE had complete control over the conduct of tests – even the pre-war series of Instructions to Establishments ceased, apparently after the last issued in late 1939.

Relations with the Royal Air Force

The MAP existed to provide for the airborne needs of the British Services. An early examination of the Establishment's wartime role was made by the RAF Inspector General, Air Marshal Sir Charles Burnett, following a visit on 31 October 1939. One telling phrase in his report was quoted during the resultant staff consideration: 'It is not perhaps generally appreciated that A&AEE is specifically designed to carry out systematic trials to cover the full scope of Service use in a minimum of time.' It was apparent that the Establishment's work became ever more vital, but, most significantly, that understanding was not complete in the RAF at large of the work done there. (It could equally have been said forty years later.) The Commander-in-Chief, Fighter Command (Air Marshal Dowding), did not rate test establishments highly; in September 1939 he wanted all 'his', ie Hurricane and Spitfire aircraft, saying, 'Comb out the back areas to the West'. A review of all R&D aircraft was instituted, and Dowding got one Spitfire and two Hurricanes from the A&AEE. Early in 1940 another cull of the 323 aircraft on the AMDP's charge resulted in 146 (of which twenty were from the A&AEE) being released – including an ancient Vickers Virginia, to terrify the Panzers, no doubt – by the end of May 1940. The disparity in the opinions of the Inspector General and a Commander-in-Chief is reflected in many surviving papers from the wartime period, with the air staffs and RAF commanders continually pressing for early results and calling into question those already to hand. Of the latter, examples are the Services' need for more handling information on the monoplanes and the experience of disappointing early performance of the four-engined bombers. These and other apparent shortcomings in information emanating from the A&AEE were remedied, but there was undoubtedly a deep-seated suspicion, particularly in the RAF, that the A&AEE's work was unnecessarily lengthy and not entirely relevant to the 'customer'. On the other hand, the Director of Operational Requirements in the Air Ministry expressed himself in 1942 as entirely satisfied with the information he received from the Establishment.

Release to Service

From May 1940 the clearance of aircraft and related equipment for Service use (later formalised as the Release to Service) was the responsibility of the Ministry of Aircraft Production on the advice of the Establishments. The system came under strain particularly with large-scale deliveries from the United States, and in 1941 a reminder was circulated to all branches within the Air Ministry: 'No new type or new mark of aircraft is to be delivered [to the RAF or RN] until released by (MAP).' With the advent of Lend-Lease, combined with more thorough testing in the USA, the MAP was persuaded to release some aircraft on evidence from America – aircraft such as the Thunderbolt, which went into RAF service in the Far East before even the limited A&AEE trials were complete. Indeed, by the end of the war most late marks of the Liberator (see Part II) were released to Service on the basis of the minor nature of changes to earlier versions. With the exception of some American types, the A&AEE remained the predominant centre for flight testing all land- and carrier-borne aeroplanes intended for Service use.

Organisation

From September 1939, when the pre-war organisation at Martlesham Heath was transposed to Boscombe Down, the growth of the Establishment was continuous, with the exception of the period in early 1940 when several aircraft were recalled to RAF Service, and one armament flight was disbanded. The growth is attributable to several causes, namely the large number of new types of aeroplane, the increasing complexity, capability and performance of most of them, and the special needs arising from wartime mass-production. The days of the competitions and of selecting the best aeroplane had long gone by 1939. A pervasive feature of the work at Boscombe Down arose from the fundamental change to the wartime policy of ordering aircraft in large numbers before testing was complete, or, in many cases, had even begun. The effect of this policy had been seen before the war, during the expansion period of the RAF when effort was concentrated on those features, eg gun turrets, that most needed testing.

It was soon apparent that a damning report by Boscombe requiring action to improve matters would mean that either the production line stopped or unsatisfactory aeroplanes were produced to be modified later. It was no part of the Establishment's remit to recommend how a deficiency was to be rectified; suggestions for improvements were, however, made both formally and informally. In drawing conclusions from tests, reports were clear as to exactly what a fault was; the ensuing recommendations in many cases were a compromise between the best solution and the most expedient for rapid incorporation. There is little existing evidence, documentary or anecdotal, of serious dissent within the Establishment to this pragmatic approach, and staff, service and civilian, were well aware of the effect on production, and thus the Services' capabilities, of an ill-considered recommendation. The Cabinet Office history notes: '…there was very little margin for vagueness and dispute … A&AEE [had a] clear and definite function.'

Two photographs illustrating the A&AEE's work for Porton: the detail shows a liquid/powder container being attached to a carrier for installation in a Wellington's bomb bay outside Boscombe's hangar, while the Wellington Mk I (possibly L4289) has its spray nozzle extended from the bomb bay.

Internal Organisation

The pre-war organisation (A, B and C Flights of Performance Testing Squadron and Gunnery (A) and Bombing (B) Flights of Armament Testing Squadron) was changed only to the extent of incorporating the Special Duty Flight of the Chemical Defence Experimental Station at nearby Porton. In the first month at Boscombe Down a bomber squadron was attached, and the Training Unit for beam approach flying formed; these and later visiting and lodger units are listed in Appendix 8.

After protracted correspondence, the Special Duty Flight with three officers and twenty-eight airmen was incorporated into the war establishment and, in January 1940, became C Flight of the Armament Squadron, reverting to SD Flt in June 1941. Three years later the Flight was reincorporated in the newly formed Communications & Special Duty Squadron; for convenience in this history, the Unit is referred to as SDF or Porton.

Early in the war a small part of the Armament Squadron was devoted to gunnery research; on 3 June 1940 this section plus six aeroplanes[2] moved to Exeter, forming the Gunnery Research Unit. With the departure of this section and the recall of trials fighters to the RAF, A Flight of Armament Squadron was disbanded; gunnery trials continued, however, in B Flight in addition to bombing. A Flight reformed, initially as the Gunnery Development Section, on 3 January 1942, on the arrival of the Aircraft Gun Mounting Establishment from Duxford.

To prepare for the expected special demands of high-altitude flying, a Wellington Flight was nominally formed in about October 1940. This small unit was soon absorbed into the High Altitude Flight (HAF), formally established on 30 December 1940. Almost a year later, on 15 November 1941, an Intensive Flying Development Flight (IFDF) appeared. In March 1942 D Flight Performance Squadron was formed by transferring aircraft from the other Performance Flights; typical tasks were compass research, engine cooling, propeller tests, target towing trials, communications and air-to-air photography. The Gun Proofing Flight (GPF) for proof-testing every 40mm gun for aircraft, was established on 17 September 1942.

Thus by the beginning of 1943 there were ten Flights within the Establishment: Per T with A, B, C and D Flights, and HAF, Arm T with A and B, SD Flight, IFDF and GPF. To these flights was added the Test Pilots' School in mid-1943. Between August 1941 and August 1943 the one, later three, Wellingtons of the RAE's Night Photographic Flight flew from Boscombe due to lack of night-flying facilities at Farnborough. The Flight was, in error, included in the A&AEE war establishment, initially in B Arm T then D Per T.

[2] Hurricane L1695, Demon K3764, Henley L3247, Glover F9/37 L7999, Monospar L4672 and Wallace K6055

The ever-changing and expanding Establishment gave those responsible for deciding the rank, skills and numbers of people needed (the establishers) a continuous task – made almost impossible using the normal yardstick of number and type of aircraft. The best that could be done was to take a typical day's aircraft holding, but, as the CO remarked, within 24 hours the information was out of date. Nevertheless, it was accepted that the war establishment was the best way of ensuring that sufficient manpower was available.

Reorganisation in 1944

On arrival in July 1944 Air Commodore J. N. Boothman (of Schneider Trophy fame and a pre-war A&AEE test pilot) immediately set about reducing the duplication he found in the support elements of the Performance and Armament Sections. Each had its own library, research section, drawing office, and report section – in addition to its own flying squadron. In August 1944 his proposals for reorganisation were accepted (with the exception of the title of the new post, which became Chief Superintendent, as the Treasury rejected the title proposed of 'Controller of Tests'). Under the CO, the Chief Superintendent (Mr E. T. Jones) had the three trials divisions, each under a Superintendent, of Performance, Engineering and Armament, and four sections – Navigation, Communications/Radar, Drawing Office and Photographic. The Maintenance Wing and IFDF came under Engineering, while the Headquarters Wing (including, for example, medical, WAAF and RAF Administration and Salvage) reported directly to the CO. The Flying Wing, also directly under the CO, was reorganised into four squadrons, A, B, C and D, and one Flight for Communications & Special Duties (C&SD). The numbers of aircraft on 5 October 1944 are given in brackets as follows: A Pert T and A Arm T lost their naval aircraft and became No 1 (twenty-two aircraft) and No 2 (sixteen) Flights respectively of A Squadron; B Pert T and B Arm T similarly formed B Squadron for four-engined aircraft (twenty-four); C Squadron (twenty-five) had all the naval machines; D Squadron (twenty-six) had the twins; while the aircraft of C&SD Flight (eighteen) fulfilled the function of its title; intensive flying occupied eleven aircraft. There were thus 142 aircraft (plus thirteen of ETPS) on the strength of the Establishment. With minor variations, the '1944' organisation lasted for more than a quarter of a century.

In March 1945 the Establishment reached its peak in uniformed personnel of 2,312, of whom 411 were WAAF, forty-eight RN and ten Allied Officers. There were in addition more than 100 civilians. With the end of the European war two months later further changes began; the defensive barbed wire was removed, aircraft were serviced in peacetime lines in their dispersal areas, the RAF Regiment Squadron was disbanded, and the first demobilisations were made in June.

C Squadron at the end of 1944. Seated, left to right: unknown, Fg Off E. Thornily, Lt Wilson, Fg Off J. R. Smith, Lt Cdr R. B. Pearson, Sqn Ldr S. W. D. (Stewart) Coll, Flt Sgt Griffiths, Cdr F. M. A. Torrens Spence, Lt Cdr J. A. Evers, Sqn Ldr K. J. ('Pop') Sewell, Flt Lt Shippobottom, Fg Off G. (Georg) Pelka, Lt ('Lion') Lyon, Fg Off K. T. Mitchell, unknown.

Relations with France and America

Before the war, the French and British authorities ordered American aircraft, frequently of the same type but to be built to their own requirements. By late 1939 France had her first Douglas DB.7s (later Boston) and Curtiss 75s (Mohawk), and invited the A&AEE to fly them in preparation for deliveries to the RAF. At the same time arrangements for a Joint Anglo/French committee were made, together with proposals for a Joint Experimental Establishment at Marignane in Southern France. The first meeting, with A&AEE representation, was held on 1 January 1940; others followed, but France was occupied by the Germans before the Establishment was formed. The balance of the French orders for American aircraft, together with some intended for Norway, Belgium and Greece, was transferred to Britain. Most types were tested at Boscombe once their more significant peculiarities had been Anglicised – for example, reversal of throttle sense and changing of metric instruments to imperial calibration.

In the USA a small team from the A&AEE made a pre-war visit in 1939, and found American flight test methods to be greatly at variance with British practice, with, in particular, no direct equivalent of the A&AEE for acceptance testing. The aircraft ordered between 1938 and 1941 for the RAF were, in accordance with the contracts, given one flight each before despatch to the UK, where the first of each type was subjected to normal Boscombe tests. The US manufacturers adhered strictly to the contract, and declined to make modifications requested by the customer; production on time was of the essence. In comparing the test methods of individual American firms, the A&AEE found wide variation in performance reduction methods. For example, Grumman made no corrections for the effects of compressibility on indicated airspeed with the result that maximum speeds were up to 19mph (true) optimistic. Up to 1941 the American services accepted the manufacturers' figures, and made no pre-service checks on operational matters. As a result, persistent problems with American aircraft remained to be discovered by the A&AEE – among them weak gun mountings, poor-quality guns, inadequate engine cooling, carbon monoxide contamination and sometimes unsatisfactory handling for combat. With these shortcomings in mind, early in 1941 a Test Branch within the British Aircraft Commission (BAC) in New York was created; from the end of the year its head was J. F. X. McKenna from the A&AEE (promoted to group captain during his lengthy appointment in America). To give impetus to the new Branch, a large and senior team of experienced pilots (only three could be spared from the A&AEE) under P. W. Bulman (made a group captain for the task) was sent in April 1941 to 'spread the word' about British knowledge from two years of war flying.

American entry into the war in December 1941 had two direct consequences relevant to the A&AEE. First was expansion of the Service testing role of both Wright Field (US Army Air Force) and Patuxent River (US Navy), at each of which two British test pilots (often from Boscombe) were posted. Second, nearly all American aircraft used by the RAF and RN were types also used by the American Services, and thus subject to increasingly thorough appraisal (but still lacking some A&AEE tests, notably armament). The change in arrangements for the supply of aircraft to Lend-Lease did not, per se, affect the work needed at the A&AEE. Flight test methods varied within the USA between the two flight test centres and between manufacturers. From January 1942 regular technical meetings, under McKenna, took place in an attempt to standardise methods based on the then current edition of the A&AEE Handbook 'Methods of Making Set Tests on Performance and Handling of Aircraft'. Agreement was difficult to obtain – even between the US Army Air Force and Navy – and in August 1943 the A&AEE learned of the existence of the transatlantic work. The Establishment was acutely embarrassed at being excluded from discussion, particularly when it learned that

the new document was intended to apply also to the UK. The war ended before the matter was resolved.

One result in the continuing disparity in the methods and extent of testing was the need for A&AEE examination of American aircraft until the end of the war. Senior RAF opinion regularly questioned the need for such work, but, with the exception of types such as the Expediter and Dakota, there were ample examples of the benefits to the Services of the Establishment's critical evaluation. With growing confidence in American methods, however, A&AEE testing gradually concentrated on armament.

Ground Defence, Air Raids and Exercises

Air raids on Boscombe Down by the Luftwaffe were increasingly considered to be a possibility, even before the fall of France. A concentrated raid on the Establishment could have led to destruction of aircraft and facilities with, at best, delays in testing, and would thus have a serious impact on both the Royal Navy and the Royal Air Force.

In July 1940 the first group of airfield defenders arrived, comprising forty-seven Aircraft Hands, Ground Gunner (ACH GG). A further sixty-eight arrived the following month. The first two Bofors guns also arrived in August 1940. By the end of 1941 the ground defences were formalised into No 786 (Defence) Squadron, with four officers, seven senior NCOs and 148 corporals and airmen; Lieutenant Colonel W. E. Pringle was the senior defence adviser from February 1941. In June 1943 No 2786 Light Anti Aircraft Squadron (as it had become) was replaced by No 2837 Squadron.

Even before the arrival of dedicated defence personnel, a scheme for the saving of lives was instituted, and tested by the AOC, Air Vice Marshal P. C. Maltby, during a visit in May 1940. By this time aircraft were maintained in dispersed sites around the airfield, with inspections and modifications inside the hangars; for the first few months of the war aircraft had been lined up south of the Officers' Mess, a sitting target for both ground and air attack. Fortunately there were no ground attacks, and only four air raids – all at night by individual aircraft.

The first was on 26 June 1940, when four small bombs were dropped, followed by a similar attack in October. No damage was caused. Two air raids in April 1941, each involving up to twelve high-explosive bombs, damaged a hangar, destroyed one Blenheim, and caused varying degrees of damage to twenty-five other aircraft, of which four had to be dismantled for repair elsewhere. After the first raid, plans were made more comprehensive, both for airfield defence and for protection against gas attack. Earlier, plans were exercised almost daily in August and September 1940 when air raid warnings were given. With the gradual reduction in German activity, air defence exercises and ground defence exercises were held only periodically, the latter usually involving the local battalion of the Parachute Regiment as the attackers. In July 1942 the MAP said, 'The exercise is not to interfere with main work on station.' The result was an unrealistic two-day event involving only the Defence Squadron. All sections of the Establishment were, however, involved in the six weekly anti-gas exercise; in time-honoured fashion, the routine became a chore. In April 1942 the CO was dismayed to see people not wearing gas masks during the exercise, and decreed that everybody was to wear his mask for a period every week. The following July's exercise was an improvement, but umpires and police were authorised to take offenders to the decontamination centre, strip them naked and treat them as being grossly contaminated. Within a few months, however. the rules were apparently relaxed, as by 1943 gas masks were not routinely carried.

Royal Visitors and Others

Regular visits by the Royal Family during the wartime period tended to favour front-line units of all three Services. The Establishment was particularly honoured by a visit on 29 September 1941 by Her Majesty Queen Mary, who expressed interest in all she saw – including the sight of some spent cartridges on the ground, when she said, pointing, 'Salvage, salvage.' Her enthusiasm was followed four weeks later by a visit by the King and Queen. Other distinguished guests during the war included Marshal of the Royal Air Force Lord Trenchard on an informal visit in August 1944, and earlier visits by the Secretary of State for Air, by General Smuts, by the Commander-in-

Chief of Flying Training Command, missions from America, France (early in 1940) and Canada, and numerous visits by senior staff from the MAP as well as officers at all levels for working meetings and demonstrations.

The impact of the arrival of distinguished visitors was felt mainly by the Establishment's more senior staff, but visits were quickly over. Of much greater impact and of a continuing nature was the very large number of Bomber Command aircraft that arrived regularly from operations over Germany and the occupied countries. There were surprisingly few landing accidents, even by aircraft suffering battle damage. Three undamaged aircraft did, however, swing off the intended landing path within a few months of each other. The first, a Lancaster of 460 Squadron, destroyed a Spitfire (180 yards from the landing path), and a Halifax of 408 Squadron savaged a Boston; the third, a Lancaster of 61 Squadron, was lucky – it careered out of control through the dispersed HAF aircraft without hitting one before ending up in barbed wire. Whether the bombers arrived in one piece or not, it required regional controllers and their WAAF assistants, a crash crew (provided by the airfield defenders) and, above all, a team of groundcrew to marshal the aircraft, refuel and inspect them, often in wet or freezing conditions. In the period 20 November 1941 to 16 January 1942, fifty four-, 176 twin- and 153 single-engined visitors (including daytime) were handled, an average of more than six per 24-hour period; the duty, ad hoc, crew could not cope with both visitors and their normal work. A Visiting Aircraft Section was established in mid-1942 with some purpose – on some mornings the south side of the airfield looked like a bomber station to those starting their day's work.

Test Pilots' School

1942 was a year of momentous events in the course of the war, reflected at Boscombe Down in continuing increase in the demands for aircraft testing. Of the critical resources, the need for experienced test pilots was most keenly felt, a shortage exacerbated at the A&AEE by the fatal accidents during the year. In December 1942 the Controller (R&D), Air Marshal F. J. Linnell, addressed the problem, suggesting that twelve above-average pilots possessing academic degrees should be selected and sent in pairs to the A&AEE, RAE and four aircraft firms for training and subsequent posting to the Establishments. By March 1943 consideration of the CRD's proposal led to the dropping of the requirement for a degree, and, more significantly, the setting up of a Test Pilots' Flight at Boscombe, where the wartime establishment would be increased by one wing commander and one technical officer to run the Flight. With these posts filled by acting Wing Commander S. ('Sammy') Wroath and Mr Maclaren Humphreys, the Flight assembled (two people) in May 1943, and the first course of thirteen students started the following month. Soon renamed the Test Pilots' School and, early in 1944, the Empire Test Pilots' School, its training syllabus relied heavily on major contributions from the A&AEE and RAE Farnborough; the School nevertheless retained its own identity, and distinct role, and is not described further here (but see Appendix 8).

The Future

Thoughts turned in 1943 to the future post-war location of the A&AEE. Boscombe Down was in an ideal position for much of the aircraft industry, but questions arose over the long-term availability of weapon ranges in the vicinity and shortage of modern accommodation. The decision to build the new runway settled the matter; in May 1944 it was agreed that the Establishment would remain where it was.

Spitfire V W3112 demonstrates the new engine running bay in March 1944. This ETPS aircraft has its armament removed and appears to be a bit ropey. *A&AEE 11707*

2Flying

The heart of the matter

Flying was the heart of the A&AEE – never more so than during the wartime period 1939-45, when new aeroplanes appeared frequently, each with its idiosyncrasies to be discovered, while new models of existing types, together with a bewildering range of armament, all needed testing to meet the insistent demands of the Services. To the aircrew, civilian observers and, most particularly, the pilots, it was a heady brew. And yet, while conscious of the dangers involved in flying untried machines to the limits of their capabilities, the challenges of the work and the sense of a really worthwhile job gave those involved a great sense of achievement. The task of the pilot, and those with him, was risky at times, accidents happened, and precious lives were lost even without the attentions of the enemy. The Roll of Honour of those killed while flying on A&AEE duty is given in Appendix 2.

A balanced view of the risks and achievements of the Establishment can be made by considering the incidents described in this chapter in conjunction with the vast amount of work recorded in Part II. The aircrew were almost exclusively RAF with up to four RN pilots and single representatives from Norway, France and the Netherlands. A small number of naval and army pilots joined air force crews on short attachments for intensive flying as required. Civilian trials officers and photographers frequently completed a crew.

The pilot's crucial role in test flying is self-evident. The broad range of tests undertaken required varying skills and experience; the more demanding handling and performance work was the preserve of a small group in the Performance Squadron. The author has been told that only the latter group regarded themselves as 'proper' test pilots. Indeed, in 1942, when considering the question of

Polish pilots of the A&AEE, probably in 1944. Left to right, they are Georg Pelka, Georg Preiss (a specialist in navigation), Toni Majcherczyk, the youngest (wearing the Polish pilot's eagle badge), who was trapped in a Hurricane in May 1944 when it overturned in a forced landing, Miedzybrodski, and Nikki Kulzycki.

production testing of heavy bombers, the CO, Air Commodore R. B. Mansell, said that B Per T had just five pilots, of whom only one was a test pilot. The number of pilots was always small in relation to the total number of people at the Establishment; in 1940 it was fewer than twenty of more than 800, and in 1945 thirty-eight in more than 2,000. In addition, some armament trials officers (never more than five) and one technical officer were qualified pilots and flew their own trials. When it is considered that the Establishment had more than 100 trials aircraft for most of the war, it is little wonder that in later years one pilot described his experience there as 'A Feast of Flying'.

The wide knowledge of new types gained by pilots at Boscombe Down was unique, and led, particularly in the early years of the war, to demands for this expertise to be spread to the Services, and to industry. The A&AEE resisted, largely successfully, the dilution of its hard-won team of experts by posting. The result was that a small core of pilots, mostly in the Performance Squadron, formed a long-serving nucleus, not only for the more demanding trials but also with responsibility for 'breaking in' pilots new to test flying. The Establishment's position in the matter of postings was strengthened by the creation in the MAP of a special post for management of RAF personnel in the Ministry and Establishments; the new post was added to the Directorate of Flying (R&D) on formation in August 1940.

The success of the A&AEE in the face of demands for its pilots may be gauged from the small number of postings elsewhere. Some departures were inevitable – Sqn Ldr H. N. Ramsbottom-Isherwood left on promotion; Sgt G. C. Brunner joined No 43 Squadron in time for the Battle of Britain; Lieutenant Commander S. W. D. Colls rejoined the Fleet; while Squadron Leader R. W. P. Collings was promoted to command No 35 Squadron – the first with the Halifax – and left in November 1940. Of the remaining pre-war pilots, plus a small number who joined later, there were several whose contributions to test flying were both lengthy and distinguished. Indeed, the bulk of all wartime handling and performance was undertaken by this handful of experienced test pilots, usually no more than two or three in each flight.

The task of commanding the flying activities of the Establishment fell to a succession of RAF test pilots (listed in Appendix 1). Squadron Leader J. F. X. McKenna AFC (promoted to Wing Commander in February 1940) left at short notice in August 1940 for the USA, to be replaced by Wing Commanders J. A. Gray DFC (a pre-war A&AEE pilot), then J. A. P. Harrison, followed by A. H. Wheeler, all within seven months. Wheeler was concerned that test pilots were becoming out of touch with current front-line operations. This deficiency was partially remedied by the arrival in the summer of 1941 of nine pilots from squadrons. Another concern was the pre-war practice, still in evidence in 1941, of the Establishment treating each manufacturer and its pilots confidentially. This restriction was swept away, and industry pilots were actively encouraged to fly aeroplanes from other makers at the A&AEE. Wheeler was succeeded by J. W. McGuire, killed, as described below, shortly after taking up the post.

Following the deaths of three wing commanders, including the OC Performance Testing Squadron, in flying accidents at the A&AEE within three months, Wing Commander H. A. ('Bruin') Purvis had an unenviable task on arrival from BAC in America in May 1942. He had a burning ambition to fly, and quickly confirmed his reputation by taking every opportunity to try new aeroplanes. He was soon promoted to group captain on the upgrading of his post, by which time he had done much to restore the prestige of the Establishment and the morale of aircrew. A spate of engine failures during yawing manoeuvres in Typhoons was investigated by Purvis, resulting in three forced landings (two in one day) without damage; a fourth engine failure in an unconnected trial led to a write-off when the wheels failed to lower. In April 1944, in a Lancaster, an overspeeding outer engine could not be feathered, leading to an uncontrollable yawing couple and a remarkable forced landing near Amesbury. Flying Officer J. Campbell, the engineer, was commended for his calmness when disaster seemed inevitable. Purvis's logbook entry says, '…port outer overspeeded arrived in Amesbury.' The story is told how, after leaving the Lancaster debris, he walked to his home nearby and told his wife, 'I happened to be in Amesbury, so I've just dropped in for tea.'

In April 1945 Group Captain 'Sammy' Wroath became Superintendent of Flying on his return from a year in the USA at Wright Field. Of those servicemen with long association with the A&AEE, Wroath is, perhaps, the most remarkable, having arrived at Martlesham Heath as a sergeant in 1936 and achieving group captain rank within eight years. Early wartime flying was in A Per T, which he commanded from 1942, and included survival by parachute of a mid-air collision while flying an early Buffalo. At short notice in 1943 he became the first CO of the Test Pilots' School.

This history is written very largely on the basis of surviving official documents, which include details of all accidents, but almost entirely omit 'good shows'. Even awards for skilful or meritorious aviating (AFC/AFM) are mentioned only intermittently in the unit's official record (F540). Private papers and logbooks fill in some missing details, and the experience of Squadron Leader A. D. (Fred) Miller may be taken as typical. Joining the new 'D Per T' (initially as a Flight Lieutenant) under Squadron Leader B. Huxtable in April 1942, Miller flew fifty-five types of aeroplane in 722 airborne hours before leaving at the end of 1944. The unusual types he flew included the Hurricane biplane, the rocket-assisted Whitley and an Airacobra with Russian instruments. Among his 'good shows' were a landing in a Beaufighter following loss of a large section of the leading edge; a similar experience in a Wellington when a whole panel of wing fabric became detached; an engine failure and successful forced landing in a Spitfire; followed

a few weeks later by undercarriage failure, also in a Spitfire, in which he stopped the engine before landing and raised the flaps to minimise damage – the aircraft was serviceable again at the end of the following day. A more serious incident was locking of the ailerons and rolling inverted at low level at night in a Beaufighter; the controls became free after climbing inverted and a foreign object in the wing was found on landing. On 20 May 1943 a Hudson was being flown to investigate the reason for fatal accidents in the RAF when making dive attacks. After careful calculations by the Technical Officer, Freddie Cook, and arranging cine photographers to record wing movements, the dives started, gradually increasing speed and 'g' on recovery. At a speed just below the maximum considered safe, the outer port wing took up a permanent extra dihedral, making control difficult. After considering bailing out, a high-speed landing was successfully made, running through a fence before stopping. As a result of the trial, limitations on speeds and dive angles were calculated for operational use (there were no 'g' meters) and no further accidents were reported from this cause.

In August 1944 Cook was approaching to land at Woodley aerodrome in the prototype Monitor when an extensive fire suddenly developed at about 1,500 feet. The observer, Mr P. F. Ainsbury, was ordered to jump. Miller delayed his own exit until he was aware of the observer's escape door opening (thus intensifying the flames); he tried to get out at about 800 feet, but only got clear at about 400 feet. His parachute did not fully deploy, but, burnt and bruised, he landed in a bog. Ainsbury had, in fact, not jumped, and was killed; at his inquest the pilot was completely exonerated of any blame and returned to flying after several weeks in hospital. Posted to C Squadron (as C Per T had become), Miller was forced in October to abandon a Wildcat, in which the central fuel tank caught fire, following ill-considered alterations to the exhaust system. He left Boscombe shortly thereafter. His skilful handling of the earlier incidents went unrecognised, and he was not awarded the AFC, possibly because his endeavours were considered commonplace and thus unremarkable among his peers; his double use of a parachute was, however, unusual at the A&AEE.

By contrast, on leaving the Establishment in February 1945 after more than four years, Squadron Leader H. G. Hastings had both the

Squadron Leader A. D. (Fred) Miller in 1946; he flew with C Per T and D Squadron in 1942-44.

AFM awarded in 1941 and an AFC after commissioning. In February 1944 he was the first A&AEE pilot to fly a jet. Boscombe pilots received four awards in July 1940, three of them to pilots of armament trials: Squadron Leaders A. E. Groom (12 years at the A&AEE) and A. S. 'Dru' Drury, and Flight Sergeant H. P. Shippobotham; Squadron Leader H. N. G. Ramsbottom-Isherwood was the fourth. Other AFCs awarded to armament pilots included those to Squadron Leaders W. P. (Pete) Whitworth and H. B. ('Mickie') Bell-Syer, and Flight Lieutenant P. S. Foy. C. E. (Charlie) Slee arrived at Martlesham Heath as a Pilot Officer in April 1937, and flew continuously with B Per T until posted as a Wing Commander to be the first Commanding Officer in 1943 of the Test Pilots' School (later cancelled as he was wanted elsewhere). His Air Force Cross (AFC) was awarded in January 1941, and today he is remembered as a most unassuming, popular man to the extent that on occasion his entry to a room was greeted by applause by airmen and officers alike. Among notable events in his career were engine failure in a production Manchester and the splitting of the rear fuselage of the first Mosquito after landing.

His colleague, the Australian J. W. McGuire (a pre-war B Per T Flight Lieutenant), had an enthusiastic and dynamic personality, and returned in 1940 to command the Flight; in February 1942 he was promoted to Wing Commander as OC Flying. His influence was immediately felt – he was first to arrive at work and would appear unannounced in any part of the Establishment, keeping everybody up to the mark. After only a month in the new post he was captain of a Liberator (standing in for a younger pilot whose wife had recently given birth) when an outer engine caught fire uncontrollably; four crew bailed out but McGuire was killed when the wing broke away and the aircraft crashed. This particularly tragic fatality was attributed to spillage from overfilled oil tanks. He was posthumously awarded a second AFC. McGuire's accident left B Per T hard pressed at a time of increasing demand for pilots; assistance from the Handling Flight of CFS was obtained for some trials, including a Lancaster in April 1942 to investigate the technique for recovery from dives. Progressive failure of rivets caused a large wing panel to detach; the aircraft crashed, killing Wing Commander P. S. Salter and four crew.

Within five months, B Per T suffered a further grievous loss when Squadron Leader W. J. Carr and three crew died in a Warwick that crashed following separation of fabric wing covering. Bill Carr had joined the Flight as a Pilot Officer early in 1938, and tested all the twin- and four-engined bombers over the next four and a half years with only a short break to fly Blenheims with No 235 Squadron in the Battle of Britain. He had survived by parachute a mid-air collision in October 1940, a write-off following nose wheel collapse on landing a Liberator, and a similar incident in another Liberator, when an inert 500lb bomb broke loose, also on landing. He had been awarded the AFC.

Investigation of undesirable and dangerous handling characteristics was stock-in-trade of the Establishment. The rudder overbalance (lock-over) in the early Halifaxes was subject to extensive testing in 1942, leading to a promising modification (described below) but at the cost of the lives of Flight Lieutenant S. F. Reiss and his crew. Reiss was one of six Polish pilots – all academically qualified engineers – at the Establishment. He had had three close shaves in 1942, the most serious of which occurred in a heavy Stirling following engine failure; the propeller could not be feathered, the crew bailed out and Reiss, alone, crashed into trees at Porton with only minor personal injuries.

The hazard of aerial collision, always present at busy airfields like Boscombe, was compounded there by the disparity of types, the nature of flying and by the proximity of another airfield at High Post, only 2 miles from the airfield boundary. A Lancaster, carrying out very low-level runs to measure airspeed system pressure errors in September 1943, was going to turn in for the fourth run when it collided with an Oxford from Upavon landing at High Post; all six men in both aircraft died. Training at the latter airfield was stopped. It is noteworthy that this is the only collision in the aerodrome area recorded in the wartime period; it is the more remarkable considering the contemporary practice of visual (ie non-radar and usually non-radio) flying in sight of the ground in all weathers when rejoining the circuit. Flight Lieutenant B. O. Huxtable had two remarkable escapes in 1940 during a lengthy tour at the A&AEE. The first, in an Albemarle, followed an uncontrollable roll and spin to the right following a loud bang (caused, it was later determined, by defective glue holding on the wing plywood). He ordered the two crew to jump, and Mr J. D. Hayhurst made a successful exit and descent. Mr Norman Sharpe's parachute fouled the port tailplane, suspending him below the leading edge. He managed to extricate himself just as the aircraft crashed, and was seriously injured. Brian Huxtable was slightly injured as the aircraft ended up in a nearly level attitude due to the drag of Sharpe's entangled parachute slowing the spin. After a long and painful recovery, Sharpe joined Hayhurst in distinguished careers in aviation. Six months later, Huxtable was to demonstrate the benefits of rockets to assist a Stirling's take-off to a group of senior civilians and service officers. Instead of firing in sequence, all the rockets fired simultaneously, tearing away from their fittings, passing through the inboard propellers, which detached, taking the outboards with them; a blur of little legs was seen by the onlookers as the crew hared away from the forlorn fuselage. It was, in the words of one witness, 'Quite the loudest, longest and most satisfying explosion yet heard on Salisbury Plain.' Such events take their toll, and Huxtable became dogged by ill health and retired. W. R. (Bill) Morris, a long-serving pilot, first as a Warrant Officer and later commissioned, had a blameless record despite the worst efforts of the engines and flaps of three Ansons (one each in 1943, 1944 and 1945) to catch him out. Arriving in October 1943, Squadron Leader Dennis Letts was promptly involved in tests of reversible inboard propellers on a Halifax, and equally promptly went on to something else when the propellers

malfunctioned on the fourth of a series of landings. Deceleration was remarkable and the aircraft landed almost vertically and was severely damaged. The crew was unhurt, and Letts remained flying at the A&AEE until after the war.

Squadron Leader H. C. D. Rex Hayter arrived from the RAE in February 1943 to take over B Per T, and was promoted to take over the newly created B Squadron in September 1944. He was joined by Squadron Leader H. G. Hazelden DFC (ex-No 1 Course of TPS), who had the alarming experience in a Halifax of a violent pitch down at high speed as fabric tore off the elevator. Hazelden was a strong man, and managed to regain control and land. Later he joined Handley Page and became Chief Test Pilot. Almost alone among the Technical Officers in wearing RAF uniform as a Volunteer Reservist, J. W. ('Al') Truran was the Senior Handling Technical Officer, and also a pilot. His claims to notoriety included writing off a Wellington VI on landing following too slow an approach in 1943, an enormous bounce that collapsed the undercarriage of a Lancaster on his first flight in the type in 1944, and a similar collapse on landing crosswind in a Firefly in 1945; his take-offs have not been recorded for posterity.

An A&AEE group in the New Forest. The only two people identified are Sqn Ldr C. E. (Charlie) Slee (seated front centre) and WO W. ('George') Morris on his left.

Four pilots looking serious. Left to right, they are Flt Lt H. J. Camps (killed in Mosquito KB209 in
August 1944), Sqn Ldr Eric Metcalfe (killed in Mosquito LR495 in January 1944), Flt Lt R. H. ('Willy')
Williams (seriously injured with Eric Metcalfe and posted to a staff appointment in August 1944), and
Flt Lt H. ('Hal') Roach (a pre-war Olympic runner who continued daily running).

A group from D
Squadron in front
of Mosquito NS586
shortly before it
crashed on 12 April
1945. Left to right,
they are Dr George
Hislop, Sqn Ldr John
Jarvis, Wg Cdr J. D.
Ronald, Flt Lt W.
('George') Morris,
Sqn Ldr Ian
Robertson and the
Squadron
Engineering Officer.

A factor very much in the minds of pilots of twin-engined aircraft was the possibility of an engine failure immediately after take-off and before a safe speed for single-engine flying had been reached; their only recourse was to close both throttles and to force-land into whatever lay ahead. With two engines, either of which may fail, the risk was double that of a single-engine machine during the critical seconds after take-off. Flight Lieutenant John Jarvis, newly arrived in July 1942, survived an engine failure taking off in a Mosquito, which ended up in a ditch having written off two parked Beaufighters in the process. Four months later the throttles jammed partially open on abandoning a take-off in a Mitchell, with expensive results. John Jarvis's immaculately written logbooks include a green endorsement for safely landing a Warwick after fabric had stripped from the rudder in 1945; he was later awarded an AFC, which he disarmingly claims was for 'attendance'.

These tales of derring-do by the small number of pilots omit the efforts over long, often uncomfortable, hours of work by a very much larger number of supporting staff, including women. 'Keeping them Flying' could well have been the motto of the WAAF, and 'Keeping them Testing' the motto of civilian ladies at Boscombe. The WAAF, of whom there were more than 400 in 1944, had among their duties MT driving (including the heaviest bowsers) and Flying Control. In cold weather, flying of Tempests and Typhoons may have stopped but for the skill of a young WAAF who alone possessed the knack of starting their recalcitrant engines. Jarvis's wife Margaret (née Young) recalls her time in the wartime WAAF at Boscombe as very intense, hard-working and rewarding in an atmosphere of great companionship, but with the constant fear, shared by all non-flying staff, of news of an accident. Her sister Betty, in the WRNS, married Freddie Cook, and her friend Brenda

Really close flying! Flight Lieutenant J. A. (John) Jarvis, in an early production Grumman Hellcat I, formates with the photographic Beech Traveller in June 1944. Camouflage is probably the standard Royal Navy Temperate Sea Scheme.

married C. B. ('Cyclops') Brown; both have similar memories. The smooth running of the Technical Office and its efficient production of reports was largely due to a small number of ladies, among them Connie Kent (later married to F. W. Myerscough) as Personal Secretary to E. T. Jones, and Margot Carter (later married to W. J. D. ('Gus') Annand) in the Technical Library. Flight Lieutenant 'Cyclops' Brown had a long association with test flying, and retired as an Air Commodore. At Boscombe he became the expert on rocket firing, although gunsight work requiring binocular vision was impossible for him as he had lost an eye in the Battle of Britain.

In the Fighter Flight of the Performance Squadron (A Per T) it is remarkable that there were only two fatalities to its pilots during the war period, although Wing Commander W. S. Jenkins of the Navigation Section died in January 1942 trying to turn back after engine failure in an Airacobra. Flying Officer D. W. Stannard, a pre-war pilot, escaped by parachute in January 1940 from a Master that broke up during diving tests; his slow descent was witnessed by many on the aerodrome.

G. C. Brunner returned as a Pilot Officer in December 1940. Engine failures and forced landings in a Mohawk (December 1940) and a Tomahawk (March 1941) were followed in May 1942 by another Master breaking up in the air. Brunner escaped by parachute, but the passenger, AC F. E. Bartlett, was killed. In May 1943 the Welkin he was flying had an engine fire (the propeller could not be feathered), which burned through the starboard aileron control; he managed to land the aircraft at Upavon by coarse use of rudder and judicious use of the port engine. He was awarded his second AFC for this feat, and remained at the A&AEE until the end of the war.

The fact that some pilots spent many war years at Boscombe was undoubtedly of benefit to the Establishment, and reflects the temperamental suitability of the individual, who could accept the daily challenge and risks of the job. Such people relished the opportunity to fly many different types of

aeroplane, often to the 'corners of the envelope'. Other capable pilots did not find test flying to their taste. One Flight Lieutenant, who had flown Hurricanes in the Battle of Britain, suffered an engine failure in a cannon-armed Hurricane and force-landed at Ashley Walk. Within two months he made a mistake after landing and later suffered an engine failure on take-off; both were in Airacobras and both resulted in the wheels retracting on the ground. He transferred thereafter to the Technical Branch.

There was also a perception in the RAF, at least, that test flying was 'dicey'. Even bomber crews, who were accustomed to facing the horror of night raids on Germany, were reluctant to fly even a single sortie in daylight in the air tests of production aircraft. Such perception by operational aircrew in the services was common. A Battle of Britain Squadron Commander recently (1996) told the author that he always held wartime test pilots in the highest regard because of the risks.

Within two weeks of arrival in November 1940, Flight Lieutenant Jack Bamber, a blunt former cane-cutter from New Zealand, had an engine failure in a Mohawk. Before leaving in February 1943 with an AFC for his work, two other incidents, both on landing (in a Blenheim and a Havoc), resulted in write-offs following

technical failures. He is remembered for his exuberance, including firing a Verey pistol when the flare sailed over a hangar and burned a Stinson on the other side. Flight Lieutenant E. S. T. (Stuart) Coles, whose RFC flying badge from the previous war was conspicuous, is recalled as a very steady performance pilot of C Per T with a natural penchant for very straight and very level flying. Flying Officer H. P. ('Sandy') Powell later commanded C Per T on reaching Squadron Leader rank, remaining very correct in dress and manner. He pulled off a remarkable crosswind landing in a heavy Hudson following engine failure on take-off, completing three-quarters of a circuit in the process. His post-war authorship includes admiring biographies of his wartime colleagues. Lieutenant Commander F. M. A. Torrens-Spence (universally known as 'TS') had earned the DSO and DSC as a Swordfish pilot prior to reaching Boscombe in January 1942. Promoted Commander to be the first CO of C Squadron, his 'rest tour' (as he later described it) included a force-landing in a Barracuda following the propeller detaching from the engine, and bailing out of a Firebrand that became uncontrollable when the air tail of the torpedo broke away and severely injured the aircraft's controls. He later became an Admiral.

Flight Lieutenant C. B. ('Cyclops') Brown in Tempest JN740 in February 1944. *A&AEE recognition 203*

The result of holding the stick too far forward on take-off and striking the propeller on the ground in March 1945. Wildcat JV782, in the hands of Lt Cdr J. A. Evers, appears to have been prevented from hitting the hangar by the intervention of the luckless Boston BZ384. The previous month, the Commanding Officer had ordered that Evers's eyes be tested following two landing accidents in Corsairs (the second of which resulted in a bounce and climb for abandonment by parachute).

High Altitude Flight

Before the war experimental aircraft had climbed to more than 50,000 feet, and early Spitfires reached about 35,000 feet under test conditions. By 1940 it was apparent that the factors affecting flight at high altitude were not sufficiently understood, and that resolution of problems found was becoming urgent in view of the threat of high-flying Germans. Among surviving papers is a letter about the need for high-altitude research dated 10 November 1940 from Philip Lucas of Hawker (previously an A&AEE test pilot), which appears to have acted as a catalyst, because two meetings at Boscombe Down quickly followed to identify the areas needing investigation. At the second, senior officers agreed to form a High Altitude Flight at Boscombe Down where all the high-flying types with the latest engines would first be officially tested. The DGRD (Air Marshal Roderick Hill) endorsed the agreement on 6 December, and the Flight officially formed on 30 December 1940. Dr George Hislop, who had been drafted to the A&AEE in November 1939, became the Senior Technical Officer, and Squadron Leader David Waghorn (brother of H. R. D. Waghorn of Schneider Trophy fame), the Commanding Officer.

Initial equipment was a pair of Spitfires and four Hurricanes, quickly followed by other types, which between 1942 and 1944 averaged about twelve aircraft. Spitfires predominated, but high-flying Wellingtons, higher-flying Fortresses, as well as Bostons, Hudsons, Mosquitoes, a Botha (!) and Lancasters, were used. The work of the HAF evolved to include the handling and performance (at all levels) of the high-altitude Spitfires, the Mosquitoes and Wellingtons; in 1944 the Flight assumed responsibility for the performance of the Mustang and other types. Meteorological investigation played a continuing part in the work of the HAF, and from June 1941 a pair of Spitfires was used for twice-daily climbs to ceiling, to establish the variation of ambient temperature with altitude. Following the transfer of the Flight's aircraft and aircrew to the new A Squadron, the Meteorological Section retained a separate identity and was formally inspected by the Director of Meteorological Services in April 1945.

From the start, working relationships within the HAF were good. and comprehensive reports on the investigations appeared regularly (149 in 4½ years). Initial tasks were threefold: to improve performance, control and stability of existing aircraft at high altitude, to investigate carburetion and ignition, and to assist research and development on oxygen and other equipment and heating. In the first group, an incident involved the grease freezing in the controls, leading to a Hurricane completing continuous rolls as the ailerons locked hard over; they were eventually freed at 18,000 feet. Thereafter lengthy trials were made of various anti-freeze lubricants. Pilots' early suspicions of an oxygen economiser in place of the earlier continuous-flow type were gradually overcome during trials – remarkable for lack of problems.

Windscreen frosting was partially cured by rubbing on a substance known as 'Gnomist' and was almost cured by heated air flow between the bullet-proof screen and the normal canopy; better was found to be a double transparency with a sealed gap (the Lobelle type), and best a double cover with airflow through the gap, as on the Welkin. In nine months in 1941 Squadron Leader N. V. ('Shorty') Longbottom, the Deputy Flight Commander, made many high-altitude flights (extremely tiring without pressurisation), including sixty-nine to about 40,000 feet in a Spitfire II (Merlin XII), specially lightened to 5,750lb. Longbottom had a particular aversion to the high-altitude Wellingtons, but was posted to the Air Ministry where his A&AEE experience could be used in formulating requirements for new aircraft. Contrails were the centre of interest of his Spitfire flights, which also included comparison of temperatures with the radiosonde balloon ascents from nearby Larkhill and distant Liverpool; among discoveries were frequent very high winds, occasional turbulence in clear air, and confirmation of large variations in the height of the tropopause. The need for measurement of humidity was soon identified, and two types of hygrometer (modified from sea-level types) were sent by distinguished scientists, but proved impractical. George Hislop, who, by late 1941 had a meteorological assistant with independent views, developed a nephelometer, testing it in a Fortress, thus becoming the first to measure humidity at altitude. Among discoveries was relative humidity of 105% – due, it was agreed, not to false readings, but to supercooled water droplets.

Among longer-term investigations was the longitudinal stability on Spitfires. Initial results in a Mark I showed a marked deterioration with altitude, a finding corroborated in the pressurised Mark VI. Later tests in 1942 using a Mark V with various modifications to the elevator controls confounded the earlier results; there was no deterioration at high altitude. Early tests of climbing Merlin-engined fighters at maximum rpm (previously reduced to conserve engine life) above 20,000 feet confirmed the benefit on ceiling (increased by 3,000 feet). Trials continued on many types to improve performance and to measure the effects on the engine, such as temperatures, and the penalty of opening the radiator flap. Notes on other trials by the Flight are included in Part II.

The demanding nature of the flying in the HAF was thought most likely to be the cause of Flying Officer L. G. H. Kelly's disappearance without trace in a Hurricane in February 1941. In July 1942, the crash of a Wellington VI killed Squadron Leader C. L. F. (Cyrus) Colmore and his crew, including Mr C. V. Abbott, the Flight's Deputy Technical Officer. Flight Lieutenant H. J. Camps was killed in a Mosquito, which crashed, for reasons not determined, in August 1944, shortly before the Flight was absorbed into the new A Squadron.

Production Testing and Rogues

In September 1942 the Commander-in-Chief of Bomber Command stated, 'Too many aircraft are rogues.' Wartime production methods led to odd handling or low performance in some aircraft; production check flights of each machine before delivery were minimal. It was initially intended to subject every 100th aircraft of every type (some sixteen per month) to a comprehensive test, involving six pilots and six observers of the A&AEE, each team with its own communications aircraft. At the A&AEE such a task would have been overwhelming, and in December 1942 it was agreed that one pilot and one senior technical officer would do production testing – limited to four-engined types only.

Rogues testing was a separate issue. Squadron Leader Dennis Clyde-Smith DSO DFC and Mr R. (Bobby) Marsh (who replaced Mr C. S. Wills in mid-1943) formed an inseparable team, and between January 1943 and May 1944 tested sixty-two Stirlings, Halifaxes and Lancasters. Several aircraft exhibited undesirable characteristics, but the majority were found acceptable (see Appendix 6). Flights lasted about 3½ hours following take-off at maximum weight. Problems were few, but initially there was a marked reluctance by RAF aircrew (a full crew was needed) to fly on these 'hairy' air tests. The team soon became well-known at the small number of RAF stations used, and both men enjoyed the unrestrained hospitality frequently extended to them. Bobby Marsh remembered with wonder the journeys home in Clyde-Smith's car, driven at break-neck speed at night (in black-out conditions); the driver no doubt enjoyed extra minutes with his loved one as a result. Scarcely was the pilot back full time at Boscombe Down when his head was dented by the handle in the roof of a Warwick following a sudden pitch down accompanied by a loud report as fabric stripped off the starboard wing in a dive at 320mph.

Early production tests were made using full power for climbs, and the Command formally complained about 'flogging' the engines; reduced power was thereafter used. All flights were followed by a comprehensive and time-consuming report. On 18 April 1944 the scheme ended.

In parallel to the arrangements being made for production aircraft, discussion on testing rogue aircraft resulted in a formal MAP administrative instruction (DTD No 11, dated 30 November 1942). This stated that suspected rogue aircraft would be flown by a visiting A&AEE pilot, and, if the reported deficiency was confirmed, the aircraft would be sent for further investigation and correction before return to Service. Details of known aircraft tested as rogues are given in Appendix 6.

Intensive Flying Development Flight

The RAF Inspector General reported in September 1939 that the A&AEE should broaden its scope to include intensive flying of new types. The Establishment had more than enough work already, consequently nothing was done, although in December 1940 arrangements were made for rapid accumulation of experience of the new bombers by the first RAF Squadron (six to twelve aircraft), the manufacturer (two) and the A&AEE. There was little coordination and the plan foundered in 1941. The need for a single organisation to fly several hundred flying hours on new aircraft led to the formation within the A&AEE of the Intensive Flying Development Flight (IFDF), under Mr Donald Fraser, and later Dr John Parker. The aim was to fly 150 hours on each of two early production aircraft, using operational air and ground crews from the appropriate Service; details of the types involved are given in Part II.

Accidents and incidents occurred frequently, attributed in part to teething problems, and in part to the quality of the aircrew – particularly pilots. The Establishment CO wrote on more than one occasion to RAF Commands expressing his concern at the abilities of pilots detached to the Establishment. Groundcrews were at first experienced and highly adaptable and proficient; the Royal Navy continued, on a smaller scale than the RAF, to supply good maintainers. In late 1943, however, a team from the RAF arrived for the Welkin intensive flying trials (a particularly unfortunate type in view of its vicissitudes) who had very little experience, to the extent of never having completed even a minor inspection in Service. Thereafter things improved somewhat.

Spitfire XIV JF318 in July 1943, some two months before failure of its Griffon 65 led to the pilot bailing out. The aircraft had completed 104 hours of intensive flying, including longitudinal stability tests at two CG. Results were satisfactory provided great care was taken in preserving the contours of the elevator shrouds made of light-gauge metal. The tests were among the first using the method of measuring stick and trimmer positions throughout the speed range for longitudinal static stability and stick force per g for manoeuvring. *A&AEE recognition 173*

The IFDF maintained an existence separate from the Technical Office and trials, both in organisation and location, being sited on the extreme southern side of the airfield. In September 1944 the Flight was placed in the Engineering Division, and the following month reached a peak of eleven aircraft: three Spitfires, three Barracudas, two Buckinghams, two Warwicks and a Halifax.

Recognition Photographs

Very early in the war, the Establishment was given the task of obtaining air-to-air photographs of new aircraft as they arrived for testing; recognition of friendly types by fighter pilots and gunners was the aim. Several incidents involving Boscombe crews underlined the necessity of the task. In May 1940 a Stirling was flying over the English Channel and was twice attacked by Spitfires; the Stirling had no guns and Mr S. A. Dean (in charge of the Radio Section and on this occasion, he relates, testing the new IFF) fired every recognition Very cartridge on board before the Spitfires withdrew. In January 1941 Squadron Leader R. G. (Gordon) Slade in a Maryland escaped the aggressive attentions of some Hurricanes by rapid (and overstressing) evasion into cloud. Slade was a

Lancaster I DV379, posing as G-AGJI in February 1944, was probably only at Boscombe for a few days, possibly for weighing and air-to-air photography. *A&AEE recognition 206*

pre-war B Per T pilot who later commanded the first Mosquito Night Fighter Squadron and, after the war, joined the Fairey Company. Later incidents included the Navy shooting at and damaging a Hurricane in Lyme Bay; as the latter was firing 40mm guns at the time, the sailors may have felt that retaliation was justified.

Boeing 247D DZ203 had only a tenuous link to the A&AEE, if any, and is included here because this image is probably an A&AEE recognition photograph.

Focke-Wulf 190A-4/U8 PE882, flown by Group Captain 'Bruin' Purvis for its 'mug' shots, flies from Farnborough in June 1943. This aircraft had landed in error at West Malling on the night of 17 April 1943. *A&AEE recognition 171*

Focke-Wulf 190A-3 MP499 poses cleanly in January 1943; there is a cockerel's head motif on the cowling. The aircraft had been extensively flown from Farnborough in late 1942 for assessment against RAF fighters. *A&AEE recognition 126*

Hind L7189 is caught by the photographic aircraft in November 1941 somewhere over Salisbury Plain, with a trench stem in the background. *A&AEE recognition 65*

Wellington VI W5798 is seen from the photographic Hampden in November 1942. This striking pose shows clearly the nose and the transparent panel for the bomb aimer. It lacks the modification of the escape panel in the extreme nose. *A&AEE recognition 118*

A Hereford, replaced by a Hampden, was dedicated to this task after early use of any available machine of C Per T; in 1944 Fireflies took over the job. Some 265 different aircraft had been 'snapped' by August 1945, many of those images appearing in this volume. Among types photographed but not in use at the A&AEE was the Curtiss Commando. The example chosen was at Prestwick, and the Hampden with intrepid crew duly flew north, only to be told by the local Air Defence Commander that the Commando could not fly as its safety could not be guaranteed due to lack of recognition information. A compromise was duly reached, and photographs were taken during one wide circuit in sight of the aerodrome.

This Blenheim I, possibly K7157 in September 1941, is in night-fighter black and has startling roundels, a four-gun pack under the fuselage and a small nose aerial. Air intake pipes extend forward of the engine nacelles. The link to the A&AEE is tenuous, probably limited to a meeting with a photographic aircraft from Boscombe. The date and unit code letters indicate that it is serving in an operational training role. *A&AEE recognition 25*

Two photographers lost their lives (and two aircraft were lost) when a Hampden and the subject Buffalo collided in October 1940 as the pilots lost sight of each other attempting to take plan-view shots. Messrs F. L. Oxley and J. W. Parsons were killed, but the two pilots escaped by parachute; the procedure for plan views was changed.

3 Performance Testing

Exploring the envelopes

Organisation

The Establishment's title inferred that the 'Aeroplane' side was responsible for all tests not falling within the 'armament' category. Such was the case at Boscombe Down in 1939-45. Indeed, for the first five years the management of tests of aeroplanes, under the Chief Technical Officer (CTO), embraced performance, handling, engineering, flame damping, contamination, radio, navigation and, initially, photographic assessment. The aeroplanes were flown by the Performance Testing Squadron with its three, later five, flights, each with its coterie of civilian technical officers under the CTO. He had, in addition, a research section and also specialists to advise on the non-performance and non-handling trials such as radio and electrical systems.

For the CTO and his small staff of technical officers, the responsibilities, already broad in 1939, became progressively more challenging as the number of aircraft types proliferated, coupled with their increasing performance and complexity. From the beginning of the war the number of technical officers was small in relation to the tests to be made. In 1940, in an attempt to speed up at least the initial clearance of new types for Service use, teams were detached to the contractors' airfields, the first, under Dr D. Cameron, went to Coventry for the Albemarle, and the second, taking six weeks under Dr G. Hislop, to Langley for the Typhoon. While this concentration of effort benefited individual types, work at Boscombe suffered to the extent that the scheme was soon abandoned.

Slight relief was afforded by the formal removal of camera testing (apart from camera guns) in mid-1941. In 1942 Mr E. T. Jones, the CTO, acquired two deputies in new posts – the Senior Performance Technical Officer, Mr Roger Cushing, and a Senior Handling Technical Officer, Squadron Leader (later Wing Commander) J. W. ('Alan') Truran. Specialist sections for navigation and radio (including radar) were formed as demands for tests on this equipment grew, while the Chief Engineer and his staff devoted more of their time to assessment of aircraft systems, in addition to their never-ending work of servicing all aeroplanes at the Establishment. One further section, formed in August 1941, was dedicated to the production of reports, and was staffed by women; in the month following its creation the section produced fifty-five reports (average fifty copies) and in February 1944 100 (up to ninety copies of each). In early 1945, following the reorganisation of the previous October, there were under the Superintendent of Performance, Mr S. Scott-Hall, four Technical Sections (one for each new Flying Squadron), a Research Section, Engine Performance Section and a Drawing Office; a further group was in Khartoum for engine cooling trials, later joined by an element of IFDF. The total scientific staff was thirty-eight (including fifteen juniors), plus fifty-one assistants and drawing office staff. Nearly a third of these people joined in the last year of the war. The embryo Engineering Division had five Technical Sections with a total staff of nineteen for trials work, plus the entire maintenance organisation.

This large, capable and efficient organisation may be contrasted with the situation in 1939. Mr Donald Lang, one of about twenty civilian staff (including seven Technical Officers) who moved from Martlesham Heath, remembers the chaos at Boscombe on arrival. Civilians were given increasingly cramped offices in the upper floor of the headquarters building, some remaining there until 1944 when they moved to a married quarter used as an office. The A Flight Technical Office, of which Lang was head in the mid-war period, moved to a wooden hut for a time after 1942. Working space, always at a premium, became progressively cosier as more staff joined. Mr Jimmy Lang (no relation) recalled up to twelve people occupying one large room on joining in March 1941 – commenting that he, in common with many others arriving with academic degrees but no practical knowledge of aircraft testing, benefited from the communal activity. The tyro technical officers spent up to a year assisting in trials, including flying as much as possible, before being given a project of their own; later they had several running concurrently. An interesting sidelight on these young graduates, of whom there were from 1944 several at the A&AEE, is that they were drafted to the job by an organisation later known as the University Joint Recruiting Board under C. P. Snow (later Lord Snow).

Most accepted their lot and made significant contributions to the work of the Establishment, but a few, it seems, found their position hard to accept and felt, perhaps, that they would be more use in uniform. A post-war synopsis by the Cabinet Office of the work of the Establishment comments that the latter group 'constituted an irritating and chronic problem'. A happier experience resulted from the recruitment of younger but able school-leavers, starting as civilian technical assistants; this number was in addition to the clerical recruits, including many women. Pay for the young ladies was low[1], and not a lot higher for the young graduates – Mr H. W. (Wason) Turner was paid £250 for his third year (1945) of work as a Junior Scientific Officer. Some youngsters were recruited locally, but most civilians and servicemen were able to travel home only infrequently. By 1942 the routine was twelve days at work followed, in theory, by a long weekend off – staggered to permit the Establishment to work seven days per week. Similar arrangements were made in the all-RAF/RN Armament Section.

So much for recruitment and domestic arrangements. The achievements of the Establishment under the head of 'Aeroplanes' are considered here in the broad categories of performance, handling and operational equipment. A nice distinction between the first two of these categories can be drawn in the definition of handling, ie stability and control,

as the motion of an aircraft about its centre of gravity (CG), while performance is the movement of the CG through the air. Handling trials were often exciting, performance trials usually dull (but busy in single-seaters); both benefited from pilots who were experienced in test work. Speaking in 1944, E. T. Jones reiterated the words of H. T. Tizard in 1917: 'Get careful flyers whose judgement and reliability you can trust and your [ie the Technical Officer's] task is comparatively easy; get careless flyers and it is impossible.'

Standard Performance

The fundamental objective of measuring performance was to establish capability, for example level speed range, climb rate and ceiling. Since performance varies with altitude and temperature, the measured values need to be corrected to standard conditions for meaningful comparison between types and for determination of the effect of changes (such as external stores). Much work was done on the correction methods to ensure sound results; the Performance Research Section under Dr D. Cameron for most of the war was largely responsible for this achievement.

Before the war, the so-called 'half and half'[2] method was in use to reduce performance to standard conditions with sufficient accuracy for unsupercharged engines with fixed-pitch propellers. From 1939 it was found that in supercharged engines, boost varied with temperature, and that variable-pitch, constant-speed propellers introduced further complications. In August 1942, after considerable experience at the A&AEE (summarised in a series of research reports), and following consultation with other establishments and industry, national reduction methods were agreed. The A&AEE, led by Dr Cameron, accepted the task of providing a suitable document, presented in its initial form as report AAEE/Res/170 of November 1942 (referred to locally as 'The Decameron Nights'). It became the basis for all UK work on reciprocating engines, and was incorporated into the Performance Handbook with tables, graphs and instructions permitting logical progress to obtain standard figures.

---

[1] Pay for a female clerk or machine operator started at 18s 6d per week at age 16, in a scale rising to 47 shillings (£2 7s) at 21.

[2] That is, applying half the correction due to pressure changes with height and half the correction due to density changes.

Compressibility was taken into account in correcting airspeed readings (as it had been pre-war), but the new document did not entirely explain some shortcomings in anticipated top speeds. The propeller tip speed in powerful types (ie fast and with a large propeller) was found to approach, and occasionally exceed, the speed of sound, leading to small losses of efficiency. In rare cases, reducing rpm and thus the tip helical Mach number increased the maximum speed achieved. In 1944, report AAEE/Res/208 included further advice on compressibility. Among other investigations was measurement of the effect of climbing into an increasing headwind; trials in a Spitfire and Boston showed that an improvement in rate of climb of 50 to 100 feet per minute could result. Consequently climbs thereafter were measured across the wind, thus avoiding wind gradient.

All reduction methods relied on accurate instruments and knowledge of the ambient temperature; only towards the end of the war was a sufficiently accurate thermometer available for use in aircraft – and then not in single-seaters. Knowledge of the daily temperatures was based initially on indifferent data from balloon ascents and occasional climbs by Gladiators of C Per T in 1939-40. From 1942 daily climbs to ceiling by two Spitfires of the HAF, modified with Cambridge transmitting thermometers, provided accurate information not only for the Establishment but all local, and not-so-local, airfields making performance measurements.

An early trial on all aeroplanes for standard tests involved measurement of the errors in the pressure instrument system due, almost invariably, to less than ideal positioning of the static source. The method involved fitting an accurate aneroid to the static source and, at various speeds, flying past an observer who recorded the actual height; the differences were compared after landing. By May 1944 more than 800 such flights had been made. The limitations of the 'fly-by' method included circuit congestion and lack of information on high-altitude effects. In 1944 a Spitfire was equipped as a calibrated datum for PE measurement using the formation method. Large, or unacceptable, errors required investigation of alternative positions for the static source, as in the Lancaster and Ventura; for the latter it was found that errors decreased towards the rear, and that the only accurate position was, therefore, some 14 feet behind the tail! With calibrated instruments, known errors and an accurate weight, flight measurements could be made, and using appropriate reduction methods the performance results presented on a standardised and comparable basis.

The original camera used for measuring take-offs and landings (the ground roll, and distances to and from 50 feet respectively were required) had a number of drawbacks, chief among them being the tiny image of the subject aeroplane. In 1940 a superior design by Mr Maclaren Humphreys was manufactured by Vinten Ltd, and adopted for use throughout the war; it was based on the F47 camera and remained a bulky instrument but had a telephoto lens among other advantages. Communication between pilot and cameraman relied on flags, but this difficulty was overshadowed by the tedious interpretation needed. Mr Terry Heffernan remembers the countless hours spent measuring image sizes, angles, times, and horizontal and vertical displacement from datum axes on each film frame. The accuracy thus attained was, on occasion, rendered useless by a small but significant change in technique by the pilot. Wind speed, ideally of a low and consistent velocity, was recorded by an unfortunate assistant holding a hand anemometer on the airfield. Landings were measured only on a small number of aeroplanes.

With known low-level pressure errors, corrections available for compressibility, and a calibrated air speed indicator, speeds were determined. Obtaining the fastest became more tricky once engines became limited to 5 minutes at maximum power, as this time was insufficient for achieving stabilised flight. The technique eventually adopted involved the use of maximum cruise power at several levels around the expected full throttle height; after selecting the best, a slight dive was made to that height while applying full power. Readings were taken during the last 2 minutes of the run, in single-seat aircraft by the pilot and other types by an observer; the indicated readings were corrected on landing. In some cases late in the war, agreement was obtained from engine companies to use the maximum settings for periods greater than 5 minutes, thus simplifying the flying.

For cruising performance (both cruise ceiling and range determination), particularly important in large aircraft, the techniques were simpler, but the flying more tedious, as up to 15 minutes were necessary to establish stable conditions at every height and condition (eg weak/rich mixture, various rpm and boost settings) and to measure fuel consumption and airspeed. The first of the objectives was to obtain the greatest height for cruising at the lowest practical airspeed, determined by the need to preserve a small margin above the theoretical minimum to cater for mild manoeuvres. In parallel to the cruise ceiling determination, range tests were usually made. For the latter, the objective was to obtain the greatest air miles per gallon (ampg) – achieved in nearly every engine by obeying the 'high boost/low rpm' rule. Thus the best range (with the engines operating at their most economical setting) height was lower than the cruising ceiling (when the engines were operating at the greatest continuous output). Having determined the conditions for maximum range, every type made a full range flight to confirm the figures. In presenting the results, the Establishment made increasingly comprehensive recommendations for the technique most suitable for operational crews to achieve the best results.

In 1941, the advice for a Wellington III with Hercules XI engines was contained in four fundamental rules: use weak mixture, optimum airspeed for weight, medium supercharger, and minimum rpm with the maximum boost needed. Three years later, for the Lancaster III with Merlin 38s (automatic mixture control), the advice was augmented by a table giving the effect on ampg of rpm and boost at various speeds, thus allowing crews to make precise settings for best results. Also given in the reports on the range flights were the maximum still air distance possible until the fuel tanks ran dry; a margin was then applied, depending on the user Command's preference. Bomber Command, for example, took 75% of the maximum and Coastal Command took 80%.

After partial climbs to determine the best speed, rates of climb were relatively straightforward to measure, but near the ceiling extremely accurate flying was required, particularly in large aircraft. Multi-engined types also made climb tests with one engine inoperative (two engines in the case of four-engined machines), and an optimum speed determined – usually with the recommendation to reduce weight if, for example, bombs were still on board. The effect of a windmilling as opposed to a feathered propeller was

Warwick I BV403 in July 1944 carrying a large lifeboat Mk II and equipped with ASV radar aerials under the wings and nose. It lacks the large window below the cockpit seen on BV-301, and weighed 1,800lb more on trials. *A&AEE recognition 228*

examined, while in four-engined types two-engine tests were usually made with one feathered and the other on the same side at an idling setting, simulating a feathered propeller.

A pressing need in performance tests from early in the war was for automatic recording of flight instruments. By 1942 the Research Section had developed a suitable device that involved tapping the static and pitot systems, and taking leads off the engine instruments; a cine camera was run at material times. In spite of the auto-observer, as the device was known, fighters' climb performance by late in the war was stretching the ability of pilots to make the necessary back-up notes on their knee pads. Particularly interesting was the Meteor, which, although not the fastest climber in its early versions, consumed fuel at such a rate that the effect of changing weight had to be taken into account; extremely short endurance added to the difficulty. The solution was to remove the ammunition boxes behind the pilot and install a set of instruments, a small writing surface and a rudimentary seat. The first flight in this configuration took place in August 1945 with Mr R. B. (Bobby) Marsh, whose short stature was considered (by others) to be ideal; Squadron Leader K. J. ('Pop') Sewell, whose attitude to civilians was less than respectful, flew the aircraft in a non-stop aerobatic sequence. After landing, Marsh, who had just managed to retain his lunch, remarked that he soon became supremely uninterested in the instruments, but that, even had he wished to do so, escape was impossible as the entrance panel had been screwed shut. The decision soon followed to develop the auto-observer for jets, although a few further post-war passenger flights were made, including those by Mr J. J. Quinn, a late wartime Technical Officer, and Vice Admiral Sir Denis Boyd.

The Meteor exercise was a first step in defining the methods of reducing jet-engined performance, and thus to update AAEE/Res/170. Coincident with the compilation of that comprehensive document, the need to expand the information presented to the Air Staffs was becoming apparent.

Operational Performance of Bombers

In service, the new four-engined bombers soon revealed capabilities well below those that Bomber Command had expected from initial Boscombe reports. As a result, early in 1942 arrangements were made for a comprehensive investigation by the Establishment of the Halifax, a particular disappointment to the Air Staff. Four aeroplanes with differing modification states and ages were received, and a major trial instigated under J. J. Unwin, J. W. Truran, D. White and W. J. D. Annand. It was immediately apparent that operational aircraft had several extra items of equipment fitted since the original trials, thus explaining much of the deterioration. A great deal of flying was, however, completed over several months to quantify the contribution of each item of difference[3]. Such an extensive trial, at a time when other large aircraft, including Halifax handling, were demanding attention,

[3] These were propellers, ice guards, air cleaners, wire-cutters and guards, upper turret, nose shape, aerials and masts, closure of bomb doors, flame damping exhausts, fuel jettison pipes, surface finish, 'Kilfrost' paste, and wear and tear.

Halifax II DG221, from No 78 Squadron, is seen in August 1942 after ten operational sorties. It was one of the aircraft used for comparative tests to investigate performance shortfall in service. This machine was the worst case, attributed to the large upper turret (Boulton Paul Type C Mk V) and the poor and worn surface finish apparent here. *A&AEE 11195*

coupled with a number of contemporary fatal accidents, was a great challenge to all involved – particularly as the whole exercise was of a development nature and thus strictly outside the normal terms of reference of the Establishment. Nevertheless, the results were considered to justify the effort, and soundly based conclusions and recommendations for improvement were made, thus allowing the Air Staff to decide on the best solutions. Perhaps the most significant results from this trial were knowledge of the effect of ambient temperature on cruising performance (the Stirling cruised 25mph (true) slower and 3,000 feet lower on a hot day), and the sensitivity of very heavy aircraft to small variations in speed, handling (even turret rotation), and engine cooling flaps. It was recommended that heavy aircraft should be cruised at least 5mph above the theoretical optimum to aid handling and engine cooling. A later trial on a Halifax Mk V established that speeds attainable were at least 5mph higher if the aircraft was unpainted.

Stirling I BF382 is at Boscombe Down in October 1942, having been confirmed as a rogue following an adverse report by No 214 Squadron. Climb and ceiling of this Austin-built machine were both poor, explained by wire-cutters visible on the leading edges, excessive 'Kilfrost' paste (seen running down the fin) and bad rigging. The Establishment adjusted the engines to give rated performance, which restored some lost performance. A&AEE 11226

Engines

The Halifax investigation of 1942 was additional to the continuous flow of aeroplanes for performance assessment under more routine arrangements. New types were received after initial handling and some speed and climb measurements by their manufacturer and, usually, brief preliminary flying by a Boscombe pilot at the maker's airfield. On arrival, weighing was followed by pressure error determination and the performance trials noted above. Wartime increases in performance were due in some measure to aerodynamics, for example the thin wing of the Tempest and later Spitfires, but to a greater degree by marked increase in engine power from both in-line water-cooled and radial air-cooled arrangements. Supercharging increases were made possible by advances in fuel. Boscombe was among the first airfields to have storage and bowsers for 150 octane petrol. British superchargers were mostly mechanically driven, while some American designs were exhaust (ie turbo) driven. An interesting comment on the Cyclones (R-1820) of the Fortress was the restriction in power at altitude due to the need to throttle back to keep supercharger rpm within limits.

By 1942 engine power and complication had so increased that the A&AEE formed a special engine section within the Technical Office to consider the developments and attendant problems, notably cylinder and oil cooling in the radial configuration. Earlier the need had arisen for special pyrometers to be fitted to enable accurate cylinder temperatures of radial engines to be measured. By 1944 all fifty-six cylinders of the four Hercules in the Halifax had pyrometers, with associated gauges, and the observer, often Flight Lieutenant M. Hermiston, had the unenviable task of frequently recording all the readings on a long flight. By the end of 1944 a Minneapolis-Honeywell auto paper recorder was received, capable of recording cylinder temperatures at the rate of one per second, but pressing needs remained for torque meters, and knowledge of charge temperatures.

By 1945 the Engine Section had five people at Boscombe under Mr Terence Pullin, with others in North Africa. The presence of an A&AEE team in North Africa resulted directly from the problem of cooling high-powered engines. Even in North European weather conditions, the early Hercules of the Stirling required considerable work to achieve moderately acceptable temperatures. With increase in power and more widespread operational use of radials in North Africa, India and, later, the Far East, the need to ensure adequate cooling became a priority by early 1944. Previously the Establishment had extrapolated results obtained in temperate climes, to indicate likely acceptability in tropical areas. Recognising that the figures were only an informed guess, the A&AEE established a small team at Khartoum in mid-1944 to determine precisely the effect of high ambient temperatures both on the ground and while flying. Wartime aircraft were a Mosquito, Typhoon, Lancaster, Halifax and later, six Tempests; the opportunity was taken to measure take-offs, rate of climb and other parameters. It was found that in general every 1°C rise in ambient temperature gave a 1°C rise in cylinder (air-cooled) and radiator (liquid-cooled) temperatures, and also in oil temperatures. These figures are similar to the 'guesstimates' used in earlier extrapolations – although oil temperatures had previously been calculated on the basis of 0.7°C rise per 1°C ambient.

By late 1944 an unarmed Liberator was regularly used to support the detachment, staging via Castel Benito near Tripoli in Libya. The record for the return trip was held by Squadron Leader J. D. Starkey in June 1945; the elapsed time of 88 hours back to Boscombe involved nearly 40 hours of flying. Those returning on this trip in a delicate state found the airborne facilities inadequate – but the unsavoury conditions in the cabin on landing deterred the customs officers from making more than a fleeting examination.

The need for cold-weather testing was less urgent, but a Lancaster did spend a few weeks in the winter 1943/44 at the RCAF testing centre at Kapuskasing.

Handling

It is doubtful if anywhere in the world had so wide an experience of handling different types of aircraft between 1939 and 1945 as the A&AEE, which flew nearly all British types, most operational American designs, and a few German machines. From this diverse collection a wealth of data was collected and disseminated, and many unusual and extreme conditions examined; here a brief description is given of the standard stability and control tests followed by examples of the more intractable characteristics explored.

On receipt of every aeroplane for handling, a thorough examination of its condition was made, and particular attention paid to critical items such as the shrouds in front of control surfaces to ensure that there was no distortion or damage. Also noted were the methods of obtaining cockpit indications of the position, for example, of the trimmer(s), wing flaps and engine cooling flaps. Meanwhile, the pilots made an assessment of the cockpit if time permitted; more often, observations on cockpit layout, reflections and view followed experience in flight.

Handling on take-off, combined where possible with distance measurements, included assessment of ease of keeping straight (both into and across the wind), trim changes on retracting undercarriage and flaps, effect of mis-set trims and, in multi-engined types, the effect of an engine cut. The last of these was explored at a safe height and at gradually decreasing speeds. Landings were the subject of qualitative investigation over a range of CG, if applicable. Of more interest was handling during a baulked approach (ie an overshoot), since many aircraft, of which the Hudson was a prime example, suffered severe trim changes, both on the application of full power with full flap selected and later when the flaps were retracted; stick forces needing two hands made operating flap and other levers particularly awkward. Such characteristics led to limitations being made on CG position. Trim changes in flight resulting from changes in speed, power and operation of ancillary controls, eg cooling flaps and bomb doors, received careful attention. In particular, note was taken of the ease of retrimming; a trimmer range of movement in excess of that required was condemned.

Stability, like all performance and most handling measurements, required calm conditions and, preferably, a good natural horizon. Lateral and directional stability usually posed fewer problems than longitudinal; discussion here is limited to the latter. Many factors had a bearing on acceptability of stability, among them aircraft role, stage of flight and lightness of controls. Quantitative measurements were made at two or more CG; for example, longitudinal static stability was recorded over the speed range (equating to the useable C_L) by noting elevator position (stick-fixed stability) and trimmer position (stick-free stability). The Technical Officer, by plotting the positions against C_L for two CG, could determine the neutral point (ie when the aircraft was neither stable nor unstable). For longitudinal manoeuvring stability, the yardstick adopted early in the war was 'stick force per g', again at two or more CG, the test pilot aiming to measure the pull force required for 5g in fighters, and 2 to 2½g in large aircraft. Stick forces decreased in manoeuvres with aft CG, and several aircraft, notably the Spitfire, Beaufighter and Mosquito, became dangerously sensitive; some Spitfire pilots in service tore the wings off, usually from this cause. The most common 'fix' was a weight in the elevator control circuit arranged to move the stick forward with application of positive 'g', thus making the pilot pull harder. Other routine tests included out-of-trim dives, with measurement of acceleration on release.

The subject of stability about all three axes is extensive and complicated, and while the quantitative data obtained for every aircraft tested were also extensive, the pilot's qualitative and informed opinion was always of value in determining acceptability. For example, a number of types displayed unstable characteristics in the climb (ie high power and low speed), but pilots found this condition acceptable as the degree of extra concentration demanded was not excessive for the relatively short periods involved. All aircraft were stalled, and the effect of flaps, ancillary controls and power noted; two standard conditions were investigated, both engine-off, namely clean and dirty (ie undercarriage and flaps up and fully down respectively). Apart from pilot training types, spins were, by 1944, restricted to examination of recovery behaviour after just two complete turns in types liable inadvertently to get into a position where a spin was possible. In both low-speed trials particular attention was paid to the warning given to the pilot (usually buffeting), the behaviour before and during the stall/spins, and the ease of recovery and the height lost doing so. Entries into stalls from turning flight usually produced the most interesting results.

At the other end of the speed range, invariably obtained in dives, handling was frequently even more interesting. Problems arose from a large number of causes, ranging from excessive stability (and possibly high stick forces), which prevented high speeds being obtained (for example in the Firefly), through feeble attachment of wing covering (for example, Albemarle and Warwick), to a series of more fundamental aerodynamic phenomena. Fabric-covered control surfaces, notably elevators (universally fitted in 1939), were sometimes the cause of unacceptable high speed handling due to distortion of the fabric;

replacement by metal usually improved matters. Structural distortion of the rear fuselage and tailplane gave rise to similar undesirable characteristics. Investigation of troublesome aircraft required considerable flying to identify precisely the source(s) of the difficulty, and needed several different loadings (changing CG and weight).

Perhaps the most daunting of the handling phenomena experienced at Boscombe Down before 1945 was associated with compressibility found during dives. The first advice to pilots on dealing with the difficulties on recovering from high-speed dives came from members of the Bulman Mission returning in 1942 from the USA, where the thin, highly loaded wings of American fighters had already revealed compressibility, ie high Mach number[4], characteristics. The basic message was to continue the dive to lower altitudes where, with increase in speed of sound, the Mach number decreased, thus reducing the effect of compressibility and allowing the elevators to become effective and permit a normal recovery.

At the A&AEE, the first recorded alarming failure to recover at high altitude occurred before the Bulman advice was received; in this incident, continuous heaving on the stick eventually allowed the relieved pilot to recover his and the aeroplane's equilibrium. It was decided that high Mach number trials on all types likely to be affected were necessary and formalised in a memorandum from the CTO (No 54 in a series) to all technical staff calling for dives at high Mach numbers – starting with a forward CG and aiming for Mach 0.7. A small number of Mach meters were received from the RAE late in 1943 and first used in a Spitfire. Fighters were primarily of interest, but even the Lancaster was dived to Mach 0.725 (350mph indicated airspeed at 25,000 feet), at which speed an escape hatch blew off.

In March 1945 a new Mosquito PR34 suffered loss of control in cloud as an engine cut momentarily when changing supercharger gear. The aircraft entered a steep dive, reached Mach numbers in the mid-0.7s and recovered from the near vertical dive below cloud after experiencing severe buffet. A few days later, and after two 200-gallon underwing tanks had been fitted to this aircraft, the crew (Squadron Leader John Jarvis and Mr H. W. (Wason)

[4] Mach number is the ratio of true airspeed to the local speed of sound; aircraft speed is expressed as the corresponding decimal fraction.

Turner) were strapping in when one of the groundcrew peered through the entrance door and said, 'I think you'd better look at this.' A crack was just visible under the starboard wing. A contemporary fatal accident to a Mosquito was attributed to structural failure following an inadvertent excessive Mach number.

An aircraft demonstrating the effects of compressibility at a low Mach number was the Welkin, where, during standard dives on the prototype to Mach 0.7 from 35,000 feet, the pilot was unable to prevent increasing back and forth oscillating of the stick until 25,000 feet was reached and the movements gradually damped out. Further dives were limited to Mach 0.65, a comprehensive investigation was made into manoeuvrability, and a table of optimum indicated speeds for various heights was produced; disappointing turning performance resulted above 20,000 feet if compressibility was to be avoided in this thick-winged design.

For lateral and directional tests, one pre-war favourite, the flat turn (ie use of the rudder alone while keeping the wings level) was soon abandoned. Other routine tests included steady heading sideslips, rates of roll, and response to aileron and rudder alone. From the resulting aircraft behaviour and the control displacement and forces needed, could be determined much information on the stabilities of the aircraft, their relative importance, and control characteristics.

Handling an engine failure in twin-engined aeroplanes on take-off had received consideration before the war when techniques were examined with a view to continuing the take-off if airborne, rather than closing both throttles and crash-landing. In the early part of the war, multi-engined aircraft were assessed for the lowest safe speed with asymmetric engine power, but the increase in engine power tended to raise the safety speed – indeed, the 25,500lb Mosquito PR34 at 200mph in 1945 was the highest found. Until reaching that speed a crash-landing was inevitable. American aircraft were, with few exceptions, praised for their asymmetric handling and relatively low safety speeds.

Awkward Handling

The Fairey Barracuda had been tested in 1941/42 and the worst of its handling characteristics improved sufficiently for entry to Naval service in early 1943. Accidents in the first squadrons led to two further investigations at the A&AEE. The first confirmed that, if recovering from a dive, during which the change of speed caused large directional trim changes and consequent sideslipping, the pilot rolled (particularly to the right) and put on coarse rudder, then an uncontrollable nose drop could occur following rudder overbalance. As a result of this trial, naval pilots were adjured not to use top rudder in sideslips. A more comprehensive investigation under Dr George Hislop was put in hand, with the flying restricted to two pilots. Instrumentation was comprehensive: control positions (Desynn indicators), control column force indicator, wool tufts around tailplane, an auto-observer and cine cameras for the tufts.

An example of part of the extensive preparations made for investigation of a puzzling handling problem, in this case the unexpected diving of the Barracuda on recovery from low-level attacks. The aircraft, P9726, was borrowed from 827 Naval Air Squadron, which called in 'M'. It was fitted with the tailplane tufts shown here to visualise flow. A camera in the rear cockpit recorded results, while extensive instrumentation was also fitted in the aircraft. The awkward undercarriage, high tailplane and wing flaps of the type are clearly visible from this angle. Compared to its tough American counterpart, the Grumman Avenger, it is, perhaps, not surprising that the type was never really liked or felt to be particularly successful.

The tests included level and dynamic (ie turning) stalls, re-examination of the trim changes with speed, power and flap settings, diving, rudder overbalance and control forces. Dynamic stalls to the right were described as vicious – the aircraft became inverted – and with flaps in the air brake position stalls were even worse. From a trimmed level attitude, a dive (rudder-free) caused steadily increasing sideslip (skidding) and needed a considerable push force. In dive recoveries the wool tufts showed that application of rudder past a certain point caused airflow breakdown; the rudder overbalanced, the elevator was pulled down momentarily and the nose pitched violently down. It was postulated that because of the high stick forces, in service a pilot would trim into a dive, recover with a large pull force, and move the flaps from dive to neutral – thus adding to the pull force required. The rapid change in speed would cause skid on recovery and, if turning (ie rolling), any vigorous use of rudder would cause the violent nose-down pitch. At low level, the results could be fatal. The recommendations by Hislop, endorsed by his superiors, included fitting a dorsal fin, a metal-covered rudder and a spring balance tab to the rudder. These modifications were incorporated immediately; other modifications suggested were to await confirmation by further trials at the RAE. This brief summary of a major trial gives some idea of the more extensive tests occasionally made, and the extent of instrumentation available in 1943.

A further example of the contribution made by the A&AEE to a development problem is provided by the Firefly, also by Fairey. The original design had, on the standard tests, demonstrated impossibly high stick forces in dives above 350mph (limit 425mph) when trimmed for maximum level speed, and also that the accelerations on releasing the stick were excessive. Six modifications were progressively tried, all in 1943, and included moving the elevator hinge line, then extending the nose of the control surface, thickened trim tabs, increased tailplane incidence, metal in place of fabric to cover the elevators, and decreased elevator circuit gearing. Improvements were made by all the changes, but all introduced other undesirable characteristics. One of the pilots involved, Lieutenant Don Robertson, recalled, after noting in flight all the multitude of handling items required, presenting the technical officer with the result; after deft work with the slide rule it was deduced that elevator distortion was the culprit. The pilots' admiration for Cameron's deductive powers was, no doubt, reciprocated by the respect for the pilots' skill. The final, and satisfactory, solution was the introduction of spring tab elevators, giving pleasant and progressive handling at all speeds and positions of the CG.

Of the larger aircraft, the Halifax had a serious problem due to rudder overbalance, found during the standard asymmetric power tests in 1940 on the first aeroplane. Cutting one, or particularly both, port engines gave the worse handling. The first major investigation of modifications to improve behaviour was made on a Halifax Mk I in early 1942, by trying bulbous leading edges to the rudders (known as 'noselings'). These aggravated overbalance to such an extent that the 'lock-over' could only be overcome and the rudders centralised by diving and cutting the running engines; much height was lost. Next, on a Halifax Mk II, four alterations were progressively made to the range of relative movement of the combined balance and trim tabs (one on each rudder); the first three reduced the tendency to overbalance but made the rudders unacceptably heavy using the starboard engines alone at maximum power. The fourth alteration gave a greater trim range to starboard (ie the trim tab was moved to port to help the pilot apply starboard rudder to counteract the asymmetric effect), and produced a curious effect in that mild overbalance reappeared but thereby assisted the pilot. Handling was described as unpleasant but manageable and this alteration was recommended for all Halifaxes. Further accidents in the RAF, however, prompted a further trial early in 1943.

Out of the three aircraft used for the new trial, one crashed in February, killing the pilot, Flight Lieutenant S. F. Reiss, and Mr J. J. Unwin, who had been in charge of the trial since early 1942. The top half of one rudder of the Halifax had broken away, attributed to the violence of the overbalance, and a spin developed. Reiss had taken over as leading pilot for the tests from Squadron Leader W. J. Carr, who had been killed flying a Warwick six months earlier. Extensive tests on the remaining pair of aircraft revealed among other things that neither reduced horn balances on the rudders nor the minor modifications tried, such as cord on the trailing edge, were effective. Limit stops on the rudder bars prevented irretrievable overbalance, and were recommended for incorporation. The strongest recommendation was for larger rudders. Fins with a 30% increase in area, known as D fins, were first tested in a Halifax Mk III with Hercules engines in June 1943, and the following month in a Halifax Mk V with Merlin engines as on the Mk II; both were satisfactory.

Operational Equipment

Flame Damping

Among the responsibilities of the Technical Office was that of measuring the night-time visibility of exhausts – work that started in earnest in 1941 under Mr Phillips, whose sobriquet of 'Flame Damping Phil' is unsurprising. Nearly all aircraft were subject to Phillips's appraisal. He was instrumental in the provision of the blower tunnel (see above) to aid testing after his initial bid in 1941 for a blower was rejected on the grounds of inadequate electrical supply. Flame damping was the cause of almost the only trials flown at night. Measurement of the effectiveness of flame damping remained somewhat subjective – photographic recording had been rejected in 1941 and ground observation by eye was always made. Even in 1944 there was discussion of the definition of a 'dark night', and the following year measurements using infra-red sensing were made. The photographs here of the various designs to reduce exhaust visibility are largely the result of the A&AEE's recommendations.

How the Germans did it! Junkers 88 PJ876 has its BMW801s examined by the A&AEE, but not, in these photographs, at Boscombe. The ducted ejector exhausts came nowhere to meeting British requirements, being visible up to 1,000 yards. *A&AEE 11578*

The stub exhausts on Heinkel He 111 AW177 in August 1942 were poor flame dampers. *A&AEE 11091*

Experimental exhaust flame dampers on the sole Boston V, BZ580, to be tested at the Establishment in August/September 1945. Originally fitted with simple individual stub exhausts, these dampers were an improvement, but still not good enough to meet the operational criteria.

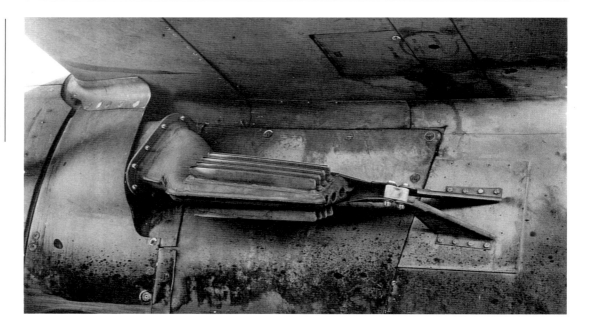

A close view of the experimental port outer engine exhaust flame dampers on Boston V BZ580 in August/September 1945. Still not good enough.

Two types of exhausts, both good, on Mosquito IX MM230. Prominent ice guards for the air intake are visible. *A&AEE 11711*

The front close-fitted anti-glow shroud on Spitfire IX AB499 in March 1943 was effective only from ahead. *A&AEE 11341*

These effective tapered and slotted shrouded exhausts on the Hercules VI of Stirling III BK649 have the 'intensifier' pipe ducting hot fresh air to the cabin. The photograph is dated about March 1943. *A&AEE 9987*

A development of an RAF design: an un-ducted fishtail saxophone exhaust with anti-glow paint. It made some improvement on Halifax II DG221 in September 1942. *A&AEE 11121*

Cockpit Contamination

The insidious gas carbon monoxide (CO), present in engine exhaust and gun-firing fumes, was a threat to aircrew – long since recognised as such by medical science, and standards of acceptable concentration laid down. Boscombe merely had the task of measurement under the leadership of Squadron Leader Fame Thompson, a pre-war Cambridge rowing blue. The early method used balloons inflated by small bellows at various times in flight, and the sample analysed later on the ground. The technique in cramped single-seat aircraft may be imagined – particularly landing with a cockpit crammed with filled rubber spheres. By 1944 large aircraft used a Type 9141 indicator (based on that used in coal mines), and single-seaters a smaller device. The most significant contribution by the Establishment was its expertise in identifying and curing the source of the contaminants, often by the simple expedient of lengthening exhaust pipes, or sealing the tail wheel opening. In some intractable cases, the Establishment was obliged to recommend the use of oxygen from take-off. Gun firing was found to produce no significant CO in crew areas apart from some hand-held nose guns; there were usually ample draughts.

Noise

Noise was not investigated on a routine basis but, if crews complained, a noisemeter was used, and analysis sometimes identified the source. Thicker material at the sensitive parts of the fuselage was fitted with varying success. Other engineering matters, such as electrical and hydraulic systems, received increasingly expert attention throughout the war period.

Heating

The draughts within the wings may have cleared fumes, but the maintenance of an acceptable temperature of the gun mechanisms was made more difficult by any airflow. A Performance Technical Officer had the responsibility of measuring gun bay temperatures – a task perhaps more appropriate for armament staff. He also assessed the warmth of all crew positions. The standard eight-gun wings of early fighters were kept reasonably warm, but new designs and modifications led to the need for measurement; the first American fighters were devoid of gun heating, and the twelve-gun Hurricane was not much better. Recording thermometers and other instrumentation (much of it invented by the Establishment) gave insights into cold areas, and, as improvements in heating and/or retention were made, a measure of success. Taping over cartridge and link chutes, as well as gun ports, was a well-tried and effective remedy. Many other suggestions made by the Establishment to increase heating supply were also effective. Crew heating was an endemic problem in large aircraft – examples of the various attempts to improve matters (eg the Gallay boiler and the Morris radiator) can be found later in this book. The situation of tail gunners in the British bombers was particularly unenviable, as no air heating penetrated to their isolated position; electrically heated clothing was often provided but was never entirely satisfactory. Not until 1944 was an attempt made to provide a special Janitrol heater to the tail gunner of the Lancaster following local modification by the RAF. It was a slight improvement.

Radio

The pre-war procedure of conducting range and interference checks continued on new aircraft, but radio appears to have been accorded low priority. Later marks of aircraft were not tested at all unless new radios were fitted. Mr Sid Dean remained in charge initially, but by 1942 Mr Bradshaw, thoroughly acquainted with spark transmitters, ruled, until Mr Chris Windley, the first leader of the radar side in June 1943, later took over the combined radio and radar section. The first major testing change accompanied the widespread adoption of IFF (Identification Friend or Foe). All aircraft types intended for Service use were assessed, initially the Mk II, then Mk IIN and Mk III (together with the American AN/APX-6 for naval aircraft). In 1944 trials were made using a mobile ground radar powered by a diesel-electric motor. Mr Henry Maidment recalls the frustrating hours, usually in winter, spent attempting to start the motor with a length of rope. With electrical power available, the team held their breath to see if the radar transmitter would work. Once the whole apparatus was running, the aircraft could get airborne (if the pilot hadn't disappeared during the frequent delays), and fly its standard triangular route with the IFF on. The radar head was rotated to follow the track (a manual procedure – leaving the operator exhausted at the end of the day).

Airborne interception and bombing radars were the responsibility of the establishment at Defford, but the Radar Section was required to maintain the serviceability of the vast variety of sets in aircraft at the Establishment, whose primary interest lay in the aerodynamic effect of radomes on handling and performance. A partial exception was the gun laying radars in rear turrets, for which the Gunnery Section had the primary interest.

Navigation

In 1939 a report, under the section headed 'Navigation', may in the case of a single-seater have had little more than one sentence stating that there was a P-type compass, and stowage for the pilot's maps. Bombers were more generously treated, with an assessment of the navigator's facilities including his view out, lighting and plotting facilities. Both types would normally have a compass swing. Reports exist on the limited number of new equipments tested in 1940/42, such as a Hughes bubble sextant and magnesyn compass. More thorough testing, however, was possible following the arrival of a specialist navigator, Squadron Leader M. A. Snowball, in March 1942, and a Wellington (later Stirling) dedicated to navigation research. Items assessed then included a gyro-stabilised drift meter, a comparison of two types of remote reading compasses, and a windfinding attachment. A comprehensive report on navigation accuracy using astro was written, and an improvement in technique recommended; later, improvements to the astro-sextants were suggested. In 1943 a further investigation (after a lapse of ten years) quantified errors due to lightning strikes, terrestrial magnetism and aircraft compass deviations changing in flight. American aircraft with electrical earth return (as in the Liberator) caused compass errors, and the effects of operating electrical services were measured. Gun firing in Beaufighters produced significant compass errors; firing again while flying on a northerly heading was shown to reduce the deviation. Air swings of compasses using the aircraft's radar were tried, and a photo-electric sun-compass showed promise.

Looking Forward

In 1944 it was planned that post-war testing of civil landplanes would resume at the A&AEE and a small team of Technical Officers under Mr Freddie Cook started looking at testing techniques. The team, with Mr W. J. D. Annand, whose statistical approach to flight testing had found little favour at first among his peers, became a separate section in 1944, and in June 1945 was renamed the Civil Aircraft Testing Section. Among the earliest subjects investigated was the question of engine failure on take-off in multi-engined types, for which a dedicated Dakota and Fortress were received in mid-1945. By the end of the war some definite conclusions on take-off and other flight regimes had been reached. From this early work developed what later became the British Civil Airworthiness Requirements – including the Grouping of types depending on the ability to cope with engine failure, the concepts of gross and net performance, the take-off gradients to be attained and the factors to be considered in defining take-off speeds. In addition the definition of qualitative handling descriptions was further considered, following a major agreement on terminology in May 1944; for example, 'immovable' was defined, and replaced the less accurate 'solid'.

4 Armament

Bombs, guns and things under wings

Armament testing was considerably disrupted on moving to Boscombe due to the abrupt separation from its workshops, armoury and air ranges. As those vital facilities were gradually arranged, trials by the two flights proceeded at a gathering pace. Invariably known as the Gunnery Flight and the Bombing Flight, the correct titles were A and B Flights respectively of the Armament Testing Squadron. C Flight was added in 1940, but was more usually referred to as the Special Duty Flight (for the Establishment at Porton). Chapter 1 described the organisational developments throughout the war (which are summarised in Appendix 3).

By 1939 recent policy changes had resulted in a fourfold increase in the testing at the A&AEE of new bombs, guns and the aeroplanes to carry them. The expertise in the Armament Squadron from its knowledge of the capabilities, limitations, handling and safety requirements of air armaments was well founded by the outbreak of hostilities, and pre-war expansion was soon dwarfed by the scale of wartime activity. The knowledge and facilities acquired in making tests of all airborne weapons (except torpedoes) intended for operational use created a unique concentration of practical experience, and led inevitably to the Establishment making significant contributions to the resolution of problems, and thus to the development of armaments. Nevertheless, the primary task remained acceptance testing.

Formalising the position in late 1943, Group Captain (newly promoted) A. E. Dark, the Armament Technical Officer, in a comprehensive guide aimed at the growing number of officers new to experimental work, laid down simple yet comprehensive principles. In listing the need for a logical sequence of tests and comprehensive recording, Dark emphasised the balance between perfection and the urgent operational requirement.

Acceptability demanded a fine judgement, starting with a decision on the minimum number of variables, such as speed, height, angle of dive, combination of weapons, types of target to be used and so on, and ending with consideration of results, particularly the significance of any shortcomings revealed. One measure of the effectiveness of the methods used is the fact that there were no ground fatalities to armament personnel throughout the war – a remarkable achievement in view of the vast range of unfamiliar weapons handled, and the firing of millions of rounds, thousands of rockets and the dropping of tens of thousands of bombs.

There were, nevertheless, accidents. In 1941 the first Liberator, with American bomb gear (vertical stowage), had no pressure plate to bear down on the safety pin, which was removed, contrary to instructions, prior to loading. One of the practice bombs fell off, detonated, and injured Pilot Officer V. L. Fisher and Aircraftsman Webb. Another accident resulted from incorrect painting by the Ordnance Factory of live bombs in the colour – black – used for inert bombs; the latter were salvaged and cut up by oxyacetylene torch. On this occasion the mis-painted live bomb exploded, killing an Italian prisoner at nearby Tidworth.

In 1939 there were about ten experimental officers, all qualified armament specialists (all had completed the Long Armament Course) and most qualified pilots, in the headquarters and the two flights. By 1945 the number was more than thirty, including several pilots in three testing sections (bombing, gunnery and rocketry), plus a research section, a drawing office, workshop, and the Station Armament Officer responsible for the explosive store, armoury and routine maintenance. All except the research section were manned by servicemen, almost exclusively RAF but including a few RN personnel.

Barracuda I P9652 carrying six Smoke Curtain Installations (SCI) units – too many for safety.

Barracuda II RK328 carries four 370lb SCI in August 1945. The SCI could contain smoke, mustard gas or other substances. However, handling and performance were the subjects of these trials, and, as a result, the number of SCI were limited to two for safety on overshoot. *A&AEE 15213*

A closer view of the SCI on RK328 in August 1945. Note the landing lamp details. *A&AEE 15213*

Bombing

In 1939 the Bombing Flight had fourteen aircraft, including five Blenheims, divided between 'type', ie new or modified aircraft, and general-purpose trials. Early work included measurement of the scatter of small bombs, and of the functioning of the pistols in anti-submarine bombs when dropped from low level at high speed. The latter trials showed that the arming vane locked on the striker spindle and prevented detonation; modifications eventually provided a remedy, but only after some 200 individual drops into Lyme Bay. By the end of 1939 the first 1,000lb General Purpose bombs were successfully dropped on Crichel Down – with unforeseen effects on a local boys' school, as related earlier. Among other novelties was a device in the form of a small bomb with pretty ribbons in which was hidden a spike to puncture enemy aircraft tyres on landing, it did not work.

Another bright idea, known as 'Apparatus AD Type H', involved the release of 1lb of explosive (the aerial mine) under a small parachute, but attached to the bomber by up to 2,000 feet of cable into which an attacking fighter would fly, pulling the explosive into it. Exeter University had the job of developing AAD Type H, and was upset when the A&AEE, without the University's knowledge, did trials in September 1940 from a Blenheim flying at speeds of up to 250mph. Of the forty dropped, half broke away or otherwise failed.

The remainder had to be pulled back into the aircraft to check for kinking of the cable – a laborious procedure. The spike and AAD were sponsored by the secret Military Department One – MDI – or 'Mad Designers' Inventions' as it was called by those in the know at Boscombe. Controversy in the Air Ministry about the effectiveness of the aerial mine did not stop trials at Boscombe Down; by mid-1941 the installation was acceptable in the Blenheim carrying two containers each with twelve mines. The AAD Type H was found to be satisfactory for use in at least the Beaufort. Whitley and Wellington.

Another very secret trial was made using the concrete target at Porton (without the Commandant there being allowed to know the details) to test the Fluvial Mine (or Royal Marine), to establish the danger to the dropping aircraft if by chance this anti-ship weapon should hit a solid object. Trials were successful there and at a reservoir at Hampton Court, but the mine was little used in service in early 1940 as the French Government objected to these mines floating down the Rhine. These interesting trials were early sidelines – but very time-consuming. The Armament Squadron soon settled into the more routine, but equally challenging, work of learning about new aircraft and their weapons.

Bombs, mines, incendiaries and flares and their modifications dominated trials by the Bombing Flight. Unfortunately, a large proportion of early relevant reports appear not to have survived. Most striking among wartime developments tested at the A&AEE was, perhaps, the increase in bomb size. The largest, and standard, pre-war bomb in service weighed about 500lb. In 1939 the Establishment dropped the first live 1,000lb weapons, and just over five years later released the 'Grand Slam' of 22,000lb. In between, all variations of British and American designs, fillings of TNT, Amatol or Torpex explosive, thick skin or thin, long tail or short, blunt or pointed nose, nose or tail arming, with or without parachute, dropped from high or low, fast or slow … the variations were almost endless, and all needed testing.

A brief synopsis of the procedure adopted gives an idea of the work involved, and the consistent, thorough and convincing results achieved. On receipt of a new or modified store, the trial officer made a thorough examination, studied the operational requirement, previous relevant reports, and documents and drawings; he then decided on the aircraft (preferably the type for operational use) and the bombing range and target to be used. The number of releases needed to clear the weapon for Service use was carefully considered. This was almost invariably a smaller total than ideal, constrained by the limited availability of hardware and shortage of time. Throughout this period, the trial officer liaised with aircrew, range staff, armourers, maintenance staff and others as required, and checked load sheets to ensure safe weights and CG. Ground trials involved not only assessment of the time taken and

practicality of loading onto an aircraft, but also the suitability of ground handling trolleys, winches and carriers, the availability of a suitable bombsight, switches, wiring, indicators and lighting, and the investigation of the path of the falling weapon on release. All this was done with safety of the armourer in mind, and consideration of the effect of cold, dark and wet conditions on operational airfields, and the need (often experienced in service) of unloading on the ground. Ground trials concluded with releases onto a mat to check clearances, and the function of release slips and arming devices. Finally, with the aircraft loaded and fitted with cameras if necessary, the crew briefed, the range available and the weather suitable, air trials could begin.

Flying trials included a carriage flight throughout the aircraft's manoeuvring envelope with bomb doors open and closed; detailed inspection followed. New weapons almost invariably included inert as well as live examples for trials; the former were dropped first to assess release characteristics and stability, and to check arming and operation of fuses/pistols. The first live drop was the culmination of the preceding work, not only by the Establishment but also by the designers, manufacturers and staffs involved. Interest was intense, and the Establishment was often obliged to arrange demonstrations for the senior people concerned. This led inevitably for a drop to be arranged for a fixed date, thus creating pressure to complete the task in weather conditions frequently less than ideal.

Dummy 'High Ball' bombs, each of 1,100lb, under a Mosquito. The A&AEE made ground assessments of this weapon and participated as observers in the dropping trials by a Vickers pilot. *A&AEE 11369*

As the Establishment caustically remarked, 'demonstrations are not conducive to the collection of data'. This comment was made in the report on the 1943 trials of the J Type Mk IB 30lb incendiary against brick buildings; the demonstration involved the release of a large number of these stores in production form, all with parachutes. The spectators observed one-third of the parachutes failing to open. An earlier demonstration, at Porton, involved the 'Capital Ship' (CS) bomb intended to be dropped from low altitude (for accuracy) against heavily armoured ships using the Munroe Effect (shaped charge principle). Damage to the releasing aircraft had already been assessed by firing 2,400lb of explosive on the ground just after the aircraft had passed overhead (trail angle 50°); height was progressively reduced. The minimum acceptable was 735 feet, when 2g was experienced. On 1 May 1942 Lord Cherwell and other distinguished visitors watched as a Lancaster dropped a single (inert) 5,000lb CS bomb to assess ballistic and functioning of the fuse. It missed the concrete target – hardly surprising in view of the scant ballistic data available. The bomb dropped was the only one available of its size (45 inches in diameter), and the Lancaster the only aircraft capable of carrying it, and then singly and with enlarged bomb doors held closed by elastic cord. Loading was very difficult. By 1945 demonstrations were rare, but in March the only live drop (on trials) of the 22,000lb 'Grand Slam' was successfully made at Ashley Walk from another Lancaster flown by Flight Lieutenant S. R. Dawson and aimed by Flying Officer C. E. Whatmore. The event was witnessed by a large group including Dr Barnes Wallis, who conceived the monster weapon, and who, it is said, counted out loud the 9 seconds between penetration and detonation.

A 'Capital Ship' (CS) bomb of 5,500lb in early 1942. Only a modified Lancaster had the capability to carry this 45-inch-diameter weapon. *A&AEE 9974*

A dummy 22,000lb 'Grand Slam' bomb under Lancaster III PB592/G. The nose turret was later removed to reduce weight. *A&AEE 15006*

The first 22,000lb 'Grand Slam' bomb to be dropped in March 1945 was carried by Lancaster PB592/G. The nose of the bomb is over the area now occupied by the Sandy Balls caravan park, and is falling in an easterly direction.

An 8,000lb HE 'cookie' on a Trolley Type F in March 1944. Apart from the long front straps and the small wheels, the trolley was considered suitable for nearly all Service aircraft. *A&AEE 11728*

Another example of the frustrations experienced concerned the American-made Bombardment flares intended to illuminate a target to allow night bombing. Of the twenty associated fuses received, five were unserviceable, and two were successful in flares dropped by day. Ten of the remaining fuses in flares were loaded in a Liberator for a night trial in December 1941 – all were inadvertently jettisoned on opening the bomb doors (just clear of Salisbury), due, it was concluded, to an electrical fault to which the early Liberators were prone. The last three flares were tested the following night. Only one functioned, but assessment of its effectiveness was not conclusive.

A 12,000lb HE 'cookie' on a Trolley Type E in mid-1943. The large and practical wheels can be seen, as can the three 4,000lb sections of the bomb. *A&AEE 11540*

A cluster bomb ready for loading. *AAEE 11848*

An unassembled cluster bomb. The details and legend of mid 1943 make an interesting comparison with similar weapons of 50 years later. *A&AEE 11848*

More success attended another American bomb – the 1,000lb M44, tested over several months. Initially incompatible with British aircraft and carriers, the A&AEE redesigned the tail and altered the attachment lugs. By mid-1942 the weapon was ready for service, and was widely used. Similar changes followed on other transatlantic bombs, including the 1,000lb M59 and 500lb M43; the 500lb M58 appeared not to have required the British tail and no fewer than twenty-four could be fitted in the Stirling's bays, and fourteen in the Lancaster's. In early 1945 a portent of the future was tested in the form of radio-controlled fins on a 1,000lb M65 bomb; gyroscopes stabilised the roll and moveable fins gave control in azimuth for use against line targets, such as railways and canals, where range was unimportant. The AZON bomb, as it was known, had a flare in the tail for visibility to assist the controller in the aircraft. Reliability was unacceptable – of twenty drops from a Lancaster, ten bombs failed to respond and three flares failed; only seven functioned 'as advertised'.

An American 1,000lb AN M65 bomb on a trolley, already fitted to its carrier – '2,000lb Mk II'. The crutching jacks and arming wire to fin assembly can be seen. *A&AEE 11850*

Flares for a variety of purposes, including navigation, target illumination and drift assessment, together with their parachutes, fuses and launching tubes, appear to have given considerable difficulty throughout the war. In particular, the launching tubes were subject to continuous experimentation. One problem was their location in the fuselage to ensure a clean separation of the flare when released, and yet placed so that they did not foul other internal equipment and were accessible to crews in cumbersome flying clothing. Many early tubes when open exhausted all the warm air in the aircraft and others sucked in exhaust fumes. Eventually, in 1945 a marginally acceptable design, the Mk III, was fitted in the nose of the Lancaster. Flight Lieutenant B. E. C. Lewis was credited with this success after many months of endeavour.

The carriage of bombs, mines and smoke apparatus on fighters from 1941, as well as external fuel tanks, gave rise to problems of damage to carriers, aiming and interference from ejected cartridge cases, in addition to stability on release. Loading, however, was straightforward although frequently cramped, and trials on the smaller aircraft were, in general, less troublesome than on aircraft with bomb bays. Fuses (and pistols) of bombs and flares became increasingly sophisticated throughout the war, and the Establishment worked on hundreds of types and variations. Trials were made as representative as possible of operational conditions for the five main types (instantaneous, air burst, proximity, long delay – some with anti-disturbance devices – and hydrostatic). Among many developments resulting from the A&AEE's experience and suggestions was the Pistol No 44, employing a diaphragm designed to be operated by the blast of the preceding bomb when dropped in salvo at low level and striking the ground at a shallow angle. (The original pistol, No 30, worked by falling on to the nose of the bomb, and only when dropped from high level.) Many trials over several years failed to produce consistent results. Air bursts, using barometric, clockwork or pyrotechnic principles, proved somewhat less frustrating; an American clockwork fuse unaffected by icing and temperature for flares gave the best results. In many trials the actual height of operation was recorded by a second aircraft. Proximity fuses tested later against the elaborate trench system at Ashley Walk were initially prone to premature operation until modified by the Establishment; accurate measurement of the height of operation proved difficult. Perfecting delayed-action devices (from 6 to 144 hours) required more than three years, and then, in 1943, the further complication of anti-

disturbance devices led to the need for more development. Finally, the Fuse No 871 was generally acceptable.

All fuses and pistols were assessed to ensure that they always worked within specified conditions, and never worked (safety tests) outside those conditions. The latter were necessary to ensure that weapons never went off if dropped inadvertently, or if on board a crashing aircraft. Both aspects were given considerable thought, time and effort at Boscombe Down, where the unique facilities and expertise became pre-eminent in the UK for armament testing. It was considered, at least by the A&AEE, that many fuses were insufficiently tested by the designers in the knowledge that problems would not only be identified, but remedied by the Establishment. Indeed, from the many surviving fuse/pistol reports, shortcomings were almost invariably found; successful modifications were equally often suggested by the A&AEE.

A group of armament staff in late 1944 in front of a Lancaster, 'Grand Slam' (left) and 'Tallboy' (right) bombs. Seated, left to right, are Mr Frank Myerscough, unknown, Flt Lt Brian Harvey, unknown, Sqn Ldr Evans, Gp Capt Fraser (Superintendent of Armament Division), Sqn Ldr Counter, five unknown. The group standing includes five RN personnel and one WAAF.

A 500lb Smoke Bomb Mk II fitted to Hellcat I JV127. *A&AEE 15021*

Other major concerns of the Bombing Flight were bombsights and calculation of the point of release. Ballistics were measured at Orfordness, using techniques evolved before the war, until about 1941. Once aircraft were available with a wing bomb-cell, ballistics of new bombs dropped from the bomb bay could be established by simultaneous release from the wing cell of one of known ballistics (usually an $11\frac{1}{2}$ or 25lb practice bomb). Having then obtained details of bomb stability from the RAE, the release point could be determined and the bombsight adjusted to indicate that point. The pre-war sight, the CSBS Mk IX, could, with a good crew, an accurate preset wind, a long straight run and a clear target, achieve very accurate results; these conditions pertained for trials, but rarely on operations. The Mk XII sight (for which most reports have not been found) allowed changes in drift, speeds, track and height to be fed continuously; its shortcoming, quantified in trials on a Wellington, was the need for a second bomb aimer to make the adjustments manually. Automatic supply of the vectors overcame this limitation in the Mk XIV sight (also known by the name of its inventor, Professor Blackett) and its American version, the T1. These sights gave a considerable advance in tactical freedom as reasonable accuracy could be obtained following turns and dives and climbs immediately prior to release. Extensive trials, using techniques formulated by Mr E. W. Myerscough of the Research Section, and Squadron Leader N. H. Carrier, investigated the capabilities and limitations of the two new marks of sight, which initially revealed

consistent line errors. The type of aircraft was found to have a significant effect on accuracy, the worst being the Wellington, and the Liberator one of the best; airflow round the open bomb doors of the Lancaster caused bomb instability and was investigated.

In 1941 improvements in calculating true height started using data from the high-flying Fortress and later Wellington VI until the latter was cancelled in 1943. A further improvement in accuracy followed lapse rate measurements by the High Altitude Flight – but all of little avail if the aircraft, like the Wellington, was a poor bombing platform. Another sight, for use by the pilots at very low level up to 300mph, employed the angular velocity principle, and was tested in late 1942; a trained pilot could achieve accuracies of 8 yards at 50 feet, and 20 yards from 600 feet. Initial trials were in a Hampden. An earlier trial using the vector principle for a pilot's sight (the Low Level Mk II (P) sight) was not successful; crews achieved better results without it.

The American 0.1 bombsight, tested in the Hudson, Fortress and Stirling in mid-1941, had many shortcomings, including the need to fly at a precise speed, which varied with height, and the inability to see even illuminated targets through the optics. Wing Commander C. L. Dann, Senior Bombing Technical Officer, personally assessed this equipment, which, contrary to the maker's manual, he found worked very well at low level for use against submarines. He confirmed this finding in a trial with No 120 (Liberator) Squadron at Nutts Corner in Coastal Command.

Bomb stowage including electrical and mechanical circuits, crutching, release mechanisms as well as ground equipment were investigated. Increasing sophistication of the equipment is illustrated by the changes in bomb selector to cater for the broadening possible loads. Manual selection of the bomb(s) to be dropped (and their arming) was widely in use in 1939. Various changes, acceptable to the A&AEE, included a simple electrical selector Mk VI. In 1943 the '6-way distributor' was tested in a Mosquito, followed a year later by a '12-way distributor', tested in a Halifax. In 1945 a '24-way distributor' was tested in a Lancaster. More remarkable, perhaps, was the range of external loads possible by 1945 on an erstwhile fighter aircraft; all had to be loaded, carried and dropped (or fired) in tests by the Establishment. An example of the comprehensive loading trials on one mark of one type, the Tempest V, is shown in Appendix 7.

On bombers, the equipment described above gave, it seems, relatively few problems; the difficulties were usually associated with the design of the bomb bay itself. Squadron Leader R. T. W. Edwards, for several years in charge of bombing trials, frequently complained of the lack of attention given by designers to the interior of the bays, where loading weapons fouled hydraulic lines, control runs and electrical cables. Edwards remarked, obviously with some feeling, that the Establishment could not reject an aircraft design because the original Air Ministry specification was wrong; this problem arose when an aircraft met the requirement but was useless. The Warwick, with totally unacceptable tiered stowage of weapons, and the Buckingham, which reintroduced features long since rejected, were quoted as examples. On fighter-bombers most problems arose from external carriage at high speed: buffeting, damage to bomb racks, instability on release and very limited aiming time. This list reflects the general concerns of the armament staff, while aircraft handling and performance with weapons carried was the responsibility of the Performance Squadron and its technical staff. The latter, for example, found that the drag of the Mosquito was greatly increased by external bombs, while comparable streamlined tanks created only 20% of the drag of the bombs; the Armament trials officer found the loading, carriage and release of the bombs to be satisfactory.

The bombing arrangement of Vengeance I AN899 in about August 1942. After the folding bomb doors opened, the 500lb bomb swung down on the arm to take it clear of the propeller arc after release. The port bomb is still stowed. *A&AEE 11107*

Rockets

Battle experience of the RAF in France and the North African desert led to the need for manoeuvrable (ie fighter) aircraft to attack small, often moving, targets. Ultimately this led in 1942 to the formation of a third section in the A&AEE Armament Squadron dedicated to rocket projectiles known as (RP)[1]. Prior to this, two sets of trials at Boscombe Down started early in 1941 to investigate the use of existing small bombs (bombards) and grenades against armoured vehicles. Using a Blenheim many sorties were flown, dropping loads of 20lb F bombs in a random scatter pattern, or alternatively No 68 grenades. Neither was successful, nor were 250lb or 500lb general-purpose bombs against tanks – the former being ineffective and the latter inaccurate. In parallel, various types of aircraft were assessed for their suitability against tanks; manoeuvrability and sighting were soon identified as the two main criteria. Of the ten types flown by the end of 1941, the Hurricane, with a GM2 gunsight, was the best, followed by the Whirlwind, Airacobra and Mosquito; the Lysander obtained accurate results with two fixed 20mm guns, but was too slow. The restricted number of pilots making the comparison included Wing Commander H. W. Dean, Squadron Leader W. P. Whitworth and Flight Lieutenant W. P. Olesen, and their

[1] Originally called Unrotated air launched Projectiles

conclusion was that, for any aircraft, heavier armament was needed. The 40mm gun was fitted to the Hurricane, and firing started in September 1941. Harmonisation was eventually achieved to give accurate shooting, although each burst caused the nose to dip 2°. This change in trim was easily held. In 1942 the dive attack assessment was broadened to include the Mustang, Kittyhawk, and even the Halifax and Lancaster; with its rudder control lightened and view over the nose improved, the Typhoon was placed ahead of the Hurricane.

On 14 December 1941 the A&AEE formally joined the RAE (where work had started earlier in 1941) in RP development; Boscombe had started flying trials on November 1941 in a modified Hurricane II. Accuracy was at first appalling, due to the complete lack of information on the behaviour of rockets after

release. The ballistic data were painstakingly obtained by many firings under carefully controlled conditions in the time-honoured step-by-step method. Data for firing from larger aircraft were obtained by an A&AEE Hudson using the Pendine ranges. The armament officer complained in the report that the trial was outside the Establishment's terms of reference; he possibly felt aggrieved by a lengthy period tramping the soggy Welsh sand. Analysis led eventually to modest accuracy and the adoption of various palliatives, ie the precise alignment of the rocket rails with reference to the flight vector, the development of a special rocket sight, and the reduction of the dispersion RPs by toe-in. An early firing sequence in a dive, at maximum speed, involved the last of four pairs leaving the aircraft at only 200 yards from the target; a violent pull-up was then necessary. Live trials using 60lb high-explosive in place of the earlier 25lb armour-piercing head led to an increase in the firing distances; both types gave very satisfactory results when a hit was scored. Based on early trials, the Air Staff said that one hit per sortie was acceptable.

The first standard RP installation, the Mk I, consisted of three or four long rails ('projectors') under each wing, with a metal blast plate for protection fitted to many types of aircraft. Various improvements were made and variations for fitting to such aircraft as the Liberator and Halifax; the latter was unsatisfactory and was not pursued. On the Typhoon IB, two rockets bolted together worked adequately on an RP Mk IA installation. Early in 1944 the Mosquito VI had longer struts to lower the rails away from the wooden wing lacking the blast plate; this Mk II installation produced poor accuracy. Incorporation of improvements, most of them developed by the Establishment, led to the Mk III, tried first on a Typhoon in 1944, and most successfully on the Tempest V in 1945. The 250lb bomb with seven rocket motors was mounted on the Mk IV installation of a Hurricane as a trial for the Beaufighter. The weapon was later named the 'Admonitor', but did not go into service.

The port side of the 'Rocket Projectile Installation Mk I' on Swordfish DK747/G in late 1942, showing details of the 'projectors' and blast plate. The Swordfish was simply too slow for grouping and accuracy. *A&AEE 11235*

Concrete 60lb heads in double rows are shown in this early RP Mk Ia version on Typhoon I MN861 in August 1944, intended to be fired in pairs; there appear to have been difficulties in firing or accuracy. However, single rockets were usually effective, and pairs did not increase the number of hits obtained. *A&AEE 11901*

Further modifications aimed at reducing drag and capable of complete jettison produced the Mk V, which was tried in a Mustang. Benefits of this encouraging RP installation were spoiled as the aircraft's attitude and thus accuracy was affected by the automatic operation of the engine cooling flaps. The Mk VI was a modification of the Mk V specially for the Beaufighter; no report on a Mk VII has been found. Trials on the 'zero length' (ie no launch rails) Mk VIII, made possible by improvements in rocket propellant, were under way at the end of the war. American 4.5-inch rocket launching tubes were fitted in a Spitfire and a Thunderbolt in 1945; trials on this installation and on other aircraft were incomplete at the end of the war. Other American installations included one known as the Mk 4, but it required essential changes to give satisfaction on the Avenger. The American Mk 5 was similar to the British Mk VIII.

This is Wildcat IV FN130, probably late in 1944, although the report (and its photograph) was not issued until July 1945, long after interest in rocket-armed Wildcat IV had waned. The installation is an American Mk 5 with 'zero length' launchers. The pressure head remains on the port wing, now more conventionally positioned but still not straight. *A&AEE 15135*

Beaufighter EL329 demonstrates another RP Mk I installation in mid-1942. Trials were incomplete when the aircraft crashed fatally in September 1943. *A&AEE 11082*

Rockets and 100-gallon long-range tanks together led to the Mk IIIA RP installation, shown here on PZ202 in early 1945 with shrouded exhaust and paddle blade propellers. The guard rail was fitted by the A&AEE to prevent damage to the rockets on jettisoning the tanks prior to firing. *A&AEE 15059*

In March 1945 Tempest V NV946 shows its 'zero length' RP Mk VIII installation, with eight 60lb head rockets. The four Mk V Hispano 20mm guns are contained within the wings, and a blanking plate in the air intake is fitted. In July 1945 this aircraft was destroyed. *A&AEE 15193*

Of the sights used for RP firing, the reflector gunsight (GM2) Mk IA and the American Mk IX were of no value. The GM2 Mk II star was of limited value at a single pre-set range, while the GM2 Mk IIL with a depressed line of sight was acceptable in all aircraft including the Master, Ventura and Liberator. The reflector sight Mk IIIA, designed by the A&AEE for the Ventura and Hudson, was the most successful model for purely rocket firing. The gyro gunsight (GGS) Mk II Series III designed for guns and rockets was acceptable for the latter, but a year's work by the Establishment produced only marginal improvements when used for gun aiming.

Various rocket heads were tested, including high-explosive, armour-piercing, smoke and inert practice types[2], and included the 250lb bombs mentioned above. The Establishment attached four 3-inch rocket motors to each of a pair of 250lb bombs, but evidence of air firing is lacking. The smaller 2-inch rockets were used to examine the possibility of carrying thirty-two RP in eight vertical stacks; the smaller rocket was so inaccurate that the idea was abandoned. These and other ideas largely emanated within the Establishment.

[2] In 1996 many thousands of concrete practice rocket heads were in use to form walls at 'Farmer Giles' open farm SW of Salisbury

Hudson VI FK689 has ASV radar aerials and rockets in May 1943. The exhaust flame dampers seem to be unbraced and above the port engine is a sensor, possibly connected with the diving trials. Four days after this photograph was taken, one outer wing bent upwards on recovery from a dive, and after a hazardous high-speed landing it broke off. *A&AEE recognition 156*

Hurricane IV BP173 (later BP173/G) poses in August 1942 in production form with eight 60lb head rockets. The protective plate under the wing is just visible, while the extensive internal armour plating cannot be seen, nor the external armour for the oil cooler. Later handling without the blast plate revealed no significant difference. *A&AEE recognition 108*

Before air firing a new installation, aircraft were flown to an airstrip near Larkhill and taxied to Enford for ground firing. A small group of pilots became the experts in RP work, and included Flight Lieutenants W. H. Else and C. B. ('Cyclops') Brown with Flying Officer R. E. ('Titch') Havercroft. Havercroft had had an unfortunate early career at Boscombe after arriving as a new pilot officer with the AGME from Duxford. He had a landing accident, in a Mustang, from failing to lock the tail wheel on landing, resulting in a red endorsement to his logbook. He later attended the Test Pilots' School's second course, after two further landing incidents for which he was not held to blame.

Armament Research

Early in the wartime period, there was a small research section within the Gunnery Flight; this section went to Exeter in June 1940. With the move to Boscombe in June 1942 of the Aircraft Gun Mounting Establishment, gunnery research was re-established at Boscombe and A Flight of the Armament Squadron reformed; Mr J. Hanson was head of the Armament Research Section from 1942 to 1945, and he concentrated on guns and rockets. The lack of a bombing specialist was remedied by the arrival of F. W. Myerscough from the RAE late in 1943. The work of the Section included advice to trials officers on the best and most efficient methods for conducting tests, trials, assistance in the resolution of problems and development of instrumentation. In 1943 Mr G. Standen evolved a method of measuring the loads on the ammunition, links, feeds and assisters when gun firing. The following year he calculated the reduction in recoil loads with the Edgewater adapter; in a Spitfire with four 0.5in guns, recoil was 6,000lb without the adapter, and 1,800lb with it – the latter still giving a stress of 0.5 tons psi on the wing spar.

A 20mm gun development in the Tempest V; this is the original long-barrel Hispano Mk II installation.

The Mk V with flash eliminators. *A&AEE 11800*

The original short-barrel Hispano Mk V.

Hurricane Z2326 around September 1941 with early guns during extensive trials to establish harmonisation. Two 0.303-inch guns firing tracer aided aiming (the ports are visible in the wings) and were recorded by the G45 camera (above the starboard 40mm gun). *A&AEE 9800*

Gunnery

Guns ranging in calibre from 0.3in (7.5mm) to 75mm came under the scrutiny of the Gunnery Section between 1939 and 1945 in nearly 100 types of aircraft. Work on individual aircraft is covered in Part II; described here are the testing and development of new and modified weapons in both fixed and free mountings, and in turrets. Procedures followed the relevant items previously described for testing bombs and were in the logical sequence of preliminary investigation, ground, then air functioning. By 1945 the original handful of gunnery trials officers had grown to thirteen,

led by Wing Commander G. A. W. Garland, who won the AFC for his work at Boscombe.

Fixed guns, ie those aimed by pointing the aircraft, ranged from the standard 0.303in of 1939, through the American 0.3in and 0.5in and British 20mm and 40mm to the 'one-offs' of 37mm in the Airacobra, 57mm in the Mosquito and 75mm in a Mitchell. Testing techniques, and instrumentation, were progressively developed, and by 1943 a comprehensive checklist had been evolved to aid trials officers. The preliminary examination had fifteen specific items, ground trials had thirteen and flight trials twenty. Advice was given on the conduct of tests, as, for example,

Mitchell FR208 is seen in September 1943 with the largest gun (75mm) tested at the A&AEE in the war. The two 0.5-inch sighting guns in the blunt nose are seen above the large opening for the plugged 75mm muzzle. Just behind the port gun is a small silver scoop, part of the instrumentation. The DF housing is on top of the fuselage and the upper turret in the rear position. *A&AEE 11528*

on stop butt trials, to ensure that firing did not shoot away essential features of the butt construction (included as a result of earlier experience, perhaps), and on the need for recording instruments for rate of fire, recoil loads, carbon monoxide and gun bay heating among others. The preparation and firing trials of an aircraft for full armament clearance was thus a time-consuming business. Pressure by the Air Staff for rapid results was resisted in the interests of early identification of problems – the wide experience of the Establishment showed that cutting corners caused delays when repeat tests became necessary. Gun stoppages were frequent and always fully investigated, while stoppages in the air required a gentle return and landing. Trials officers complained that some exuberant pilots indulged in aerobatics on the way home after gun(s) had stopped firing, thus sometimes destroying evidence, as the wings flexed under aerodynamic load.

Two views of Havoc BD126 in May 1941 with its unique battery of six upward-firing guns. The rams controlling elevation (+30° to +50°) can be seen; azimuthal movement (15°) was also possible. Control of the guns was from the gunner's open cockpit (just visible in the nose), equipped with an upward-viewing gunsight (GJ3). AI radar rendered this development obsolete, but trials continued at the GRU at Exeter, and the Fighter Interception Unit at Ford. *A&AEE 9737*

Examples of the Gunnery Section's fixed gun work, in addition to those given in Part II, include the 'worst gun installation seen' in the twelve-gun (0.303in) Hurricane in 1940. Lack of rigidity, heating, adjustment and poor maintainability were severely criticised. On the other hand, the pair of 40mm guns, also in the Hurricane, gave rise to the uncharacteristic terms 'faultless' and 'most commendable' in the Establishment reports on trials in early 1942.[3] Between these extremes was the 20mm gun. When first tested in 1939 it was clearly an effective, accurate weapon, but mounting and feed problems, among others, led to removal of development trials from Boscombe to Farnborough, then to Duxford at the AGME. Trials on Hurricanes with four 20mm guns continued, however, at Boscombe, where some ammunition feed and other improvements were made; clearance work continued from 1940 to mid-1942, and included firing with external bombs and long-range tanks fitted. A notable feature of existing gun reports on American fighters in 1940 and 1941 is the large number of serious shortcomings found – attributed to lack of testing and the peace still enjoyed across the Atlantic. Lack of strength in the gun mountings and blast tubes and absence of heating were three items identified in, for example, the Mustang, Vengeance and Chesapeake. By contrast, the Corsair installation was praised in 1944 for its well-thought-out armament of six 0.5in guns. Another characteristic of fighters from the USA was the fuselage mounting of guns necessitating interrupter gear long since abandoned in British designs. While the mechanics of the gear attracted little adverse comment, the effect in the Mustang, for example, was to reduce rate of fire from 720 rounds per minute (of which the 0.5in gun was capable) to about 400-500, ie once for every two revolutions of the propeller.

Tests of ammunition included the ball, tracer, armour piercing and incendiary types and such developments as electric firing.

An unidentified Hurricane in mid-1944 with a 'Littlejohn' nose piece, and an enlarged hopper (just visible disappearing into the wing); the latter was not successful.

[3] Production 40mm guns (virtually hand-made) were all individually tested by the dedicated Gun Proofing Flight at Boscombe, using Hurricane HD.

Blenheim V (Bisley) AZ886 was tested with this single hand-held and crudely aimed 0.303in gun in early 1943. Among criticisms was the poor durability of the rubber mounting. *A&AEE 11372*

Free Guns

Turrets on aircraft were at an early stage of development in 1939, whereas free guns and their limitations were well known. Nevertheless, the latter arrived for testing almost until the end of the war. In bombers an early modification to the Wellington in 1940 to cover areas blind to the turrets comprised two Vickers gas-operated guns mounted to fire-through apertures in the fuselage just aft of the astral (sic) dome; the main comment concerned the need to replace the old Vickers guns with Brownings. In 1943 the efficiency of a similar modification, still using the Vickers weapons, in a Whitley was restricted by the two gunners having no intercom. In the early Liberator I,

with single 0.3in guns in each beam and a third in the nose, the Establishment recommended three pairs of Vickers; later Liberators had 0.5in guns in the beam. The Royal Navy continued to use the Vickers extensively; trials in the Swordfish (1941), Walrus and Sea Otter (1943) confirmed the obsolescence of the gun, although two new mountings, one by Preston Green and the other by Rose Bros, offered certain advantages in the Barracuda in 1943. The American Chesapeake (1941), Kingfisher (1942) and Vengeance (1943) had inadequate single guns for the observer. An attempt to improve the hitting power of free guns was tried in a Hampden by using the considerably larger 0.5in guns on a powered mounting by Rose Bros incorporating belt feed for the ammunition; the poor gunner was still exposed and the complication of the installation offered no advantages over a turret. The Beaufighter had a successful compromise with a single free gun under a cupola behind the pilot – called a turret although non-moveable.

Downward-firing guns met with mixed success in trials. Those on the Blenheim and Beaufort also fired backwards but were of limited value due to very limited searching view. In the Hudson the original single gun had a similar drawback; an opening flap under the rear fuselage improved matters but was not adopted in service. A modification introduced locally by a Halifax station was not tested at Boscombe, but an Establishment team visited Newmarket to see the Preston Green mounting with a single 0.5in fitted in the fuselage hole revealed by the removal of the H2S radar. No adverse comment was made.

Wellington IA P9211 in March 1940, showing off the side gun in the opening above the wing trailing edge, which was operable up to 305mph. *A&AEE*

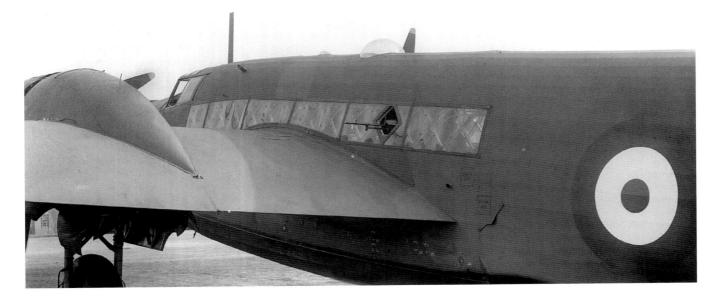

These exterior and interior views show the extendible firing position of Hudson II T9375 in about September 1940, in an attempt to provide some much-needed rear protection. The interior view shows the gunner's position, open window and relatively good searching and firing view. The notice reads 'RETRACT GUN PLATFORM BEFORE LANDING'. *A&AEE 9778*

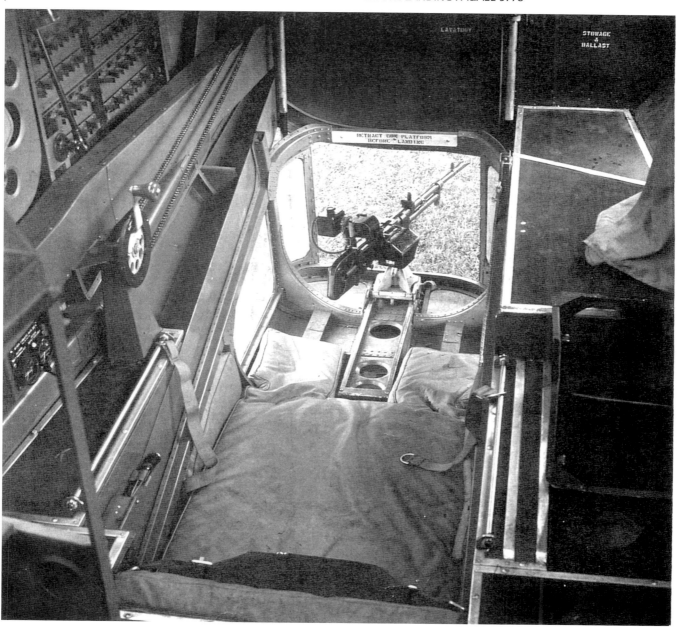

Turrets

Twin 0.303in guns on a powered mounting. The barrels are taped over and the stowage slots are well shown. No doubt the airman's headgear would be exchanged for something more easily retained when flying. The aircraft is Albemarle P1506 in passenger configuration in late 1942. *A&AEE 11207*

The Establishment's contribution to turret development started before the war – notably in making operation in rotation and elevation manageable with two levers – and at Boscombe the influence continued. British turrets throughout the war came from three designers: Bristol (almost exclusively used in Bristol aeroplanes), Boulton Paul (very widely used) and Frazer-Nash (also widely used). Early Establishment reports have largely not been found. Aircraft handling, however, was largely unaffected by rotation of nose turrets, but slight yaw was caused by rotation of a tail turret; upper turrets caused no major difficulty – with one notable early exception. Unacceptable buffeting and yawing accompanied rotation of the asymmetric FN7 turret in the Botha and, to a lesser extent, in the Manchester. In addition the FN7 was very cramped and condemned by the Establishment as a poor design.

Extendable under-turrets caused drag and a nose-down change in aircraft trim and, when raised, they blocked the fuselage. They were the FN17 (Whitley), FN21 (Manchester) and FN25 (Wellington). All had poor searching view (nil in the FN17), were cramped, cold and condemned by the A&AEE and Bomber Command alike. Smaller, non-extending under-turrets suffered similar searching limitations in the Lancaster (FN64), Halifax and Albermarle (both BP Type K) and were not much used in service. However, the slow rotation of the electrically powered Bendix Type J turret under the Mitchell in 1943 led to its replacement on the recommendation of the A&AEE by the FN64 with a rotation speed nearly doubled to 70° per second from hydraulic drive. This modification appears not to have been adopted, probably because of the reduction in firepower from a pair of 0.5in guns in the Bendix down to a pair of 0.303in in the FN64. Boulton Paul's R Mk II, tested in the Halifax, was the prototype of this under-turret; it had slow rotation and elevation and shared with other types the restricted viewing through a periscope.

This is the so-called Bristol B20 turret (actually cupola) on Beaufighter VI EL292 in about June 1943. It afforded adequate wind protection while permitting good searching and adequate field of fire. *A&AEE 11477*

A Boulton Paul R Mk I (two 0.303in guns) under Halifax I L9485 in July 1941. It suffered the usual shortcomings of awkward use, poor searching and sighting via mirrors (the lower mirror can be seen). *A&AEE 9655*

This is the standard upper turret – the Boulton Paul A Mk VIII with four 0.303in guns, but modified to increase the range of elevation and other changes The line of rivets below the turret indicates where internal structural work has been completed. The combination of unit code letters (MP-T) and prototype markings on Halifax R9375 in August 1942 is unusual. *A&AEE 11153*

The FN7 upper turret was cramped and its blunt back strained the hydraulic motors when rotated; worse, it caused severe buffeting of the fin, particularly on the three-finned Manchester. This view shows the 'saucer' fitted to the apex, which made only a marginal improvement. *A&AEE 9787*

Rose R No 2 turret in Lancaster HK543 in May 1944. This is the second prototype turret, and suffered from vibration and imprecise control, although the open panel gave gunners a good view and plenty of fresh air.
A&AEE 11801

The American approach to defence (defense?) from attacks underneath was the Sperry ball turret. The Establishment found that in the Fortress II it required a very small gunner, whose restricted view of the world was through his knees, and whose guns were very unreliable due to feed failures. Among turret improvements directly attributable to the Establishment was the change from Bowden cable to electric signal to overcome the delay in firing after the squeezing of the trigger in the Beaufort's turret (two 0.303in guns), thus creating the Bristol Type I Mk V. Side spoilers were fitted round the front turrets on Wellingtons (FN5A) and Halifaxes (BP type C Mk I) following the Establishment's recommendation, thus permitting greater rotation speeds at high airspeeds and a bonus in the case of the Wellington of a greater range of traverse. Early FN hydraulically powered turrets had superior controls to their BP electro-hydraulic equivalents and the Establishment suggested, no doubt very diplomatically, that the latter should at least try the former's arrangements. This was done in 1941 on the BP Type A Mk II, and later BP turrets received no serious criticism of their controls.

This is the Rose turret in the upper position on Boston III W8315 in November 1942, armed with a pair of 0.303in guns. The installation was too heavy, too high and had several mechanical faults; it did not enter service in this aircraft.
A&AEE 11233

A Boulton Paul T turret in Halifax II R9436 in
October 1942. It was very satisfactory, apart
from the fact that turrets with 0.5in guns had
been cancelled for production. *A&AEE 11200*

This upper turret is
a Bendix Type R in
early 1945 and is
mounted on
Mitchell III HD373;
it has a pair of 0.5in
guns. It worked
well, but the
Establishment had
to design, make
and fit collector
cases for the empty
cartridges and links.
The black-out artist
has been at work
on the negative.
A&AEE 15011

The widely used
Glen Martin upper
turret (Type 250
CE10A) on Boston IV
BZ401; two 0.5in
guns are fitted and
needed an
Establishment
modification to
prevent hot empties
raining on the
gunner below,
trying to use the
single 0.5in gun
seen under the
fuselage. *A&AEE
11990*

The Fraser-Nash FN5A nose turret was standard on several bombers. It is shown here with its two 0.303in guns (one fitted with flash eliminator) in Wellington IA P9211 in March 1940, showing the cut-away fuselage permitting greater traverse

This internal view of the Boulton Paul D turret (two 0.5in guns) in Halifax III HX238 in April 1944 shows considerable differences from the Fraser Nash installation in Lancaster JA870, including a single control stick with firing button on top, a larger reflector sight and, apparently, cocking knobs on the two guns.

This internal view of the prototype Fraser Nash FN82 (two 0.5in guns) in Lancaster III JA870 in late 1943 gives some idea of the complicated nature of the position and shows the control handles with levers which, when squeezed, opened hydraulic valves to power the turret. The two cocking handles mounted inboard of each gun and the gunner's seat are visible. *A&AEE 11643*

The Armament Workshops played an increasingly important role as their capability improved through the war. Major tasks were the fitting of BP Type A Mk IV turrets to the early Liberators, which arrived bereft, the manufacture of the turret spoilers already described, many gun blast tubes and other accessories for fixed guns, and, more precisely, alterations and repairs to the mechanisms of guns of all sorts. Most of this work was to drawings prepared in the Armament Drawing Office.

Reflections, distortion and restrictions to view through the perspex of turrets led to many attempts at improvement; the most effective, particularly in the rear position, was a shuttered arrangement where the aiming panel could be removed. Variations in design were tried to reduce the draught and buffeting induced – never completely solved. However, later American rear and front turrets had almost optically flat armoured panels affording protection to the gunner, and overcoming some problems while introducing others such as those of emergency escape and misting.

Trials of standard defensive weapons proceeded throughout the war, and in general the 0.303in gun was replaced by the 0.5in, predominantly in the tail position of the Halifax (BP Type D) and Lancaster (FN82). Both the latter had the radar aid (AGLT) by 1944 and had ingenious methods devised by the Establishment for testing it. Aerodynamically, the radar housing, first tested as a dummy in a Lancaster in 1942, caused slightly increased yaw when the turret turned to the side. Of

Few concessions to aerodynamics are made in this Consolidated nose turret (two 0.5in guns) on Liberator VI BZ972 early in 1944. The armoured glass sighting panel gave great confidence to the gunner provided there was no misting or reflection. The A&AEE said that this turret 'will do until a better [is made]'.

greater effect was the recoil when firing the guns to the side. In both the FN and BP turrets, the 0.5in gave accurate results. The FN121 (also with AGLT but retaining four 0.303in guns) was assessed for the effect on the radar of firing. The Establishment, in the course of firing more than 84,000 rounds, corrected a 1° harmonisation error between the radar and the guns, but found that the radar jittered and lagged, commenting that much work remained to be done.

Gladiator I K8042 made a swift and successful trial in September 1941 with an extra pair of 0.303in guns under the top wing (a total of six guns, each with 425 rounds); very slight damage was caused by ejected cartridges from the top guns. Noteworthy details include the channel for the starboard fuselage gun, the wooden two-bladed propeller, the contoured corrugated oil cooler on the fuselage, and the extended mast. *A&AEE 9784*

The Boulton Paul D turret (two 0.5in guns) in Halifax III HX238 in April 1944; many stoppages were experienced in the course of firing 12,860 rounds.

The Boulton Paul E Mk I turret (four 0.303in guns) is seen in Halifax II W1008 in May 1943 with an early mock-up of the AGLT. The datum for the 10-marks on the base of the turret is the centre line of the fuselage. *A&AEE 11449*

A close-up view of the ammunition feed to the Boulton Paul D tail turret of Halifax III HX238. Many essential modifications were required. *A&AEE 11828*

The Fraser Nash FN121 turret (four 0.303in guns) in Lancaster III ND794/G in the summer of 1943. *A&AEE 11877*

Long belt feeds to rear guns had been an early problem, resolved largely by the Establishment's painstaking work in developing recuperators, suitable trackways and hydraulic motors to ensure smooth feeding to the guns, albeit of 0.303in and 0.5in calibre. Further attempts to improve hitting power by a pair of 20mm guns in upper turrets were protracted. Early in 1944 the first of each type of 20mm turrets (Bristol Type 57 and FN79) were fitted into a Lancaster dummy fuselage at Boscombe; problems were found in gun operation, belt feed and, most seriously, in structural strength of the mounting. It is interesting that the first 20mm turrets reintroduced the problem of ammunition feed previously experienced in 1940/41 in fighters with the same guns. Other areas investigated were the effect of the Edgewater recoil-reducing mountings in, for example, the Bendix turret (two 0.5in guns) on a Mitchell, the capacity and power of hydraulic motors to drive turrets, the devices, often called 'taboo' cams, used to prevent upper turrets and free guns from firing into aircraft structure, and the arrangements for collecting links and spent cartridges. The last were often absent in American aircraft, even in 1945, as in the Bendix R upper turret on the Mitchell; effective containers were made by the Establishment. Two American aircraft, the Invader (1944) and Black Widow (1945), provided food for thought after each had a brief assessment made of their remotely controlled turrets (called barbettes); problems with aiming and jerky movement of the guns became apparent.

The four Browning Mk II 0.303in guns are well shown in this view in August 1941 of the FN4A turret of a Stirling I; the chutes for the links and cartridges are also evident. The centre perspex panel has been removed, and just visible is the wind defector fitted round the fuselage in an attempt (partially successful) to reduce buffeting when the turret was rotated to the side. *A&AEE 9797*

This view inside the fuselage of Halifax III HX238 shows the two ammunition boxes and the long trackway to the Boulton Paul D turret, which, over a considerable period, took a great deal of development in ensuring reliable feed to the turret at all stages of rotation. The turret installation, including ammunition feed, needed thirty essential modifications. *A&AEE 11828*

Gunsights

All types of gunsights – ring and bead, reflector and gyro-stabilised – were assessed at the A&AEE during the war. Most free guns had the simplest ring and bead sights and many fighters retained a similar system as a back-up. Of the two standard reflector types, the Mk II/GM2 was used exclusively in fixed gun applications while the Mk III/GJ3 aimed turret guns; the latter was also used for some fixed guns (eg Beaufighter and Mosquito) and a few free guns. Both were adapted for rocket firing, the first modifications being made by the Establishment to the Mk IIIA star sights of the Hudson and Ventura. Early American sights were considered inferior to the contemporary British standards, and were replaced – as in the Martlet, which

gained accuracy from fitting the GM2. In other US aircraft the effectiveness of the ST1A sight was improved by the Establishment removing the frame blocking the view. The structure supporting the sight on the Buffalo and Tomahawk was found to need strengthening, while in a Wellington with a test turret (FN120) intended for the Lancaster, the inadequately rigid structure caused severe vibrations in 1943. An American Mk VIII sight (similar to the GM2) was rendered unsuitable by the use of 24 volts for British aircraft with 12-volt systems.

Tests on gyro gunsights (GGS) started at the Gunnery Research Unit, Exeter, in 1940, and it appears that the first at the A&AEE was in the turret of a Blenheim V in early 1942. The GGS Mk I was found to be convenient to use, but bulkiness, limited view and jittery graticule were shortcomings that proved difficult to overcome. By 1943 the Mk II appeared and proved acceptable both in turrets and in fixed gun applications. Similar satisfactory performance was obtained in 1945 in an American GGS (Mk XXI), but it remained bulky and a serious risk to the pilot in a forced landing.

MUSTANG III F.B. 124. AMERICAN M.K.21.
G.G.S. INSTALLATION WITH RECORDER

(1) G.G.S. RECORDER.
(2) LEVER FOR BLANKING OUT FIXED RING.
(3) SILICA GELL CELL.
(4) RANGE UNIT.
(5) SELECTOR UNIT.
(6) SINGLE BOWDEN CABLE CONTROL.
(7) SERATED RUBBER CONTROL HANDLE.
(8) SIGHT ADJUSTMENT IN ELEVATION.
(9) SIGHT ADJUSTMENT IN AZIMUTH.
(10) SPARE BULB STOWAGE.
(11) BOWDEN CABLE RETURN SPRING
(12) SUNSCREEN OPERATING LEVER

The sprung seat of Typhoon I R7614 early in 1942, fitted in a partially successful attempt to reduce the effect on pilots' vision of the excessive vibration of early aircraft of this type.
A&AEE 11030

The cockpit of Mustang III FB124 in January 1945, showing the American Mk 21 gyro gunsight with recorder almost entirely blocking the view. The test pilots were not asked to comment on the extremely cluttered cockpit, but made their assessment solely on the gunsight, which was favourably reported. The airspeed indicator appears to be 'red-lined' at 500mph – quite fast enough if you can't see where you're going.
A&AEE 15009

The Larkhill Demonstration, July 1945

As a grand finale, the Armament Division organised a two-day demonstration, held in fine weather on 23 and 24 July 1945. Ministers and other VIPs, both Service and civilian, joined representatives from the aircraft and armament industries and some 500 servicemen and women as spectators. On the first day, at Boscombe Down, thirty-five static aircraft were on show, together with a very extensive display, including bomb loading, gun and rocket harmonisation and working turrets, all of which were continuously demonstrated. On the second day at Larkhill, flying lasted more than 4 hours, and included, as Item 7, five aircraft firing their guns – Hurricane (0.303in), Mustang (0.5in), Tempest (20mm), Hurricane (40mm) and Mosquito (57mm) – to show their effect. As Item 15, six slow aircraft (Swordfish, Sea Otter, Gladiator, Hart, Storch and Tutor) were followed by fast aircraft, including a Meteor and a Vampire. Many congratulations were received on the organisation of the demonstration.

Part II The Aircraft
Standard, weird and the not-so-wonderful

This part of the book describes the tests and duties of the aircraft at A&AEE Boscombe Down during the Second World War; excluded are 109 Squadron and its predecessors, Handling Flight and the Empire Test Pilots' School. To the remainder are added a few flown on trials at Contractors' and Service airfields. The predominant sources of information are the aircraft type reports, Weekly Returns of Serviceability (both almost complete), the partially extant series of Armament reports, and the surviving 'Res', 'Tech', 'Q' and 'Inst' reports. It is clear that formal reports for some aircraft types such as the Hillson F1/40 were never written, probably on the direction of the Project Office in the MAP following receipt of the initial verbal or written information.

The Establishment's role in testing was extensive, and every aircraft was received for a particular task, sometime necessitating only the briefest of visits. Other aircraft were on long-term allocation, particularly for general purposes in both Performance and Armament Squadrons, and for communications and photography.

The compression of the contents of nearly 4,000 reports into a manageable part of a book has led to only the briefest of details being included. Some of the highlights of the work described in this part have been included in Part 1; the aim here has been to identify every individual aircraft – more than 1,500. This figure is surprisingly similar to that for the period at Martlesham Heath, 1920-39; in that earlier period, of about 400 types nearly all were British, while during the war some forty-four (31%) were of American origin, out of a total of 140. Each chapter in Part II includes types for a particular role or roles, a somewhat arbitrary selection based on the intended role when first tested. For instance the Mosquito, first a light bomber, is in Chapter 6, and includes photographic, fighter, trainer and special duties variants. The placing of types within chapters is determined by their date of first arrival; the Index of individual aircraft gives the page.

Some performance figures are included in the Performance Tables. It was considered worthwhile to include such parameters as maximum speed and rate of climb as these are usually extracted into the summaries of the reports. Such brief details, however, can be misleading, and other meaningful limitations, such as the maximum cruising height and speed of bombers under non-standard atmospheric conditions (ie usually) are only available in a comprehensive form unsuitable for inclusion here. Indeed, although the performance figures given were produced in a thoroughly professional and scientific manner, it is possible only to assert that they relate to a particular aeroplane, on a particular day, in a particular configuration and weight using A&AEE methods of reduction to a standard atmosphere. Individual pilots, perhaps surprisingly, made little difference, except in the measurement of take-off distances.

Aircraft mark numbers are quoted as given in A&AEE reports; differences from Service nomenclature are noted. By its nature, the Establishment flew many aircraft made non-standard by features intended for later versions. Engine details are also quoted from reports; this has meant, particularly in the case of American aircraft, that early purchases made directly with manufacturers are identified by their commercial designations, while Lend-Lease aircraft and their engines are given their US military designations. The power of engines is not given, as horsepower varied with, among other things, modification state, changes in temperature limitations and fuel used. Speeds are in statute miles per hour unless otherwise stated, and are indicated values in the text, but true values in the Performance Tables. Ranges are in statute miles. The words 'control column' and 'stick' are synonymous in this work.

5 Heavy Bombers

Hampden to Heinkel He 177

Hampden and Hereford

Type testing of the Handley Page Hampden was almost complete by the outbreak of war when L4032 and L4035 flew to Boscombe Down, with Herefords L6002 and L6003 made serviceable for the journey. A total of twenty-six Hampdens and five Herefords reached the A&AEE and were allocated equally to the four Performance Flights and three Armament Flights.

Hampden

The main type report, not issued until March 1940, was one of the last in the voluminous pre-war style, and reflected earlier tests on L4032, L4033, L4035 and L4037 and later trials at Boscombe, which included L4076. The performance is in the Tables of Performance at the original gross take-off weight of 18,750lb, achieved with compromise between full fuel and full bomb load. Advice on handling at 21,000lb was included. In the lighter condition and with the benefit of leading edge slats, the stall speeds were 74mph (clean) and 65mph (undercarriage and flaps down) – remarkably low figures, particularly combined with a top speed (true) of 254mph. The four main adverse comments were the small size of the pilot's escape hatch, poor cabin heating, the inadequacy of the defensive armament, and the poor handling on one engine. The last was not emphasised, but gave considerable trouble in service, particularly when coming out of a turn with the live engine – the A&AEE had commented that there was insufficient rudder authority. Later, in 1940, additional operational equipment increased the weight to 22,500lb and extended the CG aft. The Establishment recommended that only experienced pilots should fly in this configuration, and then only in a 15mph wind on a large aerodrome with a good moon if at night. Apart from slightly better lateral control, the first Hampden built by English Electric, P2062, was otherwise similar to Handley Page's when tested from April 1940.

Meanwhile P1169 (for more than a year from September 1939) was shared with the RAE on armament work, followed by P2130 (for eighteen months from October 1940) on special bomb trials using West Freugh from time to time. P4293 was written off in a crash on 23 March 1940, shortly after arrival, and was immediately replaced for overload (22,500lb) tests by P4354 with Vokes air filters (destroyed following a collision in the air in October 1940). The filters reduced top speed by 7mph (true) and reduced service ceiling to 17,200 feet after take-off at the new loading. Locking the slats had no effect on handling: they were subsequently locked or removed in Service. The Gallay system for crew warming was as inefficient in the Hampden as other types. Distilled water, heated round the exhausts, passed to a radiator from which hot air was ducted by flexible pipes as required; 1941 improvements in L4037 raised the temperature at the pilot's position to +11°C (previously 6°C), but the poor lower gunner shivered in -10°C. Cooling the engines for tropical use was successfully achieved in P1330 on trials from January 1941. Two years later, P4369 briefly assessed the effect on handling and performance of carrying an 18-inch torpedo with its fins in the slipstream; mild vibration was felt, and top speed reduced by 7mph (true). No report appears to have been written on X3115 with Wright Cyclone G105A engines, although performance trials were completed from August 1941, before use on a general-purpose armament work until an engine fire in January 1942 curtailed further flying. As related earlier, air-to-air photography was the preserve of the Hampden AE294 for two years from July 1941, then P1215 for one month, and possibly AE439 thereafter until the latter's demise in October 1944 (the last Hampden at the A&AEE).

Hampden I P4369 is seen in April 1943, with a torpedo, ASV radar and light bomb racks under the wings. The bomb doors could not be fully closed around a torpedo, whose air tail can be seen protruding at the rear. Light buffeting was the only unusual manifestation of this configuration. *A&AEE 11376*

The extensive Yagi radar antennae is seen fitted to Hampden I P4369, with very robust mounting supports. Ground clearance for the torpedo's tail was minimal. The venturi for the gyroscopic instruments is rather anomalous in an aircraft with modern radar.

Hampden II X3115, as flown at Boscombe from August 1941 on performance and armament work. Details visible are the gunner's 'taboo' bar, the pilot's direct vision panel, what appears to be an undercarriage ground lock, the Lorenz aerial under the rear fuselage, and the aileron mass balance; part of the engine cowling has been removed.

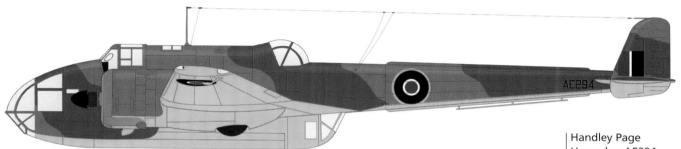

Handley Page Hampden AE294, July 1941-43, for air-to-air photography.

Lack of many relevant reports has made details of armament work difficult to establish: however, most Hampdens appear to have been employed on general trials. Following successful IFF Mk IIN tests against the ground station at Worth Matravers from December 1941, N9080 was joined by P1207, which crashed shortly after arrival in March 1942. AD925 was destroyed in dispersal by a faulty bomb falling off (July 1942) and was replaced by P4338, surviving until June 1943. X2903 endured for one year on bombing and aerial mine trials from December 1941; P5317, P5338, and AD961 were briefly in use in 1941 and 1942. X2903 later led a peripatetic life between Boscombe, Farnborough and West Freugh until January 1944, including an initial period allocated to the gunnery flight. Finally, AD982 flew for Porton for eighteen months from November 1942.

Hereford

The efforts expended at Boscombe on the Dagger engines were not rewarded by successful trials before the Hereford was relegated to a supporting role in the Service. A report dated 11 December 1939, written on the prototype L7271 at Martlesham Heath, comments that the aeroplane was serviceable for eight days in three months and that trials ceased on arrival of the production machines (L6002 and L6003). This pair, and L6006, which arrived in October 1939, were no more airworthy. Early reports on the heaviness of the elevator were noted, and alterations until early 1940 contributed to the groundings; the electric system and radio were, however, satisfactory. Trials on these three machines stopped when L6006 suffered a collapsed undercarriage following a forced landing on 2 July 1940. In the same month

Hereford L6003 in September 1939. The serial number has not been removed from under the wing, there is no direct vision panel for the pilot, and no 'taboo' bar for the gunner. Just visible is the gas diamond above the fuselage serial number. The leading edge slats are open. *A&AEE 9613*

N9075 arrived for armament trials, and departed six weeks later. In April 1941, when the Hereford was no longer welcome in the RAF, N9058 arrived for photographic work – but the excessive demands on servicing manpower led to its early demise in July.

Whitley

The Armstrong Whitworth Whitley owed its origins to a request early in 1934 by the Czech Government for a bomber to reach Berlin. The request was not pursued and when the Air Ministry removed the weight restriction on bombers, the aircraft proposal was adopted by the Air Staff as Specification B3/34 with the hope that many features of the company's existing designs could be used and thus speed entry into service. The first eighty production aircraft were ordered in August 1935, some months before the type's first flight. Testing by the A&AEE of the early versions was completed at Martlesham Heath, and three Whitleys, a Mark III (K8936) and two Mark Vs (N1345 and N1349), continued trials at Boscombe Down. A pair of Mk Is (K7183 from May 1940 and K7205 from October 1939) spent short periods with the Armament and Performance Squadrons respectively. K8936 completed full trials of the Tiger VIII-powered Mark III, and included an investigation into unsatisfactory running on weak mixture. Practical range was established at 1,070 statute miles with a full load of 512 gallons of fuel, while handling remained dominated by excessive directional stability aggravated by the heaviness of the rudder, which could not be used to produce turns. Sideslip approaches were not recommended – see Performance Table 1.

Handling of the Mk V was acceptable, stall (undercarriage and flaps down) 65mph, but performance was disappointing with a top speed some 14mph (true) lower than the original Merlin Whitley (K7208). The discrepancy was attributed to the increase in weight and the turrets of the Mark V. This version was the first with navigational facilities – a mixed blessing at night with the astro hatch open, as any hot air

inside was immediately sucked out. One very surprising recommendation by the A&AEE was for the range of elevator trim to be reduced 'so that the pilot can take off if the trimmer is mis-set to the maximum position'. Pre-take-off checks have undoubtedly become less cursory over the years.

Operational experience led to comprehensive investigation on N1346 early in 1940 when it was found that at 29,000lb (ie with bombs on) 3,000 feet could be maintained on either engine with sufficient rudder trim to relieve foot loads at 120mph (indicated). A month later Z6640 was loaded to 32,000lb at take-off; at this weight the single-engine rate of descent was 320ft/min at 4,000 feet, the standard take-off run was 665 yards, and 50 feet was reached after 1,000 yards. Heating remained a problem in the Whitley, and a modified system in Z6640 was an improvement – but even so, with an ambient temperature of -30°C the pilot's position soon cooled to -11.5°C. Two short trials in the spring of 1942 demonstrated that the radiator provided sufficient cooling for the tropics (BD231) and that flame damping (N1375) met current requirements.

The Establishment's involvement in the Whitley's new roles of glider tug and anti-submarine was limited, starting with T4223 for the latter duty for three days in November 1939. The liberal scattering of aerials on the nose, wings and fuselage reduced speeds by about 8mph (true), while the rearward shift of CG made landings dangerous unless the crew moved forward. In mid-1942 BD354 was flown with the elevator trim tab reduced in size to accommodate a towing bridle. The matt black Z9467 spent nine months at Boscombe Down from March 1942 and included tests of larger oil pumps to cope with glider towing. The maritime role demanded maximum fuel, with a concomitant increase in weight to 33,500lb and further rearward shift in CG. In this condition the aircraft was very unstable and unsuitable for Service use; in the event of operational requirements of overriding importance, the Establishment recommended early use of the

Whitley V N1349 in late 1939, in standard configuration for performance and armament trials. The thickness of the wing, and its incidence to the fuselage, are apparent; with flaps and undercarriage down, the stall was at 65mph (indicated). *A&AEE 9616*

rearmost tank. Take-off distances at 33,500lb were similar to those at 32,000lb. Single-engine performance was, however, inferior to earlier experience; the maximum weight for the maintenance of height was found to be 26,500lb. The apparent deterioration was attributed to high ambient temperatures reducing density and also causing drag from the open radiator flaps. The final trial on Z9467 with Halifax-type Rotol propellers produced a 17% increase in rate of climb at the expense of cruising speed. Aerial mines were released cleanly from Z6649 early in 1942 – the installation AD Type H being common to several types. Two Mark VIIs were briefly tested: BD621 in July 1942, to assess the original beam gun

positions (a single Vickers GO gun each side), while modified positions in Z9529 were found satisfactory, although the gunners lacked intercom and the airspeed indicator under-read by 15mph at cruising speed.

Other Establishment Whitleys were T4149, fitted with RAE rocket gear under the wings to assist take-off. Little flying appears to have been done on Z6497 in four months from November 1941 on trials intended to examine the practicability of single-lever control of the engines. Early in 1941 Z6472 was briefly with the Armament Squadron for rear turret assessment. The type was a familiar sight in the hands of 58 Squadron from September 1939 to February 1940.

Armstrong Whitworth Whitley T4149, July 1943, for rocket-assisted take-off trials. (Scale 1:72)

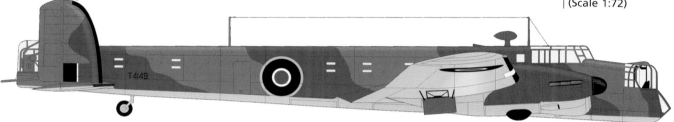

This is nearly a glider pilot's view of Whitley V T4149 in September 1943, showing the two rocket pods under the wings, and the bar around the tail turret; clearly seen are the bomb cell doors inboard of the engines. A&AEE pilots made several rocket take-offs to assess handling for the RAE; the aircraft was mostly unserviceable in the three months from July 1943. *A&AEE recognition 182*

Wellington

The twin-engined Vickers Wellington entered service as a bomber in 1938 and remained in use, as a trainer, until 1953; some 11,650 were produced. Most early wartime armament reports by the A&AEE have not been found.

Wellington Mark I

Tests of the original version were virtually complete before the Establishment moved to Boscombe Down. L4213 and R2700 flew from Martlesham in September 1939; the former completed minor items of performance (see Performance Table). R2703 soon joined the Special Duty Flight, and made a return flight to Morocco early in 1940. Armament trials employed L4285 from January 1940. In mid-1941 L4329 made a brief investigation into glidepath angles. L4359 was detached to West Freugh from November 1941 for bombing trials until well into 1942, by which time it was shown in the A&AEE's weekly return of aircraft as a Mk IC (probably in error).

September 1939 saw the arrival of the first Mk IA N2874, with rotating Frazer Nash turrets in the nose, ventral and tail positions, and with a stronger undercarriage permitting a greater all-up weight of 27,000lb; Pegasus XVIII engines were retained. In addition to performance measurements (see Performance Table), handling remained satisfactory for the role although the weight of the FN5 tail turret (252lb) made the CG further aft than the earlier version and it was recommended that the tail gunner move forward for landing. This movement was presumably made while the ventral turret was extended as it blocked the fuselage when retracted. A diving speed of 318mph was attained with the elevator trim set for maximum level speed; some wing fabric detached during the 2.8g recovery but without serious result. At the weight tested (about 26,000lb) neither engine alone was capable of maintaining height. Heating was poor – and non-existent for the tail gunner. Early in 1942 a new boiler system in N2955 was tried without success. N2955 had four containers built into the wings inboard of the engines; each container held three aerial mines, the whole installation being known as apparatus AD Type H. Release characteristics were satisfactory, but some mines failed to release due to buckled teleflex cable. Earlier, in March 1940, P9211 had turrets with increased traverse and Vickers K guns in the beam; all functioned acceptably up to 305mph, although new Browning guns were recommended. Meanwhile, armament trials, including bombsight assessment, were being made on N2865 in conjunction with the RAE until the end of 1940.

A most interesting modification was made to P2518 of the RAE with a large (50-foot) diameter ring under the wings and fuselage for exploding magnetic mines. No A&AEE document has been found relating to its short stay at Boscombe Down around late-December 1939, but pilot's log book entries state that a small number of flights were made there.

The Mk IC (a 24-volt electrical system replaced the 12 volts of the Mk IA, and without the latter's ventral turret) came from three factories. The first to arrive at Boscombe, N2761, was from Chester in July 1940, closely followed in August by T2711 from Weybridge and X3160, the very first from Blackpool. There were no significant differences between the three in handling or performance. T2711 soon departed, while N2761 measured the effect of Vokes air filters, which reduced speed by 7mph (true) at maximum power. During the measurements the cylinders ran too hot while the oil temperatures remained satisfactory; indeed, the highest oil figures were recorded on the coldest days, attributed to coring. Early in 1941 an attempt (known as saucer cowls) to improve cylinder cooling was partially effective in the cruise, but at a penalty of 3½mph (true). In the summer of 1941 W5717 was loaded to 31,600lb with ballast to simulate the weight of full long-range tanks and the take-off run measured at 1,150 yards (1,700 yards to 50 feet), a figure considered excessive. In addition, the oil temperatures were too high and the poor climb was made worse by the need to keep the gills open. The whole manoeuvre was very uncomfortable and the Establishment strongly recommended that the overload condition with Pegasus XVIIIs should not be flown in service.

Following reports from the RAF of high oil consumption, engine modifications, including new scraper rings, were flown on Z8896 between November 1941 and the following May. This protracted trial determined the optimum gill settings for controlling the cylinder temperatures. An earlier modification to T2968 introduced a pressure boiler (40psi), fitted round the port exhaust pipe, for cabin heating. While all crew positions (except the poor tail gunner) remained comfortable at all altitudes, various weaknesses were found in some components and led to the tedious task of draining the whole system after flight. Z1101 arrived in June 1942 for a lengthy spell of navigation research.

The Armament Squadron received four

Wellington Mk ICs. R1628 and Z8718 arrived in July and September 1941 respectively for development testing of the Mk XIV bombsight, and general bombing duties. X3171, soon replaced by X9984, arrived at about the same time for night photography, with the small unit detached from Farnborough. Late in 1940 R3155 joined the Special Duty Flight for work with Porton, as did DV427 in January 1942.

Wellington Mark II

The Merlin X was the first of three engines fitted as an alternative to the Pegasus. L4250 appeared in December 1939 complete with Rotol propellers and small cowlings. It was less stable than the Mk I, and in the climb exhibited unstable characteristics; these features were found to be acceptable, although the effects could not be divorced from the behaviour of the elevator, which was too heavy. Single-engine flying in straight flight could be achieved with full trim and a small bank angle. Take-off distances at 27,000lb appear to have been slightly longer than the similarly loaded Mk I, but when, in mid-1940, R3221 was measured at 30,000lb, then 32,000lb, the distances were significantly better (see Performance Table). Radio and navigation facilities were satisfactory, but heating in the

Mk II continued to be poor with the auxiliary radiator system.

Early tests had shown oil cooling to be marginal, and for tropical use the capacity of the oil pump was increased by 30%; in mid-1941 W5480 showed this improvement to be adequate. The triple ejector exhaust on W5385 successfully reduced exhaust visibility to within night-bomber limits; the aircraft then continued on compass research work.

W5389 was employed on general-purpose bombing for a short period from February 1941 and probably dropped the first 4,000lb 'cookie' bomb. Shortly before this date the AGME moved to Boscombe, together with L4250 with a Vickers turret complete with 40mm 'S' gun and predictor sight. Twin fins had been fitted after early flying by Vickers in the original configuration had produced unacceptable buffeting of the single fin. The A&AEE initially assessed the sophisticated predictor sight with its automatic allowance for height, speed, rates of elevation and rotation while the gunner adjusted for range and weapon ballistics. There was no effect on aircraft handling from operation of the turret, although firing at low elevation to the beam tore fabric off the wing. Before comprehensive testing of the sight began, L4250 went to Exeter.

Vickers Wellington L4250, December 1939, for handling trials.

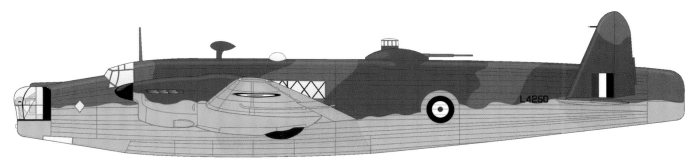

Wellington II L4250 at Boscombe in January 1942 on receipt from Duxford. This view shows the turret with its periscopic sight and 40mm gun, the twin fins and the faired-over rear fuselage. *A&AEE 9870*

Wellington III L4251 in late 1939. The Hercules SM(a) engines and the de Havilland propellers are in evidence, together with the heat exchanger on the exhaust, and the oil cooler underneath. The aircraft has a venturi under the forward fuselage, a small window above it, and an early unprotected DF aerial atop the fuselage. The mast above the roundel was a feature of the first few Wellingtons.

Wellington Mark III

The first Hercules-engined Wellington, L4251, was delivered in May 1940 to the Armament Squadron, and not, as was usual for a new version, to the Performance Squadron. This allocation was probably made as the engines were of an early standard and not representative of the production aircraft, and L4251 had the first FN20 tail turret (four 0.303in Browning guns). The two reports written appear to be lost, but the manufacturer's records indicate that the problems were few. However, in service the production turret gave trouble, and X3398 from No 9 Squadron was examined in November 1941. The Establishment found that this, and contemporary production turrets, were sub-standard, although the basic design was sound. P9238 with Hercules XIs was more representative of the production aircraft with an FN2 nose turret, mock-up FN4 in the tail and a retractable tail wheel. On arrival in May 1941 P9238 started eighteen months of tests by demonstrating a take-off run at 33,000lb of only 440 yards – a considerable improvement on the Pegasus-powered aircraft. This weight represented the standard loading, and, with full fuel of 1,030 gallons and 1,380lb of bombs, ideal range was 2,230 statute miles; with maximum load of bombs, 6,750lb, range was reduced to 520 miles. The fuel jettison system set a standard of efficiency for the later 'heavies', and gave confidence for the overload trials at 34,500lb, starting in September 1941. Performance at the new weight (see Performance Table) was encouraging, and handling remained satisfactory, except for the rudder trimmer range being inadequate for single-engine flying; the stalls were at 78mph (clean) and 64mph flaps and undercarriage down.

Engine temperatures remained marginal even after the limits were raised, both with the electrically controlled propellers and the hydraulic pair on X3223. Over the following year four major cooling modifications achieved varying success. It had been intended to use X3446 for these trials, but it made a heavy landing a few days after arrival, buckling the centre section; the task fell to P9238 later with tropical air intake and filter. The standard Gallay boiler was replaced early in 1942 in X3406 by an exhaust-heated arrangement, which initially overcooked the pilot and wireless operator and left the bunk frozen; additional heater tubes in X3945 gave better distribution, but at too low a temperature. X3476 had an improved rudder trimmer, effective in rendering prolonged single-engine flying a practical proposition at modest weight at 3,000 feet; a new leather pilot's seat may have helped. The same aeroplane had only the second Tricell flare chute, but difficulties in reloading in the air made the installation impractical. After successfully proving new De Havilland propellers in mid-1942, DF627 was fitted with unspecified special navigation equipment, thus attracting the 'G' suffix to its serial number.

Other Mk IIIs were X3282 on unreported intensive flying from October 1941 and X3475 briefly with the Armament Squadron.

Wellington Mark IV

This designation identified the version powered by the fourth type of engine – the Twin Wasp in its S3C4G variety. R1515, the first to arrive in February 1941, soon revealed two shortcomings of the Mk IV – cabin noise and high fuel consumption, particularly in the climb. The latter was at first largely attributed to the dirty and

Wellington IV R1515 in March 1941. The nacelles of the Twin Wasp engines are slightly smaller than those of the Hercules. Other features visible include a VHF aerial in front of the pilot, a streamlined DF aerial above the starboard engine and the wavy division between the matt black lower and the lighter upper surfaces. *A&AEE 9718*

continually tearing fabric of the airframe: however, a clean aircraft, Z1264, borrowed from No 300 Squadron, confirmed that cruising power in weak mixture was too low (ie speed and/or height had to be reduced), and that both oil and cylinder temperatures were too high. Later in 1942, cooling modifications improved matters; R1515 was about 12% worse than Z1264. The latter produced a maximum range of 1,500 miles (1,125 practical) following take-off at 32,000lb with 750 gallons of fuel. While the range trials were under way in late 1941 and early 1942, Z1248 flew to assess the benefit of various propellers of 11, 11½ and 12 feet diameter. The largest, although the noisiest, produced marginally the best results and gave take-off figures, at 31,500lb, of 640 yards (run) and 995 yards (to 50 feet); climb performance (see the Table) revealed a low service ceiling of 17,400 feet. Handling was similar to the Mk I, except that control column and rudder loads were too high on one engine at the previously acceptable speed of 115mph. The boiler (with its 1½ gallons of distilled water) did not adequately warm any crew position, and the flame damping (tested on Z1260 in mid-1942) failed to meet requirements. R1625 was briefly at Boscombe on navigation work in late 1941, and Z1288 a year later, fitted with a long-range tank giving a total of 890 gallons. Practical range was 1,320 miles at 15,000 feet following take-off at 31,500lb with 2,400lb of bombs; the normal reserve tanks in the nacelles were ungauged, making fuel planning difficult.

Wellington Mark V and VI

These two high-altitude versions were the first British aircraft with pressure cabins (differential of 7 psi) and were powered by the Hercules VIII (Mk V) with an auxiliary supercharger, and the Merlin 60 (Mk VI) with a two-speed supercharger. In the event W5795 (Mk VI) arrived first in November 1941, but with very limited life (10 hours) on the engines. Maximum weight was calculated at 32,000lb, but 32,300lb was achieved for the single climb made, taking 64.6 minutes to reach 30,000 feet. The restricted flying time was sufficient to reveal many shortcomings. The view was poor, aggravated by the throttles and undercarriage lever being positioned so far forward that the pilot had to lean forward and was thus unable to see out. The swing to the left on take-off could be contained only by full right rudder and trim, and by opening the port throttle first. A night take-off was interesting. The aircraft was markedly unstable in the cruise, going straight into an increasing dive or into a stall on releasing the control column. The cabin was too hot, and oil mist prevented the crew from seeing each other; propeller control was prevented by freezing of the constant speed units. Potentially the most serious shortcoming of all was the procedure for emergency escape. After depressurising the cabin, the small sealing door had to be opened, then the crew of four crawled through it, found and clipped on parachutes and made their way down the fuselage to the escape hatch, where they could escape. The report states that the rear turret (unpressurised but with electrically heated clothing) was used normally at high altitude, but the guns fired only intermittently. It is not clear what 'normal' means, but some later high-altitude Wellingtons had a remotely operated turret. So, presumably, the turret in W5795 was manned above 30,000 feet, an intriguing thought. The turret was certainly manned in R3299 in mid-1942.

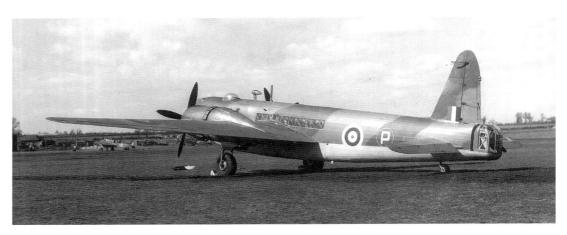

Wellington V R3298 in April 1942, probably at Filton, with the original pilot's dome and Hercules XV engines (cooling flaps closed). The DF loop housing is aft of the dome, and the Rotol four-bladed propellers are standard for the type. *A&AEE recognition 89v*

Wellington V R3299 in June 1942 with the elongated pilot's cockpit cover. The rear turret has guns and the engines Hercules VIII before flame dampers were fitted; there appears to be a small oil cooler under the engine. *A&AEE 11013*

Wellington Mk VI R5798 in February 1942 in original configuration, with very poor escape facilities, not to mention an extremely restricted view out for the pilot. *A&AEE recognition 81*

Wellington Mk VI R5798 in November 1942, showing the redesigned nose with marginally improved escape facilities and a new paint job already looking worn. *A&AEE recognition 118*

With rejuvenated engines, extended wing tips and minor improvements, W5795 returned in mid-1942. On 12 July tragedy struck when the aircraft crashed from high altitude, and all five crew were killed. The most likely cause was thought to be failure of a propeller blade, which flew off and possibly injured the pilot; the tortuous escape route cannot have helped survival, although the rear turret was presumably manned.

In the meantime R3298, a Mk V with Hercules, paid a fleeting visit, and its modified, elongated pilot's dome was judged to be no improvement. Returning in July, the Hercules XI of R3298 failed to meet the night-bomber limitations on exhaust flame damping. The intended engines, Hercules VIII, powered R3299, tested in the summer of 1942 at the slightly increased weight of 33,000lb. Performance (see the Table) was disappointing, and hopes were pinned on the Mk VI.

W5798, the first production Mk VIA with four-bladed propellers, spent its time from February 1942 on bombing trials and on flame damping measurements; the latter were an improvement but still not good enough. W5800 from October 1942 flew asymmetrically, as did DR480 and DR482; rudder trim was inadequate. DR480/G suffered a fractured tail assembly in a heavy landing in mid-October shortly after arrival. DR482 and DR484, each lacking a rear turret, with Merlin 60 and Merlin 62 respectively, could carry 1,012 gallons of fuel and 1,500lb bombs. Both were very tiring to fly, particularly during the 1¼-hour climb; controls were noticeably heavier than those of unpressurised Wellingtons. DR484, at least, had an escape hatch in the extreme nose. DR482 made a heavy landing on the very soft aerodrome in January 1943, the undercarriage collapsed and the machine written off.

Wellington VI DR482 in October 1942, during its brief visit to Boscombe. On 14 January 1943 the pilot landed heavily on soft ground and the machine tipped over; it was not repaired. The modified rudder trimmer of extra chord is visible, together with its operating levers. *A&AEE*

Wellington VI DR484 west of Salisbury in January 1943. It has the extended nose, with the escape hatch (not visible); a footstep has recently been introduced below the fuselage roundel. Note the faired rear fuselage, the original cockpit cover, and the pilot in his peaked No 1 SD hat. *A&AEE recognition 123*

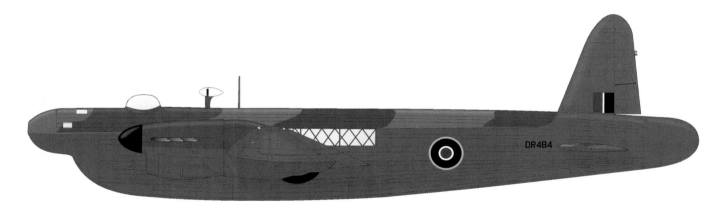

Vickers Wellington DR484, December 1942, for handling trials.

Wellington Mark VIII

The development of the Pegasus-engined Wellington for the coastal role resulted in the Mk VIII, of which only one, HX719, reached Boscombe in April 1943; no report appears to have been written on this alleged rogue. Z8713 may have had some coastal features but any reports have been lost.

Wellington Mark X

The greater power of the Hercules VI endowed the Mk X with the ability to carry 4,000lb of bombs and full fuel (750 gallons), giving a maximum weight of 34,500lb. X3374, the first prototype, was used for more than a year on performance work after initially checking engine cooling. Eventually, modified cuffs, shrouds and baffles achieved satisfactory cooling in the climb and cruise, but the problem of overcooling of the oil during descent remained. Performance is shown in the Table, and range after take-off at maximum weight was 1,520 miles (1,140 practical). X3374 suffered major damage to the tail wheel assembly from taxiing too fast over rough ground, and was replaced in August 1942 by the first production Mk X, DF609 – soon engaged on flame damping, cockpit contamination trials, and later handling with a rudder trimmer modified in an unsuccessful attempt to improve unpleasant handling on one engine. Later in 1944, with a rudder shroud and reduced elevator horn together with a geared tab, DF609 had significantly improved longitudinal and asymmetric handling. The effective rudder trim modification had been first tested on HE446 in April 1944 and the elevator modification on HE574 later in 1943; the latter was extensively instrumented for work on oil cooling, involving measurement of the efficiency of the cooler matrix and other parameters.

Two Mk Xs served with the Armament Squadron in 1943, HE736 and HE497. The latter was briefly flown to assess the sight vibration associated with the experimental FN120 tail turret; modifications were recommended before the aircraft was returned to the Bomber Development Unit at Feltwell. NA724, an unarmed training version of the Mk X, arrived in July 1945, and trials were under way when the war ended.

Wellington Mark XI, XII, XIII and XIV

These coastal versions of the Wellington were similar. MP502, the first Mk XIII with Hercules

XVIIs, spent twelve months at Boscombe from December 1942; interest centred on engine cooling, handling and performance. The engines behaved themselves provided the climb was made at a speed slightly faster than optimum. Handling differed little from earlier versions, but at aft CG MP502 became longitudinally neutrally stable at 320mph, while remarkably low stalling speeds of 73mph (clean) and 60mph (flaps and undercarriage down) were observed, even at maximum weight. At modest weight height could be maintained on one engine, provided the other propeller was feathered. Range at the operating height of 2,000 feet with full normal fuel of 750 gallons was 1,450 miles (1,160 practical). MP535, a Mk XI, arrived for investigation in April 1943 as a reported rogue.

Wellington XIV MP818 in April 1944. The Leigh light is retracted under the rear fuselage while the nose is optimised for viewing with the ASV Mk III underneath. Also seen are the fuel jettison pipe under the port wing and the rudder mass balance. *A&AEE 11731*

Wellington Mk XIII MP502 illustrates the extensive aerial array of this anti-submarine version; handling was little affected. *A&AEE 11240 dated 10 February 1943*

Two Mk XIV aircraft, MP714 and MP818, shared testing of this version from July and November 1943 respectively. MP714 had a Leigh light and an early version of the RP installation, with the blast plate under the wing divided round the fuel jettison pipes. After completing the tedious attitude measurements, the installation was approved with various minor modifications. An increase in maximum weight to 36,500lb led to tests on MP818 of handling, fuel consumption and engine cooling. Range, with 1,215 gallons, was 2,480 miles (1,980 practical), and handling unchanged. The speed at which neutral stability occurred was lower at 280mph, and the Establishment recommended this speed as the maximum. Stall (clean) was 75mph, and 64mph with undercarriage and flaps down.

A Wellington Mk XIV in July 1943 showing its Coastal Command colours and RPs under the wings. The venue is Porton range; the wall target is visible. *A&AEE recognition 172*

Manchester

The Avro Manchester had two engines and a large bomb bay in compliance with its 1936 RAF specification; these two features determined the fate of the type.

Two very powerful and new Vulture engines did not fulfil expectations, and gave trouble from the first visit to Boscombe of the first prototype, L7246. Shortly after arrival on 10 December 1939 the port engine failed during take-off, and the recovery of the large, damaged aircraft from the centre of a field was a feat in itself. Initial flying had revealed longitudinal instability and a fierce swing to starboard on take-off; in addition control forces were heavy, particularly the elevator above 260mph and on landing. At 40,000lb, and with the engines each delivering 100hp less than expected, the take-off run was 580 yards, reaching 20 feet as the airfield boundary was reached. The cockpit was generally liked. After repair L7246 returned with slightly more powerful engines, but demonstrated no real improvement; a third visit with wing span increased from 80 feet to 90 feet and with modified elevators was better.

In the meantime the second prototype, L7247 (from June 1940), and the first production aircraft, L7276 (from August

Manchester (first prototype) L7246 in December 1939 shortly before its ignominious forced landing in a cabbage field.

L7246 is seen again on 22 December 1939 following engine failure on take-off – the first of many forced landings of the type due to the unreliable Vulture motor. The pilot, Flt Lt J. W. McGuire, and three crew were uninjured, and the aircraft was dismantled and returned to its maker, A. V. Roe, by road.

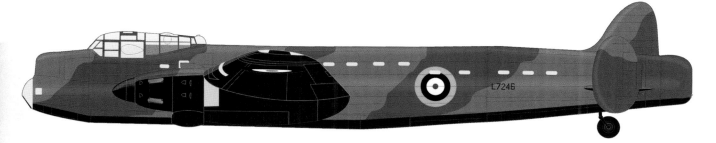

Avro Manchester L7246, December 1939, for handling trials.

1940), had arrived. The former was used to assess the armament; the aircraft was a good bombing platform, but the rear turret was jerky and, on the ground, the bomb doors could be opened only by 15 minutes of strenuous hand pumping. L7276 handled well by day and night with various modifications embodied to the controls and engines, although the incomplete navigation facilities were poor. Loaded to 45,000lb with 3,500lb of bombs and 1,160 gallons of fuel, range was 1,760 miles, performance was as in the Table, and the take-off run 600 yards.

Late in 1940 L7277 (replacing L7276 after severe damage in September 1940 following a port engine failure on take-off) and L7281, with 90-foot wings and larger tailplanes, confirmed the previous performance, but with take-off run reduced to 510 yards using 30° flap. Handling in dives to 341mph revealed unpleasant vibrations, the rudder became immovable and the pilot's position was noisy. Overshooting, with its accompanying large trim change, was, however, acceptable with the large tailplane; flap and CG limitations had already been recommended for landing (in case of the need to overshoot) with the original tailplane. Trials with and without the central fin confirmed earlier findings that the aircraft was extremely directionally unstable without it. Later trials on L7320 from March 1941 concentrated on assessing a 'dishplate' modification to the top of the FN7A dorsal turrets. Rotation continued to cause severe vibration on the central fin, to such an extent that two of them were carried away in two flights. Diving to 320mph caused the same effect. Weight increase to 50,000lb lengthened the take-off run to 880 yards. L7320 was also used to investigate remedies to many problems, including vibration in the climb, cured by removing minor oil cooler flanges on top of the cowlings. High engine temperatures were remedied by climbing at a higher airspeed, but further work stopped when L7320 was written off following an engine failure caused by overspeeding of the port propeller. L7373 tested a special bomb (report not found) in April 1941, and R5830 joined the Armament Squadron briefly in January 1942.

Thus of the eight Manchesters at the A&AEE, three suffered severe engine failures – the third occurring after the decision had been made to fit four Merlins and make the Lancaster.

Manchester I L7320 in November 1941. The centre fin was fitted to investigate buffeting caused by the upper FN7 turret. After two central fins detached in flight, two enlarged fins on a wider tailplane proved adequate for control. *A&AEE 9829*

Albemarle

Note: The Mark numbers attributed to production aircraft found no mention at the A&AEE – except for the Mk IV with Cyclone engines.

The Armstrong Whitworth Albemarle was the outcome of a requirement for a bomber to be constructed as far as possible from readily available materials, ie wood. The further innovation of dispersed manufacture was compounded by the transfer of design authority from Bristol. The vicissitudes of the resulting aeroplane are, perhaps, unsurprising and became apparent during testing. by both the manufacturer and the A&AEE, and in service. Establishment test pilots first flew the Albemarle at Baginton at the end of September 1940 and found the performance of the light prototype, P1360, mediocre (top speed 270mph (true) and ceiling 19,000 feet). The twin rudders lacked sufficient travel, were too heavy to maintain straight flight on one engine, and the aileron and rudder trimmers were poor. The nose wheel brake appeared to be ineffective. On arrival at Boscombe in November 1940 P1360 had larger rudders and balance tabs, both with increased travel rendering single-engined flight possible with the feet off the pedals. Other handling and performance trials ceased when P1360 crashed and caught fire in February 1941.

The replacement, P1361, equipped with turrets, heating and wireless, arrived ten weeks later; fully loaded it weighed 37,500lb. Take-off and climb were poor and confirmed the earlier results; the Establishment decided to limit loading to 36,500lb. Trials of the upper turret (Boulton Paul Type A Mk III, four 0.303in guns) revealed its draughtiness, and lowering the ventral turret (Boulton Paul Type K Mk II, two 0.303in guns) at speeds up to 273mph caused the aircraft to snake. Even with the turret retracted, the Albemarle was never judged to be pleasant to fly, and was distinctly uncomfortable at aft CG. A lengthy flight to determine the maximum weight for single-engine flying became a test of the pilot's endurance in the bumpy conditions prevailing. Further discomfort for the crew was expected in service from the poor heating – non-existent aft of the main spar – and the need to drain the Gallay system's water after flight was criticised.

Operational crews attached to the Establishment for intensive flying of the Albemarle confirmed the poor handling at high weight and the excessively cold upper turret. P1368 (62 hours in the four weeks prior to its crash on 28 February 1942) and P1375 (79 hours in five weeks prior to its crash just six weeks later) were used. The most damning of the comments following intensive flying was that the wooden structure of the wings warped in the rain when parked outside, in spite of the use of a cover and liberal floor polish; the Albemarle was considered unsuitable for operational use.

Armstrong Whitworth Albemarle P1361, April 1941, for handling/performance trials.

Albemarle I P1361 in August 1941, fully equipped with operational equipment. The Boulton Paul Type A upper turret and its four Browning 0.303in guns can be seen; there is no evidence of the retractable ventral turret, which may have been removed by the date of this photograph. The retracted and semi-stowed main wheel appears to be unusually large. *A&AEE recognition 9*

P1362 arrived on 23 October 1941 with a full radio fit and minor engine modifications; the IFF, radios, engine cooling and stalling were satisfactory, but performance, including take-off distances, remained poor. Among the Albemarle's unusual features were an increase in speed at maximum boost with a reduction in rpm, and an increase in take-off distance on concrete when compared to identical conditions on grass. Like the Stirling and Wellington with Hercules XI engines, range was greater at 10,000 feet (in MS gear) than at 15,000 feet (in FS gear), and calculated to be 1,560 statute miles or 1,170 miles for practical purposes. Minor control shortcomings were remedied on P1363, which replaced P1365 after the latter's crash in February 1942; elevator trim was sufficient in all configurations but the rudder balance tab needed further modification. Gunnery trials on P1372 lasted for six months prior to a crash in August 1942; draughtiness in the upper turret (Type A Mk II) was the only major criticism. Much more serious was the extreme difficulty of loading bombs (P1362 was used). The hoisting winch was attached outside the fuselage and the cable threaded tortuously down through the bay for each bomb, and it was found nearly impossible to reach round the bombs to make the necessary connections.

The Albemarle trials so far described were made in the original bomber configuration; the shortcomings reported led to new roles in passenger carrying and glider towing. P1506, modified for passengers and freight. appeared in October 1942, had no turrets and could carry 1,234 gallons of fuel (compared to 769 of the earlier version), but little else within the maximum weight of 36,500lb. At 2,000 feet maximum range was 2,340 miles. Overload tank trials had previously been abandoned in September 1942 on P1369 after a month's unserviceability. P1634 attended briefly in February 1943, probably for assessment of the twin guns mounted in the passenger version in place of the upper turret. The glider tug versions in service experienced persistent overheating of engines when towing, leading to an extensive investigation at Boscombe Down on P1523 for nearly a year from October 1942. Modified shrouds, new baffles, extra cooling holes in the nacelles and semi-flared propellers led to satisfactory oil temperatures, but the cylinders remained prone to slight overheating Two other Hercules-powered models at the A&AEE were P1367 in mid-1944 (a glider tug, reported to be a rogue, which the Establishment found to be within normal tolerance when properly trimmed) and V1743, used on photographic duties for a year from December 1944.

Albemarle I P1506 in December 1942, showing the cover over the rear gunner's position. The upper turret had been removed to make room in the fuselage for passengers and freight. Unshielded horn balances on the elevators are outboard of the fins, and the heating pipes through the exhausts of the port engine can be seen. *A&AEE 11207*

Albemarle IV P1406 in February 1943, with Double Cyclones (R-2600) revealing few external differences (notably the exhausts) from the Hercules-powered version. The beam approach aerial is mounted further forward under the fuselage than on most types.

Albemarle Mark IV

As a precaution against a shortage of Hercules engines, P1406 had Wright Cyclones (R-2600 A5B) fitted and arrived in January 1943; it was otherwise similar to the early bomber version and retained the ability to carry nine 500lb bombs. After carburettor faults were rectified the climb was found to be improved, but the ceiling even lower than with the Hercules. The engine mountings were too rigid, leading to structural breakages. Later V1760, also with Cyclones, was unserviceable during its short stay in August 1943. Hercules remained available and powered 598 production Albemarles, equipping a mere six RAF squadrons.

Stirling

The dauntingly large Stirling, designed by the flying boat firm of Short Brothers, was the first four-engined bomber at Boscombe and was dogged by poor serviceability at first. Equally poor was the performance, particularly in the early version with Hercules II engines.

Stirling Mark I

L7605, the second prototype, arrived in April 1940, followed by three production aircraft at monthly intervals: N3635, N3637 (for a stay of only eight weeks) and N3643. N3635 was unserviceable for nearly three months and N3643 for two periods totalling more than three months – all in 1940. The comprehensive performance report was, in consequence, not produced until February 1941, although the results of individual trials were made known by letter as soon as they were analysed. Nevertheless, the performance figures (see the Table) must have made dismal reading, even allowing for the low power of the early Hercules II motors, and the restricted weight of 57,400lb. Controls and stability were good, although response to the rudder was slow. Stall was normal at 115mph clean and 98mph with undercarriage and flaps down; these speeds were some 50% higher than those of contemporary Wellingtons. With one engine failed, 7,500 feet could be maintained. Consumption was measured at 1.17 ampg at 10,000 feet following take-off at 57,400lb, ie some 7,000lb lighter than the original design approval. A somewhat remarkable extrapolation to full weight and fuel (1,940 gallons) indicated that 2,000 statute miles was just achievable with 3,500lb bombs at 10,000 feet. Later, cruising speed was established at 232mph (true) at the same height. An operational trial in mid-1940 on N3635 and N3637 added further knowledge to the components requiring improvement, including undercarriages (retraction and oleos), hydraulic throttle linkage and engine reliability. N3635 ended its days on 16 August 1941 when, on the last take-off planned using underwing rockets; they all fired at once (instead of in sequence) and broke loose, severely damaging the aircraft, which was subsequently reduced to produce. The RAE report on this lethal innovation concluded that the crash ended interest in the project.

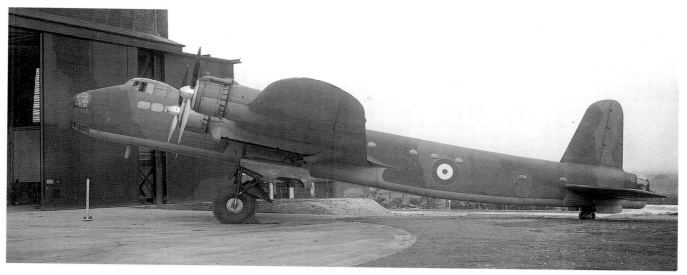

Stirling L7605 in pre-war-style markings and camouflage. *A&AEE 9637*

In October 1940 N6000, built at Belfast (earlier aircraft had been built at Rochester), arrived, followed four months later by N6008, and in March by W7426 built by Austin. All had Hercules X engines; N6008, at least, had the same four engines late in 1941 when they were designated Hercules XI. Handling the Austin-built aircraft revealed slightly heavier controls with more backlash than the Rochester machines; with asymmetric engine power rudder tramping was felt. N6000 enjoyed a lengthy existence at Boscombe,

starting with fuel jettison tests; the rate of discharge was slow and pipes were needed to direct the fuel away from the flaps. Take-offs at progressively increasing weights were measured: at 70,000lb a 900-yard run was needed (1,380 yards to 50 feet), and unstick speed was no less than 111mph. Handling, including dives to 310mph at this weight, was considered acceptable at mid CG in spite of longitudinal instability in the cruise; at aft CG lack of sufficient elevator trimmer made the aircraft tiring and unacceptable. A modified

Stirling I N3662 in August 1941. Just visible above the outer engine is the pitot head, moved on later aircraft to a position under the nose; there is no 'taboo' guard to the turret, but there are ice guards to the air intakes; and the front panel of the undercarriage housing appears to be devoid of paint. *A&AEE 9764*

Short Stirling L7605, April 1940, for handling/ performance trials.

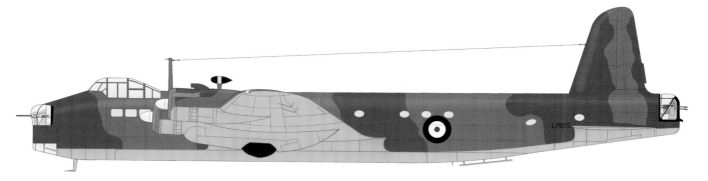

trim was later tested, but was only partially successful. Also, at aft CG overshooting from a baulked approach was particularly tricky as the control column had to be pushed to its full travel to prevent the nose rising once the undercarriage retracted (an operation taking 55 seconds on the early Stirlings). Later, flying on only two engines required unacceptably high foot loads. After modification with mock-up dorsal and ventral turrets, N6000 repeated range measurements, following take-off at 70,000lb. At a cruising weight of 58,500lb consumption was 1.11ampg at 15,000 feet in S gear, giving a maximum range of 1,940 miles (1,480 practical). In mid-1942 tropical air intake filters had no adverse affect on the 51-minute climb to ceiling.

N6000 was also involved in attempts to increase cylinder cooling. Improved baffles generally reduced temperatures by 10°C in the climb, but inconsistencies led to the measurement of the temperatures of individual cylinders. One result was the increase permitted in early 1942 in engine limitations for take-off, climb and cruise with significant gains of 3,000 feet in ceiling and up to 20mph (true) in speeds.

Meanwhile, N6008, often unserviceable, managed only one test, and demonstrated the high control column forces at forward CG that limited diving speed to 295mph. L7605 returned briefly late in 1941 with a second electric motor added to speed operation of the undercarriage, interlinked via a torque tube; no problems were reported. N3678, from March 1942, had direct air heating for the cabin (previously a steam boiler was used) and was considered an improvement after struggling to 20,000 feet (-27°C); the heating pipework had no adverse effects on the Stirling's satisfactory flame damping. H2S radar in R9254/G, from November 1942, appears to have been incidental to the investigation into the effects of carburettor heat on performance.

The Stirling suffered in Bomber Command from comparison of its performance with those of the Halifax and Lancaster, and it is not surprising that poor individual aircraft in service were reported as unacceptable for operations. The A&AEE investigated seven so-called 'rogue' Mk I aircraft (see Appendix 6); two of them were brought to Boscombe for further investigation. BF382 was found to need re-rigging and BK597 was found to be satisfactory except for a slower than normal rate of climb. An investigation by the Establishment into the type's performance concluded that the Service was unaware of the effect of the many factors involved, in particular the effect of seasonal variations in temperature, when a hot day could cause a loss of 3,000 feet in ceiling and up to 25mph (true) in cruising speed. Extra operational weight and even the anti-frost paste, if badly applied, caused deterioration. In June 1943 EF386 was found to have wing, aileron, nacelles and gill contours outside tolerance; work by the A&AEE on these defects was tedious but effected a remedy. Towards the end of the Mk I's operational life, a further increase in permitted engine boost and rpm in the cruise restored much of the lost performance when tested in July 1943 on BK645.

Four Mk I aircraft were allocated for armament work, starting with N3654 for a few weeks from March 1941, and followed by N3662 in May. The latter tested first the FN7 'Botha' dorsal turret with two Browning guns, then the modified FN7A. Details of these early gunnery trials appear to have been lost, but the nose (FN5) and tail (FN20A) turret were also probably evaluated, the latter, at least, attracting several adverse comments and recommendations for improvements. From July 1942 the servo feed mechanism to the tail turret of W7587 came under scrutiny; firing, including dives up to 315mph, was greatly improved. Later, with radar (AGLT), the rate of turret rotation decreased above 200mph. In N3678 the new dorsal turret FN50 cost 4mph,

Stirling I R9254/G in November 1942, with the 'taboo' saucer to the upper turret, but no FN64 turret or beam approach aerial. The -/G suffix reflects the fitting of the H2S bombing radar blister. *A&AEE*

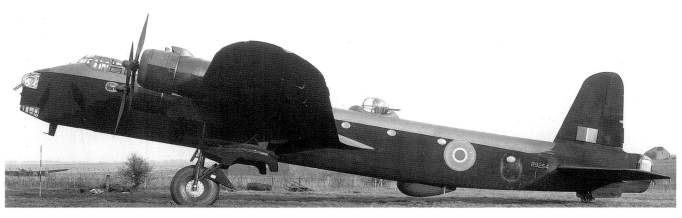

and a further 3mph on rotation to the side: the figures were similar to the FN7A. The FN64 ventral turret in N6000 cost a further 7mph reduction in speed. Early bombing reports, also lost, featured N3635 prior to August 1941, and included satisfactory release of seven 1,900lb GP bombs comprising a single load.

Stirling Mark II

All the foregoing Stirlings had Hercules engines, but two Mk IIs were flown at Boscombe with Cyclone R-2600 A5B engines, N3657 from July 1941 and N3711 from the following May. Among shortcomings that rendered this version unsuitable for operation in the opinion of the Intensive Flying Flight were poor ceiling, manual mixture control, noise and vibration. In addition, the engines ran very hot, and opening the cooling gills further reduced speed in the cruise.

Stirling Mark III and V

The Stirling Mk III had Hercules VI engines but was otherwise similar to the Mk I, and tests centred on performance and engine cooling. The first aircraft with the new engines, N3639 – a Mk I – arrived in January 1942 fitted with a Sperry O1 automatic bombsight; extensive flying proved the Stirling to be unsuitable for this American equipment due to restricted aiming view, manual flying on the bombing run and lack of directional stability. Multiple (up to eighty-eight) flare release from both bomb bay and wing bays was satisfactory from N3639, as was release of up to ninety 4lb incendiaries. The first production Mk III, R9309, arrived in July 1942; this was written off following an uncontained engine fire two months later. Performance (see the Table) measurements continued on BK649 from December; the difference in service ceiling between the two machines is not explained. It was, however,

Stirling II N3657 in August 1941. Like the previous pair, this and N3711, seen in the next photograph, show detail difference in under turrets, beam approach aerial and pressure heads. *A&AEE 9792*

In March 1942 Stirling II N3711 has an upper turret (FN7), guns in the nose, and flame damping exhausts with the gills of the Double Cyclone engines open. It also has a retractable landing light in place of the fixed arrangement of N3657. The hangar background has been deleted, with the exception of details in the undercarriage struts. *A&AEE 11025*

Stirling Mk III BK649 arrived at Boscombe in December 1942 for performance work; it was the second Stirling built by Austin, hence the 'P' marking. This pleasing image appears to be in summertime, and may not be of A&AEE origin.

concluded that the cruising ceiling of 16,000 feet was some 1,600 feet above that of the Mk I. The significance of the position of the cooling gills is striking, and engine cooling was examined thoroughly. Judicious use of the gills was necessary to achieve maximum performance while maintaining cylinder temperatures within limits. In early 1944 BK651, with flared propellers, cooling fans and spinners, was assessed as unsuitable for tropical conditions, while at the same time BK649, with fully flared propellers, ran some 10-20°C cooler and achieved the original performance at reduced cruising rpm.

The original aileron trim tabs, adjustable on the ground only, were moved inboard on the ailerons and thus into the propeller slipstream on EF517 late in 1943. Later, BK651 had aileron trimmers operable from the cockpit; the benefit was spoiled by the control being mounted in the roof in the unnatural plane; larger trims with greater operating range were also fitted to the other two control surfaces with beneficial results. EF466 joined the Armament Squadron for general bombing duties between September and November 1943. LJ571 flew for Porton a year later, and EF517 continued on navigation research until the end of 1944.

Stirling III EF503. Features visible include the streamlined DF aerial housing, twin pitot heads with static source on the roundel, and the prominent oil coolers under the engines. *A&AEE 11619*

Stirling III (Transport Conversion) EF503 in November 1943 with turrets removed and internal changes; cruising speed was up to 15mph (true) higher than the armed Mk III. *A&AEE*

EF503 was delivered in September 1943 without turrets, and was known at the A&AEE as the Mk III (Transport Conversion). Performance at 70,000lb take-off weight gave the following improvements over the representative Mk III: 1,100 feet greater service ceiling, and cruising 12 to 15mph (true) faster and 3,000 feet higher. At the higher speeds, however, the cylinder temperatures were too high for tropical summer conditions; with 2,254 gallons of fuel, maximum range was calculated at 2,270 miles. PJ992, a Mk V cargo version, arrived too late to complete any trials before the end of the war.

Production tests were made on Stirlings and are listed in the Performance Table .

Halifax

The Handley Page Halifax in its original form suffered from two major shortcomings: disappointing performance and lethal rudder overbalance. The A&AEE played its part in the resolution of both problems, the latter costing the lives of a crew in 1942. Here, the Merlin-engined versions (Mk I, II and V) are described before those with Hercules (Mk III, VI and VIII).

Halifax prototype L7244, probably in early 1940. The undercarriage doors are absent and the slats are open. Operational and radio equipment has not been fitted.

Halifax Mark I

L7244 (Merlin X), the first prototype, arrived in November 1939 and flew little, if at all, until about May 1940, while the maker's team toiled to complete modifications. Ground tests demonstrated the ability to carry various bombs up to 2,000lb in combination to a total of 11,000lb. Air tests were limited to take-off measurements (see the Performance Table) and stalling at 45,000lb; speeds were 95mph clean and 79mph with wheels and flaps down with normal behaviour. The bulk of the early testing was completed jointly on L7245, the second prototype, and L9485, the first production aircraft; they arrived in September and October 1940 respectively. Handling was good, with ailerons and elevator becoming heavy above 250mph; a Mark VII auto-pilot (rudders locked, elevator not connected) was fitted. Performance is shown in the Table, and maximum range possible with full fuel and half bomb load was calculated as 1,860 statute miles following take-off at 55,000lb. Guns, including the two beam Brownings, fired successfully in dives up to 320mph. Comments included the following: below 150mph the rudder tended to overbalance with application of trim (this appears to imply that as trim was wound on, the foot load decreased by a greater amount than expected), and that mud from the pilots' boots fell onto the W/T set. In asymmetric flight, the overbalancing of the rudder was more pronounced.

Halifax I L9485 in August 1941 with Merlin X engines. Most of the early armament trials were carried out with this aircraft. Although the mid-upper and tail turrets are not visible in this view, the rare ventral turret and starboard beam hatch are. *A&AEE*

Repairs to L7245, following collapse of the undercarriage on take-off, were combined with structural modifications to permit take-off at 60,000lb. At this weight, take-off distances (even on a concrete runway) were 50% greater than those at 55,000lb, and the aircraft felt 'soggy' at unstick. At 58,000lb the climb to 15,000 feet took an extra 8 minutes, and 20,000 feet was unobtainable. The figures were disappointing in mid-1941, just as the type was entering service, but worse was to come. The top speeds of L7245 and L9485 were re-measured late in 1941, and the turrets and other excrescences of the latter cost nearly 20mph (true) (see the Performance Table). With full fuel of 1,392 gallons and dropping 8,000lb of bombs at mid-point, maximum range following take-off at 58,000lb was calculated as 1,700 miles, down from the initial estimate of 1,860 miles. More encouraging was the change from Messier to Dunlop undercarriage; performance in L9520 was unaffected, but ground behaviour improved. The effect of large bombs preventing full closure of the bomb doors was not measurable. Minor trials, including assessment of the P24 camera, were made on L9505 in mid-1941.

reduction in rotation at speeds above 260mph; various airflow deflectors eventually raised the speed to an acceptable 310mph. Ammunition feed proved difficult to the Type E tail turret (four guns) until an effective servo feed assister was fitted late in 1941; two months later a cure was found for stoppages from empty cases blowing back into the guns. Bombing trials apparently proceeded more smoothly (early reports have not been found) and by 1942 the various loads (including 8,000lb 'cookie') had been cleared for Service use.

Halifax Mark II

A Mk I airframe, L9515, converted to take Merlin XX engines, arrived at Boscombe in July 1941 as the prototype Mark II. Performance (see the Table) at 60,000lb, even without mid-upper and ventral turrets, was scarcely improved by the more powerful engines. An extensive consumption/range trial produced figures of 1.22 ampg/1,770 miles (1,330 practical) at 15,000 feet with cold intake air from take-off at 60,000lb with 1,636 gallons of fuel; a fully equipped aircraft was expected to be 7% worse.

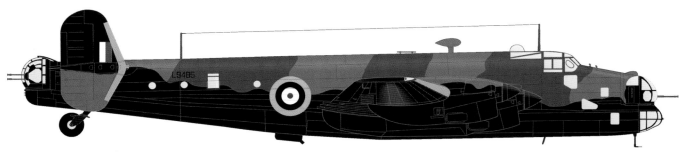

Handley Page Halifax L9485, October 1940, for turret trials.

L9485 bore the brunt of the early armament work on the Halifax, concentrating on the four Boulton Paul turrets and beam guns. The ventral, Type R, turret (the first completed) suffered from the fundamental problem of restricted view through a periscope and, even after several modifications, from slow rotation and elevation of the two guns. By late 1941 improvements to the ammunition feed prevented stoppages in firing, but the turret remained ineffective and was removed in service. The bulbous Type C in the mid-upper position (two guns) achieved creditable rotation and elevation speeds and was generally acceptable once the permissible depression angle had been reduced to prevent shooting through the flaps. The nose turret, also Type C, proved troublesome due to

The next range test was made from RAF St Eval in June 1943, using HR815/G in the maritime role with 2,746 gallons of fuel and three 600lb anti-submarine bombs. A practical range of 2,150 miles was deduced from the 14½-hour flight; the A&AEE observer said 'a rest bunk is essential'.

While range was adequate, attempts were made to improve performance with three types of new propeller on R9387 (from December 1941), W1008 (February 1942) and W1009 (February 1942); W1009 alone had a dorsal turret. The R55/17 propellers of W1008 gave the best take-off; remaining performance was similar (see the Performance Table), although the dorsal turret cost 2-3% in speed. Following reports from the Service of serious loss of performance, the Establishment joined

discussions with Handley Page and others to consider possible improvements.

During 1942 and later, the search continued for a solution to the problem of rudder overbalance, thought in view of the Establishment's experience on the Mk Is to be the cause of some unexplained Service accidents and operational losses. The worst case considered was failure (and feathering) of the two port engines with the two starboard engines at take-off power. The first modification, late in 1941, of reducing the rudder trimmer movement, resulted in excessive foot loads until, on reducing speed to 160mph, the rudders violently overbalanced to full travel and the resulting uncontrolled manoeuvre could only be overcome by throttling the starboard engines. 'Noseings' (bulbous nose to the rudders) improved matters such that control could be maintained down to a speed of 140mph with 10° bank without overbalancing, but with very high foot loads. Further changes, in mid-1942, to the balance tab and rudder tab settings reduced the foot loads to acceptable proportions, but reintroduced a mild tendency to rudder overbalance.

It was decided to check the effectiveness of the latest modifications on a representative aircraft. W7917 arrived in December 1942 from No 102 Squadron; on the first handling test flight on 4 February 1943, the aircraft crashed fatally. The top half of one rudder had detached in flight – attributed to a violent overbalance leading to loss of control. Further investigation took place on HR679 (the first production aircraft incorporating the full range of aerodynamic improvements known as the Series IA in Service but with rudders similar to W7917). Cautious reduction in speed during steady sideslips caused no indication of overbalance until at 120mph the rudders suddenly moved to full travel of their own volition. The pilot regained control at 150mph after easing the control column forward; 4,000 feet had been lost in the spiral dive. On a second attempt control was regained by opening up the engines on the inside of the spiral. Later tests with restricted rudder movement reduced the speed at which less violent overbalance occurred. Cords on the trailing edge were tried but removed after it was found that they had no effect on overbalance and again made the rudders excessively heavy. HR727 had rudders with smaller balance areas, which overbalanced at smaller angles; the modification was rejected. It was decided that larger fins were the only effective cure; in the meantime rudder restrictors were fitted in existing aircraft with the original fins, and Service pilots were carefully briefed on the overbalance of rudders.

While the rudder problem was being resolved, a comprehensive investigation was planned into the reasons for the Halifax's loss of performance. Four aircraft were involved in August to October 1942: W1008, typical of early development aircraft and flown with and without dorsal turret and air filters; W7801, a new aircraft with large flame damping shrouds, night black finish and partially closed bomb doors (due to the 4,000lb bomb); DG221, a Service aircraft in poor condition after only ten operations; and W7776, newly 'cleaned up' without nose or dorsal turret. The performances of the best, W7776, and worst, DG221, aircraft are summarised in the Performance Table. The factors contributing to the difference were individually analysed; apart from fixed items such as turrets, cable cutters, fuel jettison pipes and aerials, DG221 exhibited poor workmanship, poor maintenance and a very rough surface finish compounded with congealed oil in places. Indeed, such was the poor quality of the handling of DG221 that intended trials at the maximum weight were not made as the aircraft was considered dangerous. Two results of the investigation were the identification of a suitable standard of equipment and finish to achieve acceptable performance, and a revision of Establishment testing methods more accurately to reflect the needs of the Service (discussed earlier). At the end of the foregoing trials, L9515 reappeared in 'super cleaned up' configuration including a streamlined perspex nose; top speed was about 275mph (true).

Halifax II L9515 in April 1942. The aircraft has an unarmed nose turret, but the rear guns are visible and the beam gun position can be seen just aft of the roundel. The venturi flame damping exhausts were ineffective. *A&AEE 9888*

Halifax Mk II L9515 in October 1942 in 'super cleaned up' configuration without turrets, no flame dampers and with a streamlined nose. Top speed was about 20mph faster than previously.

Halifax II HR679 Series Ia in February 1943. There is no nose turret and the upper turret is the Boulton Paul Type A Mk VIII of lower drag but doubled fire power of four 0.303in guns. *A&AEE 11290*

In January 1943 HR679, the first production 'super cleaned up' aircraft, arrived (known in Service as Mk II Series Ia), with a low-profile Type A dorsal turret. Performance (see the Table) was most encouraging. A representative 'cleaned up' Mk II Series I (special), W7922, from 78 Squadron, also had somewhat improved performance (see the Table). Perhaps the greatest benefit from the whole 'cleaning up' was the increase in the maximum cruising height (the greatest height at which the cruising speed of 155mph could be maintained at maximum continuous rpm in weak mixture). Three other modifications to improve performance were made early in 1943. V9985 had bulged bomb doors for the 4,000/8,000lb bombs, but no significant improvement was measured. In March HR756 arrived, a Series II aircraft with slimmer nacelles for its Merlin 22 engines lowered relative to the wing; performance was similar to the earlier Series Ia. The Series II was not put into production. The third change to the Halifax Mk II was the introduction on V9985 in late 1943 of Merlin 24 engines with take-off boost increased from 14 to 18psi; take-off distances were improved by

30-40%. A final improvement for later versions of the aircraft, but tested late in 1943 on a Mk II, HR845, was a 5-foot extension to the wingspan, giving a further useful improvement (see the Performance Table).

Tests from August 1943 on BB390 with an H2S radome were limited to confirming acceptable pressure errors. The speed penalty was estimated at 5mph. The final tests on a Mk II were on a Service aircraft, JD304, which suffered from an unacceptably poor performance attributed to the excessively large exhaust shrouds. The Establishment commented that the findings emphasised the disproportionate effect of relatively minor non-standard items.

HR935 (to compare three- and four-bladed propellers) from July 1943 was in use briefly from July 1943 on B Per T, but not specifically reported.

Nine Mk II aircraft undertook armament trials. Early in 1942 W1009 continued work on the Type C nose turret with A&AEE-designed spoilers; rotation was possible up to 325mph (indicated). A Mk II version of the Type E tail turret with improved ammunition feed was approved in mid-1942 after firing more than

Halifax II V9985 in February 1943, with swollen bomb doors to accommodate the 8,000lb 'cookie' bomb. This arrangement obviated the need for conventional doors to be partially open when the large bomb was carried; no significant improvement in performance resulted. There is no upper turret, but beam gun positions are fitted. Visible in the engine nacelles are the matrices for the radiator and oil cooler, while on the outer panels can be seen the ice guards over the air intakes. The solid-looking Messier undercarriage supports the aircraft. Four raid markings on the nose reflect earlier service, probably with No 10 Squadron. *A&AEE 11277*

34,000 rounds from R9375. Also tested successfully was a Type A mid-upper turret with extended vertical movement, which was replaced by a Bristol B12 Mk I with four 0.303in Brownings and tested in mid-1943. Despite several improvements by the Establishment, the Bristol turret was found difficult to control and fatiguing with erratic shooting; thirteen modifications were recommended. Meanwhile, late in 1942 R9436 tested the Boulton Paul Type T mid-upper turret with two 0.5in Brownings with generally satisfactory results. Also, in early 1943 DT728 was used to approve a Mk VIII Type

A turret mounted lower to reduce drag. Less success attended the fitting of radar (AGLT) to the rear turrets of W1008 and R9436 where the increased torque needed for rotation led to unacceptable turret control. Following trials early in 1942 to assess the manoeuvrability of the Halifax in attacking ground targets, JD212 arrived in September 1942 armed with nose-mounted RPs. Ground firing damaged the front fuselage and no air firing took place. Triple flare chutes were judged unsafe in DT728 early in 1943, and hang-ups continued to occur later in modified chutes in JD254.

Halifax II JD212 in late 1942, showing the early troublesome fin design and rocket projectile rails.

A trial RP installation on JD212 in late 1942. Fired on the ground, the front fuselage was damaged and the idea was abandoned.

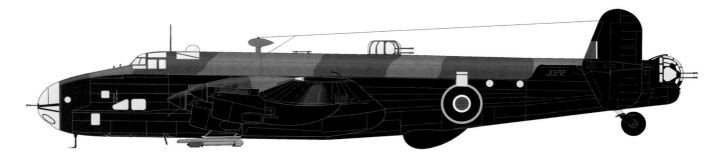

Handley Page
Halifax JD212,
September 1943,
for rocket projectile
trials.

R9435 appeared briefly from October 1942 and LW243 two years later for general armament work.

Halifax Mark V

The next version with Merlin engines was the Mk V; this version was identical to the Mk II but with a Dowty levered suspension undercarriage, first tested in L9520 in 1941. Five examples reached Boscombe Down, starting with DG235 in January 1943 for tests of fishtail exhausts at night. The need to reduce visibility was met by the shrouds fitted to DG281 in the following May with encouraging results. However, the shrouds cost 5-7mph (indicated) and 2,000 feet in cruising height. Further reduction of exhaust glow was achieved in DK256 with close-fitting shrouds and special paint. DK145 was the first Merlin-engined Halifax with fins (known as 'D' Type) with 30% increase in area. There was no tendency to overbalance, and rudder authority and foot forces were acceptable even to the extent of making turns in both directions with two engines on one side feathered. This aircraft then flew to compare three- and four-bladed propellers; the latter were marginally better on the latter stages of the climb and gave a useful increase in cruise height of 1,000 feet.

DG249 made a brief visit at the end of 1943, but after only one week it crashed on landing on 18 November due to the experimental Rotol propellers (inboard engines) malfunctioning. Reverse pitch was selected at about 50 feet prior to landing, and the engines accelerated to a very high rpm, causing the aircraft to impact near vertically; there were surprisingly no casualties.

Halifax Mark III and IV

Two variants of the Halifax with significantly increased performance were planned, but the Mk IV with Merlin 60 engines was cancelled in February 1943. R9534, the Mk III in prototype form, with Hercules VIs, reached the A&AEE in December 1942. Initial climb checks were disappointing, largely due to the drag of the gills, which had to be opened to keep temperatures within limits. Entirely satisfactory were the new large 'D' fins in all symmetric and asymmetric modes of flight. Some 85 hours were flown on these trials and a further 67 on intensive flying; however, R9534 was unrepresentative and was replaced by HX226 (the first production machine with Hercules XVIs) in September 1943. 150 hours of flying took only five weeks and serviceability was good, but crews found the aircraft noisy and draughty.

Although the Mk III was designed for take-off weights of 63,000lb, full performance trials appear not to have been made. This was probably due to the need to resolve air intake, carburetion and heating problems. HX227 and HX229 joined HX226 late in 1943, fitted with a variety of air intakes; a Vokes type was best, giving a full-throttle height some 1,700 feet above the remainder. Early in 1944 a Type 132 MF carburettor produced acceptable climb (see the Table) and ceiling, but at the expense of excessive cylinder temperatures. Increasing the climbing speed by 20mph (indicated) helped cooling up to 19,000 feet; selection of weak mixture exacerbated the problem, but a modification to give half weak mixture still produced hot cylinders. In May 1944 cooling fans in front of the cylinders made only a small improvement. The following month fully flared (previously semi-flared) propellers finally allowed climb and cruise to be made within temperature limits. With the engines behaving themselves, the long-suffering HX226 was used for fuel consumption measurements. From take-off at 63,000lb with 8,500lb bombs (dropped halfway) maximum range was calculated at 1,800 statute miles; aircraft with the 5-foot increase in span were expected to fly about 50 miles further.

Minor trials on the Mk III included exhaust flame damping, eventually satisfactory on HX229 in March 1944, and cabin heating (at all crew positions) was acceptable on HX315 in June 1944 after early criticism on HX226 in February. Top speed on LK869 in July 1944 was 241mph

Halifax III HX238 in April 1944, showing its square fins to advantage; the fixed (ie set on the ground) aileron tab and standard flame damping exhausts of the Hercules engines are visible. The radar on the rear turret was the subject of an extensive trial.
A&AEE 11721

(true) at 18,700 feet with Vokes intakes, better than with a Bristol type. A favourable maintenance report on LW125 followed a lengthy overseas trial at Khartoum and a flight to Cape Town between July and December 1944.

Three Mk IIIs were involved in armament trials. The Type D (two 0.5in guns) tail turret with radar (AGLT) caused slight yaw with rotation at cruising speeds on HX226 early in 1944; in the dive rudder forces to contain the yaw became excessive. Later in 1944 HX238 had deflectors to aid rotation at a cost of 3mph in top speed; above 320mph shuddering was felt and speed of rotation dropped from 42°/sec to 30°/sec. Some 13,000 rounds were fired, and several shortcomings discovered. LV999/G arrived in August 1944 (the -/G suffix was for the radar) and reports on its work at the A&AEE covered the new Boulton Paul Type D tail turret (with AGLT) including ammunition feed.

Halifax Mark VI

With Hercules 100s, extra wing span (104 feet), fuel and crew heating, much was expected of the Mk VI. At Boscombe, the first nine months of flying of this version were dominated by attempts to overcome the excessive cylinder temperatures. LV838 arrived in February 1944 and was immediately flown on cooling trials; the results were extrapolated to tropical summer conditions and indicated severe overheating. Palliatives over the following months included semi-flared and fully flared propellers by De Havilland and Rotol, modified gills, additional baffles, exhaust shroud seals, a new cowling, fans on the spinner, and new intakes. By November 1944 a combination of the three most promising modifications reduced temperatures for satisfactory operation in temperate climates. Cooling for the tropics appears never to have been entirely satisfactory, although NP849, in mid-1945, with fully modified engines, nearly met revised limitations. Performance was measured (see the Table), but

maximum 'all out' speed with cooling gills closed (ie least drag and minimum cooling) could be held for only a few minutes. The effect of the H2S blister, measured on NP748 from August 1944, was to reduce speed by 1mph, while retracting the tail wheel added 2½mph. The tare weight of the Mk VI, at 38,900lb, was some 4,000lb greater than the Mk II (without mid-upper turret), and 1,400lb greater than the Mk III. Initial design gross weight was 65,000lb, and the Establishment recommended that paved runways should be used above 63,000lb.

The first dedicated handling trials on the Mk VI were made in early 1945 on TW783 (renumbered from PP151) at the new gross weight of 68,000lb, when the main criticism was the very high safety speed on take-off of 170mph, leading to the conclusion that the rudder trimmer gearing and accessibility needed improving. Late in 1945 the rudder trimmer changes were fitted to LV838, in its new guise as C Mk VI with a pannier; asymmetric handling was improved. NP752 struck cables and crashed on 17 December 1944 after 109 hours of intensive flying over four months; engine problems caused the delays. Its sibling, NP753, tested a new air cleaner capable of selection by the Flight Engineer; the report is dated August 1945, one year after arrival of the aircraft.

Halifax LV838 in mid-1945 in C Mk VI guise, lacking turrets but possessing a pannier. Not visible are alterations to the rudder trimmers, which improved asymmetric handling, although safety speed remained high.

NP834 examined early in 1945 the effect of rotating the Type D tail turret on the aircraft under control of the auto-pilot Mk VIII; the rudders were not connected to the auto-pilot but the resulting skidding was judged to be acceptable. A brief but unreported visit was made by NP924 from March 1945 for research on engine cooling.

Tests on the performance of production Halifax aircraft are listed in Appendix 5.

Halifax Mark VIII

PP225 made a brief visit from March 1945; early handling trials included determination of a safety speed of 170mph on take-off.

Halifax VIII PP225 in June 1945 reveals its extended wing tips, transparent nose and faired-over tail turret, together with VHF whip aerials above the cockpit and below the nose. Trials involved considerable high-power flying, which may account for the extensive evidence of heat damage on the cowlings of the Hercules 100 engines. *A&AEE recognition 260*

Lancaster

At the A&AEE the Lancaster was represented by forty-six examples, described here under the headings of Early Aircraft, Mark II, Marks I, III and X, Mark VI, Mark VII, Special Weapons, and finally Turrets and Flare Chutes.

Early Aircraft

The Avro Lancaster was a success from the first tests on the prototype BT308 by the Establishment at Manchester in January 1941. At 38,000lb the handling was very good; minor criticisms concerned the throttle levers, length of control column and rudder trim gearing. These three items were remedied by the end of February when BT308, without its central fin but with an increase in the tailplane span, reached Boscombe. This basic configuration remained unchanged in more 7,000 production machines, although the Merlin engines were replaced by the Hercules on a relatively small number of aircraft. Full performance (see the Table) handling, including flight on three and two engines, consumption and pressure error measurements, was very encouraging. Asymmetric handling on two engines was described as excellent at 42,500lb. Concern was expressed over the 3-4 inches of play in the rudder pedals in the low temperatures at 30,000 feet, the flexing of the mainplanes and the lack of control in the hot air supply to the cabin.

With the arrival of the operationally equipped second prototype, DG595, in August 1941, full radio, gunnery and bombing trials were immediately put in hand. The IFF was the standard Mk II, and was tested acceptably, as were the HF (T1154B R1155) and VHF (TR9F) radios and intercom, although the mid-upper gunner was not, in this aircraft, connected. The automatic cut-out for this turret (FN50) failed and bullets hit the right wing, but the nose (FN5) and tail (FN20) were satisfactory with one and twenty modifications respectively being recommended, including the need for more oxygen for the tail gunner as his unenviable position was unheated. Early Lancasters had the mid-under turret (FN64) as in DG595; this position suffered from the need to search using the very limited periscopic sighting system and the risk of hitting the bottom of the

fins when firing – both serious shortcomings. Rotating the turrets at speeds up to 360mph (indicated) had small effect on handling; vigorous evasive manoeuvring, however, strained the aircraft on one sortie. It was found that recovery from high-speed dives required the use of elevator trim. A little later a trial was arranged in an aircraft (R5539) of Handling Flight to investigate recovery without the use of trim. On one dive in April 1942 the aircraft made only a partial recovery before crashing and killing the crew. It was found that rivets had progressively failed, allowing the skin of the wing to separate. Very satisfactory bombing and loading trials were made on DG595, including stores up to 8,000lb. However, the maximum approved all-up weight of 60,000lb limited the bomb load to less than 6,000lb when full fuel of 2,130 gallons was carried.

Taken on ortho film, this is Lancaster DG595, the second prototype, at Boscombe in August 1941 for extensive armament trials. The upper FN50 turret has no 'taboo' saucer. During the trials the automatic cut-out on this installation failed and some bullet damage was sustained.

Resplendent in yellow prototype colour, this is Lancaster DG595 again, now in October 1941, brought up to full production standard and fitted with exhaust flame dampers. The ventral FN64 turret is clearly seen in this view, as is the bulged belly. Note the porthole below the cabin.

Lancaster I L7528 in November 1942. Five items are noteworthy, all visible on the rear fuselage: the hook (not tested on this aircraft), the saucer cam round the upper turret, the deep-section bomb doors, for fitting two 4,000lb bombs in tandem, and the three brass plates forward of the serial number. These last were to determine the best position for the static source following the fitting of the cam and large bomb doors. Dropping the pair of bombs caused a small trim change, easily controlled with one hand. The fifth item is the unusual retention of the FN64 under turret with large bomb doors. *A&AEE 11113*

Three early production aircraft appeared from October 1941 and were allocated for intensive flying. After a total of 17 hours flying, L7527 made a wheels-up landing in November after it was found that the starboard wheel was missing. L7535 made a precautionary landing in bad weather at Cheddington and was extensively damaged on the partially made runway, while L7529 completed 60 hours without serious mishap. Six minor defects in the type were reported in 151 hours of flying.

round the engines improved but did not cure inadequate cooling; early trials with high vapour pressure fuel (suitable for tropical conditions) caused engine misfiring. Approved all-up weight was 63,000lb with full fuel, while range with normal allowances was calculated at 2,370 statute miles, reduced to 1,780 miles for practical use. At a slightly lower weight the Merlin engines gave figures of 2,500 and 1,870 respectively.

The Hercules version had two persistent problems, both associated with the engines,

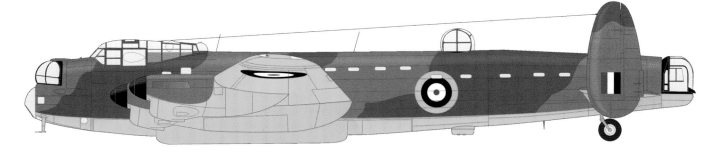

Avro Lancaster DG595, August 1941, for armament trials.

Lancaster Mark II

DT810, with alternative Hercules VI engines, arrived in February 1942; handling was soon demonstrated as superior to the Merlin version, particularly under asymmetric power. Electric control of the propellers made rapid feathering easy, and at 58,000lb the minimum control speed on the port engines alone was 127mph with wings level, while 187mph was comfortable for cruising. Various modifications to the airflow

namely flame damping and cooling. The first night visibility measurements on DT810 were initially well below requirements; they were 50% better with Beaufighter-type dampers but still unacceptable. DS602, a production aeroplane, arrived in September 1942 with two further modifications; they, and three further improvements in early 1943, were scarcely better. Eventually, in July 1943 an A&AEE-designed shroud proved effective but at the expense of a 6mph reduction throughout the

Lancaster II DS602 in October 1942. The Hercules VI motors have early and unsatisfactory exhaust flame dampers. Engine cylinder and oil temperatures were both higher in this production aircraft than on the prototype and proved difficult to control, particularly in the climb. *A&AEE 11135*

speed range. The cylinder temperatures on DS602 were at first significantly higher than those of the prototype – a problem exacerbated by an increase in climbing rpm from 2,400 to 2,500. While the time to reach 15,000 feet was thus reduced by 3½ minutes, the need for extra cooling (both for cylinders and oil) was pressing. An increase in climbing speed was ineffective, and the first modifications little better. Cylinder baffles helped but it required fans in April 1943 in front of the engine to keep the temperatures within limits. Thereafter DS602 was fitted with Hercules XVIs (see the performance in the Table); retaining the fans and with modified air intakes considerably improved the climb performance. The tendency to overheat in this engine was cured by a minor modification to the auto-mixture control. DS606 arrived in November 1942 and completed 150 hours on intensive flying until May 1943; less maintenance was needed on the Hercules than on the Merlin engines, but the propellers needed more attention and the detail finish of the Armstrong Whitworth built airframe was poor.

Lancaster Marks I, III and X

On the Merlin-powered versions, flame damping requirements were soon achieved, in December 1941 on DG595 with an A&AEE-designed box after earlier attempts using fish-tail ejectors had been unsuccessful on the first prototype. The new 'cascade box' contributed largely to a reduction of 14mph (true) in top speed; attempts by the Establishment, Rolls Royce and an RAF unit to alleviate the speed penalty were ineffective. Other engine developments examined in 1942 were the Stromberg carburettors with auto-mixture controls in the Packard-built Merlin 28, starting with W4114 (with an FN64 ventral turret) from October 1942. Consumption at 51,000lb was 1.30ampg at 15,000 feet, and at 44,300lb 1.32ampg; other performance details are shown in the Table. As with the Merlin XX, engine cooling in the climb

was just acceptable at increased climbing speed combined with the larger radiator exit doors tested first on R5546 (arrived July 1942). With cooling under control, a lower, optimum, climbing speed was used but, unexpectedly, no improvement in performance resulted.

With the arrival of W4963 in April 1943 full performance at 63,000lb (see the Table) was preceded by measurement of the effect of ice guards in front of the air intakes (a loss of up to 6mph in top speed). Engine cooling was followed by several weeks at Khartoum where Morris radiators were found to be the most suitable, although oil temperatures remained incurably high. On return the aircraft had radomes fitted for the H2S Mk I bombing aid (later H2S Mk II, then Mk III), followed by a trip to the Arctic conditions in Canada. Previously in the winter of 1943/44 DV 179, flying at 28,000 feet over England, had revealed that carburettor heating was insufficient for Arctic conditions. Experience of flying W4963 in extreme temperatures was used to confirm the accuracy of the methods of performance reduction; a gratifying correlation between actual and predicted figures proved the methods to be sound. JA894 crashed fatally in September 1943, shortly after arrival, and was replaced by JB127[1] in December for engine and propeller tests. The latter had Merlin 24s of greater power, and combined tests of wide-chord 'paddle' propellers with performance measurements at 65,000lb in mid-1944. The engines gave an 11mph increase in cruising speed; the propeller trials included range measurements and results compared favourably with JA918 with Packard Merlin 38s (2,540 against 2,440 statute miles). Boscombe received its first Canadian Mk X, KB721, also with Merlin 38s, in April 1944; it had electrical gyro instruments but was otherwise similar to JA894. JA918 was involved in an interesting trial to investigate dihedral angle, which, in the Lancaster, increased with increasing weight; the effect on stability was small and could, it was decided, be ignored.

[1] JB127 suffered major damage on landing in September 1944.

Lancaster I R5546 in about October 1942. The patches below the serial number show the six positions of the static source tried to obtain the most accurate, and the light-coloured fairings on the engine nacelles are enlarged oil cooling intakes. Not visible is the dummy radar (later called AGLT) on the rear FN20 turret; up to 360mph the only effect of the radar on handling was slightly increased yaw with turret rotation. The radar housing was tested in July 1942, and thus the first on a turret, albeit in aerodynamic form only.

Lancaster I W4963 in March 1944; this long-serving machine was on A&AEE charge from April 1943 until after the war. Under the nose are various pressure and temperature sensors, including pressure heads by Avimo (poor) and Wilkes-Berger (satisfactory). Its main role was development and validation of test techniques and reduction methods – including flights to Canada and Khartoum. What folly Flying Officer Bendall (OC B Per T Engineering) had perpetrated to merit the nose inscription 'Bendall's Folly' is not known. *A&AEE recognition 209*

Canadian-built Lancaster X KB783 in October 1943 has enlarged bomb bays and, just visible, the electrically operated Glen Martin upper turret. Unpleasant handling reported by the British team in Washington was not found by the A&AEE. *A&AEE 11942*

Short handling tests on NG408 (large H2S radome) were made from March 1945, while LM730 (flight refuelling coupling in November 1944) revealed no surprises. Pressure error measurements were made in October 1943, on ED735, with enlarged bomb doors after unsatisfactory results two months earlier on the similar ED565. R5849 appeared briefly in mid-1943, but more development was found to be necessary on its two Merlin 65s with annular radiators in the outboard positions, and the aircraft was returned to Rolls Royce.

Lancaster Mark VI

In January 1944 the first Lancaster with Merlin 85 JB675s was delivered and given full handling and cooling trials; the latter indicated that the radiator was unsatisfactory in the cruise. ND479, also re-engined with Merlin 85s, was engaged on stick force tests, but on 26 April 1944 the port outer engine oversped to 4,000rpm and could not be feathered; the extreme drag could not be controlled and the aircraft crashed, but without casualties. A third aircraft with Merlin 85s,

Lancaster Mk III W4114 in November 1942. American-built Merlin 28 engines with Stromberg carburettors (automatic mixture) characterised this mark; initial performance and range work were undertaken on this machine. The FN64 under turret is visible with its gun. *A&AEE 11191*

In May and June 1945 HK541, with Merlin 24s and dummy saddle tanks, flew to India for trials to establish its feasibility of operating in high temperatures at 72,000lb. It was calculated that maximum range with the full fuel load of 3,154 gallons (and 6,000lb of bombs) was 3,470 statute miles – a trip lasting up to 18½ hours. Oil temperatures were found to be acceptable, but the take-off was described as follows: 'The aircraft (at 72,000lb) can be pulled off in 1,050 yd, but normal squadron technique would require 1,450 yd.' The climb to 1,000 feet took 3 minutes. Similar tanks were fitted to SW244 on arrival in May 1945 for trials lasting until after the war.

ND558, arrived in June 1944 with tests concentrated on the propeller constant speed unit. After lengthy climbs to 30,000 feet the engines were set at 2,700rpm (90% maximum) and plus-2psi boost, and the aircraft dived, reaching 350mph (indicated) at about 25,000 feet (equivalent Mach number 0.72). Apart from the escape hatch disappearing, nothing untoward happened. Asymmetric handling with the higher power of the 85s confirmed failure of the port outer as the worst case on take-off. With full rudder and aileron combined with significant bank, 130mph (indicated) could just be held; without bank, 155mph was the minimum.

'Special' Lancaster III ED825/G in April 1943, showing the cut-away bomb bay (empty) and part of the mechanism used to rotate the anti-dam mines. This aircraft flew on the dams raid on 16/17 May 1943, having been flown to Scampton post-haste on the 16th from Boscombe Down. On trials at 63,000lb, the only handling effect of the mine was an increase in tail buffet at high speed. The practical range on 1,774 gallons of fuel was 1,290 miles. *A&AEE 11348*

Lancaster Mark VII

The Lancaster VII, NN801, arrived in April 1945 and initial handling was similar to earlier versions, including stick force per g of 50-90lb; the VII had metal elevators.

Lancaster VII NN801 in April 1945. Converted from a Mk I, it had the Glen Martin upper turret mounted forward of the earlier position, and metal elevators. Stick forces remained high, and trials continued after the war. *A&AEE 15016*

Armament

Special weapons

The early promise of the Lancaster on trials and in service soon led to its selection for special tasks. First from July 1942 was as the carrier of the 'Capital Ship' (CS) bomb of 5,000lb, requiring bulged bomb doors. An early ASV radar was also carried, and some aerials were near the static source; the Establishment checked the pressure error, which caused an over-reading of 8mph at 152mph on R5609. Next, on 17 April 1943, was ED825/G with no mid-upper turret, and a cut-away bomb bay for the special anti-dam bomb. Take-off weight was increased to 63,000lb (1,774 gallons of fuel and 11,500lb of bombs), and range (assuming bomb dropped at mid-point) was 1,720 statute miles or 1,290 miles practical. Maximum level speed was reduced to 256mph (true) at 11,000 feet with the bomb on. Handling was unaffected, but the bomb caused tail buffet at high speed.

Lancaster I R5609 in July 1942, modified for the anti-shipping role with Yagi aerial array on the nose and enlarged bomb bay doors for the large (45-inch-diameter) 'Capital Ship' bomb. An early form of flame damper is fitted, together with ice guards. The aerials displaced the pressure head to the port side of the nose, and at 152mph the ASI over-read by 8mph. The aircraft was on loan from No 97 Squadron.

A close view of the aerial array on the nose of Lancaster I R5609. *A&AEE 11047*

Lancaster VI JB675 in January 1944 with Merlin 85s. The deeper nacelles are in evidence but the engines were too hot in the cruise. The details are interesting, including two small aerials ahead of the pilot's position, the exhaust dampers, the H2S blister (empty) and, in the background above the main wheel, part of the airfield lighting. *A&AEE 11654*

The Lancaster was chosen to carry the 12,000lb HC bomb comprising three 4,000lb 'cookies' bolted together. L7528, engaged on armament trials since August 1942, was used in mid-1943 for trials of the new weapon. Three concrete-filled dummies proved the ballistics, and one live bomb was dropped from 10,000 feet on 25 September 1943. No special handling trials were needed, but ground transport and loading, using a special Type E trolley, were tricky on account of the low clearance above the ground. The following year the Establishment assessed and dropped the 12,000lb MC ('Tallboy') from DV405 (borrowed from No 617 Squadron as AJ-J); no report appears to have survived apart from a note about the operation of the release slip. Unlike the 'Tallboy', the 'Grand Slam' of 22,000lb

Avro Lancaster R5609, July 1942, for pressure errors.

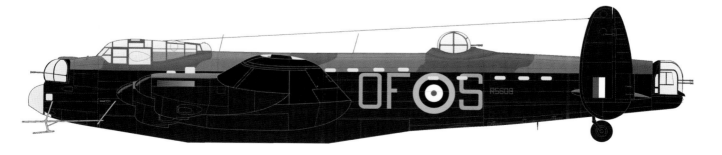

123

required extensive aircraft modification, more power and a considerable increase in weight. PB592 arrived in October 1944, was modified and flew with the new bomb, initially at the current maximum weight of 63,730lb. Handling was normal, including the overweight landing at 61,000lb; a maximum of 260mph was recommended on account of severe vibration at higher speeds.

Merlin 24 engines replaced the Merlin XXs, and gave an extra 330hp (25%) at take-off. Handling and performance at 72,000lb kept PB592/G and PD435 busy in February and March; PB592, at least, had the nose and mid-upper turrets removed. Stall (at 69,000lb) occurred at 119mph (clean) and 98mph (undercarriage and flaps down), and the Establishment recommended that only experienced pilots should fly at high weight. A high climbing speed of 165mph (normally 130-140mph) kept the oil temperatures just within limits on the 50 minutes needed to reach the cruise ceiling of 18,600 feet. Other performance is show in the Table. Trials culminated on 13 March 1945 when a live 'Grand Slam' was dropped from 16,000 feet on Ashley Walk Range, just one day before the bomb was used

operationally by the RAF. Subsequently further performance and handling trials were made on the two original 'Grand Slam' aircraft, and on PB995 with the mid-upper turret refitted. The turret reduced range by 3%, but handling and vibration remained acceptable up to 260mph.

Turrets and Flare Chutes

Armament development in the Lancaster involved the Establishment predominantly in turret testing. The first FN79 mid-upper turret with two 20mm Hispano cannon was fitted to Lancaster W4115 late in 1942; fumes, sluggish rotation and flash were early problems identified. By mid-1943 the recoil from the guns was found to exceed the structural limits of the aircraft, and standard aircraft retained the two Browning guns in the FN50 turret. A Canadian-built Lancaster, KB783, fitted with an electrically operated Glen Martin upper turret (two 0.5in Brownings) was flown in late 1944 without the unpleasant results predicted by the British team in Washington. The nose turret with two Browning guns required to be tested only for the increased speed of rotation made possible by more powerful hydraulic pumps, also in W4115.

Lancaster III PB592 in March 1945, with nose turret and bomb doors removed. The 22,000lb 'Grand Slam' is in position, and wide-chord paddle propellers are fitted. This aircraft dropped the first live 'Grand Slam' on 13 March 1945, with Captain Flt Lt Dawson and bomb aimer Fg Off Whatmore. *A&AEE 15050*

JA894, a 617 Squadron Lancaster III with bulged bomb doors, was on loan to the A&AEE for trials to check pressure errors. It collided with an Oxford over nearby High Post Aerodrome on 10 September 1943, shortly after arrival. All six people in both aircraft were killed. *A&AEE 11576*

Among the more serious problems associated with tail turrets were timely sighting, ammunition feed and heating. It was decided to develop a radar to aid sighting of enemy fighters. The first dummy radome was fitted to the FN20 turret in R5546 in July 1942 to assess aircraft handling; the effect was small up to 360mph (indicated). In May 1943 the similar but improved FN120 turret was satisfactory in W4115; two months later further improvements were flown in JA870, attracting only minor comments. Similarly, no serious criticism was made of the Rose tail turret (two 0.5in Brownings in place of earlier four 0.303in calibre) tested in early 1944 in JB456. With a gyro gunsight and radar (known by the acronym AGLT), the FN120 became the FN121 and flew in ND794/ G from May 1944. Side deflectors assisted rotation, but the effect on the aircraft was more marked than previously, to the extent that the auto-pilot was unable to cope with the yaw induced. The FN82 turret (two 0.5in Brownings and electric ammunition feed) intended for the Lincoln was successfully tested in JA870 in mid-1944. The final turret trial was an assessment of an RAF modification in PB640; the heating was adequate until the turret was rotated or the sighting panel was opened.

One unsatisfactory feature of the Lancaster that proved almost intractable was the pyrotechnic chute, first tested in September 1942 on L7528; the updraught prevented fall of the flares. A Mk II chute in ED565 in mid-1943 and a Mk III version early in 1944 were also unacceptable. Finally, in October 1944 a Mk V version in the nose (the others were in the tail) proved satisfactory.

The Armament Testing Squadron used several Lancasters not mentioned above: ED869 (gunnery April and May 1944), HK543 (bombing March 1944 to September 1945), JB415 (bombing December 1943 to February 1944), JB457 (blast effects and bombing October 1943 to June 1945), and LL619 (April 1944 to May 1945).

Tests of performance on production Lancasters are given in the Performance Tables.

Fortress

Fortress Mark I

The promise of the well-defended Boeing B-17 led initially to a small order for the -C model for the RAF; the first to reach the Establishment, AN531, was delivered on 15 April 1941. The Fortress Mk I created a very favourable impression for its ease of handling, even with two engines at idle but not feathered, and particularly for its comfort.

Small stick movement by the pilot operated tabs on the elevator or rudder, but larger movements fed directly to these control surfaces; this feature, together with an appropriate stability, made handling easy and precise. Electric motors for flaps and undercarriage (40 seconds to raise) were novel. The manual rudder trim had a wide operating range and, fully applied at 120mph (indicated), enabled straight flight to be maintained with the two starboard engines alone at maximum cruising power without the use of the rudder pedal. Most praised was the warmth of the crew area at 30,000 feet (-55°C outside), and the relative quiet achieved with copious soundproofing combined with favourable positioning of the engine exhausts. The navigator's position was roomy, with a good view; the only criticism of this first version of the type was the lack of blackout curtains.

Fortress I AN531 in April 1941. Just visible beneath the nearest engine above the wheel is the turbo-blower, which bestowed such a good altitude performance. Also noteworthy are the small fin, large rudder and ample tabs; the pilot's pedal inputs first moved the tab, making for light and pleasant rudder control. Another advanced feature is the leading edge de-icer boots. Less advanced was the armament, with no rear turret, an inadequate ventral position and two waist gun positions with blast deflectors and cut-outs to enable rearward firing. *A&AEE 9716*

Performance with the Cyclone R-1820-73 was outstanding at height with a ceiling of 34,000 feet from a maximum-weight (49,360lb) take-off, although great care had to be taken to avoid damage above 25,000 feet by overspeeding of the exhaust-driven turbocharger. Crews were carefully briefed on the special handling needed. From August 1941 AN519 also handled well at extended aft CG, but even with by-pass flame dampers of RAE design it did not meet the requirements for invisibility at night from a distance greater than 100 yards. Armament trials were limited to assessment of the American bomb gear (the maximum normal load was four 600lb), then, at the end of 1941, partially successful attempts to fit British carriers; restricted space in the bay rendered the usual bomb hoist, made by Stones, useless. A most surprising omission was the apparent absence of any trials of the five single hand-held guns; operationally the defensive armament of this early version proved inadequate.

Fortress Marks II and IIA

Improvements in the next version, the B-17E or Fortress IIA, were soon under scrutiny following arrival of the first, FK187, in April 1942. A collapsed tail wheel (necessitating replacement by FL458 in August) and the need for modifications to the gun positions, delayed completion until early 1943. The electro-hydraulic Sperry upper turret (two 0.5in guns) was smooth and positive in operation up to 300mph (indicated); some 9,700 rounds were fired. The two beam and twin tail guns were satisfactory, but the Sperry ball turret under the fuselage had a very poor view, was cramped and awkward to use, and suffered many early failures of the ammunition feed. Later in May and June 1943 FK211, with modified feed arrangements to the ball turret, was assessed as satisfactory. Reports on bombing trials included ground assessments of the bomb aimer's position, and checking of the various loads that could be carried. Seven flying hours with the Norden auto-flight system demonstrated its ability to control turns at all speeds and to hold heading even with two engines on one side fully throttled – the resulting sideslip was, however, uncomfortable. Following performance checks (see the Table) on FK187, the Establishment extrapolated the figures and assumed a full load of 1,440 imperial gallons of fuel (plus 115 gallons of oil) to give a take-off weight of 51,350lb. With standard allowances, an average of 1.42 miles per gallon gave a theoretical range of 2,020 miles (1.620 miles for practical planning). The Establishment further extrapolated these figures assuming 600 gallons in the bomb bay, and calculated a maximum still air range of 2,890 miles (2,360 practical); the exercise was to help the Air Staff to assess the type's effectiveness for the maritime role. All Fortress IIs were used in this way by the RAF.

Fortress II FL458 in January 1942. Although the image is from a second copy, the aerials under the wings, on top of the fuselage and on the nose are visible, as are four of the guns fired on trials (the starboard waist gun was not used). Some 19,338 rounds of 0.5in ammunition were expended; the total would have been higher had the ball under turret not stopped firing. *A&AEE 11108*

Fortress IIA FK187 in April 1942. Armament increases and a large dorsal fin characterise this model. The upper, ventral, port beam and tail guns are visible; the ventral (ball) turret required a very small gunner. Most Mk II and IIA models were used in the maritime role. *A&AEE recognition 91*

Flame damping was good on the Fortress IIA, and the navigational facilities adequate, including the astrodome in FA706 (a B-17F, Fortress II) in January 1943. Rocket projectiles, planned for the Fortress but never fitted, led to preliminary attitude measurements on FK211 early in 1943. A 40mm Vickers gun was, however, installed on FK185 and tested from December 1942; about

700 rounds were successfully fired. A feature of the complementary handling trials was the increase in all-up weight to 52,000lb; previous Boscombe flying had been limited to less than 49,400lb. The High Altitude Flight used FK192 for eighteen months from June 1943 on meteorological research.

Fortress II FK185 in February 1944. The modified nose houses a 40mm gun, while the worn surface finish reveals two of its previous identities. On the fin is the USAAF number 12514, and on the fuselage NR-E of No 220 Squadron. *A&AEE recognition 205*

Boeing Fortress
FK185, January 1944,
for gunnery trials.

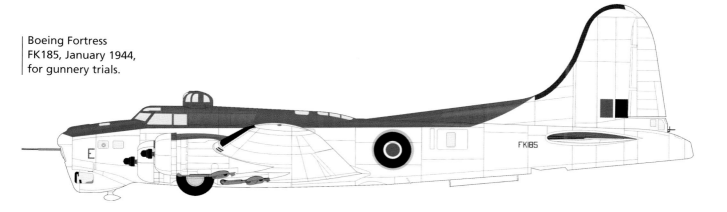

Fortress III HB796/G. A similar aircraft, HB767/G, was flown at RAF Oulton in June 1944. Handling was not significantly altered by the many aerials, with the exception of the stall, which occurred at an unusually low speed. The nose radome, seen here to be close to the pressure head, was thought to be the cause of a pressure error.

Fortress Mark III

The special electronic role of some RAF Fortress IIIs (B-17G) was cleared for Service use by brief handling trials on HB767 at RAF Oulton; the lower than expected stalling speed was attributed to the pressure error caused by the H2S radar fairing. Further trials, also in July 1944, on HB774 established that the errors were, in fact, small. The Establishment used two Fortress IIIs at Boscombe: HB762 briefly from November 1944 for gunnery, and KL835 from July 1945 to establish civil operating criteria.

Lincoln I

The Avro Lincoln was in effect a super-Lancaster, from which it was developed. Testing at the A&AEE in wartime was limited to the prototypes and the first few production aircraft.

PW925 arrived on 15 July 1944 and activity was intense. Tail and dorsal turrets were already fitted and the aircraft loaded to 75,000lb for handling, including stalls (docile) and dives to 370mph. The controls were pleasant and

adequate, but there was insufficient rudder trim for asymmetric flying. The wheel brakes were particularly liked, and the Merlin 85 engines satisfactory; even the pressure errors were small and adequate for the exacting requirements of the Air Position Indicator and bombsight. Performance is shown in the Table. In a rare oversight by the crew in an unfamiliar aircraft, the air cleaners may have been mistakenly selected in; if so, the effect would have been to reduce the top speed from 308 to the recorded 300mph (true).

In later trials on PW925, the crew were moved around the aircraft to achieve extreme CGs – the Lincoln was stable at all CGs and configurations with the exception of aft CG with power on and flaps and undercarriage down. In the extreme aft case, full forward stick was insufficient on a baulked approach; an acceptable CG position, slightly forward, was determined. Late in 1944, with rudder trimmers of 50% greater area, PW925 could be held straight at 140mph with the two port engines failed (the worse side); the improvement was marked but not considered sufficient justification

Lincoln I PW925 in July 1944, showing the 'ideal' nose allowing the bomb aimer/gunner to perform both his functions without moving. The installation, Boulton Paul Type F, lacks its two 0.5in guns. Wide-chord propellers, exhaust shrouds and the rear turret radar housing are features. *A&AEE 11853*

to change production aircraft. A larger tailplane and increased elevator down movement, also on PW925, was judged to give stability in all conditions, and thus better on overshoot. The final modification on this machine was a flap selector, improved by removal of the need to select flaps up initially when moving from mid to fully down. Further flap improvements were approved on PW929.

The specially designed Boulton Paul Type F turret was fitted to the nose of PW929 (arrival January 1945) and the two 0.5in Browning guns were remotely aimed and fired by the bomb aimer lying underneath. With rotation and elevation speeds of 45°/sec at 250mph, the turret was acceptable for Service use with eight essential modifications. The two gunners in the other turrets suffered from excessive carbon monoxide, and opening panels were recommended. The trials on the Glen Martin 250 CF23A dorsal turret started when RE227 arrived in April 1945. The Mk IIC gyro gunsight was liked, and the novel foot firing gear acceptable in the firing of 22,000 rounds; contamination appears not to have been a problem. The standard Type D tail turret was satisfactory. However, the electrical power needed for the three turrets, radar and other electrical services led to a new test to confirm the health of the generators under maximum load of 200 amps. The temperatures became excessive, and additional cooling was recommended.

Performance at the weight needed for Far Eastern operations (82,000lb) was limited initially to take-off and stall measurements,

using boost increased from 18 to 21 psi. The run of 1,040 yards and distance to 50 feet of 1,458 yards were the standard figures for UK temperatures. Stalling speeds, 112mph (clean) and 87mph (flaps and undercarriage down), were obtained on RE232 from April 1945.

Intensive flying on RE228 and RE230 took four months from March 1945. The latter had increased carbon monoxide in the front crew positions when measured after 212 hours of flying; more tests were planned. RE228 had three-blade Nash Kelvinator propellers initially, but problems led to their removal after 23 hours. RF337, with Packard-built engines and thus a Mk II, joined the intensive flying team in June 1945.

Windsor

One Vickers Windsor (probably DW512) was flown from Boscombe Down in early 1945 by the firm on armament trials. An A&AEE pilot had flown the type at Farnborough in February 1944.

Heinkel He 177

In February 1945 a Heinkel He 177A (TS429) could be seen on the eastern side of the airfield awaiting dismantling.

Heinkel 177A-5 TS439, possibly in early 1945. This aircraft languished at Boscombe, but was not flown. Markings are intriguing – it wears Allied 'invasion stripes', a 'P' prototype letter and, in small letters under the 'P', the inscription 'Prise de Guerre' (war prize) applied by the French resistance group that captured it.

Battle

Testing of the Battle light bomber was completed at Martlesham Heath, but three aircraft, K9221, K9223 and K9231, with the Armament Squadron, flew to Boscombe Down on 3 September 1939. K9223 soon left, followed by the other two machines on recall to active service in May 1940. N2087 appeared briefly, probably for gunnery work, from November 1939, while the Special Duty Flight used K7574 for a year from October 1939, and its replacement, L5280, until January 1941. P2358, allocated for SDF in January 1940, left the Establishment after a forced landing the following March.

Handling and take-off trials revealed no significant differences in the trainer version, P2277, in April 1940, nor in the target tower L5598 a month later. Comments on the trainer version included the shortcomings of the view from the rear seat for night landings and the unexpectedly short take-off run of 390 yards at a weight of 10,900lb.

Battle (T) P2277 in April 1940, during a stay of less than four weeks. The only criticism was the poor view for landing from the rear (instructor's) seat. Features include the yellow undersurface, the lack of an exhaust anti-glare shield (although there is rudimentary flame damping), the large perspex covers over the two landing lamps, the unique Battle stone guards, which retracted with the main wheels, and the exposed propeller control mechanism. *A&AEE 9631*

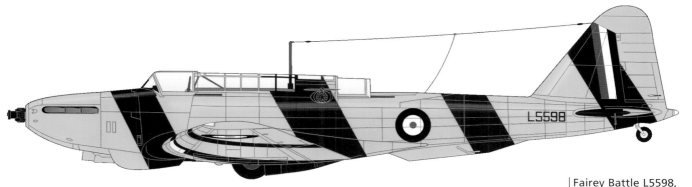

Fairey Battle L5598, May 1940, target tug version, for handling trials.

Blenheim

Blenheim Mark I

The pre-war performance of the Blenheim proved inadequate early in hostilities, and testing was concentrated on the Mk IV. Nevertheless, no fewer than seventeen Blenheim Is were used at Boscombe Down, including six flown from Martlesham. L1222, with the extra wing tanks of the Mk IV, had draught excluders, lagging and, later, four 120-watt electric heaters; only the sealing improved comfort in the cabin, measured as an increase of 5°C. More extensive modifications were made progressively to L1348 to maximise speed for reconnaissance. With standard engines, top speed was 274mph (true) (see the Table) and, with careful cleaning, smoothing (including wing fillets) and engines boosted from +5 to +9psi, speed increased to 296mph (true). Further improvements were expected from special paint (Camotint) to be applied at Heston. L1357 appeared briefly for unreported performance work in July 1940. Two early aircraft, L1173 (from April 1941) and L1407

(February 1941 until destroyed by enemy action two months later), were used by the Special Duty Flight for Porton. Other Mk I aircraft flew with the Armament Squadron.

Later in 1939 one aircraft had its turret removed and replaced by a simple mounting designed by the Establishment to fire upwards to the undefended underside of an enemy bomber. The 'no allowance' method of attack appeared promising, but trials were limited by the maximum speed of 120mph of the target towing aircraft. A contemporary modification in another Blenheim was a gun mounting in the rear floor escape hatch; sighting was by mirror and the gun's usefulness was considered very limited. K7044 (briefly), L1253 (for eight months), L1495 (eight months), L8662 (briefly) and L8689 (until a crash following engine failure in July 1941) were all used from September 1939. Later machines were L6594 (forced landing in December 1939, which curtailed tests of its lethal COW gun installation), L6787 (six months' use armed with two 20mm guns, probably forward-firing, until extensively damaged in March 1941), L8671 (from January 1940 for five months), L8669 (three months' flying from

Blenheim I L1348 in about August 1939 at Martlesham Heath, prior to the trials of its Rotol constant-speed propellers at Boscombe. Only oil on the undercarriage doors spoils its new appearance. The picqueting ropes are attached to the rear of the engine nacelle rather than to rings under the wings as on many other types. Early in 1940 performance was improved at the A&AEE before the aircraft was sent to Heston for photographic conversion. *A&AEE 9618*

March 1940), L1417 (from October 1940 until damaged by an enemy air raid in April 1945), L1274 (two months' use until damaged on take-off in June 1941) and L6777 (November 1941 until October 1942, the last Mark I). Details of the work of the foregoing are missing, but most were used on general-purpose bombing trials.

Blenheim Mark IV

One 'long nose' version (L4835) flew from Martlesham Heath; trials investigating performance at overload weight of 15,000lb were protracted by lengthy unserviceability after damage taxiing in March 1940. Using 100 octane fuel and thus permitting +9psi (instead of +5) boost, the take-off run was actually reduced to 365 yards at the higher weight (from 415 yards at 13,190lb). Performance is given in the Tables. A further addition to the load required trials in mid-1940 at 16,000lb in R3601. Handling up to 310mph was satisfactory, stalling

speeds 80mph (clean) and 68mph (wheels and flaps down), and the take-off run was increased to 480 yards. The most significant effect was in the ceiling, reduced to a mere 15,700 feet, or 19,000 feet if the engine temperatures permitted the gills to be closed. Brief performance trials earlier on L8748 had proved disappointing following cleaning up of the airframe and painting in Camotint, in contrast to the benefits from similar treatment on a Mk I. N3522, produced by Avro, demonstrated a top speed 5mph faster than the original Bristol-made aircraft, in spite of a window blowing out and needing one-third right rudder trim for balance.

From December 1940 L9387 had a Bristol X upper turret intended for the Blenheim V; the simplified hydraulic power system and ample armour were features. A year later aerial mines (four under each wing) were tested in Z6191, but results are not known. Details of other Blenheim Mk IVs are sparse. Porton used R6916 in December 1939 and L9337 from February 1940 until severely damaged in bad weather in

Blenheim IV L4835 in September 1939, the day before it flew to Boscombe Down. The long nose and fuel jettison pipe of the Mark are well shown, while the upper turret lacks guns. Our man at the front lends scale, and is, for the first time, a civilian – a sign of the changing balance from all-Service to increasingly civilian personnel. *A&AEE 9649*

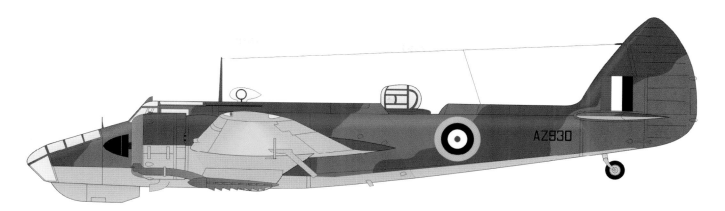

the following November; the replacement, T2354, lasted until mid-1944. The Gunnery Flight used L4838 for seven months until recalled to operational service in May 1940, and V5427, with an experimental dorsal turret, was transferred from Duxford in January 1942, flying thereafter for more than a year. The Bombing Flight flew L4893 briefly until a fatal accident in November 1940, when it spun on final approach. Premature detonation of the bombs during a low-level trial destroyed V5797 in November 1941, killing two of the three crew. V6251, borrowed from No 140 Squadron, dropped flares in April 1943. No record has been found of the work of N3552 (from May 1941) with the Performance Squadron, nor of the tests in the Bombing Flight on V6000 (also in May 1941) with 'scanning equipment'.

Blenheim Mark V (Bisley)

The low-level version of the Blenheim with Mercury XV engines, armour, and provision for four 0.303in guns in the nose first appeared at Boscombe in July 1941 when the prototype, AD657, arrived. The cockpit layout was liked, but initial problems with hydraulic power to the Bristol X turret and ammunition feed were progressively resolved by Bristol. AD661's new bomb doors led to bombs striking the aircraft structure on release. Porton then used the

machine until July 1942. Type trials on AZ930 (glazed nose) from November 1941 revealed a reduction from the Mk IV in longitudinal stability, making handling very tiring in bumpy conditions; at modest weights height could not quite be maintained on one engine at 6,000 feet. A heartfelt comment described the difficulty for the observer to enter the nose: he had to go in backwards, climb over the periscope sight (for the under gun), then straddle it. Even on the ground, and without ammunition boxes in place, this gymnastic feat took more than 15 seconds; airborne trials appear not to have been attempted. The practical range (after normal allowances for take-off and climb) was 1,090 miles on 465 gallons. The smoke/chemical containers of 500lb were not jettisonable and thus unacceptable. DJ702 from January 1942 measured performance (see the Table), the effect of air cleaners, cooling, contamination and cabin heating. Inadequate heaters made the cabin unacceptably cold at altitude, although draughts were somewhat reduced by a fairing behind the turret. A more powerful hydraulic pump rotated the turret quickly up to 325mph; the Mk I gyro sight was liked. BA248 was weighed in March 1942, and three puzzling features are mentioned: it was a high-altitude version, it had Mercury XX engines and the inboard tanks (187 gallons) had 100 octane fuel while the outboards (278 gallons) had 87 octane. A week's flying in

Bristol Blenheim AZ830, November 1941, for handling trials. (Scale 1:72)

Blenheim V (also Bisley I) AD657 in July 1941, with solid nose with four 0.303in guns for the direct support role. Just visible is the pressure head under the port wing (starboard on the earlier version), more raked windscreen, oil coolers under the engines and an intake in the wing leading edge; the undercarriage has sideways-opening doors. *A&AEE 9772*

Blenheim V (also Bisley I) DJ702 in February 1942 with the bombing nose, a Bristol BX turret with two 0.303in guns, a faired DF loop, and flame dampers. The turret has a large detachable roof for escape on the ground only; no comment has been found on this feature. Hydraulic problems in early trials (on AD657) and gun stoppages at more than 2g were overcome during frequent returns to Bristol. *A&AEE recognition 78*

AZ923 in February 1942 was sufficient to test the camera and find the dual controls dangerous on account of the second control column fouling the throttles. Gunnery tests in AZ886 from March 1943 included an unsatisfactory rubber mounting for a single Vickers 0.303in gun in the glazed nose, and the need for an Establishment modification to collect empty shells that otherwise threatened to jam the controls under the Bristol X turret. In May 1942 BA287 had four revised cams to prevent the gunner shooting the wireless mast; further modification was recommended to avoid shooting the pilot. The electrically powered turret of AZ888 from August 1942 was good, with smooth and positive action at high and low speeds.

Blenheim Mk V AZ930 in January 1942, with glazed nose and under turret for the rearward-firing gun. Movement within the forward fuselage was impractical, making use of a bombsight impossible. Under the port wing is a mast for the pitot head (nearer) and the fuel jettison tube.

Nomad

A single Northrop Nomad, AS441, appeared briefly at Boscombe from July 1940. Although designated A-17 by the US Army Air Corps, this light bomber (one Twin Wasp Junior R-1535-13) was flown by A Flight (fighters) when serviceable. No formal report was written and the type did not enter RAF service.

Nomad I AS441, seen here in August 1940, was one of a small number to reach the UK; it left the A&AEE without any trials being formally reported. Referred to while at Boscombe as 'Northrop AS441', the name Nomad appears later – indeed, a comprehensive note by the British Air Commission dated 15 March 1941 quotes its official British designation as 'Northrop A-17-A'. *A&AEE 9650*

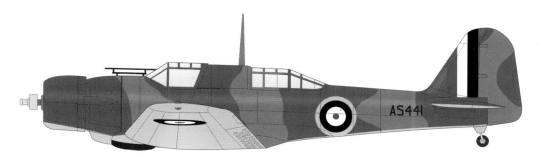

Northrop Nomad AS441, July 1940, for handling trials. (Scale 1:72)

Boston

The twin-engined Douglas DB-7B was ordered for the RAF from the American company shortly after a similar purchase by the French. The latter started to receive aircraft first, in October 1939, and six months later invited a team from the A&AEE to France. In early April 1940 an unidentified example was flown; the resulting handling report was fulsome in its praise, although no attempt was made to measure performance. It said, among other things, 'as usual with American aircraft there is extremely little friction in the control system', and the controls, with large balance areas and large trimmers, made for pleasant flying characteristics.

A feature favoured was the powering of the vacuum-driven gyro instruments by engine-driven pumps, but particularly praised was the single-engine handling. The swing on closing one throttle was much less than the Beaufighter, and the foot loads for balanced flight were small. Among matters in need of further investigating were the vertical mounting of eight 50kg bombs, and the question of optimum flap setting for take-off. No comment was made on the throttles, which worked in the reverse sense to British (and American) practice.

Boston Mark I

The very pleasant handling of the DB-7 (named Boston) was never compromised in four years of testing at the A&AEE; operational shortcomings of the early aircraft, however, soon became apparent. In July 1940 Boston I AE458 (Twin Wasp R-1830-SC3-G) arrived, having been taken over from the French contract, which had specified a fuel capacity of only 172 gallons (about twice a Spitfire's, but the Boston could weigh about three times as much). At 16,000lb performance (see the Table) was satisfactory, but range as a bomber (with 2,000lb bombs) inadequate at 880 miles (maximum). In addition to the poor range, the rear defence was ineffective and the three crew were completely isolated; the simple undercarriage design and the tool kit supplied were, however, praised. Other roles were considered, including night-fighting, and the ex-French aircraft with slightly more powerful engines, initially Boston II, were renamed Havoc (qv).

Boston I AE458 in July 1940, with its novel tricycle undercarriage and Twin Wasp (R-1830) engines. The national fin marking reflects French practice in its extent, but not the position – the French normally marked the rudders. *A&AEE 9650*

Boston Mark III

The first Boston built to British needs, including a fuel capacity of 318 gallons and powered with Cyclone engines (GR-2600-A5B), arrived in June 1941 as W8269. It was configured as a fighter-bomber, and had a bomb aiming panel and a large rudder; maximum all-up weight was 21,550lb. Performance trials appear to have been brief (see the Table); the take-off run was 585 yards. Range was initially inadequate, but extra tankage (giving 431 gallons) fitted to W8253 early in 1942 increased practical range to 880 miles (maximum 1,175), albeit with load limited to four 500lb bombs. It is interesting that more than doubling the fuel load gave an increased range of only a third. Weight increased to 23,000lb, and the take-off run was extended to 725 yards using the optimum flap setting of 15°.

Fully armed with two pairs of 0.303in Browning guns in blisters on the nose, two similar guns on a flexible Bell-type mounting in the rear cockpit, and a single Vickers gun firing rearwards under the rear fuselage, W8266 was tested from August 1941. Each forward facing gun had 580 rounds, but the rear guns, with only 100 rounds each, were totally inadequate. Prior to the gunnery trials, W8266 had been used to assess the bombing capabilities of the Boston, limited to four 500-pounders. Loading was awkward and took 50 minutes, and selection, fusing and release of the bombs was in the hands of the pilot, not the bomb aimer.

Five variations of the Boston III were tested. The criticism of rear defence was met by an air

Boston III W8269 of the first British contract is seen in pristine condition probably shortly after arrival in June 1941. It has the larger rudder introduced on this Mark, and prominent gun fairings on the nose for two (one each side) of the four 0.303in guns. The fin-mounted pressure head is common to all Bostons, and most have the bead sight in front of the pilot. *A&AEE AC897*

deflector for the gunner in W8315 from December 1941 and a glazed nose housing a Vickers gas-operated gun. The air deflector was acceptable, but the Vickers gun 'leapt about'. W8315 returned in July 1942 with an electrically operated but very heavy Rose turret. Speed was increased by 10mph (true) as a result of covering the cooling holes in the engine nacelles. In the spring of 1942 Z2184 had a searchlight (Turbinlite) in the nose. The modification was used in service by the Havoc, but in Z2184 handling was normal, except for lack of pre-stall buffet, top speed reduced by 23mph (true) and consumption increased marginally. Neither turret nor light entered service in the Boston, but the three following variations had them.

The first Intruder version, W8290, started trials in April 1942, with the benefit of earlier

work on the Havoc and with four 20mm Hispano cannons. The quality of the early prototype guns was bad, and the production version had many faults; the poor workmanship of the installation was severely criticised. The cannon and two external bombs reduced top speed (see the Table) and, despite a further increase in fuel capacity to 472 gallons, range was only 750 miles practical (1,005 maximum). Carbon monoxide contamination, measured in AL480 following 20mm gun firing, was slight, and cleared after 1 minute. Bombing trials included W8291[1], and the variety of underwing stores extended to various smoke containers as well as 500lb bombs; the main limitation was the need to jettison the containers in level flight to avoid damage to the tailplane. AL481 joined the High Altitude Flight in September 1942.

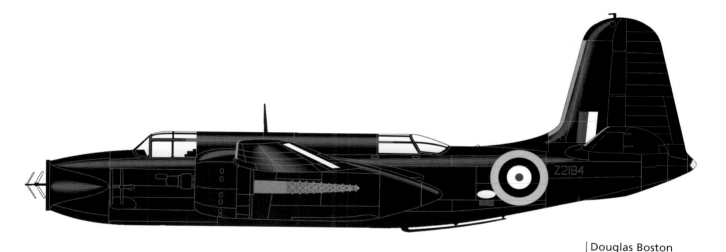

Douglas Boston Z2184, February 1942, for handling trials.

Boston III Z2184 in March 1942, equipped with Turbinlite and AI radar. The flame dampers and velvet black finish add to the impression of a night-fighter. The Havoc II (DB7A ordered to a French contract) was very similar to this British contract machine, a model DB7B. Both had the Double Cyclone GR-2600-A5B, the Havoc II in its -6 form and the Boston III in the -0 form. In both cases the nacelle size is similar to the Twin Wasp, but with the air intake further aft on the Cyclone. The white line under the wing is probably to aid visibility at night during trials. *A&AEE HA174*

[1] W8291 was later detached to West Freugh, and crashed in July 1942 in the Isle of Man.

137

Boston III W8269/G in February 1943, with distinct signs of wear, updated national insignia, an attitude reference line, flame dampers and six RP. The tube under the fuselage is believed to be for the trailing aerial. *A&AEE recognition 131*

Boston III W8315 is seen in September 1942 with the Rose Bros electrically powered turret and what seems to be a single 0.303in gun. The installation proved to be heavy and offered no advantage over existing arrangements. Nose armament has been removed, including the fairing; the unsealed gap between fin and rudder can be seen. *A&AEE 11095*

Boston III W8290 in April 1942 in black intruder guise and a pack of four 20mm guns under the fuselage in addition to the usual four 0.303in the nose. *A&AEE 9978*

On return in late 1942, W8269/G had the first rocket projectile installation Type B with the blast plate flush with the rails. In six months of trials many modifications were made to achieve an acceptable system. Handling up to 390mph was unaffected by the rockets.

The Boston IIIA had stub ejector exhausts on its R-2600-23 engines, which bestowed a useful increase in top speed (see the Table) on BZ201 from late 1942 but at the expense of a complete lack of flame damping. In mid-1943 BZ196 had only slightly improved damping with either an American or an RAE type; the usual tapered, shrouded, slotted version was eventually acceptable. On 10 March 1943 a landing Halifax crashed onto BZ201; after repairs, a new type of air cleaner and RPs were fitted. Consumption at 2.88ampg was typical with external stores. BZ199, with electrically powered traverse for the two rear guns, was rejected as the guns tended to stop firing at only modest g. No fewer than six other Mk IIIAs appear in the serviceability returns – five of them with the High Altitude Flight in 1943/44. BZ362 had a brief existence as it crashed at Worthy Down after a meteorological flight on 19 October 1943 when the pilot followed the wrong railway line in bad weather, and BZ384 was parked and destroyed by a Wildcat attempting to take off. BZ315 and BZ320 had more productive lives, flying on meteorological research, while the work of BZ311 is unknown. BZ274 was used by Porton from June 1945.

Boston Mark IV

Interest in the Boston IV, BZ401, centred on the low-drag Glen Martin 250 CE10A dorsal turret. Apart from the lack of a receptacle to retain used links and cases (remedied by the Establishment), the installation proved acceptable. The bombing arrangements were less satisfactory, and required fifteen essential and eight desirable modifications. Handling of the Mk IV led to the only adverse handling comment of the Boston, due to the aftwards shift of CG when fully loaded in BZ403. A maximum speed was recommended as a result of the need to push the control column after initiating recovery from dives at high speed; above 350mph there was a risk of structural damage if the push was delayed. Flame damping was non-existent and the standby compass unreliable.

A front view of Boston IIIA BZ201 in January 1943. Possibly of more interest is the Botha in the background – a type of which no official A&AEE photos apparently exist. *A&AEE 11241*

Boston IIIA BZ201 in January 1943, with the individual stub exhausts that identified this version; the Double Cyclone GR-2600-A5B-0s are the same as the earlier Mk III, but designated R-2600-23 in this Lend-Lease aircraft. The forward pair of nose guns have been taped over. This aircraft was extensively damaged on the ground by an operational Halifax landing at night. *A&AEE 11241*

Boston IV BZ403 in May 1944 with clear perspex nose and no nose armament but four 500lb bombs, two under each wing. *A&AEE 11755*

Boston Mark V

BZ580 arrived in January 1945 as the only representative of the Mk V, with more powerful R-2600-29s and 603 gallons of fuel; it was the heaviest Boston when loaded, at 24,453lb. Handling up to 395mph, even at aft CG, was good – the reason for the big improvement over the Mk IV was not established – stalls occurred at 125 (clean) and 112 (wheels and flaps down).

Mosquito

The story of the wooden-structured de Havilland Mosquito has often been told, but the part played by the A&AEE is related here as documented in the Establishment's reports. Outstanding performance and adaptability characterised the type, described here in five groups by role, as Photographic Reconnaissance (PR), Night-Fighters (NF), Bombers (B), Fighter-Bombers (FB) and Other Roles. The first prototype, although originally intended as a fighter, is included with PR; other prototypes were tested for specific roles.

Photographic Reconnaissance

On 19 February 1941 the first prototype, W4050, flew to Boscombe Down powered by two Merlin XXIs, then 8½ hours of flying were completed before the rear fuselage fractured during taxiing on the uneven aerodrome surface. The preliminary results were encouraging at the modest weights flown (see the Table); the controls were generally light and effective, but the rudder was found to be too heavy at high speeds up to 320mph. The stalling speeds were high (105mph clean and 90mph with flaps and undercarriage down), but behaviour benign; the cockpit was cramped but warm. The main initial criticism concerned the inadequate cooling of the engines in the climb. After repairs taking only a few days and fitting lengthened engine nacelles, stability was examined in more depth; it was difficult to trim in level flight, and a disturbance led to divergence indicating lack of longitudinal stability. Night-flying in this condition was considered to be unacceptable. Further

Mosquito I E-0234 on a misty day in February 1941. This view is one of the standard series in the A&AEE's reports, but the location is not Boscombe Down. All references to this aeroplane by the A&AEE are to W4050. The wing leading edge radiator intakes are well shown, together with the bomb aiming panel and, offset to starboard under the fuselage, the entry door, which was one of the few early criticisms as it could only be operated from the outside. *A&AEE 9691*

modifications to enlarge the elevator horn balances (and to remedy faults in the fuel system) improved but did not cure instability. Indeed, it was found worse with engines throttled back – a curious phenomenon, aggravated by large trim changes with flaps that were felt to operate too quickly. Unacceptable trim changes were also caused by operation of the radiator duct flaps; overheating of the engines continued to occur.

Stability improvements continued on W4052 (see below), while W4051 (the first PR machine, which arrived on 25 June 1941 but suffered tail damage three days later) concentrated on operational matters. The radios were satisfactory but the DF loop in the roof had to be manually rotated. The heating and operation of the cameras up to 28,000 feet were also acceptable, but needed further testing in winter conditions, duly completed in W4060 in December 1941. Oil overheating in high-level climbs was cured early in 1942 by enlarging the cooling flap opening, by which time tail wheel shimmy had been cured. W4054 produced encouraging range figures from July 1941; with normal fuel of 546 gallons, a maximum range of 2,000 miles was calculated, and, with planned bomb bay fuel, 2,530 miles – both at 19,250 feet. W4060 had tanks for an additional 151 gallons in the bomb bay: functioning up to 30,000 feet was satisfactory. The all-up weight increased to 19,130lb with the extra fuel, giving an extremely aft CG; fitting a 15lb inertia weight gave little amelioration to the poor longitudinal stability.

DK324, a bomber version converted to a PR VIII, arrived in December 1942 with Merlin 61s and tankage for 740 gallons, but it suffered a major accident the following month after being weighed at 21,184lb all up. Two PR IXs were used for tests, but largely unconnected with their role. MM230 flew in the dark air of early 1944 with two types of flame damping exhausts – both were easily visible from the rear, and MM235 had American Hamilton 'paddle' propellers but with British control units. Similar propellers on a night-fighter variant had previously oversped and led to a serious crash. On MM235 moderate overspeeding to 3,700 revs (control units should have limited them to 3,000) occurred once, but only for 2-3 seconds on a baulked landing; the British propeller controllers were acceptable.

Both Mk IX and Mk XVI were produced in PR and B versions; test-flying of both marks was generally shared without distinction between roles. The first PR XVI with pressure cabin and Merlin 73 was DZ540, which appeared in August 1943, performed very well (see the Table) and handled normally. Stalling speeds at 22,300lb were 132 (clean) and 118 (flaps and undercarriage down), and pressurisation and demisting gave no problems on trials; the report concludes with the normal caveat about exercising care on pulling out from dives due to the ease of overstressing the aircraft. Within a year, following reports of structural failure in service, the Establishment visited bomber, fighter and coastal stations to fly a total of

Mosquito VIII DK324 is a photographic variant and was converted from a Mk IV. Something of a puzzle, it arrived at Boscombe on 11 December 1942 and was involved in a major accident at High Post on 4 January 1943; the only report is on weighing, dated 8 February 1943. This photograph, clearly showing its Merlin 61 engines, was probably taken to support the subsequent uncompleted handling report, and its sequence number indicates a date very early in 1943. The white line on the fuselage was used for accurate attitude measurements, usually in connection with rocket work. *A&AEE 11359*

twenty-one front-line aircraft. The reports state that behaviour of all aircraft was consistent with loadings, and that normal variations between marks and between individual aircraft led in extreme cases to marked instability. Emphasis was placed on careful rigging of tail incidence and to observance of CG limits.

Two 100-gallon fuel tanks on the wings made little difference to handling on MM363 from March 1944, although care was needed landing with only one full tank. Maximum weight was again increased to 23,050lb, and with tanks top speed was reduced by 6mph (true). MM361 (propeller controls) and NS571 (engine cooling) were briefly flown in the summer of 1944. NS624, another PR XVI, had extensive instrumentation for engine cooling trials in Khartoum from November 1944.

Late in 1944 NS586, the prototype PR32, with lightened structure, extended wing tips and experimental Merlin RM 16SM engines, started trials. The aircraft crashed fatally on 12 April 1945 when fitted with special four-bladed de Havilland propellers with double-acting constant-speed units; the tests involved dives from 35,000 feet to investigate any tendency to overspeeding. It was considered most likely that compressibility at a Mach number in excess of the previously tested figure (about 0.75) could have led to loss of control. No fewer than six examples (RG176, 177, 178, 182, 183 and 194) of the PR34 arrived within two months from March 1944. The large number was considered necessary for clearance in view of the high-altitude supercharger surging occurring. With two

PRU blue Mosquito Mk XVI NS624 shows the standard Mosquito flaps and pressure head (covered) on the fin in the autumn sun of November 1944. It has 'paddle' propellers and a camera port for oblique shots of the ground. *A&AEE 11992*

NS586, a Mk 32, is seen in May 1943; the only apparent difference is the presence of two 100-gallon drop tanks, and extended wing tips. The engines are of Merlin RM165M rating. Early in 1945 four-bladed propellers were fitted, controlled by double-acting constant-speed units; during diving trials on 12 April 1945 control was lost and the aircraft crashed fatally. *A&AEE 11968*

RG176, a Mk 34 in late 1945, has a belly tank and 200-gallon drop tanks; from the appearance of the main tyres and the compressed tail wheel assembly it seems that it is seen fully loaded to 25,500lb – the heaviest of any Mosquito. The inscription by the receptacle for the external power reads '24 volt'. The side-mounted camera window is interesting in this version designed for both extreme range and altitude. *A&AEE 15220*

200-gallon drop tanks, total fuel capacity was 1,255 gallons, raising the gross weight to 25,500lb. The engine boost of the Merlin 113/4 was +18psi for take-off; even at reduced power (+12psi) safety speed was 200mph. Engine failure on take-off was considered very hazardous, particularly in view of the 310 gallons of fuel in the bulged bomb bay. Trials continued after the war.

Night-Fighters

W4052 (Merlin XXI) was configured as a night-fighter with four 20mm guns in the bottom of the fuselage, and four 0.303in guns in the nose, and had the AI radar aerials on arrival in June 1941. Also fitted were lengthened nacelles and a larger tailplane following early experience with the first prototype. Longitudinal stability was improved slightly while lateral and directional characteristics were praised; six months later a further 10% was added to the tailplane area with slight benefit. Persistent cutting out of the engines at 24,000 feet limited trials of gun heating and performance, although top speed was established (see the Table). Later, W4052 had air brakes fitted around the rear fuselage in an attempt to improve night interceptions, which often failed from excessive overtaking speed. The time to reduce speed by 150mph with the brakes was 30 seconds (previously 45 seconds), but such was the extreme buffeting that the installation was not acceptable.

Meanwhile, in March 1942 a check on W4070's performance had been made following de Havilland's claim that the matt black night-fighter finish reduced top speed by 26mph (true).

Mosquito II W4052 in September 1941 displays its black finish, which appears smooth and velvet-like. The wing tip and nose aerials for the radar are seen. The engine exhausts are unusual and appear to route the spent gases back into the cowling for venting below the leading edge; flame damping was satisfactory. *A&AEE recognition 24*

Mosquito II W4076 in February 1942, with four nose-mounted 0.303in and four fuselage 20mm guns in evidence. The nose aerials are not fitted, but conventional shrouded exhausts are. The aircraft was used extensively for handling trials and gunnery; some fourteen improvements were necessary for the 20mm guns and three for the 0.303in. *A&AEE 9954*

The Establishment disagreed and measured a drop of only 8mph (true) when compared to a smooth finish. The matt finish was tried first, and the Establishment delegated to the firm the tedious task of removing it and repainting in the smooth finish. From January 1942 W4076 tried a number of palliatives to the longitudinal stability problem; by the middle of the year an acceptable inertia weight was found, which, when suitably fitted in the elevator control circuit, rendered the aircraft stable at all CG and all phases of flight. The modification was introduced into the Service, but later the Establishment was dismayed to find that some night-fighter squadrons had removed the weight. Firing caused difficulty in W4076, even after fitting Mk II BSA 0.303in guns; a further seventeen modifications were recommended, most to the four 20mm guns.

W4096 arrived in October 1942 with an extra-fine propeller stop to increase drag; the results were inconclusive, but top speed on one engine was reduced by 11mph (true), and the extra drag from a single windmilling engine increased foot loads. The effect on

safety speed at take-off appears not to have been assessed. Range at 19,852lb with 690 gallons at take-off produced a calculated maximum of 2,500 miles – an outstanding figure. The tropical cowling reduced top speed by 12mph (true). Fish-tail exhausts were visible at more than 1,000 yards at night on DD736 in January 1943, thus well below the requirement. The final tests on the NF II took place in early 1945 on DD635, with double-acting governors on the de Havilland propellers, which were quick and positive in action. These 1945 tests may have been the ultimate development of the early type of governors fitted to HK196, an NF XII that had been written off (no casualties) shortly after arrival in August 1943. HK196's tests were intended to evaluate the possibility of engine overspeeding on entering a dive and throttling back. Two dives had been entered with mild and contained overspeeding; on the third dive, both engines oversped by 50% then seized, leading to a forced landing.

Handling and performance tests in early

Mosquito AV MP469, seen here in January 1943, was the first pressurised fighter version with Merlin 61s and four-bladed propellers; the small air intakes below the exhausts are for pressurisation. Features include the 'thimble' radome for the AI radar, wing tips extended by 4ft 2in each side, and the gun pack (four 20mm) under the fuselage. *A&AEE 11264*

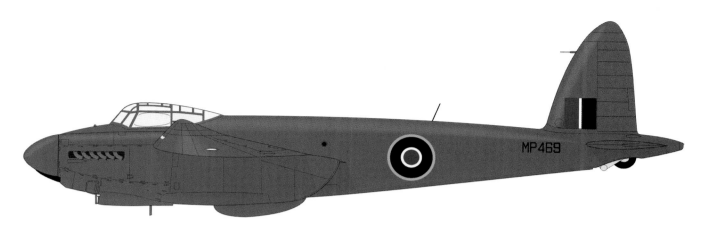

1943 of the pressurised Mk XV, MP469, with an extra 8ft 4in span and four-bladed metal propellers proceeded smoothly, after two early successful flights to 40,000 feet to check the Dunlop electro-pneumatic firing system. Performance (see the Table) was up to expectations. A year later a different result attended trials of the NF30 MM686, with a bulbous nose housing the AI Mk VIII radar. Tests were abandoned because of the very poor lateral characteristics. The ailerons were very heavy for a Mosquito, overbalanced above 160mph with only half aileron selected, and, worst of all, the left-wing-down tendency above 300mph could not be held at 440mph. A second NF30, MM748, exhibited similar but less pronounced tendencies in August 1944. At forward CG, however, handling was considered to be just acceptable, and some performance was measured (see the Table).

De Havilland Mosquito MP469, January 1943, for handling/ performance trials.

Mosquito NF30 MM748 in July 1944 was the second of this version tested, but still displayed unsatisfactory, but less marked, lateral characteristics. Three-bladed 'paddle' propellers, a bulbous nose for the radar (AI Mk VIII), small fuel tanks (50 gallons) and aerials on the wing can be seen. *A&AEE 11872*

Mosquito Mk XV MP469 shows its extended wings in January 1943. Unusually for a prototype, it has no 'P' on the fuselage. *A&AEE recognition 124*

Bombers

With the benefit of similarity to the photographic aircraft already tested, the bomber version entered RAF service just as the first bomber prototype reached Boscombe (W4057 with Merlin 21s in September 1941). It was similar to the first prototype, but had a Dowty tail wheel; at 18,980lb and with 25° flap, the take-off run was 445 yards. An early production B IV, DK290, appeared in June 1942; it was tiring to fly due to longitudinal instability in the climb, level flight and descent. Four 500lb bombs, increasing the weight to 20,670lb, did not alter handling; the Establishment recommended a limit to aft position of the CG, and adjured pilots to exercise caution on recovery from dives and thus avoid structural damage. A larger horn balance on the elevator of DK327 gave but slight improvement to longitudinal handling. This aircraft was extensively damaged on landing wheels-up in September 1942, a month after arrival.

Returning in early 1943, DK290/G had a 9lb inertia weight in the elevator control circuit with significant improvement in handling. Of equal significance was the modification (known as 'High Ball') to the bomb bay to enable two special stores (rotating mines similar to those carried by Lancasters to breach dams) to be carried. Range was measured, and showed only a slight decrease at low level. Two exhaust arrangements demonstrated the speed advantage of 15mph from the multi-stub type when compared to the saxophone design. The A&AEE made only ground assessment of the weapons.

The versatility of the Mosquito was further enhanced by the bulging of the bomb bay to take the 4,000lb bomb; DZ594/G had normal handling and release characteristics in this configuration. Tested first at the modest weight of 17,650lb, the stalling speeds were 115mph (clean) and 100-105mph (flaps and undercarriage down); dives to 360mph were safely made. Later, in 1944, DZ590 had metal elevators, and a comprehensive programme by the High Altitude Flight confirmed that the aircraft was unstable at all five CG flown, but that it was not tiring to fly. However, it was considered acceptable for experienced pilots to fly at a CG further aft (and thus nearer operational loadings) than previously.

Mosquito IX LR495 is seen in May 1943 on initial trials with two external 500lb bombs (additional to four 500lb bombs in the bay), and clearly shows the strengthening longeron (starboard side only) on the fuselage, over which the roundel is painted. The Merlin 72 motors have three-bladed narrow-chord propellers and ice guards on the air intakes. *A&AEE 11421*

LR495 in flight in June 1944, carrying the so-called 'smoke curtain equipment' that was being carried when the aircraft crashed fatally on 29 January 1944 during a forced landing following engine cutting. *A&AEE recognition 161*

The increased power of the Merlin 72 gave LR495, designated B IX, a further improvement in performance (see the Table) from April 1943; two external bombs cost 230 ft/min in best rate of climb and 1,800 feet in ceiling. Late in 1943, with permitted boost increased from +18 to +21 psi, obtainable speeds below full throttle height were increased by 13mph (true). The maximum weight increased to 22,825lb with long-range tanks (total 760 gallons) and external bombs. At the higher weights the radiators were marginally effective, and assessed as unsuitable for tropical conditions. Consumption measurements were partially complete when LR495 crashed fatally in January

1944 carrying out tests with smoke canisters; with internal fuel of 560 gallons and external bombs, range was calculated at 1,630 miles.

Following successful trials of the pressurised photographic version of the Mk XVI, the first bomber version, ML910, arrived in October 1943 for a short bombing assessment, followed by ML937 in February 1944 with a 4,000lb bomb, raising the all-up weight to 25,279lb without external fuel. Normal take-off, handling and performance (see the Table) tests followed. Excessive swing to the left on take-off limited flap setting to 20°, at which the swing could be contained, but lengthened the run to a calculated 1,000 yards at 25.280lb. At

Mosquito XVI ML937 in February 1944 reveals its bulged bomb doors to accommodate the 4,000lb 'cookie' bomb, and a pair of 100-gallon drop tanks. Ice guards and two landing lights are fitted. The entrance door forward of the bomb bays has a circular transparent fitting, while at the rear are three circular items, one housing the target camera. *A&AEE recognition 202*

Mosquito XVI ML926/G in plan form in June 1944, showing the 8-foot-long blister housing the repeater (cunningly codenamed 'Repeata') equipment for Oboe. This view shows well the extended engine nacelles of all Mosquitoes apart from the first few built, and the lack of gaps between control surfaces and adjoining wings and tailplane. *A&AEE recognition 220*

the same weight, the stall (clean) occurred at 143mph; since the flap limiting speed was initially 150mph, the small margin was considered dangerous, and de Havilland agreed to raise the limit to 170mph for flap settings of 20°. The effect of engine failure on take-off was comprehensively investigated; control with the port engine at zero thrust (the worse side) could be maintained at speeds down to 190mph. The newly defined term 'safety speed' was 195mph. Although not given in the report, the time from unsticking to reaching the safety speed must have been considerable at the maximum weight – a lengthy period at risk.

A special 8-foot-long blister under the fuselage of ML926/G in May 1944 housed repeater equipment to extend the useable range of the bombing aid Oboe; handling was normal, but breakage of the blister in June led to a limit of 350mph being imposed. The blister for the H2S radar fitted under MM175 (which arrived in September 1944) led to the recommendation for use from paved runways due to small ground clearance; handling was normal up to 450mph, but maximum level speed was reduced by 12mph. From October 1944 ML994 tested various underwing stores, including two 200-gallon tanks, which caused aileron buffet above 250mph, and 500lb sea mines. Less successful was the dangerous handling early in 1945 of PF459, built by Percival; adjustments by the A&AEE and the firm reduced friction in the elevator circuit, and by June results were just acceptable.

Three other B XVIs arrived in the summer of 1944. MM173 soon had its modified bomb doors damaged and was replaced by MM174 taken over from the HAF (on meteorological work) to continue flame damping and other tasks including a reduced inertia weight for application to night-fighters. PF391 was written off following an engine failure on take-off for a meteorological research flight in November 1944. Canadian-built Mosquitoes were represented by four examples, the first, KB328, arriving in August 1943. Performance (see the Table) reflected the lower full throttle height of the Merlin 31s. The Canadian aircraft designated B Mk 20 were heavier than their UK equivalents, and had a CG further aft. Handling was adversely affected; initially a speed limit of 420mph was recommended in view of the excessive push force at that speed in a dive following trim in level flight and subsequent risk of overstressing on recovery. KB352 from August 1944 confirmed the longitudinal sensitivity of the B 20; additional limits of speed and usage were recommended depending on CG and modification state of the elevators. KB352 also suffered an unexplained attenuation of VHF reception along the fore/aft axis. KB209, on a high-altitude test, dived into the ground in August 1944 a few days after arrival; no cause for this fatal accident was established. KB471, a B 23 with Merlin 69s, was much unserviceable until the end of the war, at which time full tests on a B35, TA638, had just started.

Mosquito 23 KB471, seen here in mid-1945 having arrived in February, was the Canadian equivalent of the British-built Mk XVI, but with Packard-built Merlin 69 motors. *A&AEE 15194*

Fighter-Bombers

The FBVI, retaining the fighter's four 20mm cannon and using the space behind them for two shortened 500lb bombs, arrived at Boscombe first in June 1942 in the shape of HJ662/G. Exceptional manoeuvrability with well-harmonised controls was demonstrated before a crash on 30 July 1942. Earlier take-offs had been measured at 20,835lb, the run being 520 yards. The first production FBVI, HJ663, did not arrive until March 1943; handling was unaffected by the jettisonable fuel tanks, and modified (Mk II star) 20mm guns were an improvement. Merlin 25s with boost increased from +12 to +18 psi powered HJ679 from May 1943; cooling (measured against new requirements) was satisfactory and performance established (see the Table). After repairs following a landing accident, HJ679 completed dropping trials of the wing tanks and external bombs. Later in 1943 HX809, with engines approved for boost of +25psi, showed gains of 22mph (true) at sea level and 25mph at full throttle height.

The fashionable rockets were fitted to HX809 and HX918 (arrival November 1943) after the normal attitude measurements to establish the exact angle to mount the rails of the Mk IA RP installation. Concern at the lack of a blast protector under the wooden wings proved unfounded, and some 423 rockets were successfully fired in the air, but with disappointing accuracy. With eight 60lb rockets, top speed was reduced by 34mph (true) at 16,000 feet. Other weapons cleared for wing carriage (up to 450mph) and release (up to 250mph) were depth charges and mines from

Mosquito VI HJ662/G in June 1942 in intruder role, with four 20mm and four 0.303in guns and two 250lb wing-mounted bombs. The shrouded exhausts of the Merlin 21 motors and the pilot's gun/bombsight can be seen. On 30 July 1942 the port engine failed on take-off and the ensuing crash destroyed the Mosquito (one slight injury) and severely damaged two Beaufighters. *A&AEE 11038*

Mosquito VI HX918 has eight 60lb head RP in April 1944, mounted well outboard to avoid the propellers. Following attitude measurements at various speeds, weight and dive angles firing trials were disappointingly inaccurate. The installation, the RP Mk II, had no blast plates and the rails were well below the wooden timings. *A&AEE recognition 199*

Mk VI HR135 in August 1944 was on loan from 248 Squadron for trials of 250lb Mk XI star depth charges (here) and mines released from the wings. Carriage of both stores up to 450mph and release (after A&AEE modifications) up to 365mph were satisfactory. *A&AEE 11908*

HR135 in the summer of 1944. Handling, jettisoning and firing trials using PZ202 with two 100-gallon drop tanks and the Mk IIIA rocket installation were completed in only two weeks in July 1944, including a local modification designed, made, flown and cleared to prevent the tanks hitting the rockets. The rockets could not be fired with the tanks in place. The greatest weight of any of the FB VI versions was 23,992lb on HR303 in mid-1945 when carrying externally the Mk XVII Torpedo.

Other FB VIs flown were LR312 (briefly with the Armament Squadron at West Freugh from November 1943), NT220, RF892 (both for the armament demonstration) and TA547. These last three arrived in July 1945.

With a single Molins 57mm-calibre gun firing 6lb shells replacing the four 20mm guns, HJ732/G was rushed to Boscombe in July 1943 as the FB XVIII. After initial disappointment with the feed of the shells into the breech, successful firing was achieved, but the flash was too bright for night operations. Ground firing took place on Salisbury Plain; the aircraft was flown to the relief landing ground at Shrewton and taxied 1½ miles to the Bustard vidette. By late October 1943 HX902/G, HX903/G and HX904/G, with armour for the crew, had completed production testing of the FB XVIII's armament, and the three aircraft entered service with 618 Squadron the same month. PZ469, the penultimate Mk XVIII, arrived in July 1945 for the armament demonstration.

Mosquito XVIII HJ732/G in August 1943 has a plug in the nozzle of its single Molins 57mm gun, weighing 1,800lb and firing a 7lb projectile – known to the Army as 'Standard Ordnance QF 6 pdr 7 cwt Mk IV' with auto feed. The top of the pilot's armoured seat is visible through the open window. Air firing started on 2 July 1943, following ground firing on Salisbury Plain, where the Army usually fired these guns. *A&AEE AC1096*

Other Roles

A rapid assessment of W4073 was made early in 1942. Known to the A&AEE as an F III, the aircraft had a special wing structure (for a previous installation of a turret since removed), and side-by-side dual controls. Apart from being cramped and the instructor having no brake control, this version was considered suitable for the pilot conversion role.

Trials had just started on LR387, a D33 (later TR33), at the end of the war; it had folding wings and a hook for deck use.

Maryland

The Martin 167 light attack bomber was ordered before the war by the French then British governments. Only the former type, with single-stage supercharging of its Twin-Wasp (R-1830SC3G) engines, was tested at Boscombe Down. First in July 1940 was No 62, a French Air Force aircraft, apparently used briefly for familiarisation. A few days later followed AR703, still with instruments calibrated in metric units and a Bendix radio compass. Handling up to 355mph and stalls at 80mph (flaps and undercarriage down) were straightforward, and asymmetric flying easy; lighting was, however, poor, there was no heating, and the pilot's windows froze over. Later, an effective glycol spray for the windscreen was spoiled by the tank

Sea Mosquito 33 LR387 in October 1945, having arrived in July. Features are the small nose radome, four-bladed propellers, two depth charges under the wings, torpedo fittings under the fuselage, and arrester hook in front of the tail wheel. *A&AEE 15282*

blocking an emergency exit. Performance (see the Table) was measured, with an Anson turret then the original American cupola. At 255mph the ASI under-read by 14mph. With 626 gallons of fuel, maximum range was calculated at 1,870 miles. Trials were suspended in January 1941 when the aircraft was overstressed evading attacking Hurricanes. AR731 from June 1941 measured the loss of speed totalling 18mph due to air cleaners (7mph) and flame damping exhausts (11mph). Tests of the four forward-firing 0.303in guns, harmonised on the ground, and the three hand-held defensive guns (two under the fuselage and one in the cupola) gave no serious difficulties.

Maryland I AR703 is seen probably in November 1940, as originally received by the A&AEE on being taken over from a French contract, and retaining French instruments, including poorly laid-out blind flying presentation. It retains the original cupola; as shown, the single gun appears to take up most of the space. Later trials on the type at heavy weight revealed a weakness in the tail wheel. Repairs of AR703 took more than two months following overstress evading eager Hurricanes, but it flew again from April 1941, including an appearance at Abingdon for a Royal visit. *A&AEE 9648*

Maryland AR711 did not appear for tests at the A&AEE, but posed beautifully in October 1941 for its portrait in the air. *A&AEE recognition 47*

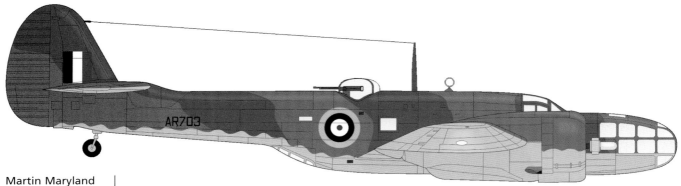

Martin Maryland
AR703, July 1940,
for handling/
performance trials.

Baltimore

From more than 1,500 of the twin-engine Martin Baltimores ordered for the RAF, only four reached the A&AEE, two each of Mk I and Mk III; the Mk II, IV and V were not tested at the Establishment.

Baltimore Mark I

On arrival in January 1942 AG691 was weighed, loaded to 23,220lb and had its pressure errors measured. Thereafter it appears to have accumulated 153 hours of intensive flying on an extensive investigation into the benefits of the auto-mixture control of its Cyclone (R2600 A5B) engines, and on flame damping assessment; the latter was judged acceptable by the RAF, although not complying with requirements. Pre-war experience had indicated that greater fuel economy could be achieved with normal control by a skilful pilot than with automatic mixture

regulation. The report concluded that auto-control was preferable in wartime as it relieved the pilot of an unnecessary task. Thus at full load (407 gallons) the practical range was 860 miles (1,140 miles maximum). After more than 150 hours, cockpit contamination had increased to a dangerous level. AG690, from February 1942, had the British CS Bomb Sight Mk IX fitted and, also successfully, dropped American bombs up to 500lb; chemical weapons were approved for dropping in straight and level flight. Gunnery in AG690 (designated Mk II in the report) involved testing no fewer than twelve 0.3in machine guns. Four of them were fixed to fire rearwards from around the bottom rear fuselage, while two guns were moveable in the hatch between them. Four more were fixed to fire forwards in the wings, and the upper position had a free pair for more conventional use. There were no serious problems – except perhaps to the Establishment's supply of 0.3in ammunition.

Baltimore Mk I AG691 is seen in early 1942, although little is visible on this unremarkable aeroplane. Engine exhausts are contained within the cooling gills, and afforded acceptable flame damping. Rearward-firing machine gun ports are visible below the fuselage roundel.

Baltimore Mark III

Armed with a Boulton Paul A turret Mk V, AG837 arrived in April 1942 powered by two Cyclones with modified carburettors (R-2600 A513-5). Range was about 3% less than the Mk I, attributed to the drag of the turret; handling up to 360mph was similar in spite of entering a spin inadvertently during stability (phugoid) tests. Performance is as in the Table, and noise in the unheated cockpit was just tolerable. Apparently the four fixed rearward guns were retained, but lacked operational effect, as there was no method of firing them. AG836 appeared briefly in May 1942, and again for a lengthier period in late 1943/early 1944; the only recorded trial, for pressure error measurement using a static vent in the rear fuselage, was cancelled.

Baltimore III AG837 in October 1942. The engines have large intakes and the turret is a Boulton Paul Type A Mk V, developed originally for the Defiant. *A&AEE recognition 115*

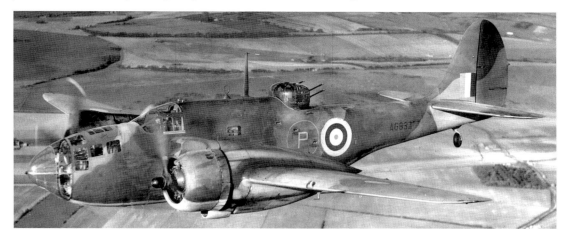

Martin Baltimore AG837, April 1942, for performance trials.

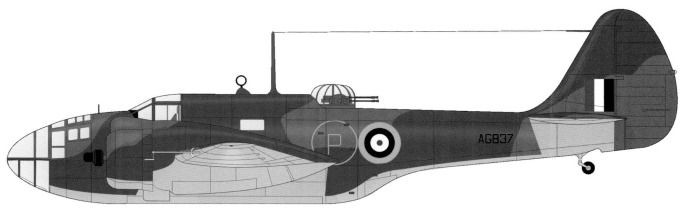

Ventura

Developed to a British contract, the Lockheed Ventura was similar in appearance to, but larger than, the Hudson.

Ventura Mark I

With 471 gallons of fuel and 2,500lb of bombs, AE748 weighed 26,700lb in May 1942. Handling was pleasant, with well-harmonised but heavy controls; there was ample power from the Double Wasp (R2800-51A 4G) engines, and single-engined flying easy with adequate rudder trim. Some difficulty was experienced in measuring consumption as the Stromberg carburettors had a novel return system that made flowmeter readings inaccurate; the problem was overcome, and range initially calculated as 990 miles (maximum) and 740 miles (practical). In 1943 a refined technique increased these figures marginally. Initial flame damping exhausts were insufficiently robust, and caused a 14mph (true) reduction in speeds. Later, a tapered and slotted type gave poor damping. The Establishment recommended that the main, P9, compass to be effective should replace the Elsan toilet (but retain its navigational function!). Performance is as in the Table; the rate of climb was slightly reduced by the need to climb at a higher speed than optimum to avoid buffet. In mid-1943 fitting the Mk XIV bombsight led to the need for an accurate static pressure source as the previous error of 15mph at 135mph was greatly in excess of the tolerance required; the ten positions tried failed to identify an acceptable error of less than 3mph with the bomb doors open. A brief check on AE683 in June 1942 revealed that firing the undergun caused contamination of the upper turret.

Ventura I AE748 in June 1942. Features include a pair of 0.3in guns in the nose with a pair of 0.303in in the upper turret, four flap track covers on each wing and black anti-icing boots visible on the fins but not on the wings. There is an unidentified cartoon strip character below the roundel. *A&AEE recognition 95*

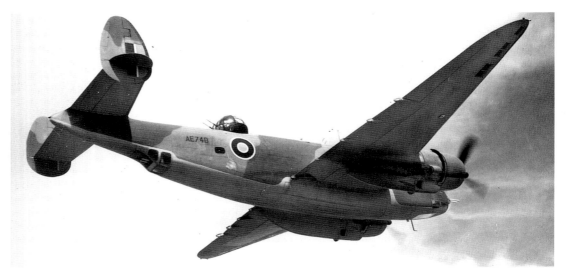

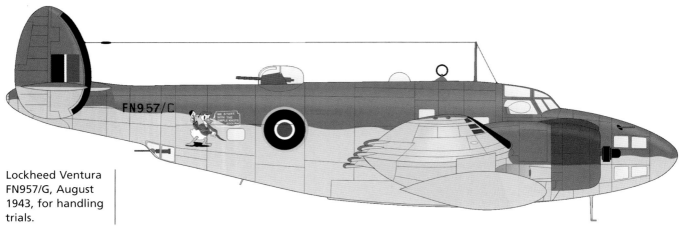

Lockheed Ventura FN957/G, August 1943, for handling trials.

Meanwhile, from May 1942 AE762 was allocated the highest priority to test the guns – a pair of 0.303in above the nose and two 0.5in on the sides of the fuselage, with a further pair in a tunnel firing rearwards plus a Boulton Paul Type C Mk IV upper turret. Firing the 0.5in guns collapsed the nose Plexiglas, and rearming was a lengthy process; strengthened Plexiglas was later satisfactory. Loading bombs revealed shortcomings in the hoist arrangements, but dropping a variety of stores was satisfactory, including, in August 1942, a 500lb LC bomb Type G Mk I.

Ventura Mark II

AJ206 with R-2800-31 engines paid a lengthy visit from June 1943, but no report appears to have been written on its RP work, possibly because of lengthy unserviceability at RAF Pembrey where firing was to have taken place.

Ventura Mark V

This version for general maritime reconnaissance was very similar to the standard US Navy aircraft, and had R-2800-25BG motors of increased horsepower. Handling of FN957/G from August 1943 up to 31,000lb remained good, including normal stalls at the increased speeds of 100mph (clean) and 77 (flaps and undercarriage down). The take-off run also increased to 960 yards; performance is as in the Table. Single-engined handling at the high weights was good, but height with the operating engine within limits could only be maintained with the weight below 28,000lb. With 1,091 gallons (obtained by use of bomb bay tanks), range at 5,000 feet was 2,090 miles (maximum) – practical range was not quoted. Armament trials were limited to examination of the low-drag Martin 250 CE7 upper turret in FN956/G from September 1943. The searching view was very restricted and elevating the guns to the maximum angle possible was very uncomfortable; handling of the turret and firing were, however, praised.

Ventura Mk II AJ206 in October 1943, with eight RPs under protective shields. The nose armament is well shown, as are the stop butts in the background. *A&AEE 11585*

Ventura V FN957/G in October 1943. Fully loaded in the configuration shown, the aircraft weighed 31,000lb and had a long take-off run. Features include a solid nose cone, 0.5in guns above the nose (not visible), drop tanks and a Martin CE250 CE7 turret (two 0.5in guns) of low drag and poor view. Donald Duck (holding a Hitler-headed snake) says, 'WE START WITH THE SIMPLE KNOTS ADOLPH'. *A&AEE 11583*

An American design that was satisfactory, but considered too flimsy on Ventura A E748 late in 1942. *A&AEE 11215*

Mitchell

The North American B-25 was supplied as the Mitchell to the RAF under Lend-Lease. Four versions were supplied and three of them entered service, of which two were used operationally.

Mitchell Mark I

The only pair of aircraft to reach the UK with this designation, FK161 and FK162, arrived at Boscombe in June 1942; the remainder formed a training unit in the Bahamas. Interest at the A&AEE centred on handling and take-off performance. At all CGs, handling was pleasant and landing on the tricycle undercarriage was easy; the only criticism was the lack of restraint to the pilot's seat, which tended to slide rearwards at awkward moments. Stalls were unexciting, but, at 29,000lb, occurred at the fairly high speed of 100mph (flaps and undercarriage down). Take-off runs at the same weight using the previously found optimum flap setting of $22\frac{1}{2}°$ took 495 yards; it was found beneficial to raise the nose wheel early in view of Boscombe's rough grass surface. Minor trials revealed no problems, but in November 1942 FK162 swung on take-off and the ensuing crash (no casualties) was partly attributed to the difficulty in closing the throttles; modification action followed.

Mitchell I FK161 in June 1942, prior to the start of handling trials. The inset hinges of the rudders gave good aerodynamic balance and were thus light to operate; the perspex tail cone appears small and of limited value. The upper turret has two 0.5in guns; the guns of the raised ventral turret are hidden in their recesses. An interesting feature of this nose wheeled type is the rigid brace under the tail to prevent embarrassing tipping up. Grass cutting was not a priority in this part of the airfield. *A&AEE AC944*

Mitchell Mark II

FL191, the prototype of this version, was written off in spectacular fashion the night it arrived in October 1942 when it cartwheeled (without casualties) following premature retraction of the rapid-acting (7 seconds) undercarriage on take-off. FL671 preceded the prototype, and started trials in June 1942; performance is as in the Tables. Lowering the under turret reduced speed by 8mph (true), and opening the bomb doors by a similar amount. At 30,000lb (559 gallons of fuel and 4,000lb of bombs), maximum range of 1,280 miles (960 practical) was achieved at 15,000 feet; with a ferry tank, range was calculated as 1,860 miles. Handling was good, although the A&AEE advised pilots to trim nose down before diving at extreme aft CG. In particular, asymmetric flying was praised in the following fulsome words: 'The Mitchell is an excellent aircraft for single-engine flying, the ample … trim available sets a new standard when compared with corresponding British types…' The long-suffering FL671 completed trials on IFF Mk II, pressure error, radios, flame damping (two types – neither satisfactory), navigation, contamination and cockpit heating – totally inadequate.

The precise attitudes of FL688 at various speeds were measured from May 1943, but rockets were not subsequently fitted. Parallel armament trials involved three machines, FL189 (July 1942), FL215 (July 1943) and FR370 (November 1942). The electrically powered Bendix Type L upper turret was slow in rotation (37°/sec – other turrets were more than 50°/sec), had bad bullet grouping, and was 'barely possible to enter'; it is not clear whether this comment implied removal of clothing. The Establishment recommended replacement by the Boulton Paul Type A, a view strongly endorsed by RAF Squadrons to the extent that FL185 (from No 180 Squadron) was received to try a modified cupola when there was no prospect of replacing the Bendix turret. The retractable under turret (Bendix Type V) suffered similarly in addition to cramped accommodation (the Americans selected small men as air gunners) and poor viewing. Changes to the amplidyne controls scarcely improved rotation, nor did replacing the under turret with a Bendix Type K in FR370. The Establishment's earlier recommendation to fit an FN64 under turret was implemented successfully in FL215 in mid-1943. The single nose 'wobble' gun (0.303in) in FL189 gave acceptable results in this early Mk II. Armament changes, flown from July 1943, in FV922 (known as Series II) included a single fixed nose gun for the pilot and a Bendix Type A upper turret with assisted ammunition feed; both were acceptable with modification, the chief requirement being ventilation for the front gunner. This aircraft successfully flew with a single M10 smoke tank under the starboard wing, then joined the SD Flight for Porton work until replaced by FW151 in February 1945.

FW143 (a Series II) from April 1944 had provision for up to eight 500lb bombs under the wings. Loading arrangements were unsatisfactory, and carriage incurred a significant performance penalty (top speed reduced by 70mph (true)) and reduced aileron response at low speed. Further radio, flame damping (still unsatisfactory) and IFF tests occupied FV903 from July 1943. Further armament changes in FW266, a Series III, added 0.5in guns to the nose (four fixed in blisters), the beam (two free), and tail (one free); only the tail position needed improvements.

In January 1944 Mitchell II FV922 was in use by the Special Duties Flight for Porton, fitted with two M10 smoke curtain containers. A single free gun and a fixed gun are fitted in the nose, and partially effective individual flame dampers are visible on the nacelles. The location of this photograph is unknown. *A&AEE 11676*

General-purpose armament trials were made in FV904 (from March 1945) and FV906 (July 1943 until damaged when landing in March 1944); the latter featured in armament research projects. Radical armament changes characterised FR208 and FR209 in July 1943 with 75mm artillery pieces in the forward fuselage. Handling of the latter without the gun and the fuselage 'fabriced' (sic) over at 34,000lb was made from a concrete runway; the take-off run was 630 yards – longer if the previous technique of raising of the nose wheel early was used. Handling remained pleasant, and stalling speed increased to 103mph (flaps and undercarriage down). FR208 (for which reports have not been found) fired at least once on the ground; the results are well remembered as the 15lb dummy shell burst through the butts and was last seen crossing a main road half a mile away. FV984 spent the last six months of the war in D Squadron on stability research, having arrived in March 1944 to be instrumented.

Mitchell Mark III

With the upper turret (two 0.5in guns) moved from the rear to the central fuselage, an additional gun in the tail and the navigator positioned in the nose, HD373 completed bombing and gunnery trials. On arrival in June 1944 the Bendix Type R turret had no means of collecting empty cartridges until a container was made by the A&AEE, but was otherwise acceptable. A second heater, for the waist and tail gunners, did not meet requirements. HD361 from November 1944 revealed that the previous aft limit for CG was unstable and could lead to excessive g on recovery from dives; a new limit of CG was recommended. The other feature of this Mark was very high static friction in the rudder controls (50lb). HD 347 arrived in March 1945 for high-priority but lengthy assessment of the new TI(b) bombsight.

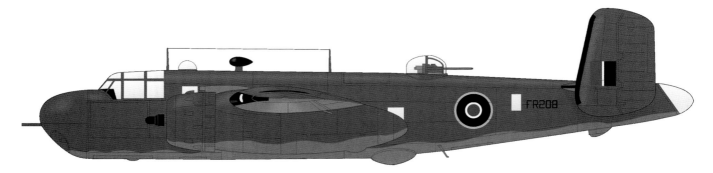

North American Mitchell FR208, July 1943, for gunnery trials.

Mitchell Mk II FR209 in July 1943, remarkable only for its huge artillery piece of 75mm bore visible in the nose. *A&AEE recognition 178*

Mitchell III HD361 in July 1945, showing the forward position of the upper turret, and, just visible, the raised rear fuselage to accommodate a gunner. There are two aircraft behind HD361 in a line, reflecting peacetime practice. *A&AEE 15167*

Mitchell III HD373 in August 1944, with lots of guns – eleven 0.5in, including the four in blisters on the side of the fuselage. The fairing for the DF aerial is under the fuselage and the anhedral of the wings is well shown. *A&AEE 11891*

He III and Ju 88

A brief visit to Boscombe in the summer of 1942 by the Enemy Aircraft Flight was used to measure the flame damping qualities of Heinkel He IIIH AW199 and Junkers Ju 88A-5 HM509; neither met current RAF requirements. A year later, JU88C-6/PJ876 was slightly better but was still poor.

Ju 88A-5 HM509 in its captors' livery flying near Boscombe for its picture to be taken in August 1942. Evidence of its previous owners is visible, 'M2-M', on the fuselage. *A&AEE recognition 104*

Vengeance

The Vultee Vengeance, ordered by the British Purchasing Commission but supplied later under Lend-Lease, was a dive-bomber that found little favour in RAF service, although more than 1,200 were ordered. The so-called 'Accelerated Service Tests' were completed by a British team in the USA, and the A&AEE's subsequent investigation was limited as a result.

500lb could be swung from the bomb bay and clear of the propeller arc. Very accurate dive bombing (radial error of 30 yards) was achieved in near vertical dives by 'tipping in' after the target disappeared under the wing. Wing mounting and jettison of the 500lb SCI were satisfactory. AN898 was fitted with various forms of slotted shrouded exhausts from February 1943; the best was just acceptable but could cause some cockpit contamination in the climb.

Vengeance I AN889 in August 1942, shortly after arrival, doing duty for its recognition photographs. The short exhaust produced alarming flames, and the occupant of the rear seat received unacceptable contamination, in addition to being unable to swivel his seat for effective use of the two 0.3in guns. A light series bomb carrier is fitted under the port wing. *A&AEE recognition 107*

Vengeance Mark I

AN889, one Double Cyclone engine (G R-2600 A5B5), appeared in August 1942 and was immediately found to be most hazardous on account of excessive flaming from the stub exhaust. With a lengthened exhaust pipe (not apparently adopted in service), handling was found to be of mixed quality. The dive brakes operated without significant trim change and proved to be very effective (a 45° dive was held to 280mph with the brakes extended, compared to 390 retracted), but the controls were heavy above 250mph, the pitch force needed for dive recoveries being considered far too high. A drill was devised for establishing the most economical cruising conditions, and the simple expedient of marking the throttle/mixture box recommended. The rear cockpit suffered carbon monoxide contamination, the facilities for astro-navigation were useless and the handling of the pair of 0.3in guns was unacceptable. Four similar guns in the wings fired satisfactorily, but were considered to be too small, particularly as ample space existed for guns of larger calibre. Two bombs of up to

Vengeance Mark IV

After taking over some RAF aircraft, the USAAC insisted on several changes. Some modified aircraft were supplied as the Vengeance IV (R-2600-13 engine). FD119 reached Boscombe in February 1944, where the new wheel brakes proved very effective (landing run reduced from 1,172 yards to 482) and contamination of the cockpit minimal. FD243 from April 1944 had American flame dampers, which were ineffective and contaminated the rear cockpit. The six 0.5in wing guns performed well, but their blast tubes proved too weak and became cracked. Bombing equipment and carriage and release (up to 200mph) of 500lb SCI tanks were all satisfactory.

Vengeance IV FD243 in May 1944 had significant improvements. Readily apparent is the lengthened exhaust pipe, with a single 0.5in gun for the rear cockpit; it has some form of muzzle fitting. There are ports for six wing guns and a grill to the rear of the engine. Not so easily seen is the positive incidence of the wing to the fuselage; the wing chord has also been increased. *A&AEE 11774*

A unique but totally ineffective flame damping exhaust on Vengeance IV FD243 in June 1944. *A&AEE 11820*

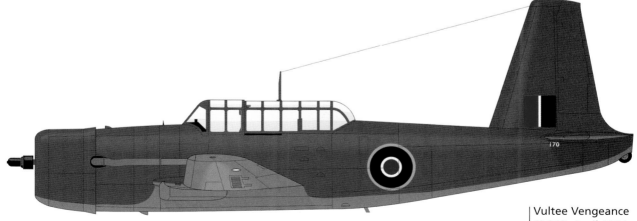

Vultee Vengeance FD243, April 1944, for bombing trials. (Scale 1:72)

161

Marauder

The standard USAAF Martin B-26 was supplied under Lend-Lease as the Marauder. A&AEE testing was minimal, even though more than 500 were supplied to the RAF and Commonwealth air forces.

Marauder Mark I

FK111, the first to arrive in September 1942, was weighed at 31,421lb, including 609 gallons of fuel and 2,400lb of bombs. Navigation facilities were spoiled by a poor American (B17 type) compass, and CO gases entered the crew area. Performance and handling trials were cancelled before completion, but not before the remarkably high stalling speeds of 120mph (clean) and 110mph (flaps and undercarriage down) had been recorded at 30,500lb. The resulting high approach and threshold speeds were aggravated by the need to keep some power on until rounded out. FK124, following

in November 1942, had two bomb cells; accessibility to the rear cell was unacceptable, and no fewer than twenty-seven modifications were considered necessary.

Marauder Mark II

With a 7-foot increase in wing span and thus lower wing loading and landing speeds, FB482 appeared in November 1943; surprisingly it was used only for armament trials. Bombing arrangements were considerably improved over the Mk I and required little testing; gunnery demanded more comprehensive attention. There were originally no fewer than twelve 0.5in guns; ground trials revealed serious shortcomings in the hand-held and nose-fixed guns, which were removed for air tests. The upper Martin 250 CE4 turret was satisfactory with minor changes, while the open beam hatches made the gunners excessively cold; heated clothing was recommended. Firing the four guns in the fuselage blisters caused the pilot's sight to

Marauder II FB482 in March 1944 carries a smoke bomb with parachute stowed at the rear. The free and single fixed 0.5in guns gave formidable firepower and a great deal of vibration; the rear guns can be seen in the Bell Sunstrand M-6 turret. Not visible is the upper turret, and the hand-held beam guns; the latter used the rectangular apertures just forward of the roundel. *A&AEE 11699*

Martin Marauder 41-35520/FB482, November 1943, for armament trials.

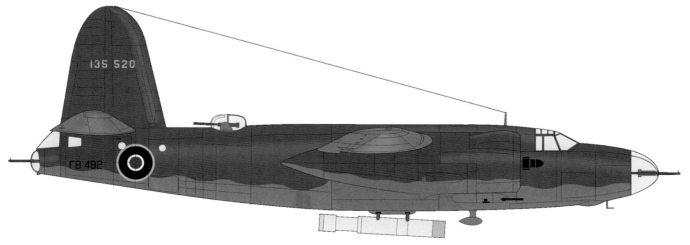

vibrate; however, acceptable accuracy was achieved using the auxiliary ring and bead. Firing from the Bell Sunstrand M-6 tail turret was inaccurate due to flimsy mounting of the sight.

Marauder Mark III

With weight increased to 38,070lb (853 gallons of fuel and 4,000lb of bombs), HD412 from June 1944 was found to be pleasant to handle, except for forward CG when the stick force per g was significantly higher than the recently introduced requirement of 10-30lb per g. At lower weight (30,500lb – similar to the Mk I) the stall occurred without warning at 128mph (clean) and with some buffet at 98mph (flaps and undercarriage down); the latter speed represented the benefit of the larger wing in the later machines of this type. The take-off safety speed was determined as 150mph. The minor changes in the bombing arrangements were acceptable. HD402 was also flown briefly.

Marauder III HD402 with a Glen Martin 250 CE4 upper turret. The pressure head has been moved from the wing tip on the Mk II to a position under the nose following an increase of 3½° wing dihedral. *A&AEE 11991*

Buckingham

The role of the Bristol Buckingham was unclear by the time it reached Boscombe; however, trials of the type as a light bomber were made.

Buckingham I DX249 in October 1943, with fins and rudders altered by the firm (Bristol) following its own trials prior to delivery to Boscombe. The Savoia-style bomb aimer's position is behind the bomb doors. The engine exhaust arrangements were changed in production. *A&AEE 11584*

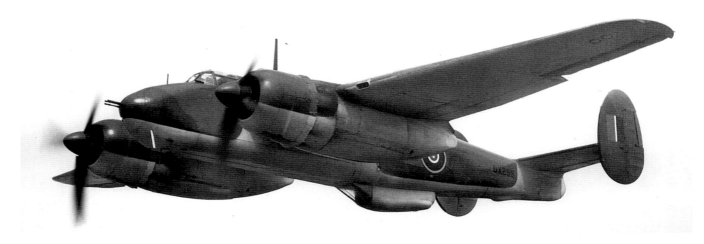

Buckingham DX255 in July 1944, with nose guns and leading edge de-icing boots just visible outboard of the oil cooling intake. Flight Lieutenant A. D. (Fred) Miller has a bead foresight, and a direct vision panel (closed). *A&AEE recognition*

The prototype, DX249, arrived in October 1943 without blind flying equipment and powered by two Centaurus IV motors. Although possessing many good features, notably the maintenance arrangement, the poor longitudinal and directional stability made the aircraft unpleasant and tiring to fly, particularly at aft CGs. Directional wander was a feature at low speed. The Bristol B12 Mk I upper turret had been hand-made by Daimler, but firing 24,500 rounds from the four 0.303in guns revealed many problems. February 1944 saw DX255 at Boscombe with Dunlop de-icing boots and nose guns. The Centaurus IV were too hot in the cruise – opening the cooling gills reduced speed by 10mph (true). Armament testing in KV303 from April 1944 proceeded smoothly for bombing; however, the flare chute required a complete redesign. The fixed nose guns (known as the Bristol Type 14 turret with four 0.303in) and the Bristol B13 (two 0.303in) under turret revealed so many faults as to make the installation unacceptable for service. From April 1944

KV304, KV306 and KV310 flew intensively until the aircraft were grounded before the normal 150 hours had been achieved. KV304 crashed on landing in June 1944 when the pilot lost control, having hit his head on the roof due to the aircraft striking a pothole; he had needed to loosen his harness to operate the undercarriage controls. To this design defect were added a long list of unserviceabilities, including repeated failure of the air intake. Before the bomber version of the Buckingham was abandoned, KV324 made creditable performance measurements (see the Table); range with 1,066 gallons of fuel and 4,000lb of bombs was calculated as 2,210 miles, and 3,105 miles with extra fuel in place of bombs. KV324 incorporated an increase in fin and rudder areas of 25%, plus enlarged tailplane and small-chord elevator with large balance. As a result the aircraft was longitudinally stable at all CG and speeds (clean), and directionally just acceptable at overload (38,920lb). KV322 flew to Boscombe in March 1945 with a dorsal fin, but unserviceability prevented wartime trials.

Buckingham I KV303 in June 1944 shows the folding door arrangement that allowed good ground loading and presented no problems in the air. The four nose-mounted 0.303in guns were, however, unacceptable due to stoppages and recoil damage. *A&AEE 11807*

Buckingham I KV337 in about March 1945, with armament removed in the passenger-carrying configuration. The large 'bath' under the fuselage is, however, retained, as is the pilot's bead foresight. The offset nose-mounted pressure head is standard on all Buckinghams. Details of the undercarriage with trailing arm suspension can be seen. *A&AEE 15237*

Armament was removed and four passenger seats fitted to KV358, a C Mk I, on arrival in January 1945. Transport Command crews flew it intensively for 104 hours, but no replacement propeller was available and flying stopped. KV337, also a C Mk I, concentrated on engine cooling both with then without a spinner; trials on this aeroplane were also curtailed as the port engine was consistently too hot.

Invader

The seventh in the wartime series of American twin-engined light bombers for the RAF was the Douglas A26 Invader. Prior to the delivery of British aircraft, the 9th US Air Force loaned an A-26B, No 41-39158, to Boscombe for five weeks from mid-July 1944, and 35 hours were flown.

The aircraft was found easy and pleasant to fly up to 35,000lb, but the rudder and elevator were heavy; indeed, at forward CG the stick force per g was 102lb (the requirement being less than 50lb). Asymmetric flying, with one of its Double Wasps (R-2800-27) windmilling, was particularly easy. The number of obstructions in the canopy frame were, however, criticised. The airspeed indicator under-read by 13mph at 320mph, and the maximum speed (348mph true at 16,000 feet) was slightly greater than the Buckingham. Among other features finding favour was the ease of maintenance of the engines attributed to the quick release cowlings. Less impressive were the restricted view of the sight for the remotely controlled pair of barbettes, each with two 0.5in guns, and the difficulty of keeping the eye on the sight in rough weather.

Invader 139158 is an early A-26B in July 1944 on loan from the USAAF. Note the heavy battery of nose-mounted guns. *A&AEE 11858*

Interest in KL690 from December 1944 centred on armament; the changes to the sighting arrangements made little improvement, and the ammunition feed to the lower barbettes was poor. Loading, carrying and dropping the wide range of bombs up to 1,000lb produced no surprises, but trials were limited to two bombs per flight, although the aircraft could carry more. Trials on KL691 were under way from July 1945.

In April 1945 A-26C Invader 322479 KL690 was the first of an order for 140 for the RAF as Invader I. The external differences are few: the perspex nose of KL690 is just visible, and its bomb doors are open. Internal changes to the remote sighting and control of the two gun barbettes afforded little improvement in KL690; the top of the sight appears to protrude above the gunner's window. *A&AEE 15069*

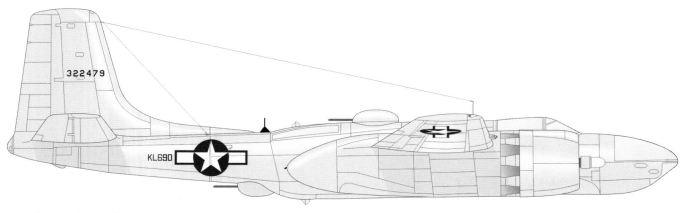

Douglas Invader 43-22479/KL690, December 1944, for armament trials.

Brigand

The first Bristol Brigand, MX991 (two Centaurus VIIs), flew to Boscombe in June 1945 and was one of the first RAF aircraft to have its airspeed indicators calibrated in knots. Early trials up to 38,060lb demonstrated good handling but with little tendency to return to trimmed conditions after displacement. Dives up to 347 knots (400mph) were satisfactory, and the stall occurred at 72 knots (83mph – flaps and undercarriage down). Airbrakes (fitted for the original torpedo role) were not tested.

Brigand I MX991 in July 1945, carrying a dummy torpedo. Its family resemblance to the Buckingham is striking although the Brigand is somewhat larger and heavier. The pitot head is under the port wing, and the static sources on the fuselage roundel. The bulge inboard of the wing roundel covers the airbrake operating mechanism. *A&AEE recognition 264*

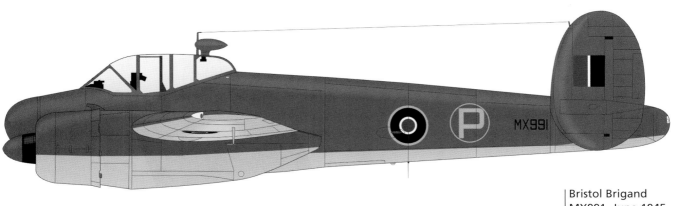

Bristol Brigand MX991, June 1945, for handling trials. (Scale 1:72)

7 Single-seat Fighters

Hurricane to Hornet

Hurricane

Already well established in Fighter Command pre-war, developments of the Hawker Hurricane were concentrated on armament in addition to increased engine power. One of the first reports to be issued after the move to Boscombe Down was the main tome of the type written on pre-war trials of L1547, L1574, L1695 and L1696 (all Merlin II); the first three had flown from Martlesham Heath with L1750 (two 20mm guns). L1547 continued on propeller, heated pitot head and radio trials when the TR9D proved superior to the earlier TR9B; it suffered a heavy landing in March 1940. L1574 and L1695 remained some months on armament work, the latter continuing at Farnborough from the end of 1939. Arriving in November 1939, L2026 had a Rotol constant-speed propeller on its new Merlin III, together adding 700lb in weight. For performance see the Table. Take-off runs of 280 yards were similar to the two-pitch version. The report comments on a novel characteristic: at 220mph, level and in trim, throttling back the engine caused a sharp pitch up with the nose nearly vertical after 8 seconds. This extreme instability appears not to have been further investigated.

Reverting to the two-pitch de Havilland

Hurricane I L1750 in late 1939, with the first cannon (ie 20mm guns) by Hispano Suiza, showing the recoil spring protruding from the fairing and the louvred recoil reducer in front. Firing trials were promising but suffered several difficulties, including lack of a local air-firing area. Aircraft handling remained unchanged, although firing one gun induced slight yaw; performance suffered only marginally. *A&AEE 9597*

Hurricane I V7360 in July 1940, during very brief trials at the A&AEE of the first fitting of four 20mm guns; the aircraft soon passed to an operational squadron. Among limitations was the short firing time resulting from the single ammunition drum to each gun. Both wings appear to have white (or light grey) undersides, and bands where the outer parts join the fuselage stubs. In the hangar roof (First World War vintage) can be seen intricate latticework. *A&AEE AC854 –original number not known*

propeller, the first Canadian-built Hurricane, P5170, started trials in July 1940. The propeller and 15½ gallons of extra fuel added 221lb to the weight and, together with a bullet-proof outer windscreen, reduced top speed by 10mph compared with L1547. In the same month P3811 arrived with twelve 0.303in guns in its metal-covered wings; handling was unaffected but excessive cooling of the gun bays occurred at altitude. The second Hispano 20mm gun installation was in V7360. The problems of ammunition feed and heating continued with these guns in the Mk II aircraft.

Bombs under each wing were tried on P2989 in early 1941; the tendency to fly right wing low could just be held at speeds up to 390mph. Later L1780 joined in November 1941 for early rocket trials in a joint RAE/A&AEE project; first firing was on 2 November 1941, and 174 rockets had been fired by mid-December.

Hurricane I L1780 (later L1780/G), in an appropriately photo dated 5 November 1941, is fitted with the first British UPs (unrotated projectiles – later RP, rocket projectiles). The original twin projectors (as the rails were called) for each rocket, the supporting framework and the mounting plate are clearly seen. Note the protective metal covering for the landing lamps and absence of normal gun armament. The pristine state of the installation suggests that the photograph was taken before the first firing from this aircraft. *A&AEE*

A new engine, the Merlin 45, was flown in P3157 from December 1940; performance (see the Table) was encouraging, but the radiator ran too hot in level flight. Handling was unchanged and the guns far too cold. A year later a similar engine in V6786 had an experimental single-lever control (the propeller and mixture levers were deleted) in the interests of reducing distractions during combat. It was initially found to give good handling results, but minor adjustments, even with the benefit of expert advice, resulted in deterioration of fuel economy to such an extent as to be reported as 'unairworthy'. The High Altitude Flight used V7709 late in 1940 to clear for operations the continuous use late in the climb of maximum (3,000) rpm; up to 3,000 feet extra altitude could be obtained. T9526, a Canadian-built machine, appears briefly in the weekly returns for performance work, and BW841/G (in the report a Sea Hurricane I) from November 1942 proved that ejected 0.303in gun cartridges did not foul the rockets under the wings. The 'slip-wing' Hurricane (with the Canadian number 321 –previously L1884) arrived at Boscombe in September 1943.

Flight Lieutenant A. D. (Fred) Miller had no trouble with a second wing on Hurricane 321 in November 1943. Previously this machine had been Mk I L1884, but was shipped to Canada in March 1939, presumably in connection with the Hurricane production programme there, returning with its new identity in 1940. *A&AEE recognition 191*

Hurricane I 321 in December 1943 is fitted with the upper wing designed to allow take-off at a high all-up weight. However, this trial installation was limited to a low weight (7,800lb) and the trial was abandoned when other Hurricanes with external stores achieved the loads projected. *A&AEE 11629*

Hurricane Mark II

The first four machines of this Mark (with Merlin XXs) to reach Boscombe went to the HAF between November 1940 and January 1941; they were Z2346, Z2398, Z2415 and Z2416.

Z2398 disappeared with its pilot on a high-altitude flight in February 1941, and Z2416 force-landed in a field the following month; replacements were Z2449 and Z2515, with Z3157 joining as a fifth aircraft in April 1941. Using the HAF Hurricanes, much of 1941 was devoted to investigating fuel vapour locking, thought to be the cause of the fatal crash as the fuel boiled and vapour starved the engine. Electric immersion heaters were used to heat the fuel before take-off, but without repeatable results; friction losses in the fuel system were held to blame. Z2885 incorporated a simplified fuel system late in 1941, and a slight improvement was reported; a modified SU carburettor designed for use above 26,000 feet also helped. The HAF also made climbs to 36,000 feet with a new make of magneto, but with little advantage. Meanwhile, after an alarming experience in Z2346 when continuous rolling with the ailerons frozen fully right-wing-down occurred, additional urgency was devoted to finding an antifreeze grease; early in 1942 a concoction by Rumbolt gave good results. Other trials included modified heating to the windscreen and cockpit.

Three Hurricane IIs in February/March 1942. All three have Merlin XX motors with three-bladed propellers.

Z2905 alone has four 20mm guns and two 90-gallon fuel tanks. *A&AEE 9883*

Z3451 lacks the Sky fuselage band but has two small bomb containers. Exhausts on Z2905 and Z3451 are similar, while BN114 has fish-tails. Z3451 is marked '100 OCT' to remind refuellers, and Z2905 is inscribed 'MI Connell's Squadron 34'. *A&AEE 9955*

BN114 carries two 500lb bombs. *A&AEE 9913*

During an uncontrolled landing a Whitley destroyed Z2905 on 8 June 1942 after only a few but busy weeks at the A&AEE, starting with trials of two 44-gallon drop tanks, then two larger (90-gallon) tanks. The latter gave a total capacity of 274 gallons and an all-up weight of 9,130lb. Even the smaller tanks enabled a 5hr 45min endurance flight to be flown, and the larger tanks gave a maximum range of 1,500 miles provided the tanks were jettisoned when empty. Handling after take-off (taking a run of 348 yards from a concrete runway) was unpleasant due to instability, and the pilot was unable to see the tanks.

Contemporary trials on V7480 with a triple ejector exhaust and an air cleaner in its tropical conversion gave only a 600-mile range (with reserves) on internal fuel (94 gallons). It was calculated initially that radiator cooling would need to be increased for tropical conditions; however, some months later the standard temperatures used in the calculations were changed and V7480 passed without modification. The aircraft was severely damaged by enemy bombs in April 1941.

Performance of the Mk II was not measured until a fully definitive aircraft with strengthened fuselage was available. Z3564, with twelve

Triple ejector exhausts on Hurricane V7480 in mid-1941 affected neither top speed nor night visibility. *A&AEE 9760*

Hurricane II Z2326 in December 1941, with the first 40mm guns; apart from inadequate heating, the installation received fulsome praise as 'very commendable'. There were no stoppages in these Vickers guns, even when pulling 4g. The clean fitting, and the ports of the two 0.303in guns, together with the small opening for the G45 camera (starboard wing), are seen. *A&AEE 9800*

0.303in guns (known as a Mk IIB), arrived in June 1941, flew with and without drop tanks and was compared (see the Table) with Z3888 (a Mk IIC with four 20mm guns). The former was longitudinally unstable, particularly with the external tanks, when it was judged unacceptable; it also vibrated 'painfully' between 380 and 410mph. Z3888 was less unstable in the climb, stalling speeds had increased to 90mph (clean) and 72mph (undercarriage and flaps down), and the spin remained docile and predictable. Uncovering the 20mm guns cost 5mph in top speed. The Mk IID with two 40mm and two 0.303in guns produced a comparable performance in Z2326 (see the Table) in January 1942. For well over a year this aircraft had undertaken a lot of work (together with Z2461 and Z2885) to improve the ammunition feed of the 20mm armament. Replacing the Vickers with Rolls Royce-designed 40mm guns reduced top speed by 20mph. Work continued in 1942 on Z3888 to clear the 20mm installation combined with two 250lb and later two 500lb bombs, thus making the colloquial 'Hurri-bomber'. Throughout these guns trials, lack of gun heating remained a problem, initially exacerbated by metal-covered wings without lagging. Investigation revealed that condensation on the metal fell into the guns, froze and jammed them. Various palliatives were tried, and even in the Mk IID the hot air supply did not meet requirements – but as the Establishment remarked, tank-busting, for which the 40mm installation was designed, was a low-level exercise. Mk II versions of the 20mm guns on modified mountings were improvements in KX862 during mid-1943.

Full trials of various types of 250lb bombs, bomblet containers and smoke installations occupied Z3451 from May 1941, including carriage up to 400mph and release to 300mph; the drag of the small bomb containers led to slight engine overheating at low level and a decrease of 40mph in top speed. Similar trials on Z4993/G stopped when it crashed fatally in October 1942. Stores of up to 500lb were flown on BN114; landings with only one bomb were possible, but not recommended for Service use. Further hitting power came from a battery of four rocket projectiles under each wing; the first were on Z2320/G from September 1942 following calculation of the datum for mounting the rails, and for sighting. Z3092/G joined in November with a Mk II RP installation; Z2457/G was also involved a little earlier.

BE173, of the HAF, investigating engine cutting under negative g, gained no benefit when all tanks were selected on. Further investigation was prevented when the aircraft was written off in May 1943, after only a month's flying. A faulty fuel gauge was blamed. Flame damping was measured on a few Hurricanes with mixed results; shrouds over the exhausts of Z3353 in the autumn of 1942 provided some improvement but did not prevent detection by infra-red sensors. The final trials on the Mk II, of which details have been found, followed complaints from the RAF of overheating of the engines; from April 1943 KZ232 demonstrated that the larger, tropical cooling air intake was effective.

This is a close-up view of the hot air muff fitted to the exhausts of Hurricane II Z2346 of the High Altitude Flight in the spring of 1941. Hot air was ducted to the gap between a special extra windscreen fitted in front of the standard bullet-proof type in order to prevent misting. The system worked, the only problem found being rainwater seeping into the pipe on the ground. *A&AEE 9715*

Hurricane Z3092/G with a Mk II RP installation in November 1942. The white line is a typical marking worn by aircraft carrying out rocket trials and was intended to assist accurate determination of attitude during fight. The projectiles seen here consist of two 3-inch rocket motors bolted together and propelling a 250lb GP bomb. Only two were made – both by the A&AEE.

Hawker Hurricane Z3092/G, January 1943, for rocket projectile trials. (Scale 1:72)

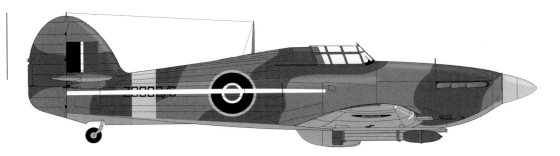

Other aircraft spent varying periods at the A&AEE, often brief and often on general duties unconnected with type trials, and there were several accidents: Z2419 (from October 1941), Z2691 (negative g carburettor November 1941), Z2749 (oil tests with the HAF – force-landed in April 1941), and LD264 (alleged a 'rogue' in July 1943), all with the Performance Squadron. For general armament work appeared KX858 (April 1943 – undercarriage jammed up in October 1943), and for gunnery LD438 (August 1943 – landed wheels-up in June 1944), LD439 (August 1943) and LE525 (November 1943). In addition, the Gun Proofing Flight had BN526 (from January 1942), BN571 (damaged by guns of the Royal Navy in February 1944, then by its own rocket four months later) and BN965 (minor crash in May 1942 just after arrival), HW182/G and HW187/G from October 1942 and KX175 a year later; KX176 flew from August 1944. KX175 had an undercarriage failure in January 1944, then on 24 August 1944 HW 187 and KX 176 collided on return from the range; one pilot was killed.

Hurricane Mark IV

Extensive armour plating, including the engine, radio and oil tank, gave BP173/G (Merlin XX), a Mk IV, a 10% increase in empty weight in April 1942. At 8,480lb for take-off, handling up to 350mph was normal with eight 60lb head rockets, but maximum speed at 12,000 feet was only 261mph (true); 75% of the extra drag came from the rocket rails. Internal fuel gave a radius of 235 miles (with rockets fired on turning); firing trials were satisfactory. In an attempt to improve range, KZ679 (from July 1943) had four rockets under the starboard wing and a 90-gallon tank under the port. It was deemed safe to fly, but very careful landing was needed with all the rockets remaining and an empty tank. With the so-called 'low attack' wings capable of accepting any of the guns, rockets and fuel tanks previously flown, HW747 arrived in December 1942. Certain combinations of stores gave an extremely aft CG leading to unacceptable handling due to severe longitudinal instability and insufficient elevator trim range. Late in 1943 aerobatics in all marks of Hurricane when carrying rockets were approved on KZ381. Other Mk IVs were KZ189 (rocket armament development from June 1944), KZ379 (for Porton from May 1945), LE756 (for the armament demonstration in July 1945) and LB743 (from January 1945 for rocket armament work).

Hurricane Mark V

KZ193 appeared in November 1943 powered by a Merlin 27 driving a four-bladed propeller. Weighing 8,710lb at take-off, handling was worse than the Mk IV with aft CG; additionally there was a large change of directional trim with power, for which the very large radiator and propeller were held to be responsible. With a three-bladed propeller, handling was acceptable and performance (see the Table) was completed with both types; armament was two 40mm guns.

Hurricane Mark X

Three Canadian-built Hurricanes with Packard-built Merlin 28 engines were used by the Establishment; BW963, JS220 and JS244 came in June 1942 for intensive flying and investigation of consumption characteristics of their Stromberg carburettors. The first two suffered engine failures, but the third aircraft completed 164 hours in the air, in spite of considerable inverted flying. An interesting feature, and contrary to normal experience, was that fuel consumption was lower at low altitude than at height for the same engine conditions; the automatic mixture control worked well.

Hurricane V KZ193 in November 1943. The four-bladed propeller, 40mm gun, large air intake with ice guard and very large radiator cowling under the fuselage are noticeable features. *A&AEE 11621*

Spitfire

Supermarine's Spitfire was established in RAF service before the war, and developments were already under way to realise the type's potential. As modifications were made and performance, handling or armament enhanced, so the Establishment assessed the innovations. A total of 156 Spitfires were flown, including aircraft used by the High Altitude Flight and for target duties. Tests of new features were frequently made on existing versions: for Service use the new version led to a new mark number. Here, the tests are described in the section corresponding to the Establishment's contemporary allocation, ie the part number of the A&AEE report.

Spitfire Mark I

Two Spitfires flew from Martlesham Heath in September 1939, but both soon departed as K9793 (Merlin II) had completed its trials, and L1007 (Merlin III) was unable to test its 20mm gun armament due in part to the lack of a suitable air-firing range. From November 1939 N3171 (Merlin III) with a Rotol constant-speed propeller, domed canopy and bullet-proof windscreen demonstrated an improved climb performance (see the Table) and take-off run of 225 yards (K9793 took 320 yards). Handling was little changed, with the stall (clean) occurring at 78mph, and with flaps and wheels down at 66mph. With the Type B wing (two

20mm and four 0.303in), R6770 and X4257 had handling and performance similar to the eight-gun version when flown from late 1940; initially the 20mm cannons jammed during tight turns, but simple modifications were effective and the installation approved. With the original eight 0.303in guns, X4782 of the High Altitude Flight undertook armament tests early in 1941 followed by work on new camouflage paint. Two particularly interesting modifications to Mk I aircraft involved P9565 and X4268 (crashed in October 1941, three weeks after arrival). X4268 had strengthened flaps, operated by compressed air, capable of extension up to 400mph. Deceleration was twice the normal, but trim change was fierce and unacceptable at high altitude. The aircraft's automatic radiator shutter kept coolant temperature too low. X4610 spent some time at Boscombe from June 1941, and X4266 was used for comparative handling with a Mk V in mid-1942.

Spitfire Mark II

P7280 was the first Nuffield-built Spitfire and had slightly more power (Merlin XII) and more armour (6,172lb all-up weight) than the earlier version. Designated Mk II, P7280 arrived in June 1940; handling was unchanged but was slightly faster up to 17,000 feet. Accidents in service due to overstressing the wings led to inertia weights in the elevator control to increase stick forces: a 3½lb weight was found ideal in the Mk II. The 'blister' hood considerably improved the view. For more than a year from late 1940 P7661 investigated the effects of fitting several types of propeller, including a four-bladed wooden Rotol version; top speed was reduced by 6mph, but ceiling was improved by up to 1,000 feet. Using maximum engine speed (3,000rpm) reduced the ceiling marginally compared with using 2,850rpm; the propeller tips lost efficiency at the higher revolutions. Reducing blades to three and

Spitfire I P9565 in October 1940 has a 30-gallon fuel tank on the left wing, weighing 440lb full; maximum weight (total 114 gallons) was 6,400lb. Take-off with plenty of right stick was easy, but as speed increased so it became progressively more difficult to hold the left wing up; above 350mph it was not possible. This asymmetric configuration was not recommended, but at least one squadron used it. *A&AEE 9654*

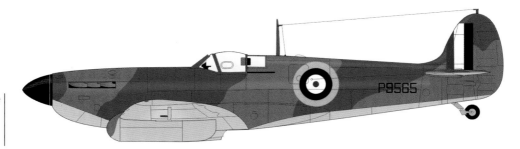

Supermarine Spitfire P9565, September 1940, for handling trials. (Scale 1:72)

the diameter from 11 feet to 10ft 3in further reduced ceiling and rate of climb.

Six Spitfire IIs arrived between February and August 1941. The HAF received P8021 (Merlin 47 fitted in August for contrail and camouflage work), P8273 (crashed fatally during unauthorised low-level aerobatics) and its replacement, P7301. The Armament Flight flew K9830 (eight 0.303in guns) and P8134 (two 20mm and four 0.303in guns); the former had hot air drawn from around the exhaust stubs, thus keeping the guns significantly warmer. P8036 had the single external wing tank, but new metal ailerons; performance (see the Table) was commensurate with weight, and handling was unaffected by the metal ailerons. Two reverse-pitch propellers showed promise in 1943. On P7884, the de Havilland model was adjusted to give very effective braking action in the air without a large trim change, while P8194's propeller was effective in reducing the landing run from 465 yards to 270. Both required further development. P8704 appeared in 1942 for armament trials.

Spitfire Mark III

The original 'Super' Spitfire became the Mk III; only two were converted and both reached the A&AEE. First was N3297. W3237 from June 1941 had a wing built to accept various combinations of guns (the 'universal' wing); four 20mm guns, then two 20mm plus four 0.303in guns were tried. Success was achieved with a few A&AEE-instigated modifications.

Spitfire Mark V

Increased power from the Merlin 45, 46 or 47 and other improvements characterised the Mk V – the most numerous version to be built. No fewer than thirty-nine appeared on the strength of the Establishment. First was K9788 (converted from a Mk I) in December 1940; performance (see the Table) was good, but freezing of the oil in the control unit led to overspeeding of the propeller and damage to the engine. N3053 soon followed with a slightly modified engine, produced an identical top speed, a lower rate of climb, but an increased ceiling of 39,300 feet. An improvement in climb and ceiling (to 40,500 feet) followed replacement of the three-bladed with a four-bladed propeller. Two armed and representative production aircraft, X4922 with eight 0.303in guns and W3134 with two 20mm and four 0.303in guns (known as Mk VA and VB respectively), flew in the spring of 1941. The weight of the VB was greater but performance

Spitfire III N3297 in October 1941, with normal wing tips for comparison with the earlier wings of reduced span. Other changes are the four-bladed Rotol propeller, fish-tail exhausts, raised cockpit cover and absence of an anti-fouling frame on the fin. Two inspection panels have been removed from the rear fuselage. *A&AEE 9805*

Spitfire III N3297 in July 1940, when interest centred on the radiator cooling of the new Merlin XX; the engine ran too hot in level flight. Features visible are the absence of armament, the wings clipped by 7 feet overall, the three-bladed propeller, the retractable tail wheel, the extra main undercarriage doors and the anti-fouling frame at the top of the fin. *A&AEE 9647*

(see the Table) similar. The latter machine tried an inertia weight in the elevator control to reduce the effect of tightening in turns produced by a rearward shift in the basic CG. A short trial in Mk VB R7337 revealed that the port 20mm gun received insufficient heating from air drawn through an exhaust muff. Later, similar shortcomings were found on the Mk VC (four 20mm guns) in AA873, but in mid-1942 some improvement resulted in Mk VB AA875 from blanking the wing air outlets. At the end of 1942 Mk VC BR351 had redesigned hot air arrangements within the wing, which kept the guns warm and the ammunition cool.

Hot weather in the summer of 1941 was suspected of causing loss of performance in P8781 of 66 Squadron due to fuel boiling at altitude. The Establishment could not reproduce the problem, even when using heated fuel in W3134. In September W3228 had pressurised

fuel tanks; even with hot fuel the Merlin 45 performed faultlessly at all altitudes, whether the pressurisation was on or off. The engine of W3322 had a Rolls Royce diaphragm carburettor to ensure smooth running when inverted; however, inversions were limited to 5 seconds by the oil pressure dropping. Later, the aircraft had a so-called balloon hood, and the view was thus further improved. With an SU injector in its Merlin 46, W3322 had good engine response; above 30,000 feet the SU unit proved very economical, and gave a slightly higher top speed than the AVT40 carburettor. However, it was considered that a fuel pump would be needed for tropical use. Finally, in 1944, W3322 flew from Hooton Park on a research project on the solubility of air in fuel; the results indicated a far greater solubility than theory suggested.

Spitfire V X4922, initially a pure A version with eight 0.303in guns, but now with a tropical intake for its Merlin 46 and a wooden mock-up 90-gallon ventral tank when seen here in December 1941. The tank cost 7mph (true) in top speed and 3,500 feet in ceiling. Note the 'H&H' inscription. *A&AEE 9848*

A striking pose by Spitfire V AB-320 behind the Hampden in March 1942. The tropical air intake, 90-gallon ventral tank, radiator (starboard wing) and oil cooler (port wing) are well shown. *A&AEE recognition 82*

With Malta and the desert in mind, the Air Staff required longer range and tropical filters. In March 1941 X4922, a Mk VA, performed (see the Table) with a filter and with and without a dummy wooden 90-gallon 'slipper' tank. AB320, a Mk VB with the two modifications, was initially unserviceable, and replaced briefly by BP866 for engineering trials of the 90-gallon tank. When serviceable, AB320 completed performance (see the Table) and range measurement; provided the tank was jettisoned when empty, a practical figure of 1,060 miles at 20,000 feet was calculated (the theoretical maximum was 1,235 miles). At 7,485lb, the take-off run increased to 413 yards. A larger, 170-gallon slipper tank on BR202 in mid-1942 produced a disappointing maximum range of 1,450 miles. With a Merlin 46

in place of the earlier Merlin 45 and with a new fuel tank (29 gallons) behind the pilot, maximum range of 1,625 miles was slightly less than the optimum as altitude was restricted by handling difficulties above 15,000 feet. The Merlin 46 gave a significantly greater ceiling than the Merlin 45.

The earlier freezing of the de Havilland propeller control led to replacement by a Rotol design; the earlier problem was replaced by a deterioration in handling on recovery from dives. A 6½lb inertia weight alleviated the risk of overstress in BM559 in mid-1942. Later that year R7306 tested successfully modifications to the de Havilland propeller, while the following year EF731 (Merlin 55 M and clipped wings) measured a small reduction in performance on a Rotol propeller with an armoured leading edge.

Spitfire V BR202 in June 1942, with a 170-gallon ventral tank giving a total fuel capacity of 284 gallons. Early leakage was cured by the Establishment, and an absolute range of 1,624 miles calculated (after jettisoning the ventral tank). This configuration gave an extremely aft CG, making handling in the cruise very tricky. At 7,835lb it was the heaviest Spitfire to date, and took 580 yards to unstick. The prototype marking and 'intensifier' pipe from the exhausts are of interest. *A&AEE 11022*

Spitfire V AA873 has the 'universal' wing, here armed with four 20mm guns in January 1942. It lacks the armoured windscreen of X4922, and has a Sky tail band in addition to the inscription 'Manchester Air Cadet'. *A&AEE 9857*

The greatest firepower of the Mk V was in the version with four 20mm cannons (Mk VC, performance as in the Table); the cost was an extra 200lb in basic weight, and a further rearward shift in CG requiring a 7½lb inertia weight in tests on AA873. Later the similar AA878 demonstrated greatly improved performance up to 13,000 feet as a result of the maximum permitted boost being raised from 12½ to 15psi. This aircraft suffered a hydraulic failure and was damaged in October 1942 in a landing without undercarriage. Further performance measurements early in 1943 on AA937 with clipped wings were followed by significant increases at low altitude (see the Table) in W3228, resulting from its Merlin 50 with a cropped supercharger impeller and a permissible boost raised further to 18psi. Other engine modifications included, in 1943, continuing trials in P7661 (now regarded as a Mk VA with its Merlin 47) with a Bendix Stromberg injector proving slightly less economical than a carburettor, but giving a ceiling of 40,200 feet. The radiator temperatures of BR288 (with tropical intake) were too high for hot countries; with a modified, copper-baked QED radiator, AB167 was marginally better in mid-1943.

Attempts continued to find a satisfactory method of preventing overstressing. Late in 1942 AB186, with larger elevator balance horns but without the inertia weights, was better, but then the horns required to be made slightly smaller to reduce the tendency to overbalancing. An alternative option was a convex-section elevator, which was less satisfactory due to loss of feel. Heavy roll control at high speed led to the usual cable runs to the ailerons being replaced by push rods in AB191; up-float was reduced but control forces were judged to be unchanged.

Following air-brake trials on a Mk I, AB213, a Mk VB, arrived in April 1942 with strengthened split flaps powered by compressed air; 24 seconds were needed to reduce speed by 100mph (previously 70 seconds) from up to 400mph. In mid-1943 AB167 intensively flew the Merlin 45M, and BL304 had a curved windscreen giving an additional 2mph.

Other Mk Vs were with the High Altitude Flight and the Armament Squadron. The former used AB488 for eighteen months from February 1942; the basic performance was below standard, but permitted comparisons to be made when testing ignition and mixture at altitude, followed by propeller efficiency measurements. The Flight used EP496 for a short time in mid-1942. P8709 (from January 1942) and EE611 (April 1944) were long-serving hacks on armament work, while AA873 was used to evaluate the conversion sets to change armament in its 'universal' wings. Comparison of British and American-built 20mm guns was made on EP654 (from August 1942); both performed adequately. Modified 20mm guns (Hispano Mk II star), fitted to EF561 on new mountings, were satisfactory. MA855 ran out of fuel in March 1944 and was written off.

Spitfire V AA937 in November 1942 has its wings clipped – the cause of reduced rate of climb and ceiling, but a small increase in top speed. Aileron up-float was of interest with the clipped wings, and the starboard indicator plate can be seen. The code letters 'AF-O' of its previous owners (AFDU) are in evidence. *A&AEE recognition 117*

AD268, on an RAE high-speed trial, appeared at Boscombe briefly, as did BL987, with a hydraulically controlled Rotol propeller. Rogue aircraft are listed in Appendix 6.

Spitfire Mark VI

High-altitude German aircraft prompted development of the Mk VI with a high-altitude Merlin 47, greater wing area and cockpit pressurisation with 2psi differential. The two prototypes, R7120 and X4942, arrived in September 1941; the former had a long duct on the cowling, routeing the airpipe round the bulkhead, while the latter had a slightly larger wing span (40ft 5 in). Early criticisms included heating, frosting of the windows, and stiff operation of the trimmer. The standard fuel of 84 gallons was largely used in the 33-minute climb to 39,000 feet, and longitudinal stability was poor. Oil and coolant temperatures were satisfactory and the best ceiling of 40,000 feet was obtained using a four-bladed propeller and weak mixture. X4942 later had balance tabs and horn balances on the ailerons, giving lateral control equal to the best Spitfires; overbalance at low speed, however, needed attention.

In January 1942 AB200, in production form with two 20mm and four 0.303in guns, started tests of performance (see the Table) followed by handling to investigate violent recovery from dives. Using an aft CG, dives at increasing speeds required increasing force (using both hands above 410mph) in addition to full nose-down trim. Relaxing the push at 450 resulted in a violent pitch up, during which the pilot blacked out; the wings were found to have buckled. It was also discovered that the elevator trim tab was masked by ill-fitting tailplane shrouds; with new wings and smooth shrouds handling and spinning were normal, but still required care on recovery. In all, 322 hours of intensive flying on BR200 (crashed in April 1942 when the pilot became lost in bad weather), BR205 and BR287 revealed no major problem with the pressurisation or heating. Six months of flying on BR309 improved but did not completely cure the original tendency of the engine to cut out around 34,000 feet; it was found difficult to match fuel temperature and feed pressure with carburettor requirements over the range of operating conditions.

With a 'Lobelle' hood, the pressurised AB528 recovered the enhanced view already enjoyed by early versions. BR247 joined the HAF in April 1942 for extensive research flying.

Merlin 61 engine

This was the first Merlin with two stages of supercharging to preserve peak power to high altitude; N3297 reappeared as a hybrid with this engine in mid-1942, sporting two large radiators under the wings. The general condition of the airframe was poor, but did not prevent an outstanding top speed (see the Table). Consumption was higher than expected at high power, and oil cooling marginal; trials with propellers made of two materials and with two ratios of rpm reduction produced small differences.

Spitfire VI X4942 in September 1941. Features of this pressurised version visible are the extended wing tips, four-bladed Jablo (wooden) propeller and the intake, under the exhausts, for the Marshall cabin blower.

Spitfire Mark VII

AB450, with Merlin 61, cabin pressurisation and extended wings, started limited A&AEE trials in July 1942; even in medium supercharger, performance (see the Table) was good. More comprehensive trials were made on BS229 from February 1943; ailerons of reduced span coupled with the extended wing tips gave a 40% reduction in normal rate of roll. With standard-span wings, rate of roll was still 10% below normal – confirming that the tip extension was largely responsible for the earlier deterioration. Longitudinal stability was poor (attributed in part to an increased horn balance on the elevator), and a gentle rocking, particularly in the glide, led to a recommendation for a larger fin and rudder. The latter were incorporated in MD176 on arrival in May 1944, together with two small fuel tanks in the wings and a special Merlin 112. Performance (see the Table) was spectacular – but, as frequently approved for test flying, the Establishment was allowed to use the maximum power settings for longer than the usual time limit to obtain the figures.

Yet another trial was made on the use of flaps as airbrakes up to 470mph; results on BS229 were also spectacular – two sets of flaps failed and the nose-down change in trim was exciting. From May 1944 the HAF used MD114, MD124 and MD190 until the end of the war, the latter pair making daily meteorological climbs to record air temperatures.

Spitfire Mark VIII

In effect an unpressurised Mk VII, the Mk VIII had no separate performance or handling trials. Five experimental modifications were, however, featured on this version. In August 1943 JF299 was received with a cut-down rear fuselage and a single bubble hood – its benefits were spoiled by lack of a winding mechanism. JG204 (from July 1944) had a high-speed wing section (intended for later Spitfires) contoured to keep airflow laminar for a greater distance over the chord. Stalls occurred at 78mph (clean) and 70mph (undercarriage and flaps down), only slightly faster than previously, but now characterised by pre-stall aileron-snatch rather than buffet. Higher than desirable stick forces and trim shortcomings were expected to be cured by later alteration of the tailplane incidence. Contemporaries were JF707, without camber or toe-in on the undercarriage, giving satisfactory ground handling and reduced tyre wear, and LV674, with 'Pacitor' fuel gauges, which functioned well except in prolonged inverted flight. With four 20mm guns (two each of Mk II and Mk V Hispano), MD347 was eventually successful after A&AEE modifications.

Spitfire VII BS229 in March 1943. The pointed wings (of 40ft 5in span) and enlarged elevator horn balance are visible, and the reduced-span ailerons can just be discerned on the original print. The two-stage supercharged Merlin 61 gave this version an outstanding top speed.

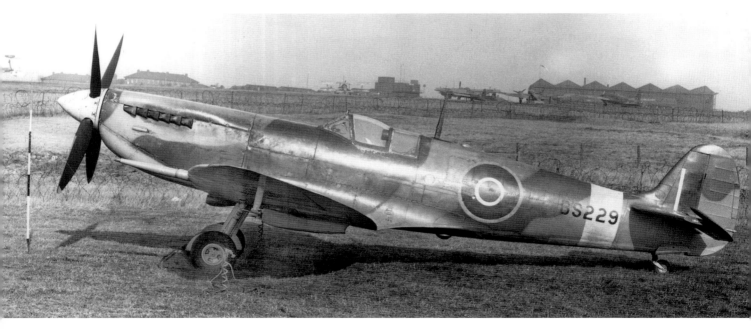

Spitfire JF299 in September 1943, regarded by the Establishment as a Mk VIII, featured a cut-down rear fuselage and a rounded windscreen. The Merlin 61 has an enlarged air intake mounted well forward.

Spitfire Mark IX

Fitting the Merlin 61 (with a four-bladed propeller) to the Mk V created the Mk IX, which appeared at Boscombe before the two preceding Marks. AB197, the first, arrived in May 1942, with Type B armament. All-up weight was 7,445lb (85 gallons of fuel); trials were initially limited to a maintenance appraisal. The following year hot air drawn from each radiator kept all guns almost warm enough, but the four 0.303in guns needed extra electric heaters. Changing to four 20mm cannons revealed further shortcomings of the heating; by mid-1944 both armament configurations had been made satisfactory. Performance (see the Table) on a standard aircraft, BF274 in mid-1942, was encouraging, using combat rating for extended periods. Cooling was assessed as acceptable for European and tropical use. With a suitably modified 170-gallon belly tank, maximum range was calculated as 1,370 miles. Prior to its fatal crash following engine failure on 23 December 1942, BS139 had completed spinning (without external fuel) trials, with attendant unpleasant pitching and buffeting, and an extended evaluation of the fuel system. This aeroplane was free of engine cutting in all conditions of flight, and also lacked the tightening

on recovery from dives, both features of earlier versions. A larger rudder on BS354 helped contain the swing to port on take-off, but otherwise made little difference to handling.

Early in 1943 BS354 (low-altitude Merlin RM 95M) was joined by BS543 (Merlin 66, also low-altitude) and BS551 (Merlin 70, high-altitude) for comparative performance (see the Table); at sea level BS543 was the fastest (336mph). Fighter Command, wishing for offensive action, modified BS428 to carry a bomb under the fuselage. Speed (see the Table) at low level was increased by a Merlin 66 with an SU Mk II injector carburettor; in MA648 late in 1943 this carburettor proved to be about 5% more economical than earlier types. Offensive capability, enhanced by two additional underwing bombs (250lb), was tested early in 1944 on MJ823. Handling was little affected, even when the 90-gallon fuselage tank replaced the centre bomb; at 8,675lb all-up weight, the stall was normal, but occurred at 87mph clean.

Spitfire IX BS428 in February 1943, with a 500lb bomb on a rack designed by Fighter Command, is seen here when a 402 Squadron machine. Handling was satisfactory up to 400mph, but top speed was reduced by 22 mph (true) and radius to only 225 miles The long nose and the inexperience of the pilots using the gunsight for bombing gave very inaccurate results. Modifications suggested by the Establishment improved only the rack.

For higher-level operations, EN524 (Merlin 70) had satisfactory cooling characteristics, but changing propellers and gear ratios gave no worthwhile improvement from standard. A contra-rotating propeller on AB505 (Merlin 77) in September 1943, coupled with enlarged fin and rudder, was found pleasant to fly, had no tendency to swing on take-off, and required no directional re-trimming with changes in speed and power. Reverting to the normal Rotol four-bladed propeller, JL165 had its Merlin 66 approved up to 25psi boost; low-level performance in early 1944 was outstanding (see the Table), but at the expense of a 30% increase in fuel consumption and marginally inadequate cooling. At the same time a five-bladed propeller was tried in BS310, but with no particular advantage, in spite of top speed remaining well below sonic speed at high altitude. BS310 was used to examine the effect of aircraft Mach number on dive recovery; pull-out could always be made as airspeed increased at lower altitude, but it was established that the maximum lift (C_L max) decreased with increasing Mach number.

Another handling trial early in 1943 involved EN314 (Merlin 61) with tailplane incidence increased by 2° and enlarged elevator horn balances. The push needed in dives was reduced to such an extent that no force at all was needed – the Establishment felt that this was undesirable, and suggested a compromise of 1½° increase in incidence. Also, the elevator hunted at low speed. EN314 was then used to examine the advantages of a Maclaren radiator protector. With a normal tailplane, but with CG further aft than normal on a Mk IX, BS310 initially required a satisfactory 25lb full force to achieve 4g, but as CG was extended aft undesirable characteristics developed; the handling limit was not established because it was found impossible to add further ballast in the rear fuselage.

Spitfire IX BF274 in September 1942 is ready for standard performance measurements of this Mark; results were encouraging. Seen here with a small belly tank, it later had one of 170 gallons, when range was calculated to be 1,370 miles (without reserve). *A&AEE 11100*

Spitfire IX MK210 in September 1944 is also the subject of the accompanying colour view. It is seen here fitted with Mustang drop tanks. The fittings under the tanks are probably to assist fuel feeding.

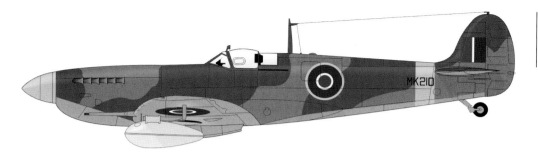

Supermarine Spitfire MK210, July 1944, for range trials. (Scale 1:72)

At 9,165lb all-up weight, MK210, in late 1944, had additional fuel tanks in the wings (16½ gallons each), two Mustang-type drop tanks (61 gallons each) and the tank behind the pilot (43 gallons), giving 283 gallons in total and weighing 2,151lb. In this configuration MK210 had previously been flown across the Atlantic; the Establishment experienced engine cutting when the rear fuselage tank was used. It is not known whether the Atlantic pilot had this problem, but it was found that the drop tanks caused a loss of 36mph in top speed.

A remarkable feature (unique in the writer's experience) of the Mk IX Spitfire was the complete lack of any pressure error throughout the speed range when tested on BS352. Four discreet trials were completed in 1945. American 4½-inch rocket projectiles on MH477 gave no adverse effects up to 450mph; firing trials may have followed. The Royal Navy designed a system of cooling gun barrels; trials on TA822 were successful and proved novel to the Establishment, which was usually concerned with raising gun bay temperatures. With the operational need to use drop tanks first, fuel in the rear fuselage was retained, causing a large rearward shift in CG. This configuration was tried in ML186 (Merlin 66) with metal elevators; instability made flying tiring and marginally acceptable for escort flying, but unacceptable for close formation or instrument flying.

Spitfire IX MH477 is carrying American bazooka-type rocket launchers in 1945, each capable of carrying a 4½-inch rocket. There were no adverse effects up to 450mph, although it is not certain that firing trials with the devices were carried out.

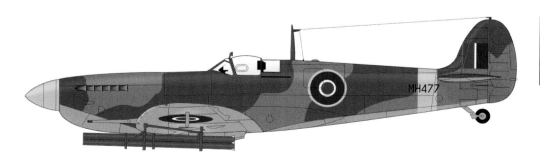

Supermarine Spitfire MH477, January 1945, for rocket projectile trials. (Scale 1:72)

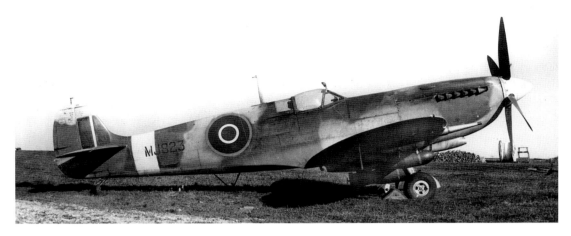

Spitfire IX MJ823 in September 1944, with two additional wing-mounted 250lb bombs. Handling and release up to 450mph posed no problems, although firing the guns armed the wing bombs; deflector plates were recommended. Jettison of all three bombs together was, however, unsatisfactory. This aircraft (Merlin 66) has a longer air intake when compared with BS428 (Merlin 61) and lacks the latter's small fairing immediately behind the spinner, but has a rear-view mirror. *A&AEE 11934*

Other Mk IXs were AB499 in early 1943, with unacceptable anti-glow shrouds over the exhausts, and BS118 with MK 197, each mounting two 20mm and two 0.5in guns requiring four essential modifications before Service use. One subsequent improvement, strengthened gun fairings, was satisfactory on SM205[1] at the end of 1944. In 1945 RR238 had three different types of stadiametric range controls, all of roughly equal merit. PT413 joined for armament work in July 1944. The HAF used BR600 and MA763 to replace earlier types, and EN397 was modified in 1945 to measure pressure errors in other aircraft.

Spitfire Mark XI

No Mark X was seen at the A&AEE, and brief trials on the photographic Mark XI, MB789 (Merlin 63), on loan at Benson, established a good top speed (see the Table) in August 1943. Six months later, PL758 was used to investigate over-cooling in the cruise. Each bank of cylinders had its own radiator and a simple modification of reducing the area of the air exit duct cured the problem.

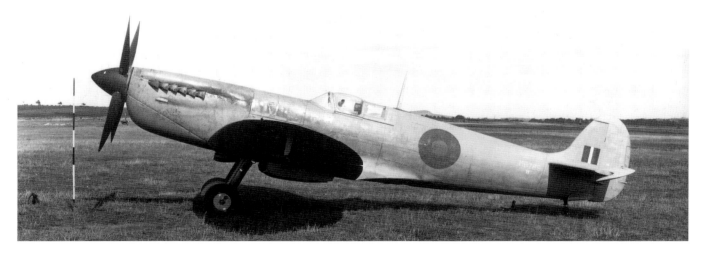

Spitfire Mk XI MB789, seen at Benson, shows little evidence of its photographic role in August 1943. It has a one-piece windscreen. The A&AEE's photographer took not only his camera but the ever-useful pole for scale. *A&AEE 11508*

[1] Given as Mk IX in report, but built as a Mk XVI.

Spitfire Mark XII

The first version of the Spitfire with the Griffon engine, the Mk XII, first appeared at Boscombe in the form of DP845 (Griffon 11B) in August 1942. In early 1943 it had a Griffon IV with reduced boost and a controllable swing on take-off (but was still felt to be excessive for aircraft carrier use); spinning with clipped wings produced the usual pitching and buffeting. In mid-1943 performance (see the Table) with the Griffon VI was further enhanced. Intensive flying of the Griffon was the aim of EN221 and

EN222. The engine proved free of serious difficulties after minor modifications to the radiator shutters, but, as may have been expected, it lost oil pressure under negative g; otherwise the system was satisfactory in MB878 in late 1943. More surprising was the small aerodynamic benefit of a fairing on the Mk III bomb rack; the installation cost 22mph in top speed. No 91 Squadron complained of very heavy aileron control in EN624 in July 1943, but only minor rectification was needed.

Spitfire XII DP845, the first with a Griffon engine, is seen here with the Griffon IIB in September 1942. The current pointed rudder of increased area is fitted, but proved too heavy and lacked authority on take-off. The propeller rotated in the opposite sense to that of the Merlin. Standard fuel remained 84 gallons, and range a mere 425 miles; other performance was good, and was improved with later versions of the engine. *A&AEE 11115*

Spitfire XII EN221 in December 1942, following repairs to minor damage caused by hitting an airfield light pole the previous month. Assessment of the cooling (Griffon III) during intensive flying resulted in minor modifications to the radiator shutter, seen open here. *A&AEE recognition 122*

Spitfire XIII L1004 in March 1943, intended for low-level work. All-up weight with 84 gallons was only 6,355lb, giving a stalling speed of 55mph (undercarriage and flaps down), the lowest recorded for a Spitfire. Handling with a large horn balance on the elevator was satisfactory, but performance mediocre. Note the armoured windscreen. *A&AEE 11330*

Spitfire Mark XIII

L1004 was the sole representative at the A&AEE, from February 1943, of this photographic version with a low-level Merlin 32.

Spitfire Mark XIV

Known initially as Mk VIII (conversion), the Mk XIV had a two-speed two-stage Griffon 65 (initially the RG 5SM) with a five-bladed propeller. Three 'conversions', JF317, JF318 and JF319, arrived over a period of four months from May 1943, and the first pair were intensively flown. After the crash of JF318, handling was completed satisfactorily at the aft-most CG on JF319. JF317's initial task indicated that the lateral and directional

behaviour was poor, with very large directional trim changes with power and speed. The rudder was too heavy, and the 'hunting' of the elevator was partially explained by bent shrouds. JF319 concentrated on performance (see the Table); although marking a significant advance, it was felt that compressibility effects may not have been sufficiently allowed for. With a combined balance/trim tab on the rudder, control forces were acceptable.

Production Mk XIV RB141 appeared in November 1943, was weighed at 8,488lb (including full fuel of 112 gallons), then flown intensively with RB144. Servicing of this mature type was exceptionally good and the engines gave little trouble, although simplified starting

Spitfire XIV RB141 in November 1943 was exceptionally easy to maintain and gave no serious problems during handling trials. This view shows the flaps well, including the open access panel above them; the left-handed five-bladed propeller, retractable tail wheel and larger rudder with its substantial trimmer are noteworthy. *A&AEE 11620*

Spitfire XIV RM784 in March 1945 spun normally, but exhibited the old Spitfire characteristic of 'tightening' in turns at aft CG, attributed to the combination of bubble canopy, cut-down rear fuselage and extra fuselage fuel. Trials continued after the war to improve longitudinal handling. The anti-fouling frame at the top of the fin can be seen, together with oil stains on the ground and fuselage. *A&AEE 15047*

was recommended. RB146 spun normally and would, it was calculated, fly a maximum of 525 miles on internal fuel. In early 1945 piano hinges and geared tabs on the ailerons improved manoeuvrability substantially. The Griffon 65 ran 20-30°C cooler than the Merlin, a feature largely responsible for the guns (two 20mm plus four 0.303in) cooling excessively. Similar results were obtained on RM766 late in 1944 with two 20mm and two 0.5in guns, although low temperatures were less serious as the 0.5in guns could function adequately 10°C cooler than the 20mm cannon. Similarly armed, NH703 had twelve gun defects on arrival in March 1944; after rectification, air and ground trials involving the expenditure of more than 8,000 rounds were successfully completed. Three features were previously flown individually without difficulty on Spitfires; cut-down rear fuselage, extra fuselage fuel, and 90-gallon drop tank were, in combination, on the Mk XIV the cause of poor directional behaviour (particularly with the drop tank), dangerous longitudinal instability with fuel in the fuselage tank (both on MV247), and a marked tendency to tighten in turns at aft CG (on RM784). In addition, the F24 camera installation on MV247 proved unsatisfactory; spinning was, however, acceptable. Trials continued after the war on RM674 (which arrived in February 1945).

Spitfire Mark XVI

The Packard-built Merlin 266 in a Mk IX airframe became the Mk XVI, and MK850 was flown to Boscombe in September 1944, where interest centred on oil cooling and radiator suitability with the engine cleared to a boost of +25psi using 150 octane fuel. Spinning in mid-1945 on SM410 was satisfactory, even at aft CG with fuel in the fuselage tank. On the other hand, handling by experienced pilots only was recommended after tests on TB232 with full fuel, 90-gallon drop tank and two 250lb bombs, due to sustained short period pitch oscillations and bad directional characteristics. Rocket trials on TB757 were under way at the end of the war using the Mk VIII RP system.

Spitfire XVI TB757 in June 1945, showing its zero-length Mk VIII RP installation, and the method of attachment to piquet ropes. Trials continued until December 1945. The small intake above the rearmost exhaust is characteristic of this Packard Merlin 266 version.

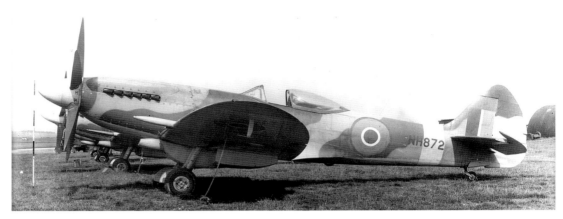

Spitfire XVIII NH872, in a neat peacetime row in July 1945, sporting a 90-gallon ventral tank, which aggravated the shortcomings of this version, both directionally and longitudinally. The tank was not recommended for Service use. *A&AEE 15118*

Spitfire Mark XVIII

NH872 arrived in July 1945, and TP279 shortly afterwards; initial handling trials revealed marked longitudinal instability.

Spitfire Mark XIX

The photographic version of the Mk XIV, PS858 (Griffon 66), appeared in February 1945 followed by SW777 in May 1945; trials continued after the war.

Spitfire Mark XXI

Lengthy development of a 'super' Spitfire (including the new wing section tested earlier) resulted in the so-called Mk XXI 'Victor' – a term briefly in use to identify PP139, which was virtually a new design. This aircraft spent two

months at Boscombe from August 1943; it weighed 9,124lb including 116 gallons of internal fuel. Other improvements included a Griffon 61, flush riveting and undercarriage doors that completely enclosed the wheel housing. Performance (see the Table) was limited to speed measurement; armament of four 20mm guns gave accurate shooting from the steady platform.

LA187 first arrived in October 1944 and exhibited unusual handling behaviour with baffling interaction between longitudinal and directional trim; when yawed the aircraft pitched, and under g it yawed; 520mph was achieved in a dive. These limiting manoeuvres caused paint and filler to flake by the time of the performance tests (see the Table). The reduction in top speed was, however, attributed more to the flat windscreen of LA187 (PP139

Spitfire XIX PS858 in February 1945, with an ice guard for the pressurisation intake, but not for the engine air. In the clean configuration it was pleasant to fly, and reached 40,000 feet with a 170-gallon drop tank, and 420mph at low level. However, directional behaviour was poor with either the 90-gallon or 170-gallon drop tank, particularly the latter at high altitude. The ailerons were unusually heavy and out of harmony with other controls; increasing aileron droop was suggested as a remedy. It was calculated that a Mach number of 0.825 was achieved at high altitude. *A&AEE 15037*

had a curved screen) than the worn surfaces. Regarded as a Spitfire 21 (Griffon 61) with an arrestor hook, TM379 was assessed as suitable for carrier operations in late 1944. LA189 and LA190 each completed 100 hours of flying in two months, testament to their serviceability, although LA189 suffered an engine failure, and a propeller change following an enthusiastic take-off in which the undercarriage was raised too soon with the resultant cropping of the blades. From February 1945 LA211 and LA215 had modified elevators with reduced horn balance and deleted balance tab on the rudder. Handling was acceptable, but the directional instability remained to a lesser degree; adverse

aileron yaw was commented on, the first time in a Spitfire[2]. Contra-rotating propellers identified LA219 and LA220, which arrived in June 1945 to continue trials after the war; initial results were entirely favourable.

LA191 suffered a temporary interruption in the gun firing trials when wrinkling of the skin was discovered. Rearming the four 20mm guns took two armourers 16 minutes.

Spitfire Mark XXII

PK315, as a Mk XXI but with cut-down rear fuselage, was delivered in July 1945.

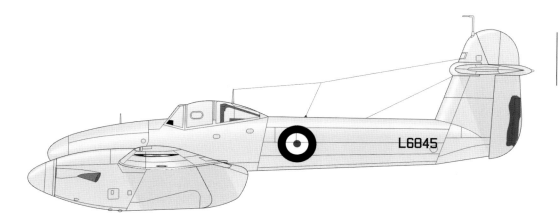

Westland Whirlwind L6845, September 1939, for handling trials. (Scale 1:72)

Whirlwind

Following brief handling checks of the second prototype before the war, L6845 was at Boscombe, mostly unserviceable, for six weeks from mid-September 1939. Enforced grounding enabled engine changes to be timed – each took more than 22 man-hours, a time extended by the freezing conditions inside the unheated hangar.

L6844 arrived in July 1940 for performance (see the Table) and handling; the latter was unremarkable apart from some tailplane vibration, heavy ailerons and the difficulty in achieving a three-point landing. The pilots were pleased to see that the colour of the light indicating a safe, locked-down undercarriage had been changed from red (1939) to green. The take-off run was 375 yards, and it was felt that an engine failure could safely be handled above 140mph.

P6980 was successfully tested from November 1940 up to 420mph with a large

'acorn' fairing between fin and tailplane to overcome vibration. In squadron service, outboard slats had torn off, so P6997 arrived in April 1941 with all slats locked closed; as a result of favourable trials this configuration was recommended for Service use. Stalling speed (undercarriage and flaps down) rose to 90mph, and landing distance increased.

Self-sealing fuel tanks thickened part of the wing, so P6997 was tested in May 1941 to examine the effect; the take-off run was improved, but top speed reduced by 16mph. It was also found impossible to achieve more than 415mph due to the excessive push force required, even with full nose-down trim; the RAF claimed to have achieved 460mph. Painting the rear of the propellers was recommended to reduce reflections at night.

[2] Maybe the pilot had been to ETPS and had recently learned about the phenomenon.

Whirlwind I P6997 in September 1942, armed with four 20mm guns and two 500lb bombs. Noteworthy are the shrouded exhausts, the camera fairing and cartridge collector (behind the port propeller), the four guns, the bead sight and aerial mast in front of the pilot, and the fin-mounted pitot head with its cover floating in the breeze. *A&AEE 11172*

On return in the summer of 1942, P6997 was equipped to carry two 500lb bombs, thus increasing maximum weight to 11,409lb. Maximum speed was recommended to be 360mph as the ailerons twitched above this speed, and snatched above 400mph; with one bomb only under the port wing, handling was poor. Performance (see the Table) suffered accordingly with bombs on.

Mohawk

The RAF received Curtiss H-75As following the collapse of Norway and France in 1940 and named them Mohawk; none of the type was ordered by Britain from the manufacturer. Powered by the Cyclone (R-1820) or the Twin Wasp (R-1830), the former were regarded by the Establishment as Mk I and the latter as Mk II; these designations differ from nomenclature used in service.

An invitation led to a small team from Boscombe flying the H-75 in France in November 1939. In spite of the throttle working in the opposite sense to British practice, the pilot found the aeroplane exceptionally easy and pleasant to fly. At high speed (not specified) the 75A was more manoeuvrable than early Spitfires or Hurricanes, and had lighter controls; the docile stall occurred at 64mph (flaps and undercarriage down), and assessment was limited to flight below 4,000 feet. Arrangements were made for a French Air Force machine to visit the A&AEE but, to acute embarrassment, the aircraft (No 188) crashed following engine failure on 14 January 1940. Repairs were made and, after waiting for new sparking plugs (a recurring supply problem), the aircraft was serviceable, but was removed before trials could start.

Mohawk AR678 in January 1941, with a Cyclone (GR-1820-G205A) engine and a weathered propeller. The bulges above the engine are for the two 0.3in guns, and the fairing below the cowling covers an exhaust. In RAF service this model was known as the Mk IV. *A&AEE 9675*

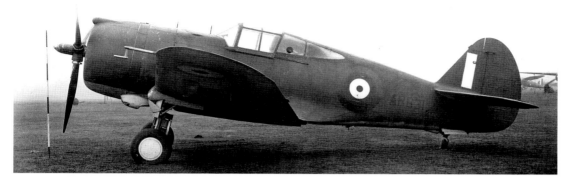

Mohawk AR631 in January 1941, with a Twin Wasp (R1830-SC3G) engine, appears indistinguishable from AR678, seen in the previous photograph. The gunsight is a ring and bead, and there are light carriers under the wing. The cranked pitot head is interesting. The engine quoted in the A&AEE report would make this aircraft a Mk III in RAF service. *A&AEE 9676*

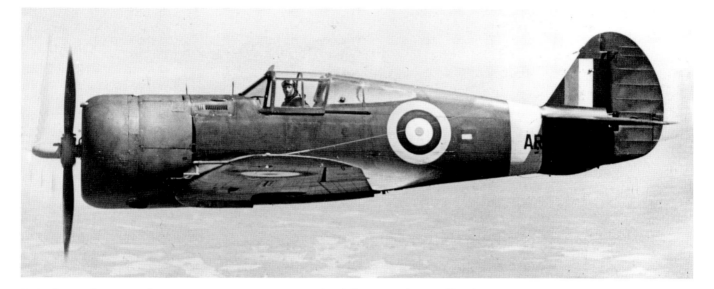

Mohawk Mark I

Seven examples of the Cyclone (R-1820-G205A) version with throttle operating in the British fashion reached the Establishment. The first, AR645, appeared in August 1940 and, following a serious crash in December, was replaced by AR678. This pair completed performance, cooling, handling and range tests. Handling remained outstanding, but performance (see the Table) was below what contemporary Spitfires were achieving, although take-off distances were similar. The 84-gallon fuel capacity gave a maximum range of 525 miles (including 15 minutes at maximum power), and it was calculated that an external tank of 48 gallons would give 960 miles. AR644 spent three months on radio and armament trials before a major crash in December 1940; the replacement, BK877, with staggered wing guns, crashed fatally in March 1941 during a test of gun heating. All four accidents were attributed to

engine failure. A Vokes air filter for tropical use in AR640 from October 1940 produced no measurable difference in performance – a surprising result in view of the penalty usually associated with filters. This aircraft was destroyed by enemy action in April 1941.

Brief tests were made on AX882 (from June 1941) and BS747 (August 1941), both with modifications to the oil system to permit inverted flight.

Mohawk Mark II

The first Twin Wasp (R-1830-SIC3G) version, AR634, made a brief visit from July 1940, and the second, AR631, a slightly longer visit from November 1940, during which performance (see the Table) was measured. The lower heights of the Mk II resulted from the single speed of the Wasp's supercharger – the Cyclone had two speeds.

A Mohawk Mk III, probably AR635, in late 1940. Its only association with the A&AEE was in the recognition photographs.

Bf 109

The Establishment took the opportunity in April 1940 to fly a Messerschmitt 109E-3 (Werk Nummer 1304) in France following its capture. The A&AEE report says that none of the expected vices was apparent, but that both directional and longitudinal stability were too great. The result was heavy handling, particularly the elevator above 250mph; a considerable pull force was needed to manoeuvre at 400mph. The consensus was of flying qualities inferior to the Spitfire and Hurricane, and lack of headroom and the toe brakes were criticised.

The aircraft briefly visited Boscombe on 4 May 1940, where it was photographed on its way to Farnborough.

Messerschmitt Bf 109E, W Nr 1304, May 1940, for handling trials. (Scale 1:72)

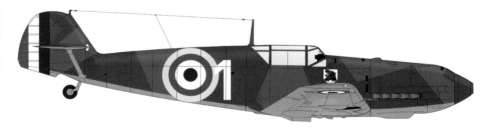

Gloster F9/37

The Gloster F9/37 L7999 (as a single-seat fighter) made a small number of flights at Martlesham Heath in July 1939 before being returned to Gloster's after a crash. The pleasant handling was confirmed on return to the Establishment at Boscombe Down in April 1940, with the controls being light and flat turns easily made. The view was excellent. Serviceability was poor, but performance (see the Table) measurements were made on the power of the Taurus T-S(a) III engines (slightly de-rated from the earlier T-5(a) version). With the cooling gills fully open to maintain acceptable cylinder temperatures, rate of climb was reduced by 540ft/min.

Gloster F9/37, April 1940, for handling trials. (Scale 1:72)

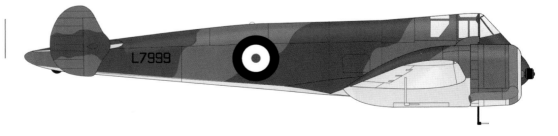

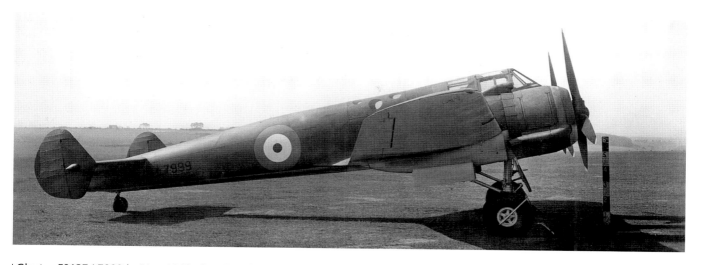

Gloster F9137 L7999 in May 1940, showing the transparent panels fitted in place of the intended turret. The extensive engine cooling gills, which created so much drag when open, are closed. Inset hinges characterise the ailerons, while the rudder has unshielded horn balances. *A&AEE 9635*

Typhoon

Conceived as an interceptor fighter, the Hawker Typhoon suffered early vicissitudes and the Establishment was asked to take the unusual action of flying the first prototype at the maker's airfield (Hawker at Langley), and to undertake such trials as were essential to clear the aeroplane for production. Flying, lasting three weeks, started on 25 September 1940 during the peak of activity in the Battle of Britain; official interest was intense. P5212, with a Sabre I, had twelve 0.303in guns, a total of 6,000 rounds of ammunition and weighed 10,620lb fully loaded. The take-off run was marked by a strong swing to the right and took 525 yards. The controls were light, effective and well harmonised. Performance (see the Table) was good, except for ceiling, and the report contains the

following, somewhat unscientific but informative, conclusion: 'It is quiet, and though fast, gets along without any obvious effort and as a result has a good psychological effect on the pilot.' Maintenance was straightforward, but cold starting was poor, twenty to forty cartridges being needed on occasions. Maximum still air range was calculated at 585 miles. The first Typhoon at Boscombe, P5216, had hardly started trials of its four 20mm gun armament before being damaged on hitting the concrete compass base in July 1941, a month after arrival.

Production aircraft (by Gloster) started arriving in November 1941, when R7614, with enlarged radiators, soon displayed serious overheating of the engine oil, and unacceptable carbon monoxide levels in the cockpit (not experienced in R7579). A sprung seat was tried to overcome vibration, previously sufficient to impair vision;

Typhoon P5212 at Langley (Hawker's airfield) in September 1940, undergoing A&AEE tests there in an attempt to minimise the time to clear the type for production. The large size of the combined radiator and oil cooler is emphasised in this view. All twelve gun ports are taped over, and the chutes for spent cartridges and links can be seen under the starboard wing. The Mk VIIID pressure head under the port wing, coupled with the high speeds attained, introduced a further complication in true airspeed calculations – the need to allow for shock waves forming on the nose of the sensor-in 1940! *A&AEE 9653*

the work of installing the seat led to the rudder pedals being refitted incorrectly, with the result that an uncontained swing developed on take-off in May 1942, causing major damage. Prior to this accident the twelve-gun armament had been severely criticised due to lack of adjustment, poor fasteners and ill-fitting blast tubes; gun heating was also inadequate. R7617, with four 20mm guns, was received in January 1942 and fired successfully, but parasitic images spoiled the aim through the GM2 gunsight, and much work was needed to resolve the problem.

Remedies to the early shortcomings mentioned above met with mixed results. In mid-1942 R7617 and R7700 had 4-inch exhaust extensions and copious sealant to rid the cockpit of carbon monoxide, while more lagging and hot air in R7646 kept the guns warm until the muzzle seals were broken on firing. A fully balanced crankshaft in the Sabre II engine of R7617 gave no improvement in vibrations; indeed, the 9½lb inertia weight in the elevator circuit caused the stick to vibrate and make the pilot's hand numb. Removing the weight improved stick vibrations without unacceptable deterioration in stability. In September 1942 oil cooling was greatly improved in R7700, permitting performance measurements (see the Table) with the four 20mm gun armament; maximum range on internal fuel (148 gallons) was 605 miles, obtained at 5,000 feet. Further alleviation of vibration was unsuccessfully attempted with sprung rudder pedals in R7577. The fitting of a four-bladed in place of a three-bladed propeller in DN340 produced a great improvement in vibration in early 1943, but at the expense of reduced longitudinal and directional stability. This aircraft also had improved (No 3 Mk II) mountings for its four 20mm guns. A Tempest-type tailplane on EK229 produced little improvement, but the 16lb inertia weight reintroduced at the same time restored longitudinal stability. From January 1944 JR333 (Sabre IIA), with the current standard of sliding hood, revealed no handling surprises; its new windscreen did, however, require further investigation on the effect of vibrations. Some months earlier, in May 1943, R8809 had suffered a forced landing; it may have had a sliding hood. Earlier spinning trials from 25,000 feet in R7673 revealed that recovery from right spins could be prolonged.

A pair of 1,000lb bombs is mounted on DN340 in June 1943. The four-bladed propeller combined with the original type of canopy is unusual, but reduced vibrations significantly. One of the four modifications considered essential was the need for a stronger hoist to raise the bombs on to the wing. The black and white stripes were peculiar to Typhoons and Tempests in 1943. *A&AEE 11642*

In February 1944 JR307 has 500lb American Mk 10 smoke tanks. These performed their function of discharging gas well, but the tanks were not acceptable as they struck and holed the wing when jettisoned empty. The aircraft crashed fatally in March 1944 on bombing trials. *A&AEE 11696*

The Typhoon's operational usefulness was extended in four ways, all tested at Boscombe. In late 1942 the Establishment made modifications on R7617 to reduce dazzle from landing lamps. Two months later R8889 (Sabre II), with a tropical air cleaner, had degraded cooling; in July 1943 R7771 was equipped with a new Gallay 'mixed-matrix' oil and radiator cooler, giving considerable improvement. For extra range the standard fit was a pair of 45-gallon tanks under the wings (giving 244 gallons in total) and, with four 20mm guns, an all-up weight of 11,834lb in R8762. The tanks reduced the rate of climb by 200ft/min and top speed by 30mph (true), but extended the range to 1,090 miles at the low altitude of 5,000 feet. The tanks were unaffected by gun firing.

The most significant operational improvement was in offensive capability, starting with two 500lb bombs on R7646 from September 1942; slight buffeting was felt above 350mph, but the aircraft was a steady platform up to 400mph. Top speed was reduced by 33mph (true), and range (on internal fuel) reduced by a mere 35 miles. The installation was considered good, once the Establishment made modifications to prevent empty cartridge cases from arming the bombs by removing the fusing links. A similar modification was made on DN340 in June 1943 on trials of 1,000lb bombs; all-up weight was 13,248lb and handling normal up to 390mph, with the stalling speeds rising to 95mph (clean) and 79mph (flaps and undercarriage down).

Typhoon R8762 undergoes performance trials in January 1943 fitted with 45-gallon fuel tanks under the wings. There appears to be a strengthening band around the rear fuselage.

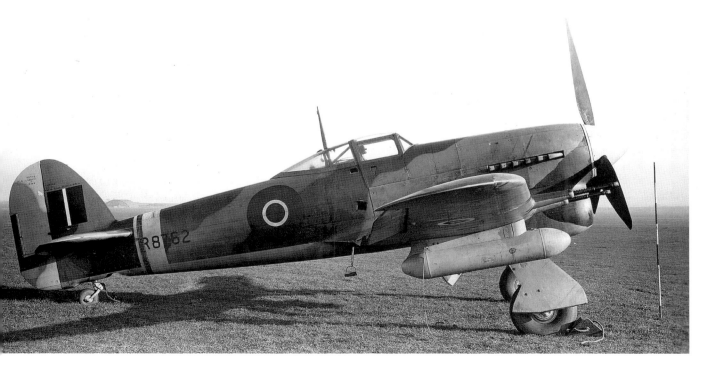

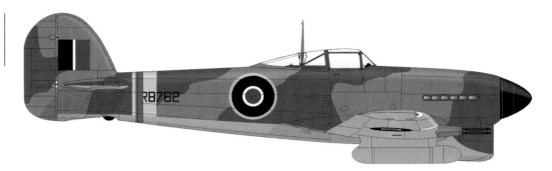

Hawker Typhoon R8762, March 1942, for performance trials. (Scale 1:72)

The range of stores was progressively widened and existing stores modified, as occurred with the introduction of later types of tail (No 26, then No 77) to improve release characteristics of 500lb bombs. Single bombs were released up to 400mph, and an asymmetric combination was tried of one 45-gallon tank with either one smoke container (250lb) or one 500lb bomb – all were satisfactory. American Mk 10 smoke tanks were tested – 500lb on JR307 and 1,000lb on JR448 (both early 1944) – but both had unsatisfactory jettisoning characteristics above 200mph and excessive vibration above 400mph. The same high-speed limitation was initially imposed on the carriage of 500lb anti-personnel clusters; however, in response to operational needs JP855 and MN466 cleared speeds up to 450mph with severe buffeting. During armament tests in March 1944, and within three days of each other, two fatal accidents occurred involving JR307 and JR448, both due to loss of control at low altitude. A year later MN551 was severely damaged following engine failure, but after raising the limit for 1,000lb to 450mph. A similar speed limit was issued following trials in mid-1945 of Mk VIII mines on SW518.

Rockets were first tested on EK497 from March 1943; all-up weight with eight RPs was 12,426lb, but the proximity of the installation to the pitot head caused the ASI to over-read by 15mph at 340mph. However, the aircraft was a very good firing platform – but much work was needed to improve the original Mk I rocket installation. A Mk II version designed by Hawker was satisfactory up to 480mph in mid-1944, but trials of the Mk IIIB installation were curtailed when EK497 force-landed at the Enford range in June 1944. Trials continued on MN861, and were followed by tests of 'duplex' RPs in which pairs of rockets were bolted together; both versions were satisfactory. The pressure error was greatly reduced in JR333 at the end of 1944 by locating a separate static source.

EK497 in August 1943, with a Mk I rocket projectile installation, modified by the removal of the blast plates under the wings; rails are fitted, but not the rockets. Rocket aiming by the use of the gunsight and ground harmonisation was difficult, but the Typhoon was found to be a very steady platform and accurate firing was eventually achieved. The proximity of the outboard rocket rail to the pressure head (just visible by the port wing roundel) caused significant over-reading of airspeed above 300mph. *A&AEE 11522*

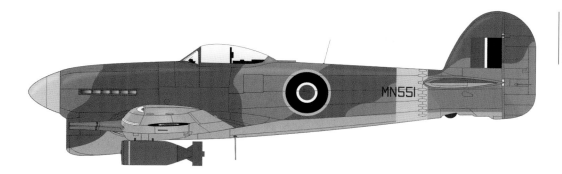

Hawker Typhoon MN551, April 1944, for bombing trials. (Scale 1:72)

While all the armament trials were under way, the boost limit of the Sabre IIA was raised from 7 to 9psi for combat. R8762 made the performance tests (see the Table) at the new rating, but at the expense of overheating of both oil and coolant. The higher power also exacerbated the existing problem of sudden directional trim change on rapid closure of the throttle. Three types of rudder were tried, but none was completely satisfactory; however, as the anticipated structural failure did not occur, the best of the three (on R7617) was adopted. The earlier trouble with vibration appears to have recurred in service, and four rogue aircraft were examined by the A&AEE (see Appendix 6).

Other Typhoons on the strength of the A&AEE were R8830 (low-altitude bombing from January 1943), JP380 (July 1943), and JP598 (August 1943), the latter two on smoke trials. JP598 was contaminated with mustard gas and had to be sent away. MN290, from April 1944, had an automatic recorder for engine cooling work; it was in Khartoum by November and was still there in July 1945. SW535 spent the last five months of the war on general bombing work.

Tomahawk

Ordered in large numbers by the British Purchasing Commission, the Curtiss Type 81A (Allison V-1710 engine) was named Tomahawk (P-40 in the USAAC). An initial batch was taken over from a French contract. Before production aircraft were available, an example intended for the American Volunteer Group in China was obtained, and, as BK853, arrived in November 1940. Interest initially was on US reports of a tendency to ground loop; test pilots, flying from grass and concrete at Tangmere, found no difficulty in keeping straight with the tail wheel interconnected to the rudder. Satisfactory operation in the tropics was predicted following cooling trials, and a flame damping modification gave good results.

Typhoon IB MN290 in mid-1944, to examine methods of determining the effectiveness of engine cooling in temperate climates. The aircraft appears to be in standard late-production configuration with four 20mm guns, bubble canopy, whip VHF aerial and, under the fuselage, the IFF aerial. The fuselage band shows the strengthening plates, while under the starboard wing is a small temperature sensor. Tropical climate trials continued at Khartoum.

Tomahawk BK853 in November 1940 is devoid of radio, guns, navigation lights and flame damping exhaust, yet ground handling, oil and radiator cooling and flame damping (fitted early in 1941) were assessed as satisfactory. The refuelling cap is visible in the rear cockpit panel. Elevator and rudder trim tabs are visible, as is the port aileron fixed tab. There is a ring and bead sight. *A&AEE 9659*

Arriving in February 1941, AH900 (mispainted as AX900) had its guns harmonised with some difficulty as considerable movement of the barrels occurred and heating was insufficient; investigation continued at Duxford. The replacement, AK 160, was similarly armed with two 0.5in guns above the engine but four 0.30in guns in the wing (AH900 had 0.303in wing guns). AK160's firing trials were acceptable, but a more rigid mounting for the gunsight was required. AK181 was intended for performance work, but damage after an engine failure in March 1941, shortly after receipt, led to replacement by AK176 the following month. The latter was fully modified for RAF use, but lacked flame damping exhausts and an air cleaner; the performance is as shown in the Table, based on overload fuel (130 gallons including drop tank). The take-off run without drop tank was a mere 215 yards, and range with drop tank 665 miles. Flame dampers reduced top speed by 4mph (true) and an air cleaner by 14mph (true). Handling, including dives up to 440mph, was satisfactory, and behaviour conventional at the stall (77mph with flap and undercarriage down). The Stromberg/Bendix carburettor found favour as the engine functioned under negative g, but the need to depress the button on the stick for 45 seconds while raising the undercarriage was criticised. AH797, regarded as a Mk II, was used to examine the automatic, variable datum boost control; the combat rating was found to creep over the permitted figure of 40 inches during tests starting in October 1941. Four months earlier, AH785, a Mk I, started successful tests of radio and F24 cameras (a second was added early in 1942) for the Army co-operation role.

Kittyhawk

A British contract (and later Lend-Lease) for the Curtiss Type 87A with V-1710 engines led to the Kittyhawk I, III and IV (later model P-40 in USAAC); the Packard Merlin (V-1650) powered the Mk II. No Mk III or IV appears to have reached Boscombe.

Kittyhawk Mark I

Similar to the Tomahawk but powered by the more powerful V-1710-E3.R, AK764 arrived first (in January 1942) for gunnery trials. Apart from a few unnecessary and confusing switches, the six 0.5in guns, together with camera and the ST1A gunsight, attracted the following comment in the report: 'Best gunnery from the USA to date.' Modified flash eliminators fitted later improved the installation further. AK572, with only four 0.5in Colt guns and lacking radio, was not representative of later aircraft, but nevertheless flew intensively in February 1942 and gave few, minor, problems. Internal fuel of 123 gallons gave an all-up weight of 8,542lb and a range (using the 1942 criteria for warm-up and climb, and 15 minutes for combat) of 650 miles. Handling was acceptable, although the ailerons became heavy at about 400mph and stiff at 460mph, and the rudder was also heavy with a tendency to lock over with power on when about two-thirds travel was applied; the stall occurred at 80mph (flaps and undercarriage down). Dives to 280mph with the belly tank fitted were satisfactory. Climb performance (without the tank) was measured (see the Table).

The first Kittyhawk I, AK764, was received at Boscombe for gunnery trials in January 1942. It was voted 'Best gunnery from the USA to date'.

Kittyhawk I AL229 in April 1942, with a 40-gallon ventral tank. The three port guns and the ring sight (but no bead) can be seen. An HF aerial appears to run from near the top of the fin to the starboard wing tip, and a VHF aerial and mast are also fitted; the aircraft carried the TR9D (HF) and TR1133C (VHF) for its intended Army co-operation role. *A&AEE recognition 90*

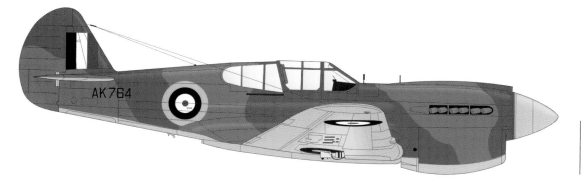

Curtiss Kittyhawk AK764, January 1942, for gunnery trials. (Scale 1:72)

AK579, from March 1942, undertook radio and successful flame damping trials, while AL229 (fully equipped) was used for comprehensive tests, including performance (see the Table), and bombing using the centre-line station. The take-off run (with belly tank) was 385 yards and the range 1,060 miles.

The discrepancy in the range figures between AK572 and AL229 is not explained in the reports dated within two weeks of each other in May 1942. Inadequate gun heating was cured by extra sealing within the wings by the A&AEE, but oil and cylinder temperatures were satisfactory. In August 1942 AK751 arrived with a Hydulignum propeller, which reduced the rate of climb slightly, but caused a marked change in directional trim with change in speed, a major drawback for gun aiming. Nearly a year later ET573, with modified air cleaners in fairings on the cowling, lost 9mph (true) in top speed as a result.

Kittyhawk Mark II

FL220 was the only representative at Boscombe of the Merlin (V-1650-1)-powered version, arriving in August 1942. Although the take-off run increased to 465 yards, performance (see the Table) was generally significantly better than the earlier version. Maximum range was 815 miles on internal fuel (131 gallons) and 1,085 miles (with a 43-gallon belly tank), both obtained using a Rolls Royce automatic mixture control. Apart from flame damping, which did not approach visibility criteria, FL220 met requirements for engine cooling, cockpit heating and contamination, while the Signal Corps Radio (SCR 274) was particularly free of interference. Handling was very similar to the Mk I.

Buffalo

Aircraft from the 1939 British contract for the Brewster 339E were preceded at the A&AEE by Belgian model 339B aircraft; all were named Buffalo by the RAF (F2A in the US Navy). AS412 (ex-Belgian) suffered engine failure shortly after arrival in July 1940, and its replacement, AS425, was found to have structural damage. The third aircraft, AS430, appeared in August 1940 and undertook some trials before it collided in October with a Hampden during air-to-air photography; the pilot bailed out. AS426, for performance, and AS410, for armament, both from February 1941, were more successful. Two British contract aircraft, W8132 and W8133, were received in October and April 1941 respectively.

The main report (dated July 1941) is an amalgam of the results from both types of aircraft, although the British contract aircraft had the Curtiss electrical propeller control replaced by a Hamilton hydraulic unit, and also a British pitot head. The Belgian aircraft weighed 5,746lb all up and the British 6,430lb. Performance (see the Table) was not outstanding, although the take-off run (with flap) was only 215 yards. Carbon monoxide was dangerously high in the cockpit; improvements were rendered ineffective later when fish-tail exhausts were fitted, although the flame damping qualities were good. It was easy to load the aircraft to give an excessively unstable (aft) CG; an acceptable limit was found and recommended for the Service. The aircraft was unsuitable for hot climates on account of predicted excessive oil temperatures. The RAF sent the type to Singapore, but what modifications, if any, were made is not known; they were not tested at

Kittyhawk II FL220 in August 1942, with a Packard Merlin (V-1650-1) in place of the V-1710 of the Mk I. Apart from the slightly deeper radiator and absence of an air intake above the engine, the only difference from the Mk I appears to be the radiator flap mounted slightly further forward and a camera gun fairing under the starboard wing. In the original print the aerial from fin to wing tip can be seen for the SCR 274 radio. *A&AEE 11067*

Buffalo I AS412 in July 1940 has recently been taken over from a Belgian contract. The large spinner houses a Hamilton hydraulic propeller control. Three of the four gun ports (two in the wings and two in the upper cowling) can be seen; the unique undercarriage proved too fragile in Service use. *A&AEE 9645*

Fish-tail exhausts were an improvement on Buffalo W8133 in January 1942. *A&AEE 9868*

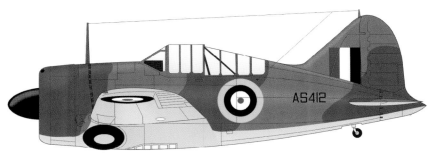

Brewster Buffalo AS412, July 1940, for handling trials. (Scale 1:72)

Another view of Buffalo I AS412, showing the extensive canopy glazing and portly lines.

Boscombe. Gun firing trials were made on both versions (Belgian reports not found); the two 0.5in fuselage and two 0.5in wing guns were generally satisfactory in the British version, but rearming the wing guns was awkward, and firing the fuselage guns at low altitude caused oil to obscure the windscreen.

Airacobra

The unique features of the Bell Airacobra (P-39 in the USAAC) ordered by the British Purchasing Commission in 1940 were the mid-fuselage mounting of the V-1710 engine, and the cannon firing through the propeller hub. To speed testing, three early-model (P39C) aircraft were received, two reaching Boscombe in July 1941. DS173 had the standard 37mm gun firing through the hub plus two 0.5in guns in the nose and two 0.3in in the wings. Firing trials were limited due to lack of spares; rearming by two men was completed in 20 minutes, but replacement of the 37mm gun (weighing 210lb) took no less than 25 hours. In November 1941 DS173 was badly damaged when the undercarriage was retracted after landing; four weeks later an engine failure in DS174 convinced the pilot (the same in both cases) to remuster as a Technical Officer. Armament of the standard aircraft, AH590 from September 1941, was a 20mm gun in the hub, two 0.5in guns in the nose and four 0.3in in the wings; the last required an excessive force of up to 180lb to cock. The whole installation was found inaccessible. Flash eliminators and flaps over the ejector openings were later modifications, the latter being made to alleviate inadequate electric heating of the guns. In early 1943 three P-39Ms (42-4723, 42-4734 and 42-4748) were assessed for the USAAF following experience of jamming of the empty cases of the 37mm gun; the Establishment found the fault to lie in bad design.

Airacobra DS173 was one of two P-39Cs received in July 1941 before the arrival of aircraft to the British order. Lack of spares hindered progress, although some tests of the unique armament were completed before the aircraft was damaged on 20 November 1941 when the pilot raised the undercarriage instead of the flaps after landing. The 37mm gun can be seen in the spinner, and the ports above the nose for two 0.5in guns; there were also two 0.3in guns in the wings.

Handling trials on Airacobra I AH573 started in August 1941 (with the type already in squadron service), following a very comprehensive cockpit assessment. The entrance door was condemned as being far too small for escape by parachute. Rudder and elevators were light, quick and effective, but the ailerons (fabric-covered) were heavy over 300mph. Stability and other aspects were acceptable. The aircraft crashed fatally in February 1942 following engine failure when the pilot turned back from 600 feet on take-off.

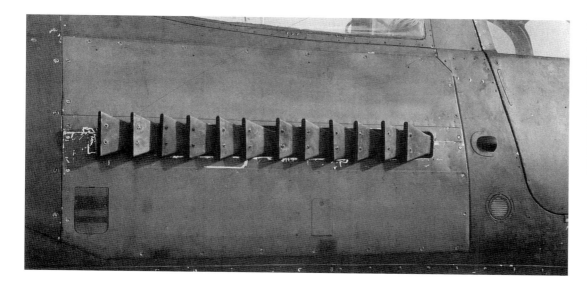

These stub ejector exhausts made but a small improvement to the Allison V-1710 of Airacobra AH573 in October 1941. After two modifications, flame damping of the novel exhausts was almost acceptable.

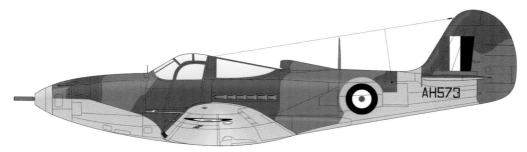

Bell Airacobra AH573, September 1941, for handling trials. (Scale 1:72)

Handling trials on AH573 started in August 1941 (with the type already in squadron service), following a very comprehensive cockpit assessment that severely criticised the cramped conditions and condemned the arrangements for baling out. The rudder and elevator were light, quick and effective, but the ailerons (fabric-covered) were heavy over 300mph; stability and other aspects were acceptable. After two modifications, flame damping of the novel exhausts was almost acceptable, but the aircraft crashed fatally in February 1942 following engine failure when the pilot turned back from 600 feet on take-off. Its replacement, AH589, arrived the following March, but was greatly unserviceable, so the armament aircraft, AH701, was used. Thus the performance trial (see the Table) of the V-1710-E4 version was spread over three aircraft, and lasted from July 1941 to August 1942, long after the type had been rejected by the RAE. Rejection was largely based on compass deviation after gun firing (up to 160°); the A&AEE aircraft (AH573) investigating this phenomenon crashed without a formal report being raised. AH574 had a V-1710-E12 engine with altered supercharger and propeller gear ratios, together with very satisfactory autoboost control; performance (see the Table) was similar to the E4 version but undoubtedly both versions suffered from the lack of the turbo-supercharger that the US authorities declined to supply. AH579 (from March 1942) and AH587 (February 1942) were briefly at Boscombe, the former for 'dives and aerobatics', according to the serviceability reports.

Tornado

Two engines, the Sabre and Vulture, were proposed by Hawker to meet the F18/37 requirement. The former became the Typhoon and the latter the Tornado. The types were aerodynamically similar, but only a few Tornadoes flew, of which one, P5224 (Vulture V), the second prototype, was briefly at Boscombe from October 1941. At 10,690lb, handling was indistinguishable from the Typhoon, with the stall at 82mph (clean) and 61mph (undercarriage and flaps down), although the engine ran rough at high rpm (up to 3,200). Performance (see the Table) was comparable to the early Typhoons; the report comments that had an extra pound of boost been available, top speed would have been over 400mph. Engine temperatures were satisfactory for temperate climates, but not for the tropics.

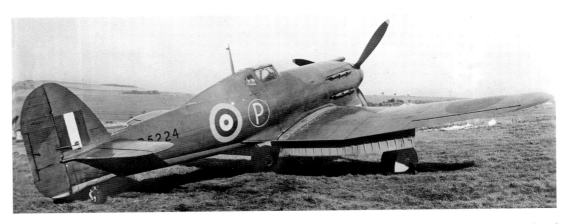

Tornado P5224, the second prototype, is seen at Boscombe in October 1941. The ill-fated Vulture engine ran rough at high rpm, but propelled the aircraft to almost 400 mph.

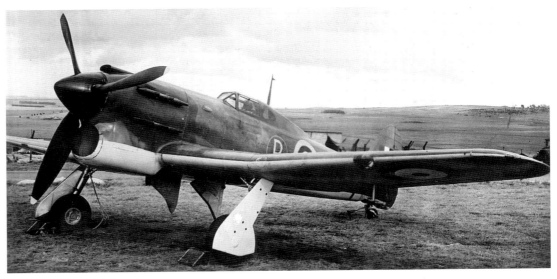

Another view of Tornado P5224, showing the brutal appearance of the beast, which has been well tied down. No armament appears to be fitted and the gun openings are covered over. Note the small air intake above the cowling.

A starboard side view of Tornado P5524, showing the type's similarity to the Typhoon. Handling of both types was virtually identical. Performance of the Tornado was similar to the early Typhoons – both were extremely fast for the time.

Mustang

Designed by the North American company in the USA to a British requirement, the Mustang represented a significant aerodynamic advance with a novel laminar flow wing.

Mustang Mark I

In November 1941 the first aircraft, AG351, arrived at Boscombe, just 19 months after design had started more than 5,000 miles away. With a 140-gallon fuel capacity (but only 130 could be used), all-up weight was 8,622lb and performance (see the Table) good at low level, but with a low ceiling attributed to the lack of power of the Allison V-1710-39 at height. The take-off run of 335 yards was comparable to other fighters with higher cambered wings, and the maximum range of 960 miles on 130 gallons was outstanding. High oil temperatures were attributed to coring in low ambient temperatures; blanks were fitted to reduce cooling and permit all oil to flow freely, but the situation was not helped by the need to keep the cooling shutters open for the radiator. The difficulty was overcome by a new Harrison oil cooler, successfully tested on AL973 on arrival in July 1942. Handling, initially restricted to low speed due to a fragile hood, was completed on AG383 from March 1942. This aircraft had a heavier duralumin propeller, giving a forward CG. Handling was pleasant at all speeds up to 500mph, and trims positive; the stall was 92mph (clean) and 80mph (undercarriage and flaps down). The ease of crosswind take-offs was particularly liked. Later, at extreme forward CG, elevator control was inadequate for safe approach and

landing; the limit was thus set slightly further aft. Stewart-Warner electric heaters gave poor heating of the wing guns (two 0.5in and four 0.3in); the two fuselage guns (two 0.5in) were adequately heated by hot air. Rearming (on AG359 from February 1942) all eight guns took two men 35 minutes, but maintenance and design features were deemed to need seventeen modifications, including stronger blast tubes. AG359 suffered a major accident when the pilot failed to lock the tail wheel and suffered an uncontrollable swing on landing. Use was made of AL997 while with IFDF from July 1942 to assess its F24 camera for the Army co-operation role, flame damping with Kittyhawk ejector exhausts, gun aiming, cockpit contamination on the ground, and other minor differences of this North American Type 83 aircraft from the earlier Type 73.

Two brief trials in late 1942 on A P206 with American multi-ejector exhausts demonstrated that the pilot was not hampered by the exhaust glow at night, but that the aircraft was visible to outside observers. AP227 (from January 1943) had significant compass deviation with use of some electrical services, while AP222, with a modified supercharger gear ratio (identified as a V-1710-F21R engine), gave increased speed at sea level, but became progressively slower with altitude.

Forty-millimetre guns and rockets were flown on AM106/G and AM130/G respectively. The former, after calibration to determine the angle between fuselage datum and flight path, achieved very good results and was compared favourably to the similarly equipped Hurricane. Top speed was reduced by 17mph (true), but range was scarcely affected. Later, AM106 was used to clear fourteen different underwing stores from its 'low attack

Mustang I AG351 in February 1942 shows its pleasing lines; not apparent are its outstanding range and low-level top speed. This early aircraft had a fragile hood, and, it appears, little headroom for the pilot, who lacked a gunsight in spite of the visible fuselage gun; wing gun positions are taped over. The radiator flap is cracked open, and equipment, probably radio, can be seen behind the pilot. *A&AEE recognition 77*

This rare underside view of Mustang I AG351 on 9 February 1942 reveals the exceptionally clean design of the wing. Points of note are the ejector ports for the wing guns, the landing lights inset into the wing leading edges, and the effect of airfield mud. Note how the engine-mounted 0.5in guns project at different lengths. The blunt wing tips gave an unsettling similarity to the Messerschmitt Bf 109E; fortunately, by the time the Mustang was in service in numbers the German type had been effectively replaced by later models with rounded wing tips. *A&AEE recognition 77E*

Mustang I AM106 shows its flaps.

Mustang 1 AM130/G in March 1943, probably at Farnborough where the A&AEE trial on the RP installation took place. The drag of this early Mk I version was high, and more marked than on other aircraft with thicker wing sections. Other items of interest visible are the pitot head under the starboard wing, the fish-tail exhausts, the blanked-over gun port behind the spinner, and the three-bladed propeller.

wing' with a universal bomb carrier; 300 rounds of 40mm ammunition were fired in various flight conditions for each store. With two 500lb bombs, aileron control was poor at low speed. AM 130/G suffered a loss of 68mph (true) in top speed with rockets (mostly attributed to the drag of the blast plates and the rails), but handling was unaffected at the increased weight of 9,400lb. Use of the rails for flares and small bombs was not acceptable as they could not be released 'safe'. In August 1943 AM130 was written off in a forced landing. In mid-1943 an installation designed by the UK 'sister' firm Air Service Training on AG357/G cost an estimated 53mph (true), in spite of having no blast plate and slimmer rails.

The prototype installation of four 20mm guns in AM190 from November 1942 was unsatisfactory due to faulty mountings leading to progressive breakages. A month later, FD446, with similar armament, suffered similar defects together with failure of all four front mounting tubes after a few weeks. Modifications included fitting Edgewater front mountings, successfully tested in mid-1943 in FD438.

Of the trio of types fitted with the Maclaren 'drift' undercarriage, the Mustang AG386 had the highest performance. A complicated system of buttons controlled the angle of the main wheels up to 20° from the fore/aft axis. The setting had to be made before take-off or landing and was felt to need simplification before Service use.

Other Mustang Is were AG647 (minor radio modifications from January 1940), AM203 (briefly for speed checks in December 1942) and AM118 for the HAF.

Mustang Mark X

One Mustang with a Merlin 65, AM208, was tested at the A&AEE from November 1942. Performance (see the Table) was markedly improved, but large changes in directional trim with power and speed, and a propensity to sideslip in manoeuvres, spoiled the handling. The four-bladed propeller was thought to be the cause, and a larger fin recommended.

Mustang I AM106 in October 1943, showing signs of more than six months of continuous testing, carries a 120lb smoke bomb, one of many stores tested. The fuselage gun position is blanked over, although a gunsight is fitted; the fuselage line was used for attitude measurements. No equipment is visible behind the pilot, although an aerial is fitted, and there is an IFF aerial under the wing. The radiator flap is open. *A&AEE 11602*

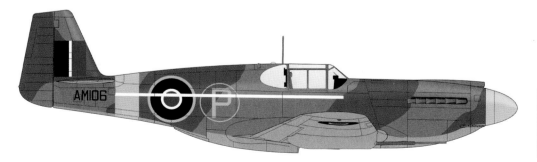

North American Mustang AM106/G, April 1943, for gunnery trials. (Scale 1:72)

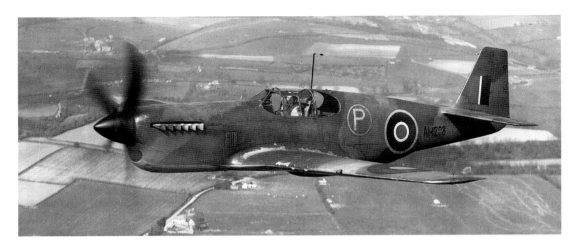

Mustang X AM208 in April 1943, powered by one of only two Merlin 65 engines made. A reflector gunsight appears to be fitted, but the two port guns have been removed and permanently sealed. As a recognition photograph for the Merlin-Mustang, it was misleading as the large chin intake and the grill above the wing root were not features of production aircraft. *A&AEE recognition 144*

A-36

March 1943 saw the arrival of EW998, the ground-attack version of the P-51 Mustang. The Allison V-1710-F21R engine was later changed for the -F3RM version; with the former, top speed occurred at 1,000 feet and was 19mph less than the Mustang I in the clean configuration. Features included removal of the pitot head to the starboard wing tip, the ability to carry two 1,000lb bombs, and dive brakes. With bombs, handling was similar to the Mustang I, except that the dive brakes allowed a dive angle of 30° (previously 13°) to be maintained at 300mph, and the time to lose 150mph was halved. Operation of the dive brakes produced a sudden change in incidence, but once extended normal sighting was possible.

Mustang Mark II

Minor fuel, armament and engine changes identified the Mk II (equivalent to the USAAC P-51A). With 150 gallons, all-up weight was 8,576lb; the wing armament of four 0.5in guns appears not to have required separate tests. FR893 from July 1943 completed performance tests (see the Table) with a change to the supercharger gear ratio (the engine was designated V-1710-F4R). Performance was superior at very low level, but inferior above 10,000 feet. From January 1944 FR894 was used to assess the GSAP gun camera, while FR932 concentrated on IFF and radio equipment. FR890 joined the Armament Squadron for more than a year from December 1943 for gunnery and bombing.

A-36 EW998 in March 1943, the sole example of this USAAF type in British markings, was distinguishable from the Mustang I and II by the dive brakes above and below each wing. The operating rams of the lower port brake can be seen, together with the carrier for bombs up to 1,000lb. Other features visible are the port fuselage gun, the ramshorn exhausts of the Allison V1710-F21R engine, and its square cooling air intake under the fuselage. *A&AEE 11319*

Mustang Mark III

The Merlin transformed the Mustang's high-level performance. Packard-built engines (V-1650-3) were standard in early Mk III aircraft, starting with FX908 briefly in October 1943, soon followed by FX899. Empty (tare) weight had increased by 10%, and all-up weight with internal fuel to 9,190lb. External fuel or bombs could be fitted, including a mixed load of one 500lb and one 65-gallon drop tank, which produced interesting directional behaviour as speed was increased. Performance (see the Table) was revealed by FX953 from January 1944, but was nevertheless some 4% inferior to figures supplied by the

American manufacturer. The effect of propeller tip speed was measured and a reduction of 200rpm (reducing the tip Mach number from 1.07 at 3,000rpm to 1.03 at 2,800) gave an increase of 10mph (true). Later investigations showed that peak boost could occur at lower than maximum rpm, but that changing from a four- to a three-bladed propeller gave no significant changes in climb or speed. Range on internal fuel (150 gallons) was 1,045 miles (maximum) – a remarkable figure – while two 65-gallon drop tanks reduced top speed on FX953 by 69mph (true), but range benefits appear not to have been measured. The tanks also caused overheating of the engine in the cruise.

Mustang III FX899 in May 1944, with 65-gallon underwing tanks, suitably braced. The four 0.5in gun ports are taped over. A four-bladed wide-chord propeller is fitted to absorb the additional power of the Merlin (Packard-built V-1650-3); the air intake is below the spinner, and flame damping exhausts are fitted. *A&AEE 11784*

Mustang III FX908 in October 1943, in pristine condition on arrival at Boscombe for its brief stay. It is equipped with a radio behind the pilot, a bomb rack and what appears to be a bead gunsight just ahead of the windscreen. *A&AEE 11573*

Mixed results of trials on the four 0.5in guns on FZ103 were puzzling, and were at variance with American experience; by May 1944, modified Dunmore feed assisters for the ammunition overcame earlier stoppages. Rockets on the RP Mk V installation on FX893 increased weight to 10,200lb, and stalling speeds to 98mph (clean) and 84 (flaps and undercarriage down); handling up to 450mph was very good, and the bulged Malcolm hood a great improvement. Production versions of the RP Mk V on FX866 in late 1944 established that the Mustang was a good platform, but with one interesting observation. With the oil and cooling radiator shutters under automatic control, the attitude was liable to continuous change; limiting shutter movement solved the problem.

Mustang III FZ103, with smoke curtain installation (SCI) of the American M10 variety, is seen here in April 1944 outside the Special Duty Flight hangar; long-serving Blenheim T2354 is behind. The SCI trial was brief, as FZ103 spent most of its life on gun heating investigation, and then firing under 'g' with a Hughes belt feed assister. During the latter, on 14 July 1944, the wing detached and the pilot was flung from the cockpit involuntarily as the aircraft disintegrated; his parachute ripcord was also pulled without effort on his part. *A&AEE AC1208*

Flt Lt R. V. Muspratt brings Mustang FX893 with eight RPs alongside in March 1944. *A&AEE recognition 210*

The first Merlin 100-series at Boscombe powered FX858 from March 1944; with 130 octane fuel and a combat rating of +25psi boost, performance (see the Table) was outstanding. More mundane trials were made on FX898 with a 71-gallon tank behind the pilot; dives to 505mph after take-off at 10,770lb with two 500lb bombs presented no problems. Asymmetric stores, however, gave the usual interesting handling and landing phenomena. Release of fuel tanks up to 360mph was eventually made acceptable, but separation of the empty M10 smoke tanks was risky above 300mph; the reason for jettisoning empty smoke tanks is not clear. FB124 arrived in August 1944 with an American Mk XXI gyro-gunsight; three modifications were needed for satisfactory operation. A little later KH550 extended clearance for gun firing up to 6g.

FX854 (with horn balances from November 1944) and HB934 (for armament five months later) were in use at Boscombe.

Mustang Mark IV

TK589, the first Mk IV (bubble canopy) in the UK, was immediately engaged in speed trials following arrival in June 1944. At 9,982lb (including 220 gallons of internal fuel), and using combat power of its V-1610-7 engine (3,000 rpm and +25psi), top speed was 25mph (true) higher than earlier versions. Specially smoothed wings undoubtedly helped in the search for sufficient speed to catch V-1 'doodlebugs'. Stalling speeds were higher than the Mk III, and considerable left rudder was needed in dives up to 480mph. In addition, for the first time in the Mustang, care had to be exercised to avoid excessive g on recovery from dives; elevator 'kicking' occurred twice on recoveries. The problem was most acute below 400mph with the rear tank full (ie aft CG).

A fatal accident to KH648 in January 1945 led at first to doubts about the strength of this version; the cause was later established as an ammunition panel becoming detached. In the meantime, and in the light of advice from the USA, speed and acceleration limits were imposed when carrying two 1,000lb bombs. Trials continued on KH766 until May 1945, and included aerobatics with the bombs on. Gunnery, radio and cockpit heating trials on TK589 in 1945 revealed shortcomings in all three areas; one fault was the tendency of the six 0.5in guns to stop firing when more than 3g was applied. TK586 was on Establishment strength for gun cooling tests from March 1945.

| Although not positively identified, this may be FX866 showing the Mk V RP installation, which was capable of being jettisoned.

TK589 was the first Mustang IV (bubble canopy) in the UK. Note the oddly positioned US serial number.

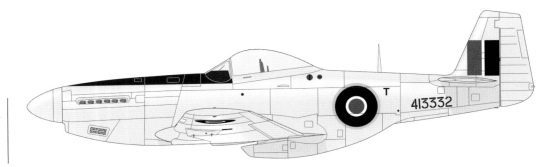

North American Mustang TK589/44-13332, June 1944, for performance trials. (Scale 1:72)

XP-51F

One of this lightweight version, FR409, was briefly flown by the A&AEE. The empty weight was a mere 5,688lb, and loaded 7.669lb (with 150 gallons of fuel). Handling was pleasant and easy, and the view outstanding; precise performance was not established, but was stated to be 'a marked improvement'. Cockpit control layout was the only point of criticism.

XP-51F (unofficially Mustang V) FR409 in October 1944, one of the three lightweight versions built and the only one supplied to the UK. The outstanding view was matched by outstanding performance. The Packard Merlin (V-1650-3) had a broad-chord three-bladed propeller; there is no evidence of armament. *A&AEE 11965*

Lightning

The Lockheed Lightning (P-38 in the USAAF) was ordered for the RAF in 1940. By the time deliveries started in 1942, several accidents had occurred in American service and, most significantly, the British aircraft were delivered without the turbo-supercharger. For good measure, the only example to reach the A&AEE, AF106 (two V-1710-US motors), had no armament and was restricted to 300mph. Trials were limited to a brief assessment from April 1942. Handling was pleasant, although the elevator was heavy, the stall at 78mph (flaps and undercarriage down) straightforward, and flying on one engine comfortable and without foot loads down to 115mph. The red and green colouring of the engine controls was praised, as was the tricycle undercarriage. The trial was of academic interest as the RAF had rejected the Lightning on the basis of unacceptable high-altitude/high-speed characteristics found by the RAF test pilots in the USA. The USAAF nevertheless flew the P-38 especially successfully in Pacific operations.

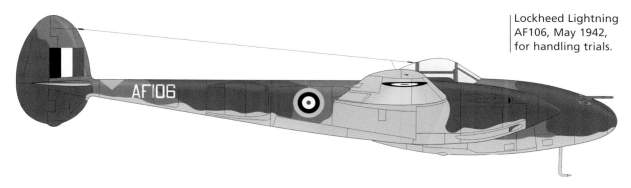

Lockheed Lightning AF106, May 1942, for handling trials.

Lightning I AF106 in June 1942 over Larkhill Camp. Lack of turbo-superchargers (notable by their absence just behind the exhausts) and high-altitude handling problems led to cancellation of the British contract by the time the aircraft reached Boscombe. Gas warning diamonds can be seen ahead of the fins. *A&AEE recognition 94*

HM595 is the prototype Tempest, then known as the Typhoon Mk II, at Boscombe from March 1943. For much of the time it was unserviceable. The white line is to assist in accurately determining attitude. Handling trials were deferred until the arrival of a production aircraft, which carried a much more elegantly shaped fin. Gun mountings were condemned for their lack of rigidity.

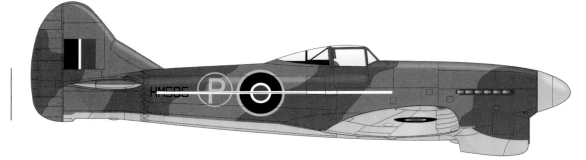

Hawker Tempest HM595, July 1943, for performance trials. (Scale 1:72)

Tempest

The Hawker Tempest was, in effect, a Typhoon with a thinner, elliptical wing. Several power plants were initially considered, but only two versions reached the A&AEE during the war – the Tempest V (Sabre) and Tempest II (Centaurus).

Tempest Mark V

The first Tempest, HM595, flew in September 1942 and reached Boscombe the following March with a Sabre II engine, in a brief visit, with much unserviceability. Performance (see the Table) was measured, and attitude accurately determined (usually a prelude to RP installation). Time was found to investigate the effect on top speed at altitude of reducing rpm from the maximum (3,900) to 3,700; speed was only very slightly reduced and was attributed to reduction of helical tip speed to below Mach 0.95. The installation of four 20mm guns was totally unacceptable due to lack of rigid mounting. Handling was deferred until the production

aircraft, JN731 (Sabre IIA), appeared in October 1943; the ailerons and rudder were considered to be too heavy, and elevator authority insufficient to achieve a three-point landing with the engine at idling. A speed of 535mph was recorded in a dive at 11,000 feet (Mach 0.8). In manoeuvres, undue concentration was needed, a fault attributed to poor longitudinal stability.

Performance (see the Table) improved on the preliminary figures of the prototype, and a maximum range (on internal fuel of 132 gallons) of 675 miles was obtained at 10,000 feet. It seems that air intake efficiency had been improved since the prototype trials. Contamination, engine cooling, IFF, radio, and gun and cockpit heating were satisfactory; gun muzzles needed sealing in extremely cold conditions. An extensive handling trial on JN731 in the latter half of 1944 revealed that airframe distortion occurred at high speed (up to 500mph) and that there was extreme torque reaction; these phenomena posed difficulties for accurate stability assessment, but it was nevertheless concluded that, at all practicable

Tempest V JN731, the third production aircraft, is seen in October 1943. Extensively used for handling trials, it was eventually dived to 500mph; its thin, elliptical wing allowed Mach 0.8 to be achieved without serious problems. More significant for piston-engined fighters as a class was the extreme torque reaction from high power settings, making stability measurement difficult; there was adequate rudder trim but no aileron trim. The long Hispano 20mm Mk II guns were replaced in later (Series II) aircraft by the shorter Mk V version. *A&AEE 11617*

Another view of Tempest V JN731 in October 1943, revealing details of the construction of its wing flaps, and the greatly refined fin extension.

CG positions, longitudinal handling was acceptable. JN730 had two 45-gallon drop tanks on arrival in May 1944, which reduced top speed by 9mph but did not appreciably affect handling. Range, after take-off at 12,345lb, was extended to 1,215 miles (maximum); corresponding endurance was 5.15 hours. The Pacitor fuel gauging system and the drop tank system (with minor improvements) were well liked.

Lengthy periods of unserviceability extended rocket trials on JN740 from June to November 1944. The Mk IIIA RP installation using a Mk IIL (depressed elevation) gunsight proved satisfactory in the course of firing 479 rockets, but later work at higher speeds revealed that the sight settings were inaccurate, causing rockets to undershoot the target. NV946

needed eleven modifications before approval could be given of its Mk VIII RP equipment, tested from March 1945; damage to the rockets by gun firing was a major concern. NV946 crashed fatally when it stalled pulling up from an RP dive in July 1945. The full armoury of twenty-five different stores (see Appendix 7) was cleared for carriage and release up to 500mph, with the exception of 1,000lb bombs (400mph). JN798 (from September 1944) and EJ891 (January 1945) appeared for a short time. Changes to the short-barrel Hispano Mk V 20mm gun in NV732 led to repeat heating trials from January 1945; complete sealing was necessary to ensure adequate temperatures, but doubts remained whether there was then sufficient purging air.

Tempest V EJ891 in February 1945, carrying a pair of 500lb 'Bombs – smoke – Mk II' during an extensive series of trials (shared with EJ798) to clear twenty-five bombing loads. All were satisfactory for carrying up to 500mph and dropping at up to 450mph with the exception of the 1,000lb bomb – up to 400mph only. The rudder has a unique colour pattern. *A&AEE 15072*

Spinning from 30,000 feet was the province of JN741 early in 1945; behaviour of the aircraft was normal in the spin and on recovery, but the programme had to be curtailed by serious overspeeding of the engine (up to 4,500rpm, the normal maximum being 3,900). EJ592 had the first spring tab ailerons in January 1945 and demonstrated superior rates of roll above 250mph. The static source on EJ723 duplicated earlier changes on the Typhoon with similar benefits on pressure error. In October 1944 EJ759 flew to Khartoum for a month and confirmed the inadequacy of the radiator cooling of the Sabre in a hot climate; the air cleaner reduced boost by 5.75psi and top speed by no less than 48mph.

The Establishment also flew JN734 on air-to-ground gun firing (from November 1943), JN799 (for gun development from April 1944 until August 1945), EJ525 (briefly in January 1945) and SN219 (from April 1945 with Porton).

Tempest Mark II

The Centaurus V powered all versions of the Tempest II tested, starting with the prototype, LA602, from 1 May 1944. Handling was similar to the earlier Mk V, but the ailerons were a little too heavy at all speeds and the range of the rudder trim was inadequate; most serious were vibrations above 500mph, although 520mph was achieved (design was 580mph). The wide undercarriage came in for

This is the prototype Tempest II, LA602, in May 1944. Powered by the Bristol Centaurus V engine, handling was similar to the Mk V, although vibration proved to be a problem above 500mph. Maintainability was praised on account of the many access panels.

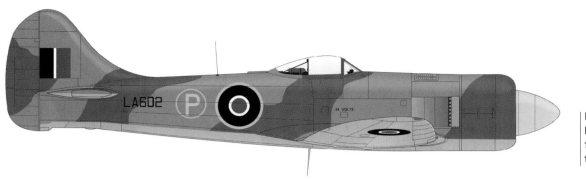

praise (surprisingly, as it was identical to the Mk V), as did maintainability with large, quickly removable panels. Performance (see the Table) just exceeded the Sabre-engined version, but measurement of top speeds needed longer periods at combat power than were usually approved.

Armament trials were limited to an assessment of vibrations on the gyro gunsight in MW736 from April 1945; sighting was satisfactory once a bracing strut was fitted. Jettison trials of drop tanks (two 45-gallon) from MW739 were under way in August 1945, following the initial 86 hours of intensive flying. Very good flame damping results were obtained on MW741.

Six tropicalised Tempest IIs (MW801-806 inclusive) flew in on 15 April 1945. After weighing (12,607lb with two 45-gallon tanks), pressure error and contamination measurements, checks were made of radiator and oil cooling. These preparations preceded the departure of the six aircraft, which spent three months flying 740 hours in Khartoum from early May 1945. There were no major defects with engines or airframes, although backfires wrecked several air intakes; the automatic cooling gills worked well, but the interconnected throttle and pitch levers were found 'tricky'. MW806 was wrecked landing at Khartoum in July, and MW801 was abandoned after catching fire on the return flight on 5 August. The conclusion was that the Tempest II was suitable for tropical use. Tempest testing continued after the war.

Welkin

Conceived as a result of the 1940 threat of high-flying German aircraft, the Westland Welkin had a 70-foot wing span and high-altitude Merlin engines. Ten of the type flew at Boscombe, but five crashed, four of them beyond repair. The prototype, DG558, arrived in May 1943 with Merlin 77 engines with two-stage superchargers. Performance (see the

Tempest II MW801 in May 1945, shortly before leaving for Khartoum with MN802-806 inclusive; they were numbered in large white characters on the fuselage '1' to '6'. Interest in the performance of this Centaurus V-powered version included, primarily, observation of engine temperatures with a view to Far Eastern operations. The aircraft caught fire in August 1945 and was abandoned. *A&AEE 15108*

Table) was established first with Rotol then with de Havilland propellers, each of 12ft 6in diameter; with the latter, the tip speed of Mach unity was calculated at 40,000 feet at maximum achievable speed. Trials were delayed by the tail wheel collapsing shortly after arrival, and a skilful forced landing in May 1943 following engine seizure resulting from overspeeding; there was no provision for feathering the propeller. The aircraft was further extensively damaged on return to the makers in September. DG562/G (Merlin 61) from August 1943 made tests of engine cooling, radio, IFF, compasses, contamination and gun heating; only the last was unsatisfactory. Tests concluded with the tail wheel structure collapsing in February 1944.

Welkin DG558 in May 1943, three days before an engine failure led to a skilful forced landing; the propeller could not be feathered. This view gives a good indication of the high-aspect-ratio wing, which was, nevertheless, of thick aerodynamic chord leading to severe compressibility problems at its design altitude. Noteworthy are the extended ladder for entry over the wing, the air intake ice guards and the bullet fairing of the tailplane/fin. The significance of the two dark fuselage bands on either side of the roundel is unknown. *A&AEE recognition 160*

Welkin I DX279 in October 1943. Handling trials on this aircraft revealed the extent of the shortcomings of all three aerodynamic controls, particularly the elevator above the relatively low Mach number of 0.65. The resulting extensive tests were the first of what later became routine in determining lift boundaries, ie the optimum indicated speeds for manoeuvring. Three of the four 20mm guns are visible in the nose, as is the small air intake for cooling the cabin; pressurisation was one of the few satisfactory features. *A&AEE 11566*

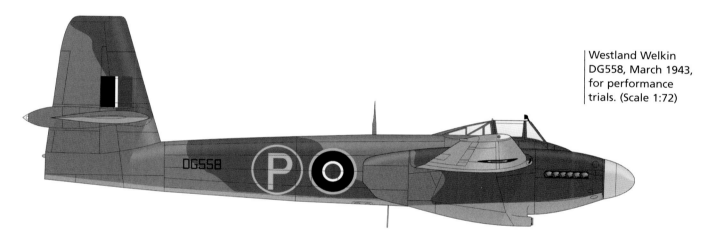

Westland Welkin DG558, March 1943, for performance trials. (Scale 1:72)

Production aircraft DX278 and DX280 (Merlin 72 and 73) went straight into intensive flying from September 1943, flown by visiting operational and company pilots, and maintained by very inexperienced RAF tradesmen. Servicing was complex, but access was easy; in the air many major faults were found, the most serious being an engine fire. In October 1943 the port engine of DX278 caught fire after oil was lost (the propeller could not be feathered) and the aircraft burned out after another skilful forced landing. The replacement, DX282, force-landed a few days after arrival in November 1943 when the port engine oversped. Two weeks later damage on landing, wheels-up, resulted indirectly from loss of oil pressure in the replacement port engine. The machine was written off after a crash on take-off in January 1944, from a third engine failure – this time the starboard.

Meanwhile DX280 was burned out in December 1943 following port engine failure and a forced landing; in this case the cause was attributed to a servicing error. Intensive flying was abandoned, with a strong recommendation for feathering propellers, and work concentrated on handling. DX279, in use from September 1943, exhibited several unsatisfactory features. The ailerons gave a slow response in spite of spring tabs also acting as geared balances; the rudder oscillated when its trim tab was deflected, as in asymmetric flight, and the elevators exhibited an alarming tendency on dive recoveries from high altitude. It was found that in a dive from 35,000 feet the control column moved back and forth of its own volition at 30,000 feet, and only at 25,000 feet could a gentle recovery be attempted. A comprehensive examination of this phenomenon established that Mach effects could render the elevator ineffective, and also determined the optimum speeds (equating to Mach 0.65) for manoeuvring at various heights. High-altitude handling was poor, and the top set of rudder pedals (fitted to raise the pilot's legs to increase g tolerance) were superfluous. Additional mass balance in the ailerons coupled with other modifications failed to increase rates of roll in DX327 early in 1945. DX333 joined the High Altitude Flight briefly, but no reports, if any were made, have been found. DX285 returned to the RAF shortly after arrival, probably without use.

Armament trials in DG562 were, the report states, protracted by the reluctance of Westland to incorporate the eight modifications recommended by the Establishment. The changes were, nevertheless, carried out on DX287 and firing trials (of 3,548 rounds) of the four 20mm guns were successful in early 1944. A ground trial of the installation proposed for the two-seat Welkin was partially inconclusive due to the difficulty of simulating flight conditions.

Thunderbolt

The Republic P-47Ds supplied under Lend-Lease arrangements were almost exclusively sent to the Far East, leaving only a handful for UK flying. Thus the first trials at the A&AEE were on a machine (42-7922) loaned by the 9th USAF in May 1943, but similar to RAF Thunderbolts. Handling was exceptionally pleasant, particularly at high weight, ie more than 12,000lb. Stability, controls and manoeuvrability were satisfactory, and the almost total absence of vibration was noteworthy. Minor criticisms were made of the view on the ground, the tendency of the ailerons to overbalance and the similarity of the rudder and aileron trimmers. Performance (see the Table) was very good, although the turbo-supercharger oversped at 25,000 feet, thus artificially limiting the height at which maximum boost (of the Double Wasp R-2800-21) could be used. More than a year later, in July 1944, FL849 appeared for IFF and radio trials, as well as clearance of two 55-gallon drop tanks (13,660lb all-up weight), and

Thunderbolt I FL849 in September 1944, with two 145-gallon external tanks; handling remained pleasant once the aircraft had been coaxed to a safe height. Dropping trials of the tanks were done on another aircraft. The panels behind the fuselage roundel are partially open to regulate airflow to the intercooler of the turbo-supercharger inside, which exhausts immediately underneath. The three blister covers of the skew hinges of the ailerons can be seen. *A&AEE AC1317*

P-47D-1-RE No 427922 in May 1943, on loan from the USAAF prior to delivery of Lend-Lease aircraft. Handling was pleasant, and few adverse comments were made. The armament of eight 0.5in guns is seen in the wings, and the extensive cooling flaps behind the engine are open. The cuffs round the roots of the propeller blades are interesting, possibly associated with cooling of the large Double Wasp (R-2800-21). *A&AEE 11406*

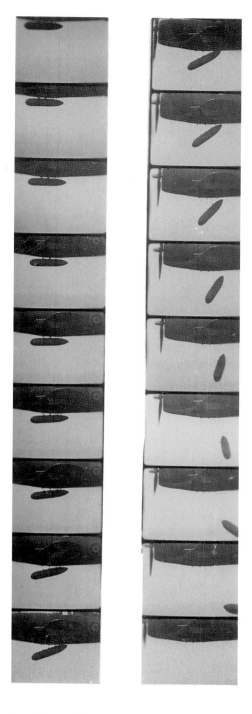

This fuel tank, holding 150 US gallons (125 Imperial), is under Thunderbolt FL844. Tanks of various capacities were flown on wing and fuselage stations in trials in early 1945. Handling, fuel flow and jettison characteristics were all investigated. *A&AEE 15614*

This sequence from a ciné film taken during the trials with Thunderbolt FL844 in early 1945 shows the behaviour of the tank at 200mph. This is typical of such trials late in the war. *A&AEE 15614*

handling with two 500lb bombs The latter increased stalling speed to 102mph (flaps and undercarriage down). FL844 (R-2800-59 engine) came in October 1944, and investigated the effect of carrying and dropping a variety of stores; the only problem was dropping 145-gallon tanks at 320mph, when the flaps were damaged. The take-off run at the maximum weight of 14,130lb was 475 yards minimum; unusually for an A&AEE report, a figure of 620 yards was given for an individual pilot using a 'safer technique'.

A bubble canopy identified HD182 received in March 1945, and, in addition on KJ298, a dorsal fin. There were no wartime reports on these two Mk II aircraft.

Trials in the summer of 1944 on the eight 0.5in guns were satisfactory, although the USAAF aircraft (42-74699) had had extensive prior use; some 27,000 rounds were expended. The same aircraft also dropped a wide range of stores including 1,000lb, 500lb, 250lb and smoke bombs; minor modifications were recommended to the release mechanism. Late in 1944 42-28916, also on loan and serviced by US airmen, tested American 4.5-inch rockets from M14 tubes.

P-47D-28-RA No 42-28916 in the stop butts in November 1944. The wet ground typified the weather during the eight-week trial of the 4.5-inch rocket tube, Type M14. The aircraft had many differences from RAF models, and was frequently unserviceable. Only fifty-three rockets were fired (another three fell off), revealing many faults, some attributable to poor design, including lack of stability. *A&AEE 15010*

Republic Thunderbolt 42-74699, July 1944, for armament trials. (Scale 1:72)

Meteor

The Gloster Meteor, the RAF's first jet aircraft, entered squadron service just as the first of the type arrived at Boscombe. Indeed, two aircraft were received for trials after two months with No 616 Squadron. Earlier, in February 1944, an Establishment team including four pilots had visited Gloster's airfield and flown the prototypes DG205/G (five flights) and DG208/G (one flight). At an 11,300lb all-up weight and mid CG, the aircraft was found easy to fly but the controls were badly harmonised. The elevator was too heavy and the rudder immovable at high speed, but the ailerons were too light; the need for continuously reading fuel gauges was stressed, and the report concludes, 'the 10 second minimum for throttle opening should be abolished'. The engines (W2B/23) were of an early standard.

Meteor Mark I

In June 1944 three pilots made a further visit to Gloster and flew four aircraft, including three production versions with various modifications. The extra thrust of the -/37 engines in DG209/G greatly improved the take-off, but, as with EE211/G and DG208/G, there was no reduction in directional oscillations. EE212/G, however, with a combined rudder balance and trim tab, was judged satisfactory.

Meteor I EE212/G in November 1944. Differences from Meteor III EE249, seen later, are apparent in the canopy, jet pipe size, fin, rudder, and marking details. EE212 lacks the lower fin surface, and has a slightly taller rudder that extends only down to the line of the top of the fuselage; also apparent are the end plate to the rudder and trimmer. The aircraft was progressively modified in an attempt to cure the directional oscillations that ruined gun aiming. *A&AEE 11935*

The priority task for Boscombe was to clear the armament for use by the Service; EE215/G was rapidly assessed on the ground and in the air in June 1944 before itself joining the RAF Squadron on 23 July 1944. The four 20mm guns functioned with some stoppages, and the empty cases and their links struck the fuselage/nacelles in seventy-six places prior to modification.

September 1944 saw the arrival of EE212/G with the area of fin and rudder below the fuselage deleted; directional oscillations were worse than previously experienced. The engines (W2B-23C) were standard, but the ailerons had apparently been modified as they were heavy;

stick forces for manoeuvres were too high and the rudder 'rather ineffective'. The critical Mach number was judged to be too low at 0.74. All-up weight of 11,670lb included 300 gallons of fuel, although at some stage a small ventral tank was fitted. Tests from January 1945 of the 105-gallon belly tank on EE214/G introduced no adverse handling effects, apart from increasing the weight (13,125lb), lengthening the take-off run, and reducing top speed by 15mph (true) at 20,000 feet. Radio (TR1143) and IFF (Mk IIIs) were satisfactory before April 1945, when the nacelles were damaged following premature undercarriage retraction on take-off.

Meteor I EE214/G in March 1945 with a 105-gallon ventral tank, which reduced top speed to 409mph (true) at 16,000 feet, but did not affect handling. The hole in the nose is for the G45 camera gun (mounted on an improved structure following early trials); also seen are the castoring nose wheel with white creep lines, four 20mm gun ports, the extended footstep and the early sideways-opening canopy. *A&AEE 15084*

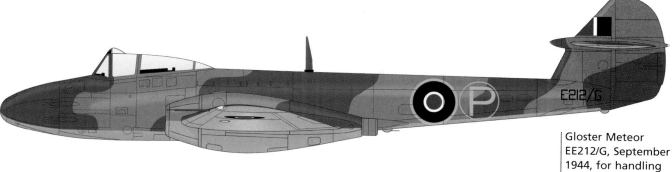

Gloster Meteor EE212/G, September 1944, for handling trials. (Scale 1:72)

EE213's gunnery trials (limited to firing below 15,000 feet) from October 1944 were trouble-free, and the Mk I ID gyro gunsight was well liked; the camera gun was satisfactory after strengthening the mounting. However, while firing was acceptable, the aircraft again exhibited a natural high-frequency directional oscillation that spoiled the aim (the Spitfire IX was 2.3 times as accurate); it was thought possible that this phenomenon was a characteristic of jet aircraft. More research was planned, and EE212/G spent two months at the RAE from February 1945.

A further characteristic, most decidedly a feature of the early jets, was the need for frequent and accurate readings of instruments for performance measurement. These readings were beyond the capability of the pilot, so EE212 was modified by removal of the ammunition behind the pilot, and a small writing surface and seat installed with the necessary instruments. The first jet passenger at the A&AEE was carried on 9 August 1945; there was no practical possibility of escape. The performance in the table was recorded. EE212 also had a metal-covered elevator and exhibited excessive stability above 400mph when stick forces became too heavy. An early W2B-37 (later named Derwent I) was fitted in EE223/G (which arrived in February 1945); top speed increased to 465mph (true) at 16,000 feet.

Meteor Mark III

EE249/G (replacing EE245/G, with faulty engines), with Derwent Is, 30 gallons more fuel,

a sliding hood and structural strengthening, was weighed in February 1945, while EE230/G, the first Mark III, retained the W213/23C engines and was used for the first jet flame damping trials. Looking directly from the rear, the flames could be seen more than a mile away. On the gunsight, an RAE range control was preferred to another by Gloster. Handling the Mark III was similar to the earlier version, with criticism of elevator heaviness. Trials of EE269 with the standardised 185-gallon ventral tank were under way in August 1945, after earlier experience on EE214/G with a 105-gallon tank. Functioning and jettison up to 405mph were satisfactory, although the take-off run at the new weight of 14,516lb was 'increased', but no measurements are given in the report.

Vampire

Designed initially to take advantage of the Halford jet engine, the first de Havilland Vampire to reach Boscombe was the third prototype, MP838/G, in April 1944, beating the first Meteor by two months. Initial handling was compared favourably with contemporary fighters, but excessive snaking occurred in turbulence. From a maximum speed of 490mph, deceleration was very slow in the clean configuration; the stall was uneventful at 80mph (undercarriage and flaps down). Engine inspections were made after every 5 and 12½ hours flying time, and many minor suggestions were made to improve maintenance, including the need for fuel drain

Meteor III EE249/G in March 1945, revealing details of the canopy, jet pipe size, fin and rudder, small elevator horn balances and anti-balance tabs. *A&AEE 15048*

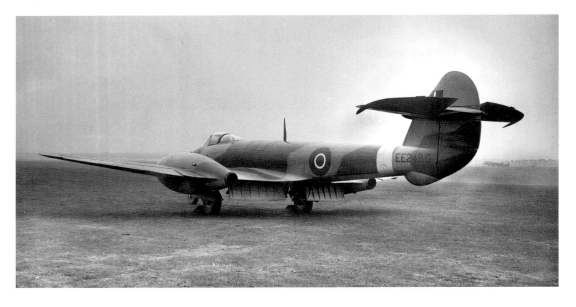

holes round the engine to prevent fire damage in the event of a 'hot' start, of which there were many during the four weeks.

The prototype's Halford H1A engine was replaced by a Goblin I in the first production aircraft TG274/G (received in May 1945); handling at 8,610lb (202 gallons of fuel) revealed mixed characteristics. From the gentle stall at 85mph (flaps and undercarriage down) to 510mph handling was pleasant, and 5g, an exceptional figure, could be obtained at 30,000 feet. An inertia weight of 13lb overcame very low stick forces in manoeuvres. On the other hand, the rate of roll (70°/sec) needed improvement, and the ailerons overbalanced at a high Mach number. Misting outside the canopy on descent was an unusual feature and the fuel gauges very inconsistent. The report contains, to modern eyes, the extraordinary statement that 'rigorous application of elevator [is] necessary to get aircraft airborne in a reasonable distance'. Finally, the report concludes that the levers for flap and for undercarriage are easily confused – a statement from experience, as the wheels were inadvertently raised after landing in August 1945. The maximum speed of 526mph (true) at 25,500 feet exceeded that of all other aircraft tested in the period.

Gunnery trials on production aircraft had not started by August 1945, but MP838/G had earlier revealed many shortcomings, requiring twelve essential modifications; the trial was stopped after only four air firing sorties in May 1944.

Vampire I TG274/G was the first production aircraft, arriving at Boscombe in May 1945, and one of the few aircraft to be dwarfed by the 8-foot pole. The rudders are split by the tailplane, the pressure head is on the port fin and a small fairing is just outboard of the starboard undercarriage. In the background the completed runway stretches into the distance, but the contractors' plant remains.

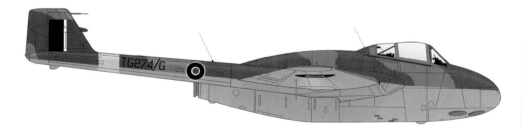

De Havilland Vampire TG274/G, March 1945, for handling/performance trials. (Scale 1:72)

Fury

The Hawker Fury prototype, NX798, spent two brief periods at the A&AEE – a week in October 1944 and the month of May 1945 – both involving handling. Weighing 11,307lb with 181 gallons of fuel, both airframe and engine (Centaurus 12 SM) were exceptionally serviceable. The report says that the Fury was the first aircraft with really effective spring tab ailerons and rudder, and set a new standard of manoeuvrability at very high speed – up to 470mph. There were three major criticisms: nose-heaviness with increase in speed, a violent wing drop on landing (not predictable from stalls), and vibrations. Fitting a larger tailplane and elevator and moving the oil cooler to the port wing for the second visit cured the instability (nose-heaviness) and the wing drop at the stall. The Establishment felt that a few minor modifications would make the Fury outstanding. On being collected by a firm's pilot on 14 May, the engine failed due to oil leaking from the crankcase.

Hornet

The long-range de Havilland Hornet, like the jet aeroplanes, was used first at the A&AEE for gun firing trials. On RR919/G (non-handed Merlin 130), unserviceability and the need for testing modifications extended trials for six months from November 1944. The arrival of a production aircraft, PX210, in February 1945, followed by PX211 together with PX217 and PX218 for intensive flying in June and July 1945, enabled full trials to get under way. Weighing – 16,136lb with 358 gallons of fuel – was followed by gun heating, engineering appraisal, navigation and cockpit contamination trials. The Merlin 131/2 engines with left and right propeller rotation were in particularly compact nacelles, giving rise to awkward maintenance.

Hornet I RR919 in November 1944, in the butts where the first tests on the type were made on the four short-barrel Hispano Mk V 20mm guns. The armament installation was eventually satisfactory after modifications, mostly strengthening, were made following ground and air firing. The uncomplicated undercarriage and neat engine cowling are apparent, as are the blanking plate for the leading edge intake and the faired carrier for the starboard bomb or fuel tank. The propellers are non-handed. The formidable earthwork of the butts is noteworthy. *A&AEE 11987*

Hornet I PX210 in March 1945 in production form. The elegance of the type apparent in this view was matched by outstanding performance and handling both in trials and RAF service. *A&AEE 15053*

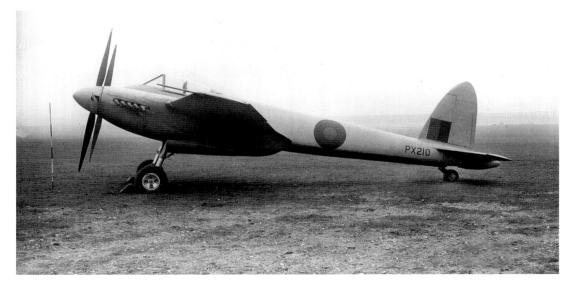

Spiteful NN664 in June 1945, shortly after arrival; trials were under way at the end of the war. Its development from the Spitfire is obvious; changes include the thinner wing and radiators of reduced drag. Only the tail section appears to have been painted, while the remainder of the aircraft has not; damage and modifications to the empennage had been completed by Supermarine. *A&AEE AC1351*

Spiteful

The first Supermarine Spiteful, NN664, the first to arrive, appeared in June 1945; trials continued after the war.

Gladiator

Two biplane Gloster Gladiators flew from Martlesham Heath in September 1939: K6129 (Mercury VIII), with some Sea Gladiator features, and K7964 (Mercury IX), flown by the Armament Squadron. They departed in May and June 1940 respectively. K7919, probably retaining its pre-war blind flying panel, was in use from October 1939 to June 1940. N5903 appears in the serviceability return from July 1945 for use at the armament demonstration at Larkhill. No reports of the work of these four has been found. K8042 made a swift and successful trial in September 1941 with an extra pair of 0.303in guns under the top wing (a total of six guns each with 425 rounds); very slight damage was caused by ejected cartridges from the top guns.

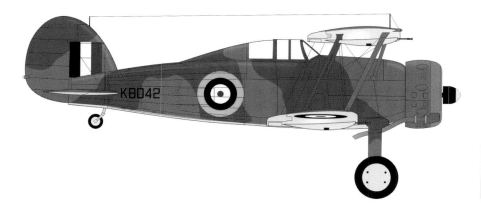

Gloster Gladiator K8042, September 1941, for gunnery trials. (Scale 1:72)

The Hillson Bi-mono in October (flying) and November (on the ground) in 1941 in its biplane and monoplane configurations. Anecdotal evidence suggests that the upper wing was jettisoned, but any formal reports have not been found; it is likely that only a 'Letter' report was made. There are protective frames round the rudder and elevator horn balances, presumably to protect the control surfaces when the top wing was dropped. This interesting experiment continued with the biplane Hurricane. The open ground behind would soon be home to many other aircraft. *A&AEE recognition 48*

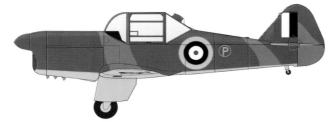

Hillson Bi-Mono, October 1941, for handling trials. (Scale 1:72)

Hillson Bi-Mono

The recorded purpose of the un-numbered Hillson Bimono was 'Trials as biplane and monoplane'. It arrived in mid-October 1941 powered by a de Havilland Gipsy Six, and was allotted away in mid-November. Any reports on this interesting aeroplane have not been found – but one anecdote suggests that it was, at least, interesting to fly. The pilot reported that the maximum level speed as a biplane was less than the stalling speed as a monoplane; in other words, jettisoning the top wing caused an immediate stall. The company pilot had earlier reported a gentle sink of a few hundred feet on jettisoning. The monoplane landing was described as 'like a high-speed kangaroo'.

Gloster F5/34

Gloster F5/34 K5604 (Mercury IX) spent five months at Boscombe after the outbreak of war, with the Performance Squadron.

Focke-Wulf FW 190A

From June 1943 Focke-Wulf FW190A-3 PN999 appeared on the list of aircraft held by the Establishment; it seems to have been unserviceable for most of its five-week stay. In the same month an A&AEE pilot flew FW 190A-4 PE882 at the RAE; it was photographed, possibly as a replacement for the unserviceable PN999.

8 Multi-seat Fighters
Defiant to Black Widow

Defiant

The pleasant handling of the Boulton Paul Defiant was established at Martlesham Heath, then the prototype K8310 (Merlin I) flew to Boscombe in September 1939 fitted with an experimental turret, together with K8620. The standard turret (four 0.303in guns) proved smooth in operation, and could be rearmed by two men in 30 minutes (a long time); other details are missing, although it returned to the A&AEE briefly in August 1940 with a single 20mm gun in the turret prior to some trials at Exeter. K8620 was joined by the production L6950; both departed in June 1940 after joint performance (see the Table) and handling. Performance (with Merlin III and two-pitch propeller) was somewhat disappointing to the Air Staff, but the 104 gallons of fuel was expected to give a useful patrol time. Handling remained conventional and aerobatics straightforward; comments include the difficulty of opening the pilot's hood at more than 200mph. L6950 had provision for bombs under the wings; the results are not known. Three months of tests included electrical and radio assessment on L6953 from September 1939; the T1119/R1120 radios were satisfactory and powered by batteries of sufficient durability. The de Havilland constant-speed propellers introduced to the Defiant in L6954 (from May 1940) conferred a useful increase in performance above 10,000 feet (see the Table); the take-off run remained at 305 yards. This aircraft returned in late 1940 with a tropical radiator and oil cooler, with an air cleaner in the air intake; times to height were slightly increased by climbing at a speed faster than optimum to keep temperatures down. L6954 was damaged in a German raid in April 1941. L6968 put in a very brief appearance in April 1940 prior to flying to France early in May for assessment in the Army co-operation role. A new Morris-type radiator assessed in N3397 from August 1941 gave disappointing results even with other improvements to the tropical arrangements in 1942. The performance of N3488 from May 1941 was not greatly affected by an increase in wing fuel to 160 gallons and the resulting increase in gross weight to 8,380lb.

Defiant Mark II

The two-speed supercharger of the Merlin XX bestowed an improved performance (see the Table) on the prototype Defiant II N1551 when tested from November 1940. Handling was not completed, but at best range speed (162mph) 5.65 air miles per gallons could be obtained. The first production aircraft of this mark, AA370, arrived in August 1941 adorned with radar aerials and carrying extra fuel (a total of 162 gallons); performance suffered

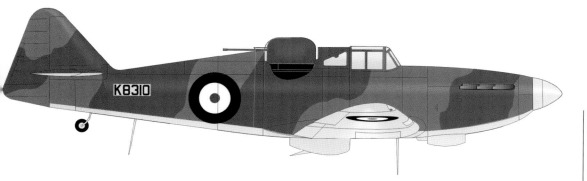

Boulton Paul Defiant K8310, October 1939, for turret trials with a single 20mm gun109. (Scale 1:72)

231

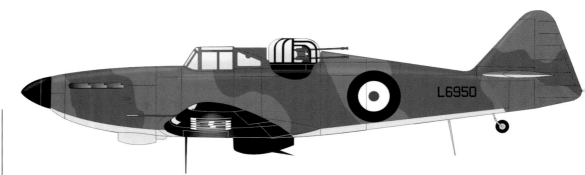

Boulton Paul
Defiant L6950,
September 1939,
for turret trials.
(Scale 1:72)

accordingly (see the Table). A smaller-diameter (11ft 3in) propeller produced disappointing results. In spite of the extra drag and weight, AA370 achieved 5.78 air miles per gallon at 20,000 feet, giving a maximum range of 810 miles (695 practical). Handling revealed a sudden reduction in push force as speed was increased above 360mph, and, at lower speeds, an unacceptable overbalance of the rudder. The latter was cured by modifying the rudder trim tab. Engine cooling remained marginal, and a Marston radiator was no improvement. Longitudinal characteristics with an inertia weight in the elevator controls were no better in N1550 in July 1942, and handling was unaffected by the large fairing for the tropical radiator; engine cooling was at last satisfactory. AA378 (in September 1941 with a modified rudder) and N1579 (from January 1944 for use with Lancaster JA870) joined the Performance Squadron, while AA354 (August 1943) flew with the Armament Squadron.

The prototype Defiant II, N1551, in December 1940. It has extra internal fuel, a large oil cooler housing and national markings appropriate to the period. The fuselage ramp is raised, but the radiator flap is lowered. A section of the wing root fillet lowers to make a step. The rudder has only a single trim tab. An HF aerial runs under the rear fuselage. *A&AEE 9661*

Defiant II N1550 is at Boscombe in July 1942 for handling trials in connection with the enormous tropical oil cooler fairing. It also has extra internal fuel and national markings appropriate to the period. The fuselage ramp is lowered, as is the radiator flap, and a section of the wing root fillet is lowered to make a step. The rudder has an extra tab above the trimmer. *A&AEE 11041*

Defiant II AA370 in August 1941 in night-fighter version with black finish, radar aerials, flame damping exhausts and the aft top fuselage ramp lowered. *A&AEE 9780*

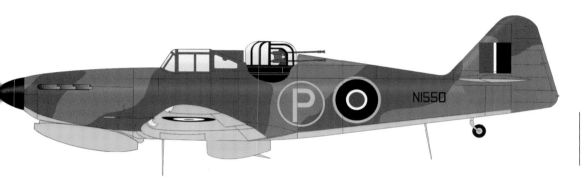

Boulton Paul Defiant N1550, June 1942, for handling trials. (Scale 1:72)

Defiant Target Towing Mark I and III

Known to the Establishment as a 'TT Mk I', DR942 arrived in September 1942 and was flown with both a windmill winch and the lighter electrical version. Fitted with a Merlin XX, handling was normal, and engine temperatures (oil and coolant) were satisfactory when towing a 4-foot sleeve target. DR936 (from January 1943) with a Mk IIN IFF produced mediocre signals. DR863 left in May 1942 after five weeks of unserviceability.

Defiant TT III (converted Mk I) N3488 in January 1943, with the winch stowed and a target visible in its housing under the fuselage. Under the fuselage (aft of the radiator) are the pulley wheels to the target. There is a guard for the tail wheel and the starboard elevator to prevent fouling. Just visible under the wing are the target towing stripes. *A&AEE 11254*

Defiant TT III (converted Mk I) DR863 in July 1942 after leaving Boscombe Down over what appears to be Church Crookham near Farnborough. The winch has been removed and the hole blanked over; the winch operator is out of sight but his hole is left open. This view clearly shows the camouflage pattern: Dark Green and Dark Earth above, Night and Trainer Yellow stripes below. Maybe if the Defiant had had wing guns... *A&AEE recognition 99*

Boulton Paul Defiant N3488, May 1941, for performance trials. (Scale 1:72)

N3488 returned late in 1942, retaining its Merlin III but equipped for target towing as a 'TT Mk III'. Handling was 'just like other Defiants', but oil cooling initially needed improvement when towing the 4-foot sleeve target; an enlarged oil cooler was fitted in mid-1943 and proved satisfactory.

Havoc

The Douglas DB7 aircraft taken over from France and powered by two Twin Wasp R-1830-S3C4-G engines had a small (171-gallon) fuel capacity, rendering them unsuitable for the intended light bomber role as Boston IIs; they were renamed Havoc I.

The first two Havoc Is, AW397 and AW410, flew to Boscombe in October 1940, the latter for armament trials in conjunction with the RAE. They were followed by BB899 for performance

work in November and BJ471 early in 1941; none of these four stayed long, and no reports have been found. From February 1941 BJ474 had a Rose mounting for two Vickers K guns fitted by the A&AEE in the rear cockpit; results were encouraging and superior to the Browning installation in the Boston, but the Vickers guns were not adopted for operational Havocs. Heating of the nose-mounted guns by air passed round the engine exhausts became acceptable after modification. A most interesting trial on BD126 took place in May 1941. A battery of six upward-firing machine guns with freedom in elevation between 30° to 50° from the vertical and 15° traverse was remotely controlled by a gunner with a sight in the nose. Although several stoppages occurred, the firing, feed and ejection were satisfactory following modifications by the Establishment. Perhaps most remarkable of all was the time of only 5 minutes taken by two armourers to replace all six guns. Trials continued at the Gun Research Unit, Exeter, in June. The last of the Twin Wasp-engined Havocs, AW392, appeared in July 1941 with a Turbinlite (searchlight) in place of guns in the nose; the extra weight, including batteries, was 2,440lb.

Havoc II

A change to more powerful R-2600-A5B (Cyclone) engines identified the Havoc II. AH433, with a battery of twelve 0.303in machine guns in the nose, was tested from February 1941, having the throttle sense reversed so that forward gave maximum power, but retaining some metric instruments. Gun heating, giving a 50°C rise in temperature, was lavishly praised – 'all aircraft should have it' – and firing trials (using 17,336 rounds) were trouble-free. The take-off run at 17,000lb was 435 yards with full flap (30°), but handling considerations after unstick limited the flap angle to 15° with a penalty of only 25 yards. Hardly had the report on AH433 been issued than a similar gun heating system for the four

20mm cannon of AH444 was found inadequate due, it was thought, to the larger gun ports sucking the hot air out. Conversely, AH464 was used to check for overheating (twelve machine guns); full power at 2,000 feet produced a steady, and acceptable, temperature of +68.5°C. A snag with the twelve guns was a temporary but dangerous concentration of carbon monoxide after firing. AH471 crashed shortly after arrival due to a servicing error, unconnected with contamination.

Indistinguishable from its bombing sibling, AH450 and AH467 completed performance measurements in mid-1941 for both Boston III and Havoc II (see the Table); holes in the cowlings materially assisting cooling but reduced top speed by 15mph (true). The similarity between types was used to test the Boston's four 20mm armament in Havoc AH517 late in 1941.

Flame damping, a success on the first Cyclone aircraft, was removed on AH509 (from October 1941); stub exhausts increased the top speed by 23mph (true). Damping was re-established by fitting ejector fish-tails on

Havoc II AH450, seen in about October 1940, was the first aircraft powered by the ubiquitous Double Cyclone (R-2600-A5B); the cooling holes round the nacelles were made by the A&AEE in an early attempt to improve cooling. No guns were carried on this aircraft. A 'French'-style fin flash is visible. *A&AEE 9690*

This early Vickers (RAE) design on Havoc II AH433 in June 1941 has 'intensifier' pipes for gun heating. For flame damping this exhaust was entirely satisfactory. *A&AEE 9740*

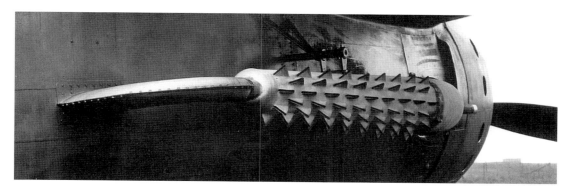

Havoc II AH470 in January 1942. This much-published image was taken during trials by the A&AEE and depicts the Turbinlite nose with AI radar aerials and matt black finish. The aircraft spent two months at Boscombe from 7 December 1941. *A&AEE 9849*

the stubs, reducing the earlier benefit to an extra 13mph (true). Overload tanks in the bomb bay added 180lb and 110 gallons of fuel (for a total of 382 gallons) to AH526, which was also burdened with ineffective Avro-type flame dampers.

The long-suffering AH509 was the last Havoc at the A&AEE in July 1942, having started its career there in July 1941 testing the effect of the undercarriage as an airbrake. Speeds up to 350mph were satisfactory, but the wheels would not lock down if selected at speeds greater than 290mph. In December 1941 Havoc II (Turbinlite) AH470 arrived and appears only to have been used for weight measurement; at 18,994lb maximum, even without guns, it was some 240lb heavier than AH509 with guns and an extra 110 gallons of fuel. AH437 appeared in April 1941 for brief, unrecorded flame damping trials.

Beaufighter

Prototypes

Designed as a cannon fighter (four 20mm guns) and based on the Beaufort, the Bristol Beaufighter was rapidly designed and subsequently comprehensively modified before and during service. By the beginning of July 1940 four aircraft had arrived at Boscombe (R2052 and R2054 in April, R2055 in May and R2060 in July); by the end of the September all had left without a formal report having been written. These four aircraft were returned to the makers for modifications to rectify the many problems discovered, notably in handling and stability about all three axes; also the first three aircraft were originally each fitted as an expedient with a

Beaufighter I R2052 has the original windscreen (and bead sight) of 1940. The heavy windscreen structure obscured the pilot's vision. *A&AEE*

An improved windscreen was fitted to Beaufighter R2054 in early 1941. This also shows the camera gun above the cockpit cover. Visibility for the pilot was greatly improved, both by day and by night. *A&AEE*

pair of Hercules II engines. The first of the unsatisfactory features to be remedied was the windscreen on R2054 on return in late 1940, by which time Hercules IIIs had been fitted, and the radios (TR9D and blind approach equipment R1124A and R1125A) tested acceptably. Four early Hispano 20mm guns were fitted (probably in R2060), together with Bristol's own slim drum feed mechanism; the latter was not adopted for Service use, possibly as a result of the A&AEE's experience during trials in July 1940. Full tests of the 20mm armament involved R2060 from February 1941; a comment was that 1,000 rounds per gun took an excessive time to load (11½ hours). R2055 reappeared from AGME Duxford in January 1942, where trials of two 40mm guns (one each side, by Vickers and Rolls Royce) had been made; at the A&AEE the aircraft was used to test modifications as the need arose over eighteen months.

Beaufighter Mark I

Three further Hercules-engined aircraft arrived in quick succession from December 1940, R2063, T4623 and X7540; the last pair were the first made by two shadow factories. The 'shadow' aircraft, with Hercules Xs, produced markedly superior performance figures (see the Table) when compared with the earlier prototypes, but the differences could not be explained by the new mark of engine. Dives to 400mph were satisfactory, and the minimum speed for single-engined flying was 130mph. Prior to severe damage in an air raid in April

1941, a brief trial on R2268 with a 20% increase in tailplane area and unshielded horn balances showed a marginal increase in longitudinal stability at low speed, but still not sufficiently safe for night-flying.

R2057, with a 12½° dihedral tailplane (taking much of it out of the propeller wash), was initially judged a great improvement, and this finding was confirmed after repair following a heavy landing in July 1941. The same machine was then fitted with Hercules Xs and split trailing edge airbrakes, eventually developed to operate without trim change and to allow a 40° dive to be made at 285mph (without the brakes a dive of only 13° could be made at constant speed). Late in 1943 the source of the vacuum for operating the speed brakes was moved from an external venting tube (7mph (true) speed penalty) to a duct in the wing leading edge. Unfortunately, asymmetric brake operation was experienced, as well as automatic retraction at 300mph; the interesting flying undoubtedly involved is ignored in the report.

Damage to R2063 on landing in May 1941 followed extensive measurements of cockpit and gun temperatures; copious sealing and, later, lagging failed to cure ineffective heating. Returning for a third time, the aeroplane had non-feathering hydromatic propellers; control was judged sufficient for a return to base following an engine failure. A fourth visit, but with Hercules XIs, was used to establish range figures at 19,600lb (550 gallons of fuel); the optimum height was 15,000 feet, giving 1,560

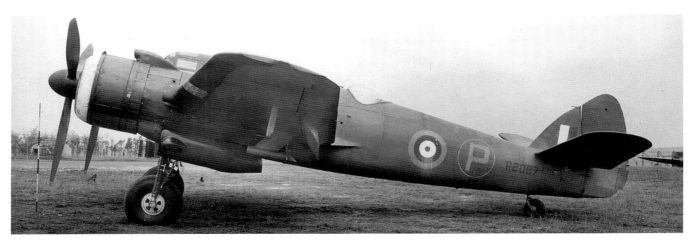

Beaufighter I R2057 in May 1942 shows the venturi under the wing, which operated the airbrakes; the lower port section is seen lowered; the upper section was similar. The dihedral tailplane is fitted, and no engine exhausts are visible. *A&AEE 9995*

miles (maximum) and 1,150 miles (practical). The extra power was sufficient to climb on a single engine at 13,000 feet. Performance was not comprehensively reported for the Mk I, and flame damping (unsatisfactory) was measured only in late 1942 on T4791. T4770 (in October 1944), V8319 and X7574 (both August 1945) had target towing equipment fitted.

Beaufighter Mark II

R2058 with Merlin XXs spent three months with the Performance Squadron from December 1940, but apparently no formal report was written. R2270, the first production Mk II, bore the brunt of testing for nearly a year from May 1941. The Merlin engines exacerbated the poor stability characteristics; a dihedral tailplane was then fitted, together with an inertia weight in the elevator control run. Both gave a great improvement, and the report concluded that 'now … [the modifications] will give a sufficient

degree of stability in the climb to make the Beaufighter II satisfactory when flying at low speed on dark nights.' It seems, however, that the Service found the modified aircraft too stable, and the straight tailplane was investigated on R2329 in September 1942 with a view to determining an acceptable CG. The Establishment recommended a limit of 55 inches aft of datum for experienced pilots, and for average pilots 54 inches by day and 52.9 inches by night. Such guidance cannot have been easy to follow in service. The lateral and directional deficiencies were addressed successfully early in 1943 on T3032 with a large extension to the fin; swing on take-off was eliminated and single-engine flying considerably improved.

Performance tests, on R2270, concentrated on the effect of removal of the undercarriage doors (14½mph (true) penalty), fitting flame dampers (14mph penalty), and fitting tropical filters (see the Table). Consumption was least

Beaufighter II R2058 in December 1940, with the fin and rudder submitted by the firm following its early experience with handling the Merlin-engined version. The A&AEE's comments are unknown. The pressure head is under the port wing and the inner portions of the propellers are painted white. *A&AEE 9665*

Beaufighter Mk II T3032 in February 1943, with the 13.1sq ft addition to the fin that finally cured the directional problems of this version. Aerials can be seen on the nose, ahead of the wing roundels, on the starboard wing and above the fuselage. *A&AEE recognition 127*

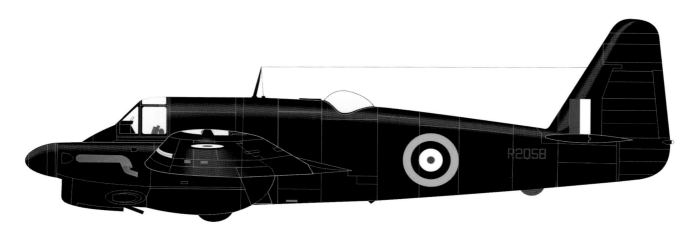

Bristol Beaufighter R2058, December 1940, for handling/ performance trials.

at 20,000 feet, giving 3.05ampg, the same as the Mk I; 376 gallons of fuel were carried at the start. Much effort was expended on flame damping, starting with two Rolls Royce types on R2270, then a modification on R2310 in late 1941, several RAE types on R2391 (until March 1943) and further Rolls Royce designs on R2061 (May 1942).

Late in 1941 T3031 arrived with four production 20mm guns; the belt feed of ammunition was found to be robust, positive and almost trouble-free, in spite of heating in the gun bay failing to meet previously determined criteria. Previously trials of the six

wing-mounted (two port and four starboard) 0.303in guns had been abandoned in spite of many A&AEE improvements on R2347 in the course of firing more than 32,000 rounds in the summer of 1941. A year later there were further trials of the wing guns, but results are not known. R2311 was destroyed on the ground in July 1942 after returning from Farnborough; R2375 (from September 1941) was due to undertake stall warning tests, but no report has been found.

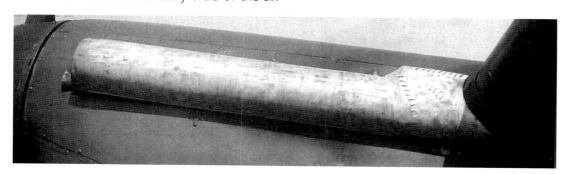

An ineffective flame damping exhaust on a Beaufighter II, R2061, in June 1942; this design was by Rolls Royce.

An RAE design for
the Merlin
Beaufighter R2391
was effective in mid-
1942. *A&AEE 11027*

An RAE design for the Merlin Beaufighter R2391 was effective in mid-1942. *A&AEE 11027*

Beaufighter Mark V

A Bolton Paul turret characterised R2274, the only aircraft of this mark to reach Boscombe for short tests in May 1941. There was little effect on handling (a straight tailplane was fitted) or top speed, but the wing guns and two nose guns had been removed. Rotation and elevation speeds were satisfactory, but draughts and the limited elevation angle achievable (less than 21° above fuselage datum) received criticism. Most unsatisfactory was the removal of the pilot's emergency exit, which was blocked by the turret.

Beaufighter Mark VI

X7542, the prototype Mk VI, appeared in October 1941 powered by Hercules VIs optimised for high altitude, and soon approved for +8psi boost. Performance (see the Table) later included measurement of the effect of tropical intakes, 'bracket' and hydromatic propellers, and with spinners. The tropical filters reduced top speed by 8mph (true), and spinners added 5mph (true). Later, a simple technique for service use was evolved to give the most economical cruise; maximum range with 550 gallons of fuel (21,000lb all-up weight) was 1,500 miles at either 5,000 feet (MS gear) or 15,000 feet (FS gear). Acceptable handling, including single-engine flying, was dependent on keeping the CG forward of 53½ inches aft of datum. X7881, with a modified oil cooler duct, gave satisfactory cooling from December 1941, and other changes in X7882 from November 1941 satisfactorily cured violent

Beaufighter V R2274 in May 1941, with the Boulton Paul Type A turret with four 0.303in guns. Turmoil in 1940 in both trials and their reporting resulted in R2274 being the subject of the first formal report on Merlin-engined Beaufighters. The black finish is streaked, and visible are the exhausts of the early, but ineffective, flame damping standard, and the aerials on the wing leading edge and below it. The blind approach aerial is under the fuselage, and the blanked-over position above it. *A&AEE 9750*

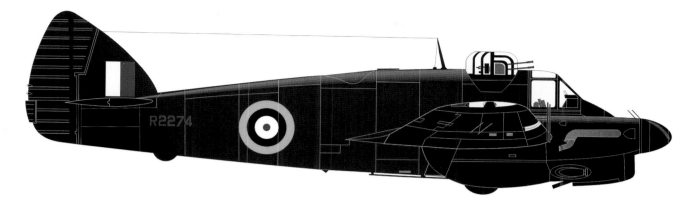

propeller surging at altitude. In the new year, 1942, X7883 had A&AEE-installed non-magnetic gun blast tubes to overcome the compass deviations previously experienced after gun firing; results were confirmed in EL343 a year later. EL151, a matt black aircraft, had a second form of airbrake intended to use split trailing edge; the inoperable mechanism reduced top speed by 9mph (true).

All Beaufighters so far described were for use in the fighter role; Coastal Command equipment requirements differed slightly from those of Fighter Command. The former added torpedoes to the aircraft's repertoire, and after weighing of a standard fighter, X8209, in July 1942 and EL223/G in the Torpedo role the following month, the maximum weight (with 679 gallons of fuel and Mk XIII torpedo of 2,127lb) rose to 24,299lb. EL223, with a dihedral tailplane fitted at the A&AEE, handled well, and, unusually, the Establishment released a torpedo to check trim change; there was none. Performance is given in the Table. EL292 was armed with the simple but effective single 0.303in gun in a so-called turret (Bristol B20) from February 1943; it later released 250lb and 100lb bombs successfully. Rockets

used to great effect later by the RAF were first tested on EL329/G from August 1942. With eight RPs the aircraft seemed to wallow in the climb and the stalling speeds were slightly raised, but otherwise it handled normally. Carriage and firing trials were curtailed by a crash on 24 September 1942; after firing at 50 feet, the port engine seized on pulling up into an irrecoverable position, and the two crew were killed.

The replacement, EL285, was in fact used in tests of long feed chutes to the guns until it, too, was extensively damaged when a 20mm round exploded on firing in March 1943 while T5103, an 'old' aircraft with 260 hours flying to its credit in six months of existence, revealed no deterioration in performance on account of its age. X7880, with individual exhaust pipes, failed to meet the night visibility requirement early in 1943. The Hercules XVI powered later Mk VI aircraft, including V8442, which was engaged on engine cooling measurements from November 1942, while JL876 from February 1943 concentrated on asymmetric handling. With the port engine windmilling, height could be maintained at weights up to 23,000lb, while handling was unaffected by position of the CG.

Bristol Beaufighter R2274, May 1941, for turret trials. (Scale 1:72)

Beaufighter VI X7881 in January 1942 in the rain ready for tests of the revised oil cooling duct (the unpainted intake beside the engine). The Hercules VI engines have tapered, shrouded, slotted flame damping exhausts, and the wing tip aerials of this night-fighter are well shown. *A&AEE 9852*

Beaufighter VI EL223/G in August 1942, with evidence on the fuselage of the work done by the A&AEE to fit the dihedral tailplane for performance measurements while carrying a torpedo. The transparent cover for the DF aerial became standard, while the wing tip roundel is apparent on only a few Beaufighters. The fuselage panel on which the roundel is painted appears to have been fitted recently, and is less faded than the remainder. *A&AEE 11055*

EL329/G, a Mk VI, in August 1942, with the first RP installation on the type, shows the long projectors (rails) of the RP Mk I; small 25lb heads are fitted to the rockets. There is a roundel under the port wing. *A&AEE 11181*

The Beaufighter was prone to losing hatches in moments of excitement, but JL876 (Hercules XVII) showed that up to 240mph hatchless flight was uneventful. Similarly powered aircraft (later designated Mk XI) were JL948 and JM119, on navigation and compass work respectively, both in May 1943, while JL871 investigated the feed mechanism to the guns.

Beaufighter VI V8442 in February 1945, during a long series of engine trials. Nose and wing aerials can be seen on this coastal aeroplane with Hercules XVI motors. The entrance door is open with the ladder lowered, and the gun ports are taped over. The notice on the hangar exhorts visiting pilots to report to the watch office west of the tarmac. *A&AEE 15018*

Beaufighter Mark X

With Hercules XVIIs optimised for low level, engine cooling was the first priority for EL290 on arrival in December 1942; temperatures were satisfactory after a minor modification to the cowling nose rings. Performance (see the Table) at 24,000lb with a Mk XII torpedo was better than the Mk VI below 15,000 feet, handling (including use of dive brakes) was unchanged, and the take-off run was only 440 yards. With 679 gallons of fuel, range was 1,550 miles (maximum) and 1,240 miles (practical), using the current allowances for take-off and climb. Late in 1943 LZ293, with a heavy torpedo, flew at 25,500lb; the Establishment recommended that this configuration should not be flown in cloud or at night. Then followed

NE343 (from January 1944) and NV612 later, with a 200-gallon auxiliary fuel tank under the fuselage, then NE352 (from July 1944), with a windscreen wiper; all three gave satisfaction. In mid-1944 another configuration on NT921 (two 500lb bombs under the fuselage plus two 250lb depth charges under the wings) caused both longitudinal and directional instability to such an extent that only the most experienced pilots were advised to fly on night operations. Greatly improved handling at aft CG on NV451 from September 1944 resulted from an increase in elevator aerodynamic balance coupled with two anti-balance geared tabs and a dorsal fin; the acceptable aft limit for experienced pilots was extended by 3 inches – a significant operational benefit.

Beaufighter X NT921 in June 1944, resplendent in black and white 'invasion' stripes and revealing much detail. On the wings are two 250lb depth charges, and under the fuselage two 500lb bombs mounted clear of the torpedo crutches. The camera aperture on the nose is blanked off, and just behind are two VHF aerials, while above is the fresh air intake for the cabin. Air intakes for cabin heating are seen in pairs at the front of the engine exhaust pipes. *A&AEE 11817*

In late 1944 NV451, a Mk X, retains the early Mk I RP installation. Greatly improved handling resulted from the dorsal fin, the 40% increase in rudder aerodynamic balance and the inset hinges of the elevator with its anti-balance tab (visible outboard on the starboard side). On all the aircraft the proximity of the RPs to the pressure head is noteworthy; the resulting pressure error was small. *A&AEE 12002*

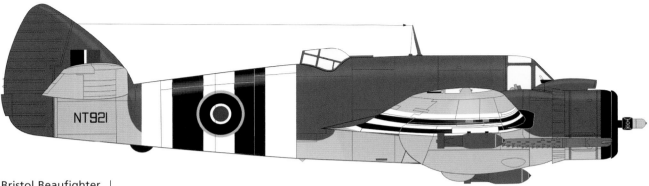

Bristol Beaufighter
NT921, 1944, for
bombing trials.
(Scale 1:72)

Development of RP capability led to a Mk III installation with jettisonable rails late in 1944, when NE352 measured an increase of 7mph (true) after release; handling was unaffected. This was soon followed by a satisfactory RP installation on EL393; an interesting result from the attitude measurements gave a correlation of 1 degree pitch change per 0.0850 change. Accuracy and jettison trials continued on NV246 into 1945, by which time tests on NV535 carrying a 1,000lb bomb had been suspended. LZ437 had the smoke curtain installation for Porton from October 1943.

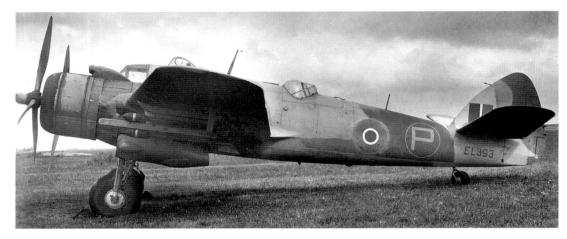

Mk X EL393 in December 1944 has the RP Mk VI installation with vertical pairs of rockets (60lb heads). The Bristol B20 turret is well shown, but is without its guns. An extra VHF aerial is mounted above the roundel. *A&AEE 15186*

Boulton Paul P92/2

Boulton Paul P92/2
V3142, July 1943,
for handling trials.

The Boulton Paul P92 cannon-turret fighter had long been cancelled by the time the half-scale P92/2, V3142, appeared at Boscombe in July 1943. Enthusiasm to fly this novel twin Gipsy Major II toy was blunted when the emergency escape arrangements were discovered. The narrow cramped cockpit had a jettisonable panel in the floor through which the pilot fell after collapsing his seat backwards; not least of the problems was the inability of the pilot to reach the jettison handle. A piece of cord to the handle gave peace of mind, at least to those not flying. Other features included effective airbrakes operated by a non-rechargeable air bottle and a one-piece cockpit hood, entirely removed for normal entry and exit. In the air, handling up to 190mph was very pleasant, particularly on asymmetric power, but lateral characteristics needed some unspecified improvement.

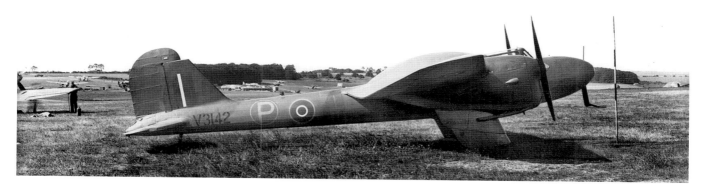

Boulton Paul P92/2 V3142 was present in July 1943 only as a curiosity. This view shows well the aerodynamic shape designed for a gun cupola on the full-scale aircraft, the trousered undercarriage and the pressure head. *A&AEE 11482*

Boulton Paul P92/2 V3142 shows some of its aerodynamic features – the horn-balanced elevator and rudder, inset hinges to the ailerons and fixed slots at the wing tips. *A&AEE recognition 174 dated 12 August 1943*

Black Widow

A single Northrop Black Widow (P-61A-1-NO), 42-5496, was loaned to the Establishment by the US 9th Air Force, and flew 30 hours from May 1944. The cowlings of the two (R-2800-10) engines and the fuselage had many quick-release panels; other advances included large spoilers instead of full-sized ailerons, and hydraulic flow equalisers to prevent asymmetric operation of the flaps. The spoilers led to a lack of feel in roll and needed large control inputs in rough air at cruising speeds. The view from the cockpit was reduced by the pilot sitting a long way from the front window, and the layout was overcomplicated, leading to the pre-take-off checks becoming 'a puzzling procedure'. The worst handling feature was the large changes of trim with operation of the undercarriage and flaps and with power changes. Although the elevator was heavy, handling was generally pleasant and single-engine flight was easy.

P-61A Black Widow 25496 in May 1944, on loan from the USAAF. Many of the interesting features, for example the spoilers, are not visible, but the remotely controlled 'barbette' on top of the fuselage can be seen, as can the large white radome, the pressure head under the nose and the large cooling intakes on the wing leading edges. *A&AEE 11782*

9 Maritime Aircraft

Hudson to Warwick

Hudson

The Lockheed Hudson was the first operational aircraft ordered from the USA by the British Purchasing Commission; the priority arose from the limitations of the Anson in the maritime reconnaissance role. Comfortable and quiet crew stations, a feature common to the larger American aircraft, was first noted on the Hudson.

Hudson Mark I

With the radio operator and his R1082/T1083 HF sets and the bomb aimer with either a Mk V II or Mk IX bombsight both comfortably settled, it was disappointing to find the gunner's position very cold. Handling and performance continued on N7205 and N7206 into the winter of 1939; straightforward stalls occurred at 76mph (clean) and 62mph, and the three aerodynamic controls were good. The major criticism was reserved for the large trim change with flaps (take-offs were initially made with flaps up); the push force needed on overshooting and on raising the flaps was considered excessive.

In 1940 an investigation into the maximum benefit of flaps on take-off at overload weight of 18,510lb resulted in a setting of 20% being recommended. At the new weight either engine alone produced a slow climb (125 ft/min) at 4,000 feet. On N7206, a lengthy trial was made to try and reduce the drag of the Boulton Paul Type C Mk II upper turret (see the Performance Table); some improvement was made, although the maximum range with 440 gallons of 1,315 miles appears to have been measured on N7205 with a low-drag dummy turret. Bomb loads of up to ten 112lb bombs were carried (and possibly released) without adverse comment; the only surviving gunnery report comments on the inadequate canvas covers for the beam gun positions on P5145 in June 1941. In 1942 interest in this aircraft centred on the effect of moving the pressure head due to forthcoming carriage of a large dinghy; the two positions tried both gave large and unacceptable errors.

In June 1940 T9266, without a turret but possessing a tunnel and gun under the rear fuselage, was briefly assessed, while bomb sight trials on T9340 and T9352 started in

Hudson I N7205 in September 1939, with a mock-up turret that was not representative of the drag of the real thing. The five flap track covers on the trailing edge are a striking feature. A windscreen wiper and faired DF are fairly advanced features for 1939. *A&AEE 9579*

December 1940; results from all three aircraft have not been found. Satisfactory tests were made on the beam approach equipment on N7280 from November 1941.

Hudson Mark II

With new Hamilton Standard hydromatic propellers, T9375 handled normally from September 1940, at the increased weight of 21,500lb, but take-off distances were increased by 25%, and the pilots reported 'slight tail heaviness' – a non-scientific term repeated in the official report. A few months later another report covering all extant versions of the Hudson (Mks I to V) concluded that at up to 20,000lb there was little appreciable difference in handling at aft CG.

Hudson Mark III

T9418 arrived in November 1940 with Cyclone engines (GR-1820-G205A) of increased power; the air cleaners and ice guards together reduced speeds by up to 7mph (true). In service the Hudson had stops to prevent more than 70% of available flap travel from being selected; in mid-1941 Coastal Command asked for 100%. The Establishment, which had recommended the restriction, made another trial on T9422, which confirmed that overshooting from an approach with 100% flap required both hands on the control column to prevent the nose rising, and was thus dangerous and unacceptable. A compromise and manageable figure of 80% was agreed. At the end of 1942 V9158 arrived with a large dinghy under the fuselage and the pitot head moved in front of the windscreen. Large pressure errors were measured – indicated stall speed increased from 66 to 86mph and the approach speed was raised from 103 to 115mph as a consequence. Handling appears to have been normal, but the Establishment recommended that a plaque should be placed in the cockpit to remind pilots of the higher speeds needed.

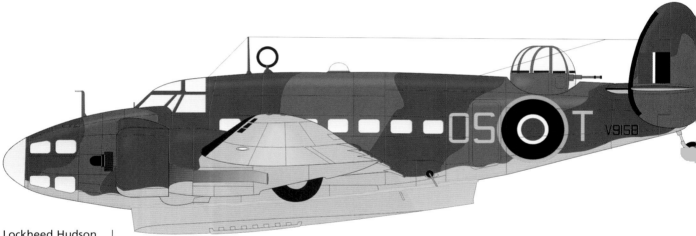

Lockheed Hudson V9158, November 1942, for handling trials. (Scale 1:72)

Hudson III V9158 is seen in November 1942 with a 'dinghy', later lifeboat Mk I, under the fuselage and, as a consequence, the pitot head mounted above the nose. This trial installation proved the feasibility of dropping a lifeboat from the air; the drops were made in 1943, probably by the RAE. The low sun emphasises the apparent ridges caused by the batons holding the anti-icing rubber on the leading edges. The aeroplane had previously served with No 279 Squadron. *A&AEE 11185*

A number of complaints from squadrons about aileron snatching at 40-45 knots on take-off resulted in a pilot and technical officer flying FK747 in the Azores; the phenomenon was confirmed but no remedy could be suggested. The cause of aileron snatch at the stall in FK803 was successfully cured in mid-1940 by a repair to the anti-icing rubber boot on the wing.

Hudson Mark IV

The single aircraft (AE610) of this mark with Twin Wasps (R-1830 SC3-G) flown at Boscombe from December 1940 demonstrated an increase of 21mph (true) in top speed, provided the cooling gills were closed; handling was unchanged. Some armament trials were flown from Exeter.

Hudson Mark V

Two-speed superchargers of the Twin Wasps (R-1830S3C4G) and the increased fuel capacity of 538 gallons introduced in late Mk III machines characterised the Mk V. Performance of AE650 from August 1941 at the standard load (18,500lb) is shown in the Table; take-off distance at overload (22,000lb) was marginally greater with the benefit of 15% flaps. AM823 arrived in August 1941 and became involved in a further examination of the use of 100% flaps for landing. Six months later, after the CFS had made its own assessment, yet another trial was mounted. In both the A&AEE tests, the conclusions were the same as previously, that 85% flap was the safe limit.

As part of an investigation into the use of the Hudson for paratroop use, AM823 had its bomb doors removed; handling and performance were virtually unchanged. With the latest shrouded and slotted long exhausts, AM526 had excellent flame damping, a considerable improvement over the long flames visible on early Hudsons.

Armament trials on Mk Vs included very successful electrical firing of the front guns in AM526, and, probably, AM520, and an opening hatch (single 0.5in gun) that could be wound down under the rear fuselage of AE650. The last was a considerable improvement on the earlier arrangement of firing through a hole in the floor. Rocket projectiles were tried first on AM526 in mid-1942; ground firing caused the under surface of the wing to collapse. With a metal plate under the wing, AM753/G fired rockets successfully on the ground and in the air – the latter at the Pendine ranges late in 1942 – and accurate results were achieved in 20° dives. An earlier trial at Boscombe had used a 7-foot-diameter parachute, released by the pilot as he began his dive, to keep the speed close to the optimum of 200mph for attacking submarines. Handling trials with RPs followed firing, and revealed a violent stall at 82mph (clean) when the left wing dropped suddenly following pitching, which occurred at 86mph. The RP installation caused a loss of 20mph (true) in top speed. After removal of its turret and installation of seats, AM553 was used for communications for the last year of the war.

Hudson V AM526 in January 1942. This mark introduced the Twin Wasp engines (R-1830-53C4G) with cooling gills. An ice guard and flame damper are fitted, and HF aerials run from the mast to each fin. Two piquet posts restrain the tail wheel. *A&AEE 9850*

Hudson V AM753 in May 1943, over what appears to be Wilton Park. Rocket projectiles are in evidence as is, just visible, the cable from under the cockpit to a point under the tailplane, parallel to the white attitude reference line. By the time this photograph was taken the requirement for a 'G' suffix to its serial number had been cancelled – hence the light-coloured patch. *A&AEE recognition 156*

Hudson Mark VI

EW890, with fittings for a 200-gallon bomb bay tank, appeared in September 1942; with a total of 837 gallons, a practical range of 1,950 miles was calculated following take-off at 22,500lb. This aircraft also made the usual cockpit contamination, flame damping and engine cooling trials following weighing. FK689, with a full array of radar aerials and rockets, was used in June 1943 to evolve a technique for recovery from dives to stay within the 2.5g structural limit, and thus avoid the wing buckling experienced by enthusiastic pilots in service. FK406 joined the High Altitude Flight briefly from August 1943, probably for meteorological work.

Beaufort

The Bristol Beaufort prototype (two Taurus II engines) had been briefly tried at Martlesham Heath; a number of odd handling characteristics were reported but gave little insight into the problems later found in this torpedo-bomber. Production Beauforts entered service before the results of further A&AEE trials were known.

Beaufort Mark I

L4456 arrived in December 1939, but bad weather prevented performance flying, so loading trials on the ground were made. Torpedoes up to

Hudson VI EW890 in July 1942 is without spinners, ice guard or DF aerial fairing, but possesses an astro-dome and, unseen, a 200-gallon bomb bay tank. The flame damping exhausts were particularly effective on this aeroplane. *A&AEE 11183*

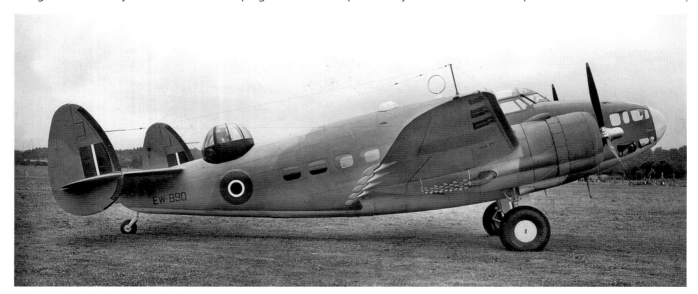

2,000lb projecting into the airflow and bombs in various combinations up to the same weight could be fitted in the bomb bay, while the crew compartment housed the standard compass, flares, smoke floats, signal pistol and sea markers. Handling was marginally improved since before the war by a larger and more powerful rudder trim; rapid engine failure, however, still caused a violent swing. The type retained the earlier continuous rolling motion, making it a poor bombing platform. Performance is as shown in the Table, as well as, in mid-1941, for W6503 at 21,000lb and fitted with Taurus VI engines originally intended for Australian Beauforts. The engine temperatures of W6503 were marginally acceptable after the limits were raised; L4510 at 21,000lb (original Taurus II) required the gills to be open for cooling. The latter had an engine failure on take-off and was seriously damaged in May 1941. Flame damping tests with Beaufighter-type exhausts on its Taurus XII engines were quickly made on L9863 in February 1942 before the aircraft joined the SDF for Porton, being replaced in April 1943 by EK996.

Gunnery reports were written but are now lost. It is probable that L4445 (in July 1940) and L4473 (from January 1940) were used in 1940 to assess the Bristol Type IV Mk IE upper turret with two Vickers K guns, the Bristol Type 1 Mk II (two Browning 0.303in guns) and, in 1941, the twin 0.303in guns in the nose, and the single Vickers gun firing to the side. W6482 from December 1940 had satisfactory electrical firing of the guns in place of unacceptable Bowden cables in the upper turret; six months later a Type B1 Mk V replaced the Mk II turret and, with six modifications, was acceptable for service. In late summer 1941 the aerial mine

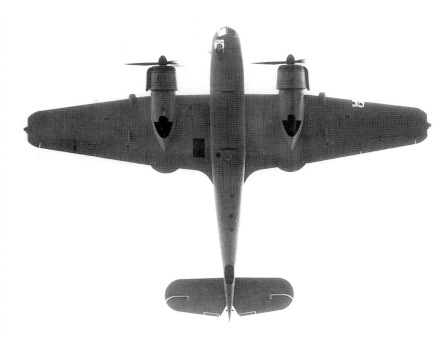

An unidentified Beaufort poses for its recognition photographs. Of interest are the handed exhausts, the twin landing lights on the port wing, the 'bumps' on the trailing edge and the sealed control surfaces (apart from the horn balances and trim tabs of the elevators). The bomb aimer's position is well shown, with external fitting alongside for a drift sight. *A&AEE recognition*

containers were found to be too fragile, otherwise the AAD Type H (later known as AD) installation of AW219 was satisfactory for carriage and release. Another aircraft, probably AW204, from December 1941 was used to clear four types of American bombs for operations. N1156 (Taurus IIA) flew for a short period from December 1940.

In January 1940 Beaufort I L4456 has red/blue roundels as the sole national marking. The nose, oil cooling intake on the leading edge, empennage and fuel jettison pipe are characteristic Bristol items. *A&AEE 9626*

The Mark I with Taurus XII engines resumed production after the supply of Twin Wasps for the Mk II ceased, and in October 1943 an early aircraft, N1038, was received for comparison with LR894, reported as a rogue by the RAF. The latter, with only 20 hours total flying, was immediately grounded on arrival after an uncomfortable delivery flight. The Establishment spent many man-hours in rectification, but with limited success; the consensus was that this aircraft in particular and the Beaufort as a type was useless as a multi-engine trainer.

Late in 1943 EK997 arrived and was fitted with a device known as an aeroflame container attached to the torpedo crutches; 1,500lb of fuel could be discharged through a pipe pointing aft and 2 feet below the rear fuselage and ignited at very low level. It is not known if ignition trials took place from the A&AEE.

Beaufort Mark II

Twin Wasp R-1830-S3C4G engines were fitted to N1110 on arrival in August 1941 for performance (see the Table), handling, navigation, range and cooling trials. The new engines gave a feeling of confidence, particularly on take-off and in the climb, while in level flight there was less wallowing – the words 'confidence' and 'wallowing' coming from the report. The only adverse comment was that the gills, when open, caused vibration. The navigation facilities were similar to the Mk I and range was calculated as 1,380 miles (maximum) and 1,130 miles (practical, assuming that the bombs were dropped halfway). However, cylinder temperatures were too high in the cruise. Later cowling modifications cured the problem until a new carburettor was fitted, adapted for the lower-octane fuel available in the Far East; extrapolated results indicated that the gills would have to be fully open to keep temperatures down. Late in 1943 LS129, with carburettors set for a weaker cruising mixture, initially ran far too hot; cut-back gills alleviated but did not cure the overheating. Fitting a jettisonable cupola with two aft-firing 0.303in guns under the front escape hatch increased airspeed error from 2½ to 14mph (under-reading) at 240mph indicated in AW244 from December 1941. ASV Yagi aerials mounted on the cupola of AW369 in mid-1942 made no difference to the errors in the airspeed system. In early 1942 AW304, with fin and rudder enlarged as on Australian-built aircraft, was loaded to 22,500lb in anticipation of the weight achievable with armour and a four-gun turret. At the higher weight and mid-CG, the aircraft was unstable in the climb, and rolled continuously in the cruise; trimming was difficult and most careful flying was needed. These unacceptable characteristics led the Establishment to recommend no increase in the existing maximum of 21,000lb.

Botha

Pre-war trials of the Blackburn Botha were curtailed on the first aircraft due mainly to unsatisfactory rudder control. The second aircraft, N6105, flew to Boscombe in September 1939 for bombing trials; the capacity was 2,000lb, consisting of either a single bomb or a torpedo (Mk XII or XIV). Although the pilot could see the target in low-level flight until the point of release, accurate aiming was impossible owing to continuous yawing with a 3-second period. Initial modifications to the rudder gave only a marginal improvement. L6109 had further modifications, including gearing of the rudder tab and trailing edge cords, a horn balance to the elevator and an increase in tailplane area. Cockpit and handling criticisms were still damning. The undercarriage and flaps were operated by a single lever on the right, while the elevator trimmer was on the left. Changes in rpm, gill setting and undercarriage/flaps all gave large trim changes – no problem for a pilot with three hands. Retracting flaps after take-off caused a large sink, and their use was not recommended; on the approach, elevator control was very poor once flaps were lowered. It was just possible to maintain height at low weight on the power of one engine. Performance (see the Table) was measured with the original Perseus X engines, and partly measured on changing to Perseus XAs; the latter were abandoned in June 1940, probably when the type was rejected for operational use, although one squadron had already started re-equipping.

L6212 with Perseus XA engines was in poor condition on arrival in August 1940; the Establishment had to devote considerable effort to make the machine serviceable. Even then, a single engine would not maintain height under any conditions; the maximum range was 880 miles and dives were restricted to 215mph due to increasing nose-heaviness. The restriction was lifted on L6254 with shrouds to all three controls, after successful dives to 300mph prior to a double engine failure on take-off in December 1940; the fuel cocks were set to 'off' and inaccessible from the pilot's seat. Production-standard aileron shrouds on L6188 in

August 1941 were a slight improvement, and satisfactory up to 255 knots (294mph). Changing to Hampden propellers (12 feet in diameter) in place of the standard 11½-foot-diameter gave a marginal benefit on take-off distance. The Botha failed to meet the requirements for flame damping in December 1942 when L6235 had Hercules-type exhausts fitted. Before the war a second factory had started to make the Botha; the first produced, L6347, was checked at the A&AEE from November 1939, but no differences were found.

No reports have been found on L6133 and its gunnery trials from February 1941, nor on L6336 from a brief visit to the Performance Squadron in July 1941. Photographs of Bothas at Boscombe were, apparently, not taken.

Liberator

Well over 18,000 examples of the four-engined Consolidated Type 32 (USAAF B-24 and C-87) were completed in the USA; the Commonwealth air forces received more than 2,000, known as the Liberator. Twenty-four of the type were tested by the A&AEE, comprising six Marks. Trials were not considered to be necessary for the following: C Mk IV, a conversion of the equivalent to the USAAF B-24E, B-24G and B-24H to troop carrying (released to service 1 March 1946); C Mk VI, a conversion to troop carrying of the B VI and GR VI (30 May 1946); C Mk VII, USAAF C-87 (10 July 1944); and B Mk VIII and GR Mk VIII, with handling similar to the Mk VI (4 October 1944). Trials at Boscombe concentrated on take-off, armament, range and, to a lesser extent, handling; all versions had a small pressure error throughout their weight and speed envelopes, and carbon monoxide levels were very low or absent.

Liberator Mark I

The first, AM912, arrived at Boscombe Down on 14 May 1941, and was the first large aircraft there with a tricycle undercarriage. Interest centred on the take-off performance at the maximum weight of 56,000lb, when 760 yards to unstick and 1,065 yards to 50 feet were measured before persistent shimmy led after only two days to the nose wheel collapsing and the abrupt end of further trials. Coastal Command also received its first Liberators in the spring of 1941, and was most concerned at the long take-off run when loaded for maximum range. Rapid work by the Heston company resulted in AM910 arriving with representative operational equipment for extensive trials from August 1941 of its anti-submarine gear (ASV) and pack of four 20mm cannon under the fuselage. The major criticisms included the ineffective defensive armament – only three pairs of hand-held Browning machine guns – particularly as after only 5 seconds of firing, a cooling period of 1 minute was required; Vickers guns were recommended. Nine modifications were considered essential to make the aircraft compatible with RAF armaments; use of the cockpit heater caused a 15° deviation of the compass, and use of the ASV caused radio interference. Handling of AM910 at maximum weight with the new gear was acceptable on four, three and two engines, and at 5,000 feet maximum speed was 262½mph TAS (emergency boost), and 253mph TAS (normal). The novel gun pack under the fuselage was satisfactory, and could be rearmed in the air by two men in 75 seconds; 1,243 rounds were fired on trials. IFF was tested later.

Trials were held on AM924 at RAF Nutts Corner, Belfast, using the bomb sight at low altitude in conjunction with the ASV, and a

Liberator LB-30A G-AGCD (formerly AM529) in May 1941 does not feature in A&AEE servicing returns or in reports. It is seen here at Boscombe, and was also photographed in the air. Most nose windows are blacked out and the bomb doors have been replaced with fixed panels. The pressure heads are on both sides of the nose. *A&AEE 9723*

Liberator I AM910 in July 1941, with plenty of aerials (ASV) to find ships and schnorkels – and to cause interference on the radios. The blister of four 20mm guns is under the fuselage, but there is no sign of the three pairs of hand-held guns, although the nose and hatch positions (above left of the roundel) are visible. The Fowler flaps are extended and the gills open. *A&AEE 9769*

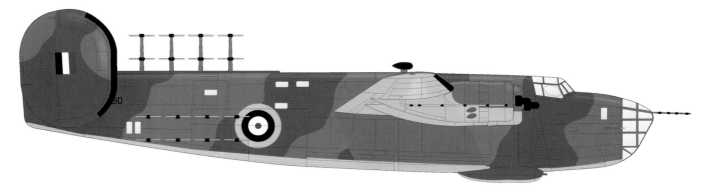

Consolidated Liberator AM910, July 1941, for armament trials.

successful attacking technique was evolved by the A&AEE team. Also in September 1941 a brief trial of modifications on AM929 raised the maximum diving speed from 275mph to 307mph (a significant increase for submarine attacks), but later trials lasting until May 1942 and involving a great deal of work by the Establishment failed to make the advanced Sperry 01 bombsight acceptable, both when in use coupled to the A5 auto-pilot and when used alone.

Liberator Mark II

The first British order for the Liberator was for 165 aircraft designated Mk II; they were delivered after the batch (Mk I above) taken over from the USAAF. The first to arrive at Boscombe, AL510, had turret mounting rings fitted, but the aircraft skin remained uncut. The turrets (Boulton Paul Type A, mid-upper, and Boulton Paul Type E, tail) were very rapidly fitted by the Establishment and satisfactorily fired before the aircraft suffered an accident on 2 November 1941, just three weeks after arrival. The Releases to Service for the Mk II were 1 November 1941 for pilot training and full release on 27 March 1942. The British armaments (turrets and bombs) specified for the Liberator II were given concentrated testing on AL546 (from December

1941) and AL505 (from January 1942). The total of fourteen Browning 0.303in guns included six hand-held: one in the nose, one in the belly and four on the beam. These needed little work, which concentrated on the two Boulton Paul turrets (four guns each). The Establishment made some improvements and recommended twenty-two others, including an essential change in the arrangements for the entry and exit for the rear gunner. The British CSBS IX bombsight gave no difficulties, but some work was needed to make the various bombs fit satisfactorily into the aircraft's carriers in four vertical tiers; a special loading winch by the firm of Stones was eventually made acceptable.

The original flame dampers on AL510 proved useless. The A&AEE-designed cascade dampers on AL546 were better and the RAE fish-tail model was eventually adopted in mid-1942. The IFF Mk II and pitot head accuracy escaped criticisms, while the beam approach equipment was unsatisfactory; ground handling proved acceptable providing a rear CG was restricted to avoid the embarrassment of tipping up, as occurred in the RAF. The practice of using the earth return in the electrical system caused errors at times in both compasses, an interesting phenomenon resulting from American design philosophy.

Liberator II AL510 in October 1941 has the Boulton Paul Type A upper turret installed by the Establishment. The paint sprayer has tested a mask against the window above the roundel. A ladder leads from the rear into the interior. *A&AEE 9815*

There were no performance trials on the Liberator II; both AL505 and AL546 were written off in accidents on 17 August and 24 March 1942 respectively, the latter killing the OC Flying.

Liberator Mark III

The first major production version, the B-24D, was ordered by the RAF as the Liberator III. A small batch, obtained before the main delivery in 1943, included two tested at the A&AEE in 1942. LV336 crashed on 16 April 1942 within two weeks of arrival; the following day LV337 arrived and was extensively flown. Interest centred on the Glen Martin electrically powered upper turret; some 4,500 rounds were fired from the two 0.5in Browning guns, and the only criticism concerned the restricted downward view. Performance and range measurements on the four Twin Wasps (R-1830-43) established the characteristic loss of range at high altitude with exhaust-driven superchargers, although exhaust flames were barely visible. With 1,950 gallons of fuel, maximum ranges were 2,510 miles at 1,000 feet and 2,280 miles at 20,000 feet – giving practical distances of 2,010 miles and 1,825 miles

respectively. From the main production order came FL927/G in April 1943, fitted with the Type C rocket projectile (RP) pack, the first to be fitted under the fuselage for use against submarines. Trials included measurement of attitude in flight, harmonisation and firing; the ground firing buckled the bomb doors and broke perspex windows, but air firing was without damage to the aircraft. With strengthened bomb doors, the Liberator was a good platform in a 15-20° dive, pulling out at 250 feet using about 2g. Reloading RPs in the air was successfully completed, and the Mk IIIL sight was acceptable. Handling, including stalling with RP, was unaffected, top speed was reduced by 2mph and range reduced by 5%. Minor radio and beam gun trials justified the presence of BZ857 from August 1943.

Liberator III FL927/G was photographed in May 1943 (chin radome), with eight RP launchers. It has ten guns (two 0.5in in the upper turret, four 0.303in in the tail turret and two in each beam); the four bomb doors are clearly seen, together with the turbochargers (one under each engine nacelle). The aircraft wears the classic Coastal Command Temperate Sea scheme colours of Dark Slate Grey, Extra Dark Sea Grey and White, designed to give maximum concealment when stalking U-boats. *A&AEE recognition 153*

Liberator III LV337 in May 1942. The upper turret on the forward fuselage was given extensive trials; the Glen Martin design was well received. This view gives some idea of the high aspect ratio wing; coupled with ample fuel, very good range was obtained, but at the expense of take-off distances. *A&AEE 11052*

Liberator III FL927/G is seen in July 1943 (starboard wing radome) with eight RP launchers. It has ten guns, and the four bomb doors are clearly seen, together with the turbochargers (one under each engine nacelle). *A&AEE recognition 175*

Liberator Mark V

BZ791 arrived on 28 June 1943 and completed the bulk of this version's trials. Fitted with an extendible 'dustbin' housing the scanner of ASG III, it also had the so-called 'paddle' blade propellers and heat exchanger flame dampers. All three modifications reduced speed slightly, but handling was unaffected even at aft CG, where the Service had reported control difficulties on the approach. Overload trials at 62,000lb produced exceptionally long take-off distances, and range figures were disappointing until weight was reduced in the cruise; range was scarcely affected by extension of the 'dustbin' unless rich mixture was needed to maintain speed, increasing consumption by 15%. Late in 1943 BZ801, with an RP pack extendable from

Liberator V BZ791 in October 1943 shows its 'dustbin' radome; just visible above the fuselage roundel is the wind deflector for protecting the beam gun position behind. The static source is some 10 feet behind the deflector, but pressure errors remained small. *A&AEE recognition 189*

the bomb bay, handled normally, and early in 1944 BZ714 tried two types of tapered flame dampers; the Havoc type was satisfactory. In BZ945 from December 1943 the tail turret by Motor Products (two 0.5in Browning guns) proved generally acceptable up to speeds of 290mph but immovable above 315mph (indicated); the poor view to the side and down was common to most American turrets. The last Mk V to be tested, in November 1944, BZ916 from Ballykelly, had normal errors in its pressure instruments despite the addition of extra aerials. BZ774 was not used, as intended, for rocket and radio trials in July 1943.

Liberator Mark VI

This version of the Liberator flew in service in three roles, powered by two variations of the R-1830 engine (the -43 and -65), with two types of nose turret, and with and without a Leigh Light under the starboard wing. BZ972 was assessed for its Consolidated nose turret after arrival on 29 November 1943; the turret proved too small and frequently unserviceable. The replacement EV828/G completed the trials by March 1944 with a turret slightly enlarged internally, but still requiring better accessibility, view and comfort. Some 8,335 rounds were fired, many after a flange was fitted by the A&AEE to prevent cartridge cases from striking the propellers. Empty cases proved a major problem in BZ970

because there was an unacceptable disposal arrangement in the Emerson nose turret; trials between March and July 1944 proved the greatly improved view of this model. For the last five months of 1944 BZ970 did not fly, but accepted a large variety and combination of bombs in its bay. The later -65 version of the engines enabled EW126 to take off at the heaviest weight, 65,000lb, flown on a Liberator from the new runway at Boscombe Down. After a year in the GR role, EW126 made range tests in mid-1945 in the bomber role, when the ball under turret reduced cruising speed by 7mph when extended. It was also found that cruising speed had to be slightly increased from the optimum to prevent the engines from overheating.

A Leigh Light under the starboard wing, retractable Anti-Submarine Gear and -65 engines characterised KG902 on arrival in August 1944. Handling was acceptable with appropriate use of rudder and aileron trim. The light, which reduced speed by 2mph, could be jettisoned in an emergency, and engine failure on take-off was assessed as acceptable. In August of the following year, trials of new 'paddle' blades were reported, and a small decrease in consumption was measured. The A&AEE declined to make range estimates but consumption trials were extensive – 1.44 air miles per gallon at low level and modest weight were outstanding; the RAF regularly flew sorties of more than 24 hours duration.

Liberator VI EW126 in July 1944. In between lengthy performance trials for both maritime and bombing roles, this aircraft made several return trips to the tropical testing site in Khartoum. On take-off trials, it made the longest run to unstick at 1,550 yards, and 2,630 yards to 50 feet, of any measured during the war. It has the 'SNAKE' marking and '30-186' in white on the nose, below the pitot head, braced well out of the turbulent air flow from the Emerson turret. *A&AEE 11874*

Mk VI BZ970, with an Emersen nose turret, a single nose aerial and the 'dustbin' retracted. *A&AEE 12001*

Ex-US Navy Liberator IX JT978 in March 1945, dominated by its single fin and rudder. The solid nose, lack of armament, windows and proper door proclaim its passenger role. There are two HF aerials up to the fin, and a third under the nose; the tail bumper/skid is a novelty. The fin inscription is 'NAVY 90026', and the rudder 'RY-3'. *A&AEE recognition 253*

Liberator Mark IX

The tall single fin and rudder distinguished JT978 on arrival in July 1945. The -94 engines had two-stage mechanical superchargers, but tests were limited to handling. The captain's view was restricted by many aerials on the nose, but the major criticisms concerned the extreme buffeting, shaking and aileron snatch near the stall, and excessively light ailerons. The geared tabs of the latter required modification. The navigation facilities were, however, judged to be acceptable.

Sea Otter

Supermarine's amphibious flying boat, the Sea Otter, had a definitely dated appearance on arrival in prototype form as K8854 in December 1941, powered by a Mercury 30 and with ASV aerials on the outer wing struts. Handling for the air-sea rescue role was sedate, pleasant and very stable; on the ground an observer was needed to direct the pilot, whose view was

poor. With flaps down, the stall occurred at 54 knots (62mph), but the flaps operated far too slowly. Later, flap operation times were reduced, while twenty-six strokes on the pump were needed to raise the wheels. Other aspects of the prototype were satisfactory with the exception of inadequate flame damping.

In August 1943 JM738, then JM739, flew into Boscombe, both with partially effective anti-glow paint on their exhausts: a later paint gave a further slight reduction in visibility. On gunnery in JM738, the Establishment commented that the Vickers gas-operated gun in the rear was obsolete, and that the nose gun was inoperable due to slipstream effects. Range with 206 gallons of fuel (10,470lb for take-off) was 680 miles (maximum) and 545 (practical). Later, with the Mercury 30 replaced by the Mercury 27, a small increase in range (up to 720 miles maximum) was obtained, but following advice on carburettor adjustments from the Bristol company the original figures pertained. JM742 and JM743 flew 100 hours each in the hands of visiting naval pilots in four weeks from 7

Sea Otter I K8854 in January 1942. HF aerials run from the wing centre section to a mounting on the fin, and from each wing to the top of the rudder – an unusual location. The frame on top of the fin may be to avoid the aerials fouling the rudder on wing folding. ASV aerials are mounted on the nearest strut below the pitot/static heads, and there is a structural member diagonally below the aft window. *A&AEE 9869*

Sea Otter I JM739 in April 1944, with a slightly lowered nose decking and light series carriers under the lower wing. Although a production aircraft, it carries a prototype marking. *A&AEE 11732*

Supermarine Sea Otter K8854, December 1941, for handling trials. (Scale 1:72)

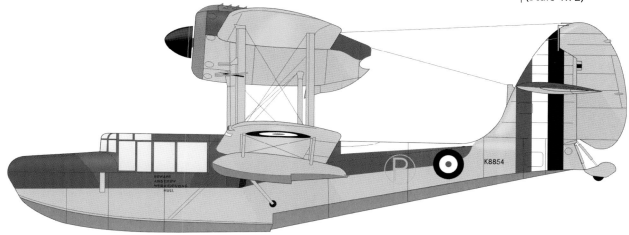

September 1943; there were no major faults in these serviceable machines. Earlier complaints about heavy stick forces on landing at forward CG were partially met by a modified elevator tab on JM824 late in 1944.

JM747 (for unreported gun trials from March 1944), JM913 (for flame damping in July 1945) and JN180 (for the armament demonstration in July 1945) also flew.

Walrus

Three air-sea rescue Walrus amphibians were tested at the A&AEE during the war. The normal single 0.303in gun in the rear fuselage was replaced by a single 20mm gun in L2271, but the report of the trial in August 1940 is missing. In December 1941 W2725 had a satisfactory installation of twin 0.303in guns in the same position, and in May 1942 W2774 flew the standard route to test its IFF Mk IIN with acceptable results.

Warwick

Vickers conceived the Warwick as a heavy bomber to complement the medium Wellington, but policy changes caused largely by problems with the original power plants led to delays. Although work on the Warwick had started in 1935, it was well into 1942 before the A&AEE received its first example of the type; however, L9704 had been flown by the firm at Boscombe in May 1940 (Centaurus engines) and August 1941 (Double Wasps). A fire on take-off in September curtailed further flying. Equipped as bombers, the first aircraft were nevertheless assessed for other roles; then followed civil and military passenger machines together with a batch for air-sea rescue. These all had Double Wasps (R-2800), while the later general reconnaissance versions had the Centaurus.

Warwick Mark I

BV214 arrived in August 1942, was weighed, started handling flights and crashed fatally on the 26th of the month when fabric detached from the port wing; the Establishment insisted on improved attachment to the geodetic structure. Nevertheless, a similar separation of wing fabric on another aircraft occurred in April 1944 during a dive at 320mph, fortunately with only slight injury to the pilot's head. Handling trials had established two unacceptable features: dangerous backlash in the mixture controls, and excessive foot loads with asymmetric power exacerbated by an inadequate rudder trimmer. In addition, the control column hunted in bumpy weather, caused, it was believed, by the large elevator horn balance. The weighing had shown that at the maximum approved weight of 46,000lb, full fuel (1,010 gallons) and a useful load of 6,500lb could be carried. The replacement, BV224, did not arrive until December 1942; the airspeed under-read by 15½mph at an indicated 120mph. Returning later in 1943, BV224 had an FN64 under turret added to its previous FN5 (nose), FN50A (upper) and FN20 (rear), and in this configuration fuel consumption was measured for the air-sea rescue role; 1.61 air miles per gallon were achieved, giving a practical range of about 1,200 miles. Engine temperatures were satisfactory but flame damping was not, and there were minor criticisms of the navigation facilities.

Warwick I L9704 in May 1940 with Centaurus CE15M engines on Vickers trials. It is unusual for the Establishment to have photographed a visiting aeroplane, and some official flying may have taken place, although no formal report was issued. The resemblance to the Wellington is striking, even to the fabric covering of the geodetic structure of the fin. Attachment of the fabric, particularly the wing, became a serious problem. *A&AEE AL853*

Warwick I BV214 is seen at Brooklands in May 1942, a few weeks before delivery to Boscombe. Shortly after arrival it crashed fatally due to fabric detaching from the wing.

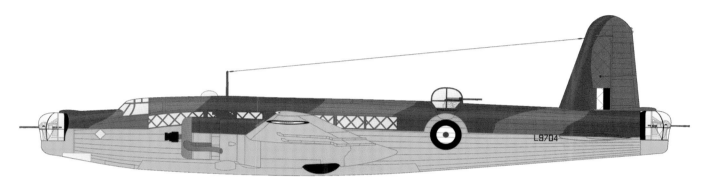

Vickers Warwick L9704, August 1941, for Vickers trials.

Any reports on gunnery trials have not been found, and there were no bombing trials of the early Warwicks. Further asymmetric trials were made (but not apparently reported) from April 1943 in BV218.

Three aircraft joined the Intensive Flying Development Flight in the summer 1943, but all had crashed before that autumn. BV295 completed 25 hours before an engine failure led to extensive damage in the ensuing wheels-up landing. BV298 made an extremely heavy landing and was written off after 70 hours' flying, while BV242 managed 120 hours before another 'firm arrival' resulted in extensive damage. The latter two accidents were ascribed to pilot error, but the Warwick's reputation was tarnished. This was a pity, as the main conclusion from the 215 hours of intensive flying was that the type had exceptionally few snags. Prior to its crash, BV295, with modified rudder trim and balance tabs, had established a minimum speed of 135mph flying on the port engine alone and 145mph on the starboard. Similarly, on BV298 the reduced horn balance on the elevator had proved acceptable.

Contemporary with the IFDF aircraft were BV243 and BV255, modified as civil freighters (G-ALEX and G-AGFJ respectively) without turrets, but with twelve passenger seats and luggage in the nose and tail. With the modified rudder tabs, it was found that 130mph could be held with wings level but without foot load on either engine alone, and down to 120mph with 5° bank towards the live engine. On take-off the pilot could just maintain control following engine failure provided that 100mph had been achieved. BV243 crashed in July 1943 at West Freugh (without casualties) following a precautionary landing on a short runway; altogether there were four Warwick crashes in three months. BV255 was devoted to performance (see the Table), consumption and handling. Take-off at 44,700lb (1,010 gallons of fuel) gave a maximum range of 1,710 miles (1,370 miles practical). Handling concentrated on longitudinal characteristics as the elevator had a friction damper in the controls; hunting was reduced, as was sensitivity, but a maximum diving speed of 330mph was nevertheless imposed. Stall (flap and undercarriage down) occurred at the remarkably low figure of

Warwick G-AGEX in June 1943. The inset hinges of the ailerons, four fuel jettison pipes, four damped exhausts landing lights (port wing) and pitot head (starboard wing) are clearly shown. In July 1943 the aircraft (as BV243) was extensively damaged on landing and probably never entered service. *A&AEE recognition 165*

65mph; it seems likely that the ASI under-read by up to 30mph at the stall. Handling was acceptable at forward and aft CGs. Other trials revealed that the passengers' heating was very poor. In mid-1944 the cooling of the Double Wasp engine of BV296 was considered sufficient for tropical operations.

Trials of the first Mk Is for service, in the role of air-sea rescue, were BV301 (from July 1943) and BV403 (from February 1944). The former had a Mk I (17-foot) lifeboat, giving an all-up weight of 44,594lb, including internal fuel and fittings for a 400-gallon tank in the fuselage. After a lengthy investigation the best position for the static vent was found, reducing the previous large pressure error to insignificance. The engines of BV403 with a Mk II (30-foot) lifeboat remained

within limits throughout the flight envelope, and handling was generally pleasant with the exception of the hunting of the unmodified elevator in bumpy conditions. Also, at forward CG both hands were needed on overshoot to prevent the nose rising on raising the flaps. With normal fuel (1,010 gallons), range was reduced from a maximum of 1,595 miles with the Mk I lifeboat and only 1,445 miles with the larger Mk II. An interesting experimental aerodynamic modification on BV217 was tested from April 1944. A spring tab was fitted to the rudder together with an aerodynamic limiter to prevent overstressing at high speed; at 300mph foot forces were found to be double the figure at low speed and thus acceptable.

Warwick I BV301 in October 1943, carrying a 17-foot (Mk I) lifeboat and retaining the defensive armament, including the FN50A (two 0.303in guns) and FN20 (four 0.303in guns) in the upper and tail positions respectively. Well shown is the fixed arm between the fin and rudder tab, arranged to move the tab in the opposite sense to the rudder, to act as a balance; rudder pedal forces remained high. The three positions tried for the static vent are visible behind the fuselage roundel. *A&AEE recognition 187*

Warwick I BV403 in mid-1944, showing the proximity of the Mk II lifeboat to the ground; wing-mounted ASV aerials can also be seen. The paint job on the lifeboat assisted analysis of behaviour after release. *A&AEE 11921*

Warwick II HG343 in November 1944. The upper turret, a Bristol B12 Mk V (seen without guns), proved unacceptable. In the background, under the flap, are at least five of His Majesty's bicycles, of which the Establishment had 485 at this date. *A&AEE 11970*

Warwick Mark II

Numerically second but chronologically last, the Mk II general reconnaissance version first appeared in October 1944, some months after the Mk V, to which it was similar. With two Centaurus VII engines, handling on HG343 differed little from earlier versions, although the ailerons tended to overbalance and opening the bomb doors above 200 knots (230mph) caused directional oscillations due to weakness in their construction. In June 1945 HG363 arrived with a dorsal fillet added to the fin and with an extra 5° of rudder travel. The rudder did not overbalance and pedal forces were high but acceptable. Extra fuel and an upper turret gave this mark a maximum weight of 52,164lb. Trials continued after the war, after the Bristol B12 Mk V upper turret had been found unacceptable due to inefficient gun functioning. HG362 made brief and successful cooling trials in June 1945.

Warwick Mark III

The earlier Double Wasp engines (reported by their military designation of R-2800-47) were retained in this unarmed transport version with a large ventral pannier, and internal seats for twenty-four troops. HG215 (from April 1944) and HG217 (June 1944) shared the limited trials work; in addition, HG217 completed 150 hours of intensive flying in forty days with only minor unserviceability. However, the report states, 'Remove the Christie Taylor utility seats … [as they] are a very poor advertisement for the future of British civil aviation.' This is the first of a recurring theme about the long-term implications of wartime utility standards. The Performance investigation concentrated on cruising speed (219mph (true) at 11,000 feet); range was, surprisingly, not established at the A&AEE. Cabin heating for the passengers remained poor in spite of improved hot air supply, and there was no lighting for the navigator's compass. In September 1944 HG252 was flown with reduced horn balances on the elevators, together with geared balance tabs and internal seals (ie no shrouds); the heaviness that Transport Command reported was cured.

Warwick III HG215 in June 1944, with its large pannier and faired-over nose and tail. The fuselage has side windows and a rear entrance door with opening extension, while there appear to be two large removable panels on the pannier. The rudder has a small horn balance, which helped reduce asymmetric foot loads. *A&AEE 11792*

Warwick Mark V

Four of these Centaurus VII-engined Warwicks arrived within eight weeks from June 1944 (thus preceding the similar Mk II by four months). PN697, the first arrival, was fully equipped, including a retractable Leigh Light under the rear fuselage and a radar blister under the nose; it made extensive flights, which showed that cylinder and oil cooling were satisfactory, except in the climb. Increasing airspeed and decreasing rpm, thus reducing rate of climb and ceiling, gave satisfactory cooling. Pressure errors were small (but exceeded the 1mph tolerable by the air position indicator), and contamination was nil. Handling up to 51,250lb (at take-off) started in August 1944, but extended periods of unserviceability delayed progress; at high weight the stall was sudden when one wing and the nose dropped violently. Harmonisation of the controls was poor generally; ailerons were light, rudder heavy and elevators hunting. Meanwhile the IFDF had completed 150 hours on PN698 and PN701 and identified poor design of the engine cowlings for the high engine power and flexible mountings.

The delay in the trials of PN697 was fortuitous, as Vickers' pilots had experienced chronic overbalance of the rudder early in 1945, losing three Mk V aircraft (one fatally) in quick succession. The investigation during grounding of all Warwicks resulted in modifications. PN710, previously on armament trials, returned in the spring of 1945 with an additional dorsal fin, reduced rudder travel (17½° to port, 12½° to starboard), reduced chord and gearing of balance tab. No overbalance was found, although foot forces were higher. LM777 arrived for compass tests in August 1945.

No fewer than forty-four essential modifications were listed following protracted bombing trials in PN710, the chief objection being the tiered stowage of stores (bombs and mines) in the bomb bay; this arrangement imposed unnecessary limitations on the size, weight and type of store that could be carried.

Catalina

Amphibian Catalina Mk IV JX242 spent less than two days at Boscombe in September 1943 to demonstrate that its IFF Mk III was satisfactory over the standard route.

Warwick V PN697 in June 1944 has a radar blister under the nose and retracted Leigh Light under the roundel. The beam guns (starboard in view) replaced the upper turret. Apart from the lack of a flame damping exhaust, the appearance of the Centaurus VII motors is surprisingly similar to the Double Wasp (R-2800-47) of the other versions. *A&AEE 11818*

Bombay

A single Bristol Bombay (two Pegasus XXII engines), L5809, quickly completed the type's trials at Boscombe Down after assisting the move from Martlesham Heath. The Air Staff were very keen for its return to the RAF, but appear not to have pressed for the Establishment's formal report, which is dated August 1940. Performance is as shown in the Table. The controls were summarised as: elevator – spongy and heavy; ailerons – sluggish and heavier; rudder – heavier still and too heavy for flat turns at high speed. The use of the word 'high' to describe a speed of about 150mph appears odd, even for 1940 usage.

L5812 joined the Bombing Flight in September 1939 and departed in May 1940 to assist the RAF leaving France.

Lysander

The Westland Lysander Army Co-operation machine had completed trials before the war in its Mk I (Mercury XII engine) and Mk II (Perseus XII) versions, although L4739 (a Mk II) was at Boscombe until December 1939.

Lysander Mark I

Five aircraft flew with the Special Duty Flight for Porton. L4737 and L4738 arrived in October 1939, the latter, surviving until mid-1944, also being used for development of chemical apparatus, while L4682 and L4691 joined in February 1940, although L4682 was severely damaged following an engine failure the following March. Long serving was R2613 from April 1941 until at least the end of 1943; an electrical fault caused a particularly tragic accident in October 1943 when the whole Smoke Curtain Installation fell off the aircraft and killed seven and injured eight of the troops who had been planned to experience only the gas spray. The installation (SCI) is shown in several of the illustrations.

Lysander I L4738 is seen in 1943 after four years of work, mainly for Porton. It continued in use at Boscombe for another year.
A&AEE recognition 125 via Key Publishing

Lysander Mark III

P1728 (Mercury XX) flew in from Yeovil in July 1940 for handling (unchanged) and performance (see the Table). Next in September 1940 came R9126 (Mercury XX) with an experimental 7-foot-long dive flap on each wing operated by a hydraulic jack powered by a battery through an electric motor. 260mph could not be exceeded in the steepest dive, but the trim change was so violent as to be completely unacceptable. Another trial installation, also not adopted, was flown from June 1941 on T1571 in the form of a tailplane of increased span, elevator with increased horn balance, and larger servo tabs on the ailerons. Both controls were greatly lightened in operation, but the elevator tended to overbalance and was thus considered unsafe at high speed. In July 1941 T1771 appeared with a 150-gallon fuel tank under the fuselage, but lacking armament. Weight increased to a maximum of 7,850lb, and handling was noticeably affected, particularly by a deterioration in longitudinal stability; performance is as shown in the Table. An E-type winch on V9815 from February 1943 was intended for target towing. The A&AEE trials were limited to measurements of the engine cylinder and oil temperatures, both being satisfactory.

Lysander III T1771 is seen in June 1941 with long-range fuel tank, slats open and flaps down. The balance tab is deflected by the raised starboard aileron. A VHF aerial is mounted just forward of the fin, and a beam approach aerial features under the fuselage. The bead sight, fitted above the cowling, is standard. *A&AEE 9746*

Lysander IIIA V9815 in February 1943 shows off its target towing stripes; the E-type winch is on the starboard side. The carburettor intake can be seen within the cowling, and the relatively small oil cooling intake (under the cowling) was sufficient to keep oil temperatures within limits. An external fuel tank is carried. *A&AEE recognition 130*

Porton used two Mk IIIs, Tl428 from August 1940, until written off after overturning in bad weather two months later, and T1501, the replacement, until it too was severely damaged landing the following June.

Lysander Experimentals

K6127, the first prototype but powered by a Perseus XII, reappeared in July 1940 armed with two 20mm guns on the undercarriage legs; the report has not been found. A more drastic modification of this aircraft, known as the 'Delanne' conversion, involved in effect a second wing with twin fins in place of the tailplane, and a rear turret. With a CG at 45.5% to 58.2% of mean chord (of the front wing), the aircraft was longitudinally stable and easy and pleasant to fly up to 300mph. The slats, however, gave a large trim change and were difficult to operate in that speed had to be reduced below the normal approach figure of 75mph to ensure full extension before increasing speed again. Trials of the FN turret appear to have been satisfactory after improvements by the Establishment to the continuous belt feed of the ammunition.

Lysander K6127 in late 1941, with the rear wing of the so-called 'Delanne' conversion. The FN20 tail turret can be seen, and, just visible, two of its four 0.303in guns; firing trials may have been made. The wing leading slats, shown retracted, gave minor problems on the approach, otherwise handling was similar to conventional Lysanders *A&AEE 9812*

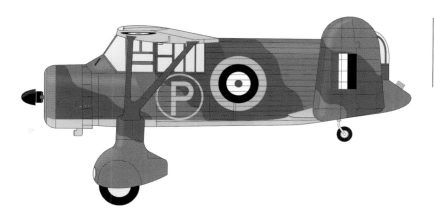

Westland Lysander K6127 'Delanne', July 1940, for handling trials. (Scale 1:72)

Henley I L3247 in December 1939 in use as a target tower for the Establishment; no reports of trials on this aircraft have been found, but photographs were usually taken only for trials machines. The stowed winch is seen, but the arrangements for stowage of the drogue/target are not apparent. Of interest are the black and yellow stripes on the upper as well as the lower surfaces, and the diamond patch just ahead of the fin to indicate the presence of gas. Note the foot wells in the wing root. *A&AEE 9615*

Henley I L3276 in March 1942, with carriers under the wing for two 500lb and eight 20lb bombs. The Merlin V engine has a large filter fairing, and the first aid locker is just impinging on the fuselage roundel. Under the serial number is a bobbin, normally associated with a trailing HF aerial. *A&AEE 9914*

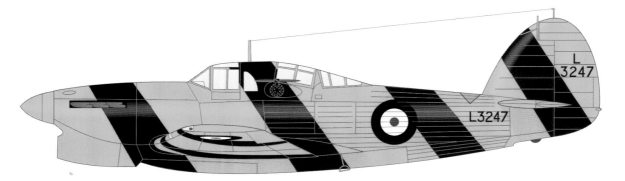

Hawker Henley L3247, September 1939, for target/towing trials. (Scale 1:72)

Henley

The Hawker Henley was relegated to the target towing role before the war and, with tests complete, L3243 stayed at Boscombe for a few days after arrival from Martlesham. L3247 (Merlin II) towed targets for gunnery trials from September 1939 until the Gunnery Flight moved to Exeter in June 1940. Final tests on a Henley started in January 1942 on L3276 with no target gear, but equipped to carry two 500lb and eight 20lb bombs. At an all-up weight of 9,506lb (1,000lb more than target towing), the type retained its good handling, and the straightforward stall was at 70mph (flaps and undercarriage down). One test, strange for 1942, is reported thus: 'In turns of 30°, rudder alone could not prevent the nose from dropping'. The need for a test pilots' school was urgent.

Flamingo I R2765 in March 1940, with exhausts above the engine, an HF aerial secured by a mast on the rear of the fuselage, and a blind approach aerial under the cockpit. No fin flashes are carried, but the serial number is in large figures under the wing. *A&AEE 9628*

Flamingo

The civil de Havilland 95 Flamingo was recommended for civil Certificate of Airworthiness before the war. Early in 1940 a military version, R2765, was tested for the King's Flight with an increased all-up weight of 17,600lb, increased wing span, reduced wing dihedral and other changes, including full leading edge de-icing. The Perseus XIIC engines worked well, but the de Havilland variable-pitch propellers tended to overspeed above 260mph, although 285mph was achieved successfully on one occasion. The major criticism was of the Exactor engine controls needing frequent adjustment.

Cunliffe Owen Flying Wing

The Cunliffe Owen OA-1 (Flying Wing), G-AFMB, failed its civil airworthiness tests before the war, on the basis of an excessive take-off run and very poor workmanship. It was left behind

at Martlesham for a comprehensive independent inspection. The Air Staff, desperate for air transport, ordered investigation of the type's performance, duly completed (see the Table) in September 1939, presumably after a satisfactory inspection, although the A&AEE trials were at a weight 1,000lb below the pre-war figure.

Proctor

The military version of the pre-war Vega Gull, the Percival Proctor Mk I, P6107, arrived in April 1940 for performance (see the Table), handling and cooling trials for the communications role. It handled in typical light aircraft fashion, but the Gipsy Queen II engine overheated considerably on the climb. Returning later in 1940 with the tailplane enlarged from 35 to 41 square feet, the aircraft was dived to 225mph and stalled (flaps down) at 50mph. In May 1941 P5998 was received with a Serek oil cooler under the port wing and a tropical cowling; the oil temperatures were satisfactory for tropical conditions, but the cylinders were 31°C too hot.

Proctor I P6107 in April 1940 with spatted undercarriage, an HF aerial and mounting for a drift sight under the rear window. Some attempt has been made in the design of the exhaust to reduce flames, but flame damping was not measured. The picqueting ring is under the starboard wing. *A&AEE 9636*

Proctor IV LA586 in May 1942 is without spats, but has an extended passenger window and a DF loop. It is shown before intake modification to improve cooling; the small intake under the wing root is probably for cockpit ventilation. *A&AEE 9997*

Proctor Mark IV

This version had seating for three in addition to the pilot and was intended for training wireless operators of the RAF and RN. Handling of LA586 from February 1942 remained unchanged, but performance (at the same weight as the Mk I – see the Table) was inferior. Cylinder temperatures were still too high for the tropics, but improved cooling was later obtained by redesigning the air intake. With naval equipment (including T1115/R1116 sets in place of the RAF's T1154/R1155), weight increased to 3,550lb, leading to marginal performance on overshoot with full flap down. Handling at forward CG on LA589 early in 1943 was assessed as just acceptable. In June 1943 MX451 had a rudder trim tab, satisfactory but considered unnecessary. Two new types of radio were acceptable in NP336 (October 1944) and HM344 (January 1945); the layout of the former with American SCR 522 equipment was praised.

Vigilant

Plans for the RAF to receive a substantial number of Stinson Vigilants did not materialise for reasons unconnected with the A&AEE, where the type was well received. Two seats for Army co-operation, high lift devices and a Lycoming R-680-9 motor gave an outstanding view, a stalling speed (all devices in play) of 28mph, and a take-off too short to measure; the landing run was 50 yards. The aircraft could be climbed safely at 25/30mph; other performance is shown in the Table. The Vigilant was summarised as being 'very suitable for its role'. HL429 and HL430 were used from November 1941 for the trials described, while HL431 (May 1943) and HL432 (January 1943) joined for Porton until mid-1944.

Vigilant I HL429 in December 1941, in one of the few recognition photos taken on the ground. The full-span slats are open but the flaps are raised; crude (or undercoat) touching up has been made on the port wing. A bracing wire joins fin to tailplane. *A&AEE recognition 57*

Vultee Vigilant
HL430, November
1941, for handling/
performance trials.
(Scale 1:72)

Reliant

Manufacture of the pre-war Stinson Reliant ceased in 1941, but was put in production again in 1942 for 500 of the type for the British forces. The example tested, FK818, from June 1943, was a three-seater for RN observer training powered by a Lycoming R-680-13. At 3,980lb, handling was unremarkable, and the stall at 56mph (flap down) was accompanied by pitching. Eleven modifications were recommended to improve the layout of the radios (British equipment). There was concern that various canvas seals would, with time, admit exhaust fumes. The effect of the weight increase due to ASV equipment was investigated and a weight of 4,300lb approved early in 1944. Two Reliants were used for communications, FK917 briefly from November 1944 and FK894 from March 1945.

Reliant I FK818 in
June 1943, in its role
for training naval
observers. The
apparatus visible in
the rear window is
intriguing – a
signalling lamp or
stowage for flags?
The shielded horn
balance of the
rudder is of unusual
configuration, and
the HF aerial extends
from fin to wing
tips. *A&AEE 11439*

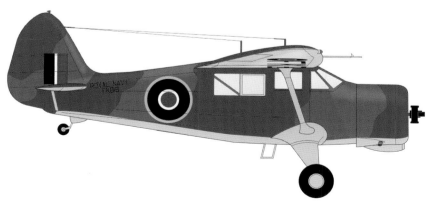

Stinson Reliant
FK818, June 1943,
for handling trials.
(Scale 1:72)

Argus

The four-seat Fairchild Argus was represented at the A&AEE by HM164 and HM167 from November 1941. The type was stable at all CG and handled well with a suitable range of trim available up to 188mph. Take-off run was 276 yards; other performance seems not to have been measured. The technical staff found the pitot static system unique for a light aircraft, with the head on a strut and the static vent on the port side. The pitot gave a large over-reading on the ASI, partially offset by the under-reading from the static source. The report cynically comments, 'The net effect is to make the top speed appear higher, thereby aiding sales.'

'Expediter'

A solitary Beechcraft made the 150-mile circuit to the north of Boscombe while its IFF was successfully tested in April 1942. The aircraft had Wasp Junior engines and was the Beechcraft 'PB1' for Prince Bernhardt of the Netherlands.

Argus I HM167 in November 1941, with fixed-pitch airscrew, slotted ailerons and a small windmill on the undercarriage strut for an unknown purpose (a fuel pump?). *A&AEE 9826*

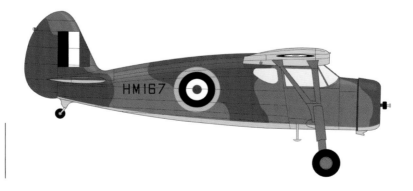

Fairchild Argus HM167, April 1942, for handling trials. (Scale 1:72)

Curtiss Wright CW20 Commando G-AGDI makes a quick circuit round Prestwick chased by the photographic Hampden in November 1941. The local defence commander initially forbade the flight because his gunners did not have appropriate reference material to identify the Commando! The aircraft later came to Boscombe for IFF tests. *A&AEE recognition 56*

CW-20

The Curtiss-Wright CW-20, G-AGDI, spent a day at Boscombe in May 1942 on Mk II IFF tests. A modified aerial gave acceptable results.

Auster

Licence manufacture of Taylorcraft aircraft in the UK led to the Auster, all five wartime variants being tested at the A&AEE.

Auster Mark I

LB263 (from May 1942) and LB266 (June 1942) with Cirrus Minor engines were intensively flown by Army observation pilots; each machine achieved more than 150 hours in less than eighteen days, involving a total of 2,322 landings, which included major damage to LB266 on 19 June 1942. There were no dedicated performance or handling trials, but the design was found to be very simple and robust with remarkable take-off and landing distances. Several minor improvements were suggested. LB264 (from May 1942) had experimental split trailing edge flaps, and was flown to assess suitability for ship duties. It was considered that at 1,400lb a take-off run of 80 feet would be possible into a 15-knot wind, and a similar landing run achieved with an arrester hook.

Auster Mark II

The Lycoming 0-290-3 characterised this version, the first, MZ105, arriving in February 1943. Performance is given in the Table, and the stall speed was 28mph (flaps down); handling was satisfactory although the elevator trimmer range was insufficient. The major deficiency was engine cooling, particularly in one very hot cylinder. On return with new wings (as fitted to the Mk III),

Auster II MZ105 is seen over the Salisbury Plain Training Area in February 1943. Changing from the Cirrus Minor to the Lycoming was the main difference from the Mk I. However, both photographs show an HF aerial from wings to the fin; only MZ105 has the official radio bonding markings on the fin, rudder and fuselage. *A&AEE recognition 132*

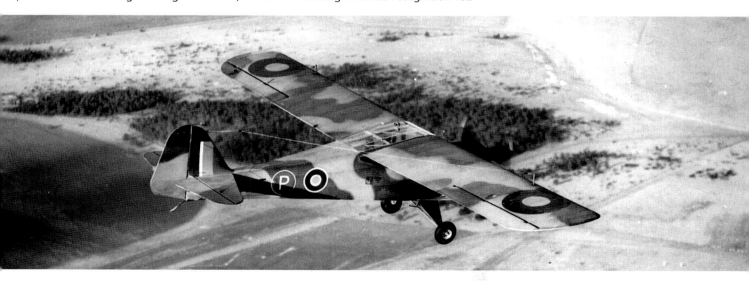

MZ105 completed 163 hours up to February 1944. MZ110 came in July 1943 with the engine temperature limits raised; a new propeller (the Z5600) cured previous slight overspeeding without affecting performance, and reduced overheating to only a single cylinder. Contamination, radio and flame damping (including removal of the fish-tail exhausts) all met requirements. Cabin heating, however, was judged inadequate for Arctic conditions.

Auster Mark III

The Gipsy Major I powered this version, which included LB319 converted from a Mk I and appearing in October 1942. The heavy engine, plus 40lb of compensating ballast in the rear fuselage, permitted a crew of pilot only in this aircraft. Performance is given in the Table, and handling between the stall of 51mph and diving speed of 135mph was satisfactory, although there was a slight tendency to nose over on landing. In fact, LB319 suffered major damage in January 1943 when it tipped up landing in bad weather. Tests on production aircraft MZ126 (from October 1943) and MT407 (October 1943) were brief. With 10 gallons of fuel, the take-off weight increased slightly to 1,555lb, and at forward CG the tendency to nose over on landing was increased. Flame damping of the engine and lighting of Army Wireless Set Type 22 were unsatisfactory.

Auster Mark IV

A transparency behind the pilot, and a Lycoming 0290-3 engine, were features of this mark; both were acceptable on MT454 at Taylorcraft's airfield in June 1943. MT100 (from March 1944) weighed 1,679lb at take-off with 15 gallons of fuel, and was later flown at 1,700lb; ground handling with a tail wheel was more difficult. MS935 (also from March 1944) had a conventional elevator trim in place of the less satisfactory auxiliary surface, and acceptable heating with the exception of the observer's feet. He was interchangeable with a Wireless Set, for which heating was not criticised.

Auster Mark V

The loaded weight of NJ730 in September 1944 was 1,813lb, the increase due in part to extra fuel and a blind flying panel. An improved method of inducing cooling airflow kept the Lycoming engine temperatures below limits, while handling up to 144mph remained satisfactory. Fifteen gallons of fuel gave an endurance of 2hr 9min. In service, serious exhaust burning was experienced; RT540 tested a satisfactory modification from November 1944. NJ630 and NJ631 (the first Auster Mk V to arrive in June 1944) flew for Porton.

Auster III LB319 is seen in November 1942, with simplicity as a keynote – the fuel contents indicator is the 'mast' in front of the windscreen, the venturi just below it, and there is fabric covering throughout (apart from the engine cowling). The pitot/static heads are on the port strut and the rudder has a large mass balance. The fixed rudder and elevator tabs (ie fixed on the ground) can be seen. *A&AEE 11184*

Auster IV MT100 in March 1944, revealing the lowered top fuselage and the excellent all-round view enjoyed by the pilot. The tail wheel and the elevator trim tab (just visible) are also novelties. *A&AEE 11690*

Martinet

The Miles Martinet was the first British aircraft designed from the outset as a target tug – albeit adapted from the Master. LR244 arrived in July 1942 powered by a Mercury 30 moved forward to compensate for the weight of the towing equipment in the rear. With an E-type (motorised) winch and 130 gallons of fuel, weight was 6,555lb; performance is given in the Table. Similarly equipped but powered by a Mercury 25, LR244 weighed 6,620lb in May 1943; with a 4-foot low-drag sleeve target, top speed was reduced by 25mph, accompanied by slight engine overheating.

York

Contemporary accounts attribute to development of the York a degree of subterfuge by the designer, Avro, which was officially fully stretched on Lancaster production. Nevertheless, LV626 was flown to Boscombe in August 1942 for preliminary handling and performance assessment (see the Table) in the freighter role. With water ballast 60,000lb was achieved, and the 1,898 gallons of fuel gave a range calculated at 2,350 miles. Lateral stability and its ratio to directional stability were too high, but otherwise handling was unremarkable; the stall occurred at 97mph (flaps and undercarriage down).

Martinet I LR244 in July 1942 is bereft of the interesting paraphernalia of a target tug, even lacking the striped underside. The only clues to its role are the circular blanking plate under the centre canopy, the pulley arms under the fuselage and the cable between the tailplane tip and the rear fuselage. Other features are the box-like oil cooler and the pair of lengthy exhausts. *A&AEE 11051*

HN862, in production form and with the alternative B-type (wind-driven) winch, weighed 6,678lb. The Establishment turned the exhausts 70° away from fuselage and thus cured cockpit contamination. The maximum continuous towing speed was 200mph (true) at 4,100 feet, and the modified rudder trim contained the yawing moment caused by the side-mounted winch. Handling including spinning was satisfactory between 330mph and the stall at 58mph (flaps and undercarriage down). Endurance at 200mph (true) was 3.44 hours. HP201 underwent minor radio trials from August 1943, but was rarely serviceable.

JN302, JN303 and JN509 appeared in May, August and December 1944 respectively as target tugs for the Establishment until well into 1945, while PX172 and PX173 appeared briefly in August 1944 for a similar purpose.

Comprehensive asymmetric trials demonstrated good 'Lancaster-like' characteristics; even with the port inner feathered and the outer idling, full power on the starboard engines could be contained down to 140mph in straight flight. Rain obscured the flat windscreen. and the roof mounting for the throttles was novel in a landplane.

On return to the A&AEE in mid-1944, LV626 had Hercules XVIs and a third, central fin. Extrapolated results indicated that in the cruise in tropical conditions the cylinder temperatures would be excessive. The permissible aft-most position of the CG was determined by elevator control on overshooting; with the elevator modified to give 6° greater down movement, control was satisfactory on overshooting, but unsatisfactory for a three-point landing at forward CG. LV633 (Merlin 22), specially modified for the use of the Prime Minister, was given priority at the A&AEE; comprehensive trials took fourteen days from 30 April 1943 and involved 31hr 20min of flying. Apart from domestic accommodation, a fuselage fuel tank brought capacity to 2,478 gallons (and the calculated range to 2,950 miles), all-up weight increased to 63,000lb, the windows were square and there was a third fin. Heating was adequate up to 10,000 feet in all climates, but the Establishment noted that the aircraft was 'furnished to austerity not luxury standard'. More serious, perhaps, was the high level of cabin noise except in the rear compartment, which was nevertheless plagued by a continuously whistling wash basin.

Cabin noise was measured again in MW132 (Merlin 22) from November 1944 and, for some passengers' positions, found to be unacceptable at 112 decibels at 100 Hertz in the plane of the propellers. Handling at 70,000lb was acceptable, but at aft CG excessive friction in the control circuits gave an impression of instability on the approach; the stall was at 103mph (flaps and undercarriage down). A metal elevator fitted in May 1945 made no appreciable difference. Performance at the high weight was slightly degraded in the climb by reducing rpm to keep engine temperatures within limits.

York I LV626 in July 1942, with wings and empennage of Lancaster design bestowing good handling. Features include mass balances on both sides of both fins, a tired-looking tail wheel (oleo collapsed?), lots of round windows, ice guards on the air intakes, and twin landing lights on the wing roundel. The stub exhausts and propellers were easily heard in the cabin. *Probably A&AEE 11087*

York I LV633 in May 1943 has some interesting visible modifications to suit the Prime Minister. There is a third fin, flame damping exhausts, a small number of square windows, an HF aerial, DF loop, VHF aerials under the fuselage, a longer tail wheel (or normal but serviceable), a second nose fairing (probably extra heating), and windscreen wipers *A&AEE 11382*

York II LV626 in June 1944, showing well the Hercules engines with their outboard flame damping exhausts and long oil coolers. A third fin is fitted. *A&AEE recognition 224*

York II LV626 in June 1944, showing well the Hercules engines with their outboard flame damping exhausts and long oil coolers. A third fin is fitted. *A&AEE recognition 224*

Dakota

In October 1942 the Establishment made one successful flight to test the IFF Mk II for the US 8th Air Force in Douglas C-47 41-7838. Eighteen months later two C-47As (42-92681 and 42-100678) were similarly tested with two new types of aerial, but with only mediocre results. Meanwhile, a Dakota I, FD903, completed flame damping trials in August 1943; although standard damping exhausts were fitted, results were disappointing.

Miles M28, M38 and Messenger

Designed privately, but with official blessing, the Miles M28 was intended for communications and training. The second of the type, HM583 (known as the M28 Mk II), had a Gipsy Major IIA engine, and weighed 2,013lb all up with 20 gallons of fuel on receipt in November 1942. It was easy and comfortable to fly between 225mph (diving) and 45mph (stall with flaps and undercarriage down); seven minor points were raised concerning the cockpit. The next aircraft

Dakota I FD903 in August 1943 has the tapered, slotted shrouded type of exhaust widely used; for some reason on these trials, this design was well below requirements, being visible at up to 930 yards. *A&AEE 11526*

Miles M-28 Mk III PW937 on a wet day in November 1943. This exterior shot gives only one clue to the third pilot's position; there is a raised perspex section above the rear seat. *A&AEE 11600*

built, PW937 (known as the M28 Mk III), arrived in November 1943, retaining twin fins but powered by a Cirrus Major III; it weighed 2,306lb and had three sets of basic flying controls (ie a third set for the rear seat). It also was easy, pleasant and safe to fly throughout the speed range, although it was easy to overspeed the engine. Apart from the need for a third elevator trimmer, the Establishment made no comment on the philosophy of a third set of controls.

Preceding the M28 at Boscombe by a month, U-0223, with a Gipsy Major IIA and known as the Miles M38/28, was assessed for Army observation and communications. Handling was marred by the inability to trim in the glide at any speed, and ineffective ailerons near the stalling speed of 30-32mph (flaps down); the engine

was prone to overspeeding, even in level flight. The overriding comment was that the aircraft was too fragile for army work – even with all-up weight reduced to 1,965lb from the normal 2,110lb. The next M38 (later named Messenger) arrived in mid-1944 in the form of RG327, also with a Gipsy Major IIA, but having a third, central fin. With 18 gallons of fuel, gross weight was 2,190lb and handling was safe and easy, although the improved ailerons remained unsatisfactory at low speed. A coarser propeller was less prone to overspeeding. With a Gipsy Major ID, the production Messenger, RH373, was briefly tested from February 1945. Weight had further increased to 2,435lb, and range on 18 gallons of fuel was calculated as 245 miles. The take-off run was 150 yards.

Miles M28/38 U-0223 in October 1942, resplendent in bright yellow finish. The spindly undercarriage and large perspex cockpit cover illustrate the Establishment's comment of general fragility based on other constructional features. All three rudders had horn balances. An area of the engine cowling appears black in this photograph. *A&AEE 11159*

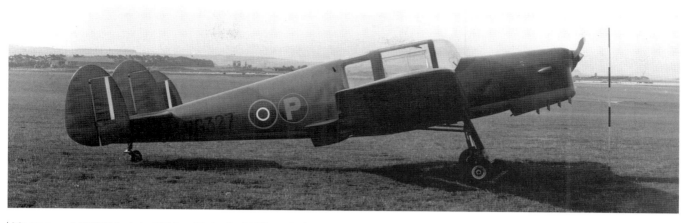

Messenger I RG327 in July 1944, with typical Miles windscreen and three fins and rudders. The flaps are raised, and there is a hand-hold just behind the top of the rear window. In the distance construction of the runway proceeds apace. *A&AEE 11838*

A front view of Messenger I RG327 in July 1944. The fragility of the undercarriage is readily apparent from this angle. *A&AEE 11838*

Messenger I RH373 in February 1945, looking forward to peacetime conditions in silver finish. The VHF aerial and 'W/T' stamped behind the window indicate that a radio is carried. The AID-approved inspectors' markings liberally applied to the exterior all bear the prefix 'PP' (Philips and Powiss – still in use some years after the firm was known by the name of Miles). *A&AEE 15028*

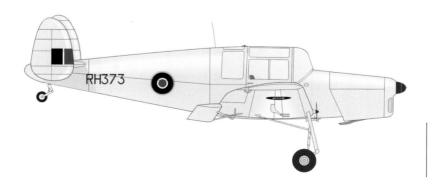

Miles Messenger RH373, February 1945, for handling trials. (Scale 1:72)

Traveller I FT461 in March 1944, with distinctive backward-staggered wings and a retractable undercarriage. The single interplane strut is well braced. The inscription on the fin reads 'NAVY 23657', and on the rudder 'GB-2'. The mass balance of the elevator looks vulnerable. *A&AEE 11718*

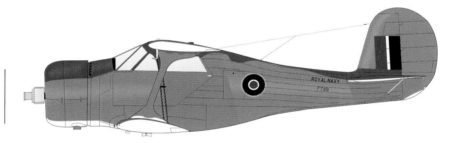

Beech Traveller FT461, March 1944, for handling trials. (Scale 1:72)

Traveller

As a biplane, the Beech Traveller was something of an anachronism when first tested at the A&AEE following the arrival of FT461 in March 1944. With a Wasp Junior R-985-AN3 engine and 101 gallons of fuel, testing was limited to brief handling, contamination, navigation and radio. On the ground, the view was poor and operation of the rudder/brake combination awkward; in the air, handling was straightforward, although the pilot's leg room was restricted. Fumes entered the cockpit with the undercarriage down, and the only navigational equipment was stowage for maps; excessively long cables to the aerials reduced the effective range of the radios. At the end of 1944 complaints by the Royal Navy of contamination in FT520 proved to be fumes other than carbon monoxide. FT446 joined the Communications Squadron in November 1944.

Skymaster

Four days only were permitted for a brief handling assessment of Douglas Skymaster KL977 in March 1945. The engine limitations of the four R-2000-11s were not known, but modest settings allowed flying at 51,500lb. Take-off using nose wheel steering required two pilots, probably the first time at Boscombe that normal operational drills made such an arrangement necessary. The aircraft was very easy and pleasant to fly, and stability about all three axes good.

Skymaster I KL977 in March 1945 on the new runway, during a stay of less than a week. Note the nose wheel layout, extensive leading edge anti-icing, ample VHF and HF aerials, and a large double door surrounding the roundel. *A&AEE 15046*

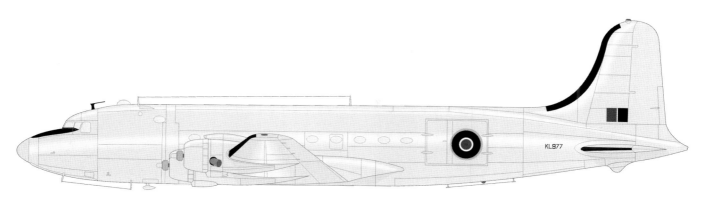

Douglas Skymaster
KL977, March 1945,
for handling trials.

Aerovan

The first aircraft built for the post-war civil market to be tested was the Miles Aerovan, U-0248, arriving in June 1945, powered by two Cirrus Major III engines. Although in normal flight it was easy and pleasant to fly, the Establishment severely criticised the type, including the inability to maintain height on one engine, lack of sufficient elevator and rudder trim, absence of heating and leaking cabin in rain. The severest comment was the generally flimsy construction.

Miles Aerovan U-0248 in June 1945, the first new civil design to reach the A&AEE for more than five years. It was very austerely equipped and built, and condemned by the Establishment as too flimsy. *A&AEE 15154*

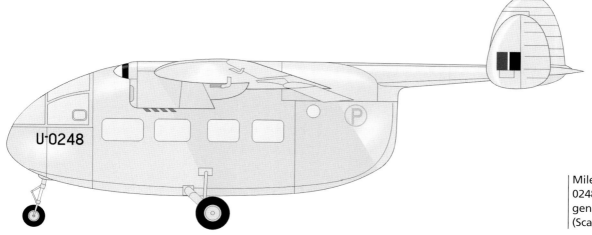

Miles Aerovan U-0248, June 1945, for general assessment. (Scale 1:72)

Monitor

The Miles Monitor, designed as a high-speed target tug with two Cyclones (R-2600-31), had a very unhappy association with the A&AEE. In August 1944, during Establishment preliminary testing at the firm's airfield, NF900 caught fire rapidly on the approach to land and was destroyed; one crew member was killed. The second prototype, NF904, suffered hydraulic failure and a wheels-up landing in August 1945 shortly after arrival at Boscombe. The same month NP409 on intensive flying crashed into the sea, killing both crew members. More successful was NP406 following arrival in May 1945, although flying was delayed. The cockpit was poorly laid out, including the rudder trimmer being positioned much too near the throttles and undercarriage levers and the trimmer's (electrical) action being too fast and powerful. However, the operation of all three trimming switches in the instinctive direction was praised. Trials continued after the war.

Monitor I NP406 in August 1945 was the only one of four of the type flown by the A&AEE during the war that was not written off in a crash. Above the fuselage is the winch operator's cupola, the only evidence in this view of the target towing role. *A&AEE 15192*

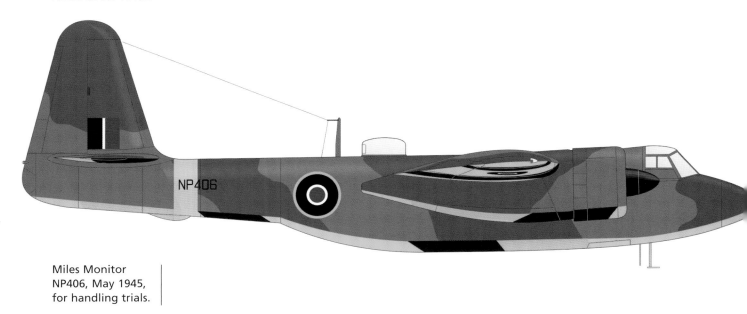

Miles Monitor NP406, May 1945, for handling trials.

Storch VG919 in May 1945. Considerably larger than the Auster and generally more robust, its advantages included the tall undercarriage, full-span slats and drooping ailerons, all seen here. The Cross of Lorraine on the fin indicates the French origin of this machine. *A&AEE 15124*

Storch

A captured French-made Fieseler Storch, VG919, arrived at Boscombe in January 1945, and was flown until after the war. The landing was exceptionally short by virtue of the long-stroke undercarriage being placed well forward of the CG, thus permitting full use of the powerful hydraulic brakes. When measured later the run it was 42 yards (still air); the take-off took 150 yards (still air). At 3,060lb it was twice the weight of the Auster.

Phoenix

One of the few Heston Phoenix was at the A&AEE as X2891 for four months from May 1941 on radio work. No report has been found, but the weekly returns state its purpose as 'VHF', probably in connection with the Beacon Approach equipment.

Miscellaneous types

The following heterogeneous group of aircraft of types not described elsewhere fulfilled a wide range of support duties during the war.

Blackburn Shark

K8485 presented itself for its recognition photographs in November 1941.

Hawker Demon

K3764 remained with the Establishment as a target aircraft on the outbreak of war and moved with the Gunnery Flight to Exeter in June 1940.

Fairey Fantome

L7045 left the Establishment in December 1939 after a year with the Gunnery Flight.

Shark Mk II K8485 in November 1941, en passant for air-to-air photographs. The camouflage, open rear cockpit and a device just visible in front of the lower wing are features. *A&AEE recognition 53*

Fairey Gordon

K2749 spent the first six months of the war towing targets; it was too slow by early 1940.

Hawker Hardy

K5919 flew with 'B' Flight of the Performance Squadron until April 1940.

Hawker Hind

K2915 towed targets for the Bombing Flight until departure in May 1940.

Miles Mentor

L4393 was in use before the war and was written off in June 1944 following a landing accident; the continuous use for more than five years made this the longest-serving Establishment aircraft during the war. To A Flight Performance Squadron goes the credit for this longevity on communications work.

General Aircraft Monospar

K8307 flew from Martlesham with the Gunnery Flight, but soon transferred to A Flight Performance Squadron until it was damaged on landing in October 1940. Monospar L4672 replaced K8307 on the Gunnery Flight until prolonged unserviceability led to its removal in August 1940.

Hawker Osprey

K5750 was on Establishment strength from November 1941 to April 1942; it was, in fact, used by Porton as a 'wind maker' – presumably without flying.

Pitcairn

PA39 BW833 appeared for a month from December 1941; the reason is not known, and BW834 was photographed.

Pitcairn PA 39 BW833, December 1941, for unknown trials. (Scale 1:72)

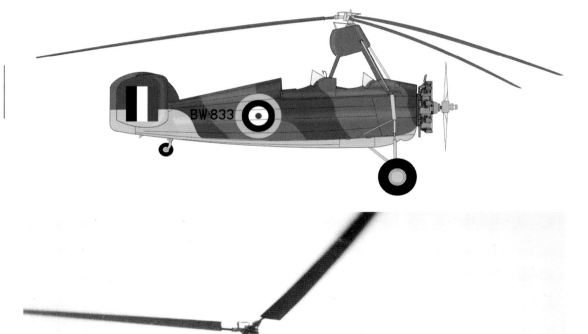

Pitcairn P39 BW834 in flight in January 1942. This Establishment photograph shows an aircraft that does not appear on the servicing returns, although BW833 does. *A&AEE recognition 74*

Piper Cub 31404 shortly before becoming VM286 in June 1945 for post-war trials of the Brodie suspension gear. The aircraft has many similarities to the Auster, including details such as the fuel content indicator in front of the pilot and a small windmill between the undercarriage legs. Longitudinal trimming was, however, by means of varying tailplane incidence. The purpose of the 'windsock' on the fin is unknown.

Piper L-4

VM286 arrived in June 1945 for post-war trials of the Brodie Suspension System of take-off and landing.

De Havilland Puss Moth

X9378 flew hither and thither for C Flight Performance Squadron between October 1940 and February 1941.

Avro Tutor

K6105 arrived in July 1945 for the armament demonstration on Larkhill, and K6100 was photographed in November 1941.

Vickers Virginia

J7130 was pressed into service with the Bombing Flight between March and October 1940.

Westland Wallace

K6055 departed to Exeter in June 1940 with the Gunnery Flight after six months at Boscombe. Wallace K8679 was recalled for RAF training duty shortly after arrival in January 1940.

Tutor K6100 in November 1941 was less than ten years old, but looks distinctly dated. No attempt has been made to seal control gaps; ailerons have inset hinges and the elevator shielded horn balances. *A&AEE recognition 61*

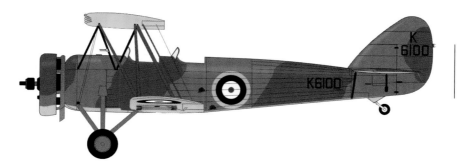

Avro Tutor K6100, November 1941, for recognition photos. (Scale 1:72)

11 Trainers
Tiger Moth to Buckmaster

Tiger Moth

The Establishment's association with de Havilland's Moths in general and the Tiger Moth in particular had virtually ended by September 1939. K4281, on communications duty with the Gunnery Flight, was the sole representative to fly from Martlesham, and left Boscombe in June 1940. In late 1940 the desperate war situation called for desperate measures, including the arming of Tiger Moths with eight 20lb bombs. Handling and release trials on N9454 and T5610 were made, with only one seat occupied, in October 1940; bombs released cleanly. Spins, with the pilot in either seat, were straightforward, and diving normal up to 170mph.

Following a spate of crashes in service, three 'difficult' aircraft, N6221, R4760 and R5129, arrived in the summer of 1941. The Establishment investigated all possible variables that could affect the spin – one and two pilots, slats locked and unlocked, with and without instrument hood. All three machines were confirmed as unusual, taking up to four turns to recover. After further investigation by the RAE, R5129 returned with the mass balances removed from the ailerons and with strakes on the upper rear fuselage; recovery from spins always took less than two turns. In mid-1943 T7809, with a new type of hood for simulating night-flying in daylight, showed no significant differences from normal.

Dominie

New wireless equipment in Dominie X7323 was installed well aft. When the instructor moved back along the fuselage, the CG moved outside the previous aft limit, making the aircraft very unstable. Following tests from December 1940, the Establishment recommended that only experienced pilots should fly the machine in this configuration. For nine months from September 1941 K4772 (the pre-war prototype) communicated for the Bombing Flight.

Dominie I X7323 in January 1941, displaying its classic 1930s de Havilland lines. The only evidence of the new wireless equipment fitted appears to be an aerial under the fuselage between the engines. *A&AEE HA162*

Magister U6 in September 1939, a private venture with wings of the later M-18. Front and rear cockpits have windshields of differing designs, there are long strakes on the fuselage ahead of the tailplane, an anti-spin parachute with its attachment round the rear fuselage, and its operating cable leading from the rear cockpit. A protective bar is just visible ahead of the rudder horn balance – the bar casts its shadow on the fin. Spin recoveries were consistent. *A&AEE 9609*

Magister

One aircraft in the throng flying from Martlesham Heath to Boscombe Down in September 1939 was the Miles Magister U-6 fitted with the wings of the later M18 type. With a Gipsy Major I, the aircraft was simple to fly and lacked the standard Magister's wing drop at the stall; spin recovery was consistent and rapid. Judged suitable for primary training, the wing modification was, however, not adopted for service. A further Magister, L8168, arrived in October 1939 with the outer leading edge of the wing built up, and the inner leading edge fitted with a sharp triangle section. These modifications by the RAE produced a gentle, predictable stall, but at the expense of a stalling speed higher by 7mph.

A third experimental modification on the Magister was tested from August 1942 on P6456 in the form of the Maclaren drift undercarriage in which the main wheels could be turned 30° left and right. Even with an aft CG, landings in crosswind components of up to 25mph were found feasible, and the Magister was assessed as suitable for training with this modification. P3939 is mentioned in the report of the Maclaren undercarriage, probably for comparison only, as a standard machine.

Other Magisters for which formal reports were not written were P2381 (from September 1939 until damaged on landing in March 1940), L8211 (August 1941 until it crashed the following November) and its replacement on the Bombing Flight for communications, L8295, in use for more than a year. In January 1945 L8253 and N3782 appeared in the Communications Squadron for the newly instituted scheme for training trials officers to fly.

Heston and Miles T1/37, and M-18

Two contenders in the pre-war T1/37 competition returned with modifications and flew in 1939 at Boscombe; by then both had Gipsy Queen I engines and two-pitch propellers. The Heston, L7709, had improved but still

Miles M-18 Mk II U-0224 in May 1941. It was a pre-war design that returned re-engined with a Gipsy Major. The windshields appear to be identical. Note the semi-fairings to the wheels. *A&AEE 9726*

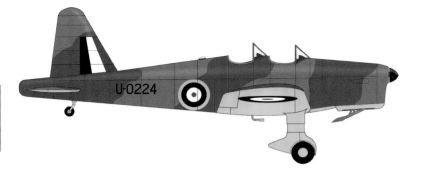

Miles M-18 U-0224, October 1941, for handling/ performance trials. (Scale 1:72)

unsatisfactory ailerons, and an unacceptable performance (see the Table). The Miles, P6326, had its weight reduced and cockpit changes; the ailerons still gave a poor response, the stall was like a 'falling leaf' with aft stick, and the performance (see the Table) was poor. The brakes were, however, praised. The pre-war private venture by Miles for a primary trainer, the M-18, U-0224, returned in May 1941, powered by a Gipsy Major. Handling was better than the Magister; it was impossible to spin and very good at night, and performance is shown in the Table. However, the M-18 lacked robustness. In October U-0224 returned again as a Mk II and performed with a Cirrus Major engine (see the Table).

Harvard

The rapid pre-war tests of the North American Harvard at the A&AEE had identified two remarkable features: undesirable wing drop at the stall and excessive propeller noise.

Harvard Mark I

N7001 flew from Martlesham, and had 12-inch-long thin rods glued on the wing leading edges. The stalling speeds were 4mph higher

and behaviour the same; no advantage in the rods was apparent. A wartime report of pre-war tests says that noise was slightly ameliorated by a reduction in rpm; the effect on performance was small. N7108 spent a few days testing the receiver Type 3002 in April 1941, possibly in connection with its imminent departure for Rhodesia.

Harvard Mark II

BD134, with clipped wings, metal-covered fuselage and pointed fin, was briefly handled from October 1940; the Establishment pilots found the large loss of height on recovery from spins to be undesirable, and thus no advantage over the similar Mk I recovery. In level flight the oil was too hot. Canadian-built FE788 arrived in November 1943, with an R1340-AN-1 engine, almost identical to the Wasp S3H1 of earlier aircraft. The former military designation was applied to Lend-Lease supplies, and the latter to the directly purchased aircraft. Handling of FE788 was made at extended aft CG caused by equipment fitted in the aft fuselage; stick forces reversed approaching the stall but other characteristics were normal.

Harvard II BD134 in October 1940, showing its smooth, metal-covered rear fuselage and pointed fin, all changes from the Mk I. The large air intake on the port side of the nose is comparable in size to the oil cooler underneath. The lever for the aileron balance tab can be seen, as well as the protective structure behind the pilot's position. The surface finish appears to be in a single colour, but different from the yellow of the roundel. *A&AEE 9856*

Canadian-built Harvard II FE788 in October 1943 differs only in details from BD134 by a lack of undercarriage doors, VHF whip aerial and possibly the exhaust. *A&AEE 11630*

Harvard Mark III

The only Harvard of this version, FT958, was examined following complaints from the RAF. The aircraft was found to possess a spin with high-speed rotation, but the consensus was that this aircraft was only a little worse than normal.

Moth Minor

The light (1,550lb) de Havilland Moth Minor, G-AFTH, was evaluated in October 1939 as an ab initio trainer with a Gipsy Minor engine. It was easy to fly up to 190mph with viceless stall and spin, but during aerobatics controls were too heavy and the cockpit was cold and draughty.

Airspeed AS45

Four pilots visited Airspeed's aerodrome in February and again in March 1942 to fly the company's AS45 design (unofficially named Cambridge). T2249 had a Mercury VIII engine, plenty of fuel (130 gallons) and a high gross weight of 7,372lb. The rudder control was good, but otherwise all comments were uniformly adverse. Taxiing was difficult due to lag in brake operation, acceleration on take-off was poor, the ailerons with variable gearing lacked response at low speed, and the elevator was ineffective on landing. The maximum permitted speed of 330mph could not be achieved due to uncontrollable roll to the left at 300mph. The pilots had two interesting days out, but heard nothing more of the AS45.

Moth Minor G-AFTH in October 1939, being photographed from another aeroplane judging by the anxious look over his shoulder by the pilot. Mass balances under the outboard sections of the ailerons and the pitot/static heads under the starboard wing can be seen.

De Havilland Moth Minor G-AFTH, October 1939, for handling trials. (Scale 1:72)

Anson

Chosen as a twin-engined trainer for widespread use, the wartime trials of the Avro Anson (predominantly Mk I) started in August 1940 with N4947 with C Per T; it apparently completed normal handling and performance tests, including use of the windscreen wiper. R9816 (Cheetah IX engines) had nacelles intended for Canadian use; the port engine supplied cabin heat, which was unsatisfactory, but performance was unaffected. Contemporary trials on R3320 with an intensifier in the starboard exhaust manifold gave better results – indeed, the pilot's hands were too hot even with an ambient temperature of -13°C. The aircraft was later used for communications. Unreported compass trials occupied R9689 for three months from March 1942. A Bristol BI Mk VI turret with two 0.303in guns graced AX254 on arrival in July 1942. The turret door was too small, servicing difficult and the hydraulic pump on the port engine overheated after 10 minutes; modifications, including a cooler, were successful.

Various exhaust designs were tried on EF940 from September 1940 to improve both flame damping and cabin heating; an extra-long version was the best. Trials of LT298 with a turret were incomplete when it crashed in July 1943 at overload, ie 9,850lb, following engine failure. It had already been demonstrated that height could not be maintained on one engine at the new weight. The aircraft was also slightly but acceptably unstable throughout the speed range; the engine oil and cylinder temperatures were just within limits in UK conditions. Performance with air intakes similar to those on the Oxford is shown in the Table. MG244 from September 1943 completed the trials of LT298, and a combination of baffles and Oxford-type cowlings reduced engine temperatures; an investigation into the effect of humidity on air-cooled engines was inconclusive because of large scatter in the results after flying in cloud. The notorious hand pumping needed to raise the undercarriage on the Anson Mk I was absent on LT764 in February 1944; a hydraulic pump operated the undercarriage successfully but was inadequate

Anson I LT764 in February 1944, with an engine-driven pump on a Cheetah IX engine to operate the flaps and undercarriage. The modification required further refinement before incorporation in production aircraft with Cheetah XIXs and known as the Mk X. The rudder mass balance is standard, and the pitot head is under the nose. The astrodome and Bristol turret indicate two of the training roles possible on this machine, which has fixed-pitch propellers. *Probably A&AEE 11884*

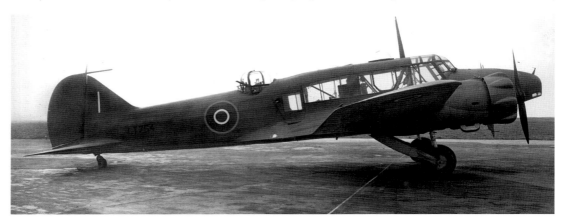

Avro Anson R9816, December 1940, for engine trials. (Scale 1:72)

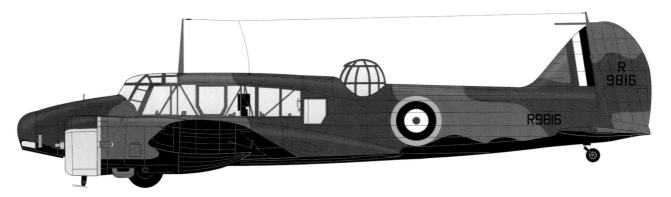

for fully lowering the flaps. After the tests the aircraft remained as a taxi until the end of the war. LT595 was quickly approved in April 1944 for launching 4-inch training flares.

Eight Anson Mk Is were in use at various times on non-reported work, mostly communications: K6157 (from October 1944), K6161 (October 1940 until a major accident in bad weather the following December), K6260 (September 1940 until damaged the following month), N5163 (for Porton from June to August 1943), N9595 (September 1939), DG717 (communications from October 1942), EG239 (with a smoke installation from August 1943), and LT112 (single-engine trials from February 1943).

Anson Mark XI

Tests of NK870 with a powered hydraulic system (Cheetah XIX and fixed-pitch propellers) took place from August 1944 at a take-off weight of 9,583lb. Handling was easy and pleasant, although 2,000 feet could not be maintained on the power of a single engine and

the range of the rudder trimmer needed to be increased. IFF and radios were satisfactory. 'Tail-heaviness' on Anson XIs was reported by the RAF, and NL227 was flown from February 1945 at increasingly aft CG. During the trial, a fault caused the flaps to extend of their own volition on take-off; the aircraft was written off (without casualties) in the ensuing forced landing. NL141 was used as a hack from February 1945.

Anson Mark XII

MG159 was a civil Avro XIX representative of the version for the RAF (known as the Anson XII), with deepened fuselage, more powerful Cheetah XV and constant-speed feathering propellers. Handling from June 1944 remained pleasant with a straightforward stall at 50mph (undercarriage and flaps down) at 9,900lb. 3,000 feet could be maintained on either engine alone, although greater rudder trim range was required and the undercarriage wheels needed to be fully retracted. It suffered major damage in August 1944. With a further weight increase to 10,600lb and a Cheetah XV, NL171 was tested

Anson XI NK870 in October 1944, with a raised cabin roof but retaining the fixed-pitch propellers for its Cheetah XIX motors in smooth cowlings. Just visible above and below the port aileron are the mass balances. The HF aerial runs from the nose via the large mast to the fin; there is a VHF aerial above the door and an IFF aerial under the roundel. *A&AEE 11955*

Anson XII MG159 in June 1944; when first tested it was referred to as an Avro XIX. Its Cheetah XV and constant-speed propellers permitted flight on one operating engine; however, the powered engine failed on an asymmetric overshoot in August 1944 and the aircraft crashed, but without injury. Square windows have replaced the earlier 'greenhouse', and curtains are visible. *A&AEE 11825*

from September 1944; performance is given in the Table. Maximum range with 140 gallons of fuel was 660 miles, and cabin heating was judged barely acceptable for the rear seats.

Oxford

Testing of the original version of the Airspeed Oxford was virtually complete by September 1939.

Oxford Mark I

The Mark I with Cheetah X engines was represented by N6327 for test pilot training for three months from March 1940; this aircraft later had experimental twin fins, tested elsewhere. The fourth Oxford built by the Standard Motor Company, V3868, handled normally in March 1941, but the intended engine trials of N6250 were cancelled just after arrival in August 1941. Assessment of L4539 with the Maclaren undercarriage took eight months from December 1941 due to the need for suitable winds to test the swivelling properties of this novel feature. The installation, in prototype form, had practical limitations, but the pilots considered that a development could allow continued operation from a single runway in crosswinds, which would otherwise prevent safe flying. A more practical innovation, electrical operation of the undercarriage by push buttons, was found very good on HN610 from September 1943. HN782, used for training, was written off after fifteen months in September 1944 by an out-of-practice pilot.

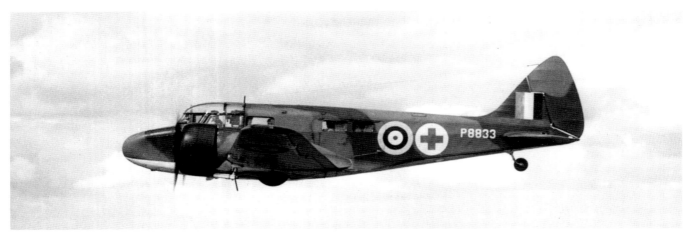

Oxford I P8833, in ambulance guise, poses for its recognition photographs; dated 12 March 1941, this is an early example. P8833 never belonged to the A&AEE.

Oxford I L4539 in April 1942, during lengthy trials of its swivelling Maclaren undercarriage intended to permit safe take-offs and landings across the wind. All three wheels could be turned to align them with the runway, but in this trial installation adjustments were possible only on the ground. Some details can be seen including the frame behind the gunless turret to protect the empennage from enthusiastic tyro gunners; the mast height looks unusually tall. *A&AEE 9938*

Oxford Mark II

The turret-less N4720 left less than a month after flying from Martlesham Heath. With standard Cheetah X engines, P1070 was received from Percival's in November 1939; it was faster and climbed better than a similarly loaded Airspeed aircraft for reasons that are not elucidated in the report. It had a markedly improved flap system that automatically set the mid position on overshooting with full flap selected. The side-by-side seating in T1387 and the single fixed gun was designed for pilot air-to-ground gunnery. The technique on trials was to tip in at 75-85mph, dive at up to 30° and pull out at about 2.5g. The gun functioned without problems. DS845 made the standard IFF tests late in 1941.

Oxford Mark III

P1864 was the only Mk III and had Cheetah XV engines with constant-speed propellers; it was tested from September 1940. Take-off and climb benefited from the changes; later, Seafox propellers gave further improvement (see the Table).

Oxford Mark V

A pair of Wasp Junior AN6B engines powered EB424 on trials from September 1942. Six training roles were planned in service: wireless, bombing, gunnery, beam approach, navigation, and intermediate pilot. Although handling was affected only to the extent of increased buffeting near the stall, the most striking feature of this version was the reduction in range from a maximum of 740 miles in the Mk I to 595 in the Mk V. Two types of propeller were tried but without significant difference.

Oxford II P1070, seen in November 1939, was built by Percival and was marginally faster than the Airspeed-built machines tested. There is no turret. The flaps are shown fully down, and were automatically set to the take-off setting on overshooting. It appears to be in training yellow overall. *A&AEE 9617*

Oxford V EB424 in October 1942, with its Wasp Junior engines well hidden in cowlings. Ice guards are fitted to the air intakes above the nacelle. *A&AEE 11118*

Master

Master Mark I

The Miles Master, an advanced trainer with a Kestrel XXX engine, was tested before the war in prototype form. Trials on production aircraft N7409 and N7410 continued in September 1939 at Boscombe; handling was good, although the rudder was heavy but responsive. Stalls at 59mph (undercarriage and flaps down) were usually marked by either wing dropping; spins were normal with the hood open or closed. The view from the back was poor, particularly for dive bombing; performance is shown in the Table. In July 1940 N7893 arrived with strengthening modifications to the fuselage and fin structure; following tests the Establishment recommended removal of the restrictions on aerobatics in all Masters, imposed earlier following several accidents in the RAF, and one at the A&AEE (see below). The fitting of radios moved the CG aft, and T8559 was flown from March 1941 with radio and a larger tailplane. Stalls with the rear

hood open were described as 'vicious wing drop', although there was ample aerodynamic warning. To reduce the risk of wing failure (as had occurred in the RAF), various inertia weights to increase stick forces on recovery were tried; 12lb was found to be the most suitable.

In 1942 T8559 returned with wing span reduced by 3ft 3in, and a slight deterioration in stalling behaviour was noted. In service the clipping of the wings caused experienced instructors to condemn the modification. One aircraft, N7757, was regarded as a rogue in this respect, but when flown by the Establishment in October 1942 was found to be normal. The explanation postulated was that the low power of the type led to some loss of speed in steep turns resulting in an accelerated stall; no accelerometer was fitted in RAF aircraft.

Master Mark II

Testing of the Master Mk II was delayed following the crash of the first, N7422 (Mercury VIII), in January 1940, a few weeks after arrival. A

Master I T8559 is seen in March 1942 following modifications that included a larger tailplane, clipped wings and practice bomb equipment. Anti-spin parachute and rudder guard are fitted, but there is no aerial for the radio, the weight of which in the rear fuselage led indirectly to the modifications. The spinner and exhaust arrangement of the Kestrel XXX give the nose a fighter appearance. *A&AEE 9930*

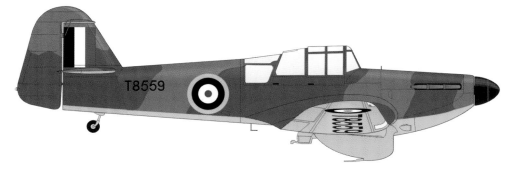

Miles Master T8559, February 1941, for handling and radio trials. (Scale 1:72)

comprehensive investigation determined that during a high-speed dive with the cockpit open, at about 290mph the tailplane attachment failed and the tailplane detached. The pilot bailed out. Trials continued in February 1941 with N7447 (Mercury XX) – performance as shown in the Table – with pleasant and easy handling up to the maximum diving speed of 330mph. Comments included the heaviness of the rudder, the poor view past the radial engine when taxiing, and the good view on the approach from the rear seat in the raised position with the hood open.

N7447 force-landed and was replaced in May 1941 by AZ104 for tests with the propeller diameter reduced to 9ft 6in following RAF experience of the original 10-foot version hitting the ground on night take-offs. The improved performance with a de Havilland propeller is shown in the Table; T8886 was briefly tried with a Rotol version. The latter also flew in mid-1942 with a modified oil cooler intake in an unsuccessful attempt to reduce oil temperatures,

and also with a thickened wing section at the tip, with noticeable benefit. Finally, in mid-1943, T8886 had the strengthened centre wing section being fitted in Service aircraft; the main effect was to raise clean stalling speeds. AZ543 repeated from January 1942 the earlier tests of reduced-span wings; spin recovery was judged to take marginally longer, otherwise behaviour was normal. On return in mid-1942, AZ543 had a Mercury XXX and a 'g restrictor'; the latter, designed by Miles, was unacceptable because the device snatched at the stick and was thus not progressive. An RAE design, weighing a total of 30lb, was better, but still produced a jolt on the stick as it operated on DK810 in October 1942. DL302 had a cut-away rudder and hook for towing gliders. Its Mercury XXX oil temperatures were within limits, but tended to be so cool that the plugs oiled up; removing the spinner raised temperatures again. Handling was normal, but more left rudder trim movement was required for the slow climb.

Master II N7447 in May 1941, with electric pitch control of the propeller; the exhaust has been extended to take gases clear of the fuselage. Four practice bombs and a rudder guard are fitted. *A&AEE 9680*

Master II N7422 in December 1939, with original hydro-mechanical pitch control of the propeller, eight practice bombs (four under each inboard wing) and anti-spin parachute fitted. The original full-span wings are fitted and the static vent is forward of the roundel. The aircraft broke up in January 1940, and the observer was killed. *A&AEE 9620*

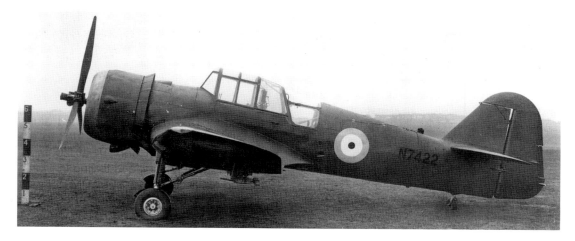

Master II AZ543 in January 1942. Although extensively used for spinning trials with reduced-span wings, the anti-spin parachute has yet to be fitted, but the inevitable practice bombs are in evidence. The scowling figure present in the front cockpit is unusual, no doubt sheltering from Boscombe's fresh air. The wavy line between the upper and lower surface finish is also unusual. *A&AEE 9907*

Master II DL302 in July 1942, with the lower rudder cropped for glider towing. The exhaust has been further extended, spinning was normal, and did not require use of the anti-spin parachute. The spinner was later removed from the propeller to raise oil temperatures. *A&AEE 11045*

Rockets were successfully fitted to and fired from DL852/G from February 1943; six RPs were fitted under blast plates on the wings, and aimed by the Mk IIL sight. Handling was affected to the extent of causing the left wing to drop at the stall; other Masters usually dropped the right wing. Measurements of attitude using the datum line painted along the fuselage showed an angle of 9½° to the flight path at 100mph and 1° at 200mph. DL852 was severely damaged taxiing in March 1943, and replaced in August by DM159 with modifications to make RP training effective.

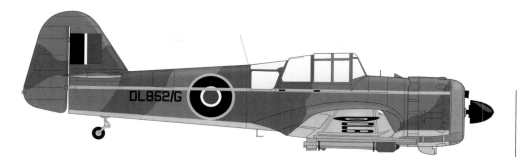

Miles Master DL852/G, February 1943, for rocket projectile trials. (Scale 1:72)

Master Mark III

Handling of W8437 with a Twin Wasp Junior SB4G was normal in early 1941, while the performance of N7994 from February 1941 was the best of the Masters (see the Table). T8852 arrived in April 1942 with a device acting on the elevator trimmer to increase stick force under acceleration. The device suffered a snatch in operation, similar to those on the earlier Marks. On 6 May, on the eighth dive of a series, the aircraft reached 7g and the port wing failed, due, it was later discovered, to defective gluing of the plywood skin. The observer was killed.

Buckmaster

The training version of the Buckingham, the Bristol Buckmaster, was represented at the A&AEE during the wartime period by RP122 in March 1945 for weighing (33,649lb all up) and successful contamination tests. It was followed by RP137 from June for handling, until a minor engine fire in August. Longitudinal stability was just satisfactory, with negligible stick forces needed to change speed by 50mph from the trimmed condition, and no tendency for the stick to return to its original position. There were no trimming controls for the instructor, but the aircraft was considered to be a good and suitable conversion from the original bomber.

Master III N7994 in February 1941, with a Twin Wasp Junior engine prior to the start of its A&AEE trials. The mechanism for raising the centre cockpit cover can be seen; the instructor in the rear seat was thus shielded when he raised his seat to see where he was going. The static vent is between the roundel and the serial number.

Buckmaster I RP122 in pristine condition in March 1945. Minor criticisms of the type were made in the wartime period of this pilot trainer conversion of the Buckingham. After the war it was used for training for the similar Brigand. *A&AEE 15068*

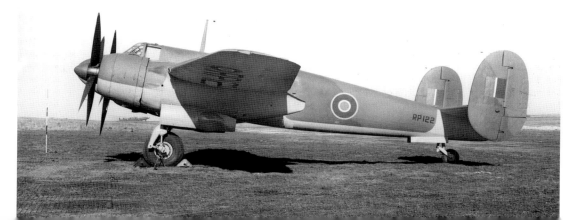

12 Wings for the Navy

Fighters and Observers

Roc

Pre-war trials on the Blackburn Roc with its turret with four 0.303in guns were soon completed at Boscombe on L3057. The low top speed and rate of climb of the type were marginally changed by fitting a Skua-type propeller, and slightly improved by a Tiger (Whitley) type in L3058 from December 1939; details are given in the Table. Armament trials occupied L3069 for eight months from September 1939, but reports have not been found.

Fulmar

The Fairey Fulmar had no prototype, as the design was based largely on the pre-war P4/34; two seats allowed an observer to be carried, primarily, it is said, to help find the aircraft carrier for landing.

Fulmar Mark I

N1854, the first Fulmar, arrived in May 1940, only five months after its initial flight; N1855 and N1858 soon followed, all powered by the Merlin VIII. Performance (see the Table) was disappointing and handling inferior to that of the Hurricane, with heavy ailerons and poor response to elevator and rudder on the approach. The latter shortcoming was most marked on carrier trials on HMS *Illustrious* approaching at 68 knots (78mph) into a 30-knot (35mph) wind over the deck. Two deck landings were made by an A&AEE pilot. Among good features noted were instantaneous spin recovery and stability in dives up to 415mph. However, there was criticism of the high cockpit noise, the voice pipe intercommunicating system, the absence of cockpit heating, and, on the powerful elevator trim, the tendency of the datum to alter. N1888's guns were quick and easy to rearm from July 1940; other details are lacking. N1859 had modified but still ineffectual heating in December 1940, and oxygen was recommended for use above 5,000 feet as some contamination was measured on trials.

Fulmar N1855 in May 1940, showing the general arrangement of the type. Features include the lowered split flaps, the starboard undercarriage door, and a line from the back of the rear cockpit taped on the top of the fuselage. Extensive spinning was completed on this aircraft and it is possible that the anti-spin parachute had yet to be fitted. The lighting makes it difficult to establish whether the fin and rudder are, indeed, painted white. *A&AEE 9638*

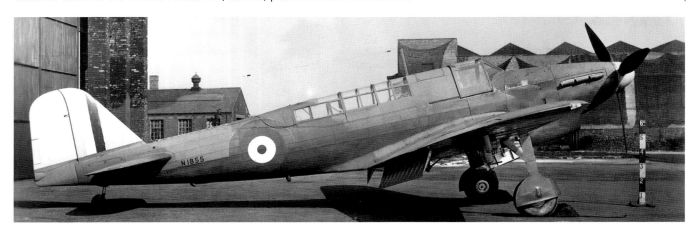

Fulmar Mark II

Increased power from the Merlin XXX gave the Mk II a small improvement in performance (see the Table), even with a tropical cowling. Range (without bomb carriers) was 980 miles (maximum) – unchanged from the Mk I. These figures were obtained on a re-engined Mk I, N4021, badly damaged in June 1941, some six weeks after arrival. After repair, engine cooling proved satisfactory, but a new type of air thermometer was not. N4079, the first Mk II to appear in March 1941, had a mass-balanced rudder acceptable up to 415mph in a dive of 11,000 feet. Later, an assessment was made of the Ministry system of electrical wiring – the Establishment acknowledged that it had 'some good points'. Earlier, an interim system had been fitted to X8741. Flame damping of the triple ejector fish-tail exhaust was improved with anti-glow paint.

A standard modification on N4126 in July 1941 eliminated contamination, and an external 60-gallon fuel tank on X8641 from October 1941 increased weight to 10,500lb and maximum range to 1,100 miles. IFF Mk IIN (R3109) proved acceptable on X8756 in February 1942, the same month that X8697 arrived armed with four 0.5in wing guns; rearming by two men took a lengthy 40 minutes and thirteen modifications were recommended. In June 1942 X8757 appeared with a rack to carry a single 250lb or 500lb bomb; American bombs could not be carried as the rear crutches were too long. There was adequate clearance from the propeller on release in dives up to 60° and 310 knots (357mph). Smaller bombs were released at 50 feet without problems after a diving approach.

Martlet/Wildcat

Grumman's stubby carrier fighter, ordered by France before the occupation, was added to the subsequent British contracts, as were later machines intended for Greece. These were originally designated Martlet Mks I, II and III respectively in the Royal Navy; the name was changed to Wildcat for Mks IV, V and VI supplied under Lease-Lend.

Fulmar II N4021 in May 1941 has a standard cowling, showing the air intake to the carburettors The aircraft was later damaged on 22 June when it suffered a forced landing at night with the undercarriage retracted. After repair, it was returned to service with the Navy. *A&AEE 9818*

N4021 now has a revised cowling for tropical use. The air intake has been moved to the side; an air cleaner could also be fitted. The larger cowling had only a marginal effect on performance (2% slower climb) and the air filter caused a further slight deterioration. *A&AEE 9818*

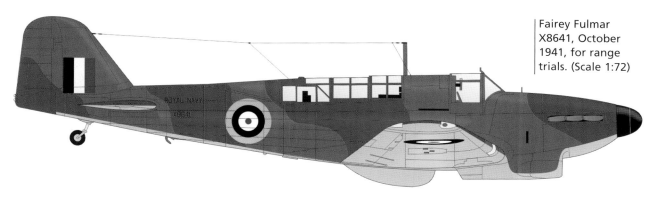

Fairey Fulmar X8641, October 1941, for range trials. (Scale 1:72)

Martlet Mark I

Grumman removed many French features before delivery of the Cyclone G205A-powered Mk I, and AX826 and AX828 reached Boscombe in September 1940 for handling and armament respectively. At 6,810lb the aircraft was pleasant to fly, with straightforward stalls at 83mph (clean) and 70mph (flaps and undercarriage down). The take-off run was 280 yards (160 yards into a 20-knot wind), but the narrow undercarriage was described as 'twitchy', and took 30 seconds to retract manually. Other comments included the lack of a direct vision panel, and the placing together of the similar flap and fuel levers. A creditable maximum range of 930 miles was calculated on 136 gallons of fuel. Contamination by carbon monoxide was bad, but was improved by sealing the cowling and cockpit. In June 1942 BJ570 proved worse at first, but in this case a cure was found by sealing the holes round the tail wheel and arrester hook. The six reports on the armament of two 0.5in Colt wing guns have not been found, but investigation included high-altitude firing trials not made in the USA. AL247 had triple cascade flame dampers on arrival in February 1943 and just met the relaxed Naval requirement of invisibility at night at ranges of more than a mile. BJ525, an ex-Greek contract machine, appeared briefly for IFF work in September 1942, followed in December by BJ514 for Porton; both had Cyclone (R-1820) engines and were thus regarded as Mk Is.

Martlet I AX826 in 1941 with a Cyclone (R-1820) engine, air intake at the top of the cowling, conventional pressure head on the port wing, and four wing guns. The wing did not fold. *A&AEE 9852*

Triple cascade exhausts have been fitted to Martlet I AL247 in early 1943; the design just met the Naval requirement of invisibility at more than a mile. *A&AEE 11286*

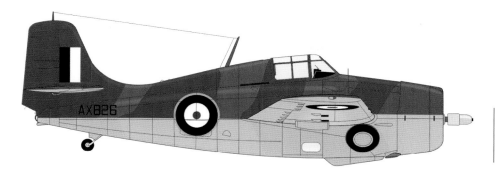

Grumman Martlet
AX826, April 1940,
for handling trials.
(Scale 1:72)

Martlet Mark II

A Twin Wasp S3C4-G, folding wings and six 0.5in Browning guns were features of this version. AM969 arrived in December 1941, joined briefly by AM980 the following February and by AM991 two months later, all for handling and performance. A large pressure error of 15mph over-reading was found at stalling speeds, attributed to the Z-shaped pitot head being mounted on top of the port wing; later the type had a more familiar pitot tube ahead of the leading edge, although errors remained large. Handling at aft CG was 'viciously unstable', but forward of the limit consequently imposed it was acceptable. Performance (see the Table), not outstanding for 1942, resulted from the weight used representing full catapult equipment and a 25-gallon external tank. Range was reported as 890 miles. AM987, with a GM2 gunsight, completed satisfactory gunnery trials with ten recommendations for improvements.

Wildcat Mark IV

FN111, a Mk IV, was similar to the Mk II (same engine but with US Navy designation R-1830-86) with provision for two 100lb bombs; arrival in September 1942 was followed by uneventful handling. While improvements had reduced rearming time of the six wing 0.5in guns from 30 minutes (in the Mk II) to 20 minutes, the gun heating was inadequate, even after modifications by the Establishment. Six 25lb head rockets on an RP Mk I installation were fitted to FN202 on arrival in November 1943; the all-up weight increased to 8,120lb and unchanged handling followed attitude measurements. Firing trials appear to have been cancelled before completion, but in October 1943 FN130 had the American RP Mk 5 installation without rails; accuracy was unaffected although gravity drop on release was greater on the American system. FN224 was photographed in October 1944 but is otherwise undocumented.

Martlet II AM969 in 1941 with Twin Wasps (R-1830), folding wings (reducing guns to one per side) and a forward-raked HF mast. Clues to the wing folding are the 'D' ring by the serial number, a small fitting on the top of the wing outboard, and a fairing and small lever (all just visible) inboard. Just above the 'D' ring can be seen the uniquely shaped pressure head on the outboard rear port wing. The pilot's bead sight can also just be seen. *A&AEE 9851*

Wildcat IV FN202 in December 1943 with the RP Mk I installation, illustrating well the thick blast plate on which the rocket projectors (rails) are mounted. Under the wings can be seen oil cooler intakes, and the exhausts have short extensions in an attempt to reduce flames entering the cockpit. *A&AEE 11627*

Wildcat VI JV642 in May 1944, showing the taller fin and rudder of this mark to cope with the more powerful Cyclone (R-1820-56). It has a pair of drop tanks (starboard shown), and HF and VHF whip aerials. *Probably A&AEE 11875*

Wildcat Mark V

JV336, from June 1943, a Mk V with only four guns but the ability to carry two 250lb stores, had the same R1830-86 engine as the Mk IV, but required an 8-inch extension to the exhaust (3 inches on the Mk IV) to cure contamination. Stick forces became dangerously light at aft CG, and a limit (based on a pull of 2lb per g) further forward than earlier Marks was determined; the ailerons were assessed as heavy for a fighter. Rearming the guns took an additional man to support the weight of the ammunition box while the other two lifted the ends; each box had 430 rounds compared with about 240 in earlier Marks. 250lb smoke apparatus was carried and jettisoned successfully up to 240mph before the aircraft was damaged following engine failure on take-off in August 1944. Two months earlier an RAE-designed flame damper had not proved successful on JV468, and damage to JV528 due to undercarriage collapse on take-off curtailed rocket trials. In October 1944 JV397 caught fire during contamination measurements and the pilot bailed out. The following month JV431 appeared for bombing, but soon became unserviceable.

Wildcat Mark VI

The more powerful Cyclone (R-1820-56) and large fin and tailplane identified JV642 as a Mk VI on arrival in April 1944. With two 48-gallon drop tanks the weight was 8,175lb and handling excellent, although ailerons remained slightly heavy. A safe deck take-off and landing with a single fuel drop tank could, it was considered, be made. Top speed was raised (see the Table), but contamination and gun heating remained problems. Water injection (R-1820-56W) in JV782 from December 1944 gave an increase of 14mph (true) in top speed up to 10,000 feet; the aircraft was destroyed in March 1945 when an over-enthusiastic pilot hit the propeller on the ground during take-off. Rocket trials on JV783 (RP Mk II installation) and JV875 (American RP Mk 5) were under way at the end of the war; the latter again experienced unacceptable cockpit contamination. After six months of unserviceability in the Armament Squadron, JV651 was removed in October 1944.

Wildcat VI JV875 in early 1945, although the report was not issued until August 1945 – long after interest in rocket-armed Wildcats had waned. The installation was an American Mk 5 with zero-length launchers. *A&AEE 15135*

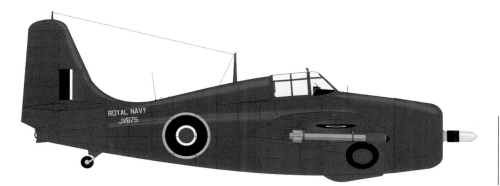

Grumman Wildcat JV875, March 1945, for handling/ performance trials. (Scale 1:72)

Miles M20

The second prototype Miles M-20, U0228, was offered for a short assessment in April 1941. Seventeen comments on construction and layout were made, and included poor hood operation and lack of wing venting, although the view was excellent. At 7,560lb, powered by a Merlin XX, U0228 had somewhat heavy and slightly overbalanced controls and conventional stall, but with the stick in the central position. Acceleration in a dive up to 450mph was rapid in spite of the fixed undercarriage.

Miles M20 U0228 is ready for its first visit in April 1941; assessment as a naval fighter (DR616) followed three months later. The bubble canopy was an advanced feature and the view was praised; the fixed undercarriage was simple, but dated, although speed and climb were creditable. The Merlin XX and propeller lend scale to this small aeroplane.

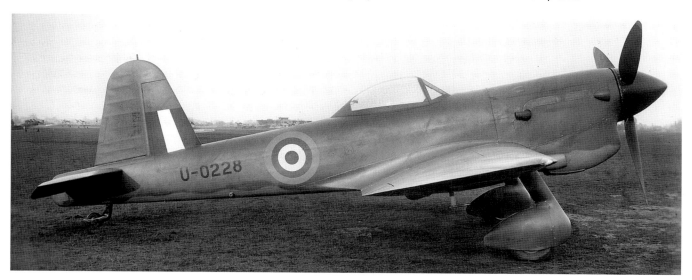

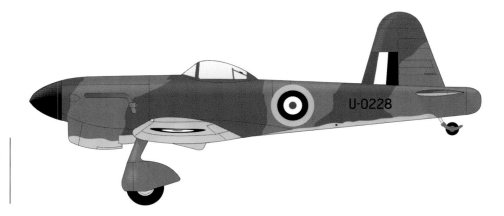

Miles M20 U0228/DR616, April 1941, for handling/ performance trials. (Scale 1:72)

On return to the A&AEE in mid-1941, the same machine was numbered DR616 and examined as a possible naval fighter. Performance (see the Table) was measured, and was faster and at a greater height than the Wildcat three years later. Greater oil cooling was required, while the cockpit needed more warmth; the eight 0.303in guns were adequately heated. The internal fuel of 110 gallons gave a calculated range of 610 miles at 9,000 feet.

Firefly

The Fairey Firefly required considerable development of all three flying controls before satisfactory handling was achieved; equipment changes and concomitant CG alterations exacerbated the difficulties. The A&AEE tested each modification.

Firefly Mark I

The first prototype, Z1826 (Griffon IIB), appeared in February 1942; after weighing to give 11,498lb all-up with 193 gallons of fuel, handling followed determination of pressure errors – 11mph over-reading at 130mph. Excessive push force in dives limited speed to 360mph, while at slower speeds the elevator hunted continuously in bumps; the large horn balance area was blamed. The aircraft was without guns, radio or a sliding hood, there being no time to fit a replacement.

Firefly I Z1826 in May 1942, with no cockpit cover and no radios but many aerials – HF from wing tip to fin and from mast to fin, and a VHF whip aerial. Points of interest include the Youngman flaps extended from their stowage in the wing to the cruise position, and the horn-balanced elevators with balance tabs, together insufficient to reduce stick force in dives to an acceptable level. *A&AEE 11003*

Late in 1942 ailerons with altered gearing and reduced deflection were found better, but still too heavy. A full analysis of the elevator characteristics indicated that the tail twisted such that elevator reversal would, it was estimated, occur at 500mph; also, the forces in dives were still excessive. A larger and more robust tailplane and elevator were recommended. Removal of the wing tips had no measurable effect. In mid-1943 two alternative types of three-bladed propeller were tried, but top speed scarcely improved; loss of efficiency at high tip speeds was blamed. Z1828 had control changes on arrival in September 1942, including the elevator hinge moved slightly aft, a reshaped horn balance on the rudder and smaller, metal, ailerons. The elevator forces remained high in dive (350mph only was achieved, although 425mph was permitted) and the ailerons were much improved at low speed, but immovable at high speed. Repositioning the static source reduced pressure errors, and the conventional stall was at 74mph (flaps and undercarriage down). Handling remained poor, but the small improvement allowed 204lb of ballast to be removed, reducing the weight to 11,285lb. Trials on Z1828 included radiator cooling, which was inadequate for tropical conditions; a minor modification improved but did not eliminate the problem. Spinning at three CG was normal.

Z1830 came to the A&AEE in March 1943, mainly for armament work with alterations to the gun mountings following unsatisfactory trials at Fairey's Works in December 1942, when flexibility and resonance had occurred when firing the four 20mm guns. The same problem had curtailed earlier trials on Z1828. By May 1943 a No 3 FMU (feed mechanism), together with strengthened mountings, met with limited success, but further redesign was needed; satisfaction was achieved in the following August. Meanwhile Z1834 and

Z1837 each flew 150 hours with the IFDF, and each had two engine failures, which at least allowed shortcomings in the engine changing arrangements to be identified. A range of 805 miles was calculated from the intensive trials. The conclusion was that the Firefly was a good aeroplane for its task – apart from completely unacceptable handling!

These sentiments were confirmed in handling trials from June 1943 on Z1842, a representative production machine. Excessively high elevator and aileron forces remained the main culprits. Z1832 had stiffened ailerons and an increase of 2° in tailplane incidence. Aileron forces remained high but elevator forces in the dive were acceptable; however, manoeuvring stick forces were too great at forward CG. The versatile Fairey-Youngman flaps were praised, but metal elevators on Z1867 in July 1943 were rejected due to high manoeuvring forces; at the end of 1943 Z1888, with production-standard metal elevators, was deemed acceptable for all roles, ie fighting, reconnoitring and training. Stick forces were a maximum of 16lb per g (forward CG) up to 4g and 418mph. Z1838 attended in October 1943 with an improved sequence valve for operating the flaps. The final, and successful, modifications to the Firefly's controls were spring tabs on the ailerons and elevator fitted to Z1839, tested from October 1943. In March 1944 the aircraft crashed fatally during rate of roll measurements at 420mph; the starboard wing failed, suggesting that aileron forces had been made too low.

Rockets, bombs, fuel tanks and radar pods were fitted externally to the Firefly. An RP Mk I installation in 1944 on Z1867 was used to fire 316 25lb and 208 65lb rockets, eventually clearing the weapon for Service use; the aircraft was badly damaged on landing in April 1945. Z1909 from May 1944 had improved Mk V gun

Firefly I Z1867 in February 1944 displays its battery of eight 25lb RPs on a Mk I installation. The 20mm guns are of the Hispano Mk V variety. *A&AEE 11684*

mountings for its pair of 20mm guns; later tests with sixteen rockets (double the previous loads) on an RP Mk VIII installation and two 45-gallon fuel tanks gave no problems. Ninety-gallon tanks had a small adverse effect on the handling of DT985 from August 1944, and a similar deterioration was noted with two 1,000lb bombs; handling with a single bomb was unpleasant, but manageable. In May 1945 spent cartridge cases impinged on bomb fins in an area of great turbulence. Z1970/G from March 1944 had a pod for anti-shipping radar under the engine, causing some reduction in directional stability and 8mph (true) loss in top speed; engine cooling was, however,

satisfactory. Late in 1944 the Establishment confirmed annoying vibrations in MB395 (Griffon II); a rubber buffer in the control circuit of MB394, flown at Heath Row early in 1945, cured the problem. The new radio in MB295 worked well. Z1844's Griffon XII had, in early 1945, satisfactory cooling while the exhaust caused no contamination, although flame damping was poor and the hot gases damaged the fuselage. Z1882 checked guns in March 1944. MB465 was used for routine photography from February 1945, and MB576 investigated the gyro gunsight from April 1945, while MB647 continued gun development after the war.

Firefly II Z1831/G in March 1943, with a 15-inch fuselage plug to move the engine forward to counteract the weight of equipment planned for the rear of this mark. The aircraft has ballast in the rear cockpit and a representative searchlight. Extensive protection for the rudder is provided in the event of deployment of the anti-spin parachute. *A&AEE 11324*

Firefly I DT985 in about July 1945, armed with a pair of 250lb GP bombs. A pair of wedges under the wing probably held a camera for flight trials. The aircraft looks a bit tired. The bomb carrier has the fairings introduced to reduce drag, and the tip of the arrester hook is just visible under the serial number. *A&AEE 15207*

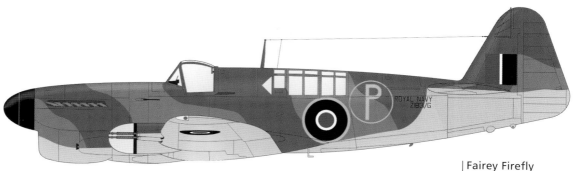

Fairey Firefly
Z1832/G, March
1943, for handling
trials. (Scale 1:72)

Firefly Mark II

Intended for night-fighting, Z1831/G was representative of the Mk II in March 1943 with the Griffon II engine moved forward 15 inches, radar pods on the wings, and ballast in the rear cockpit. At 11,655lb, the stalls were 96mph (clean) and 82mph (flaps and undercarriage down); at aft CG the aircraft was unstable, but satisfactory at forward CG. When the basic aircraft CG was moved forward by 1.7 inches, the directional characteristics were worse. With the current standard of aerodynamic 'fixes' (ie +2° incidence on tailplane and metal elevators), Z1840 arrived in August 1943; the high but improved stick forces were judged acceptable for a night-fighter. Cockpit lighting was generally good, but exhaust dampers were needed and the landing light reflected from the propeller. Spinning was unpleasant but safe, after initial trials on Z1831 with an anti-spin parachute. Z1875 completed unreported handling in April 1945.

Firefly Mark III

A larger chin radiator for the Griffon 71 identified Mk III Z1835 on arrival in July 1943. Top speed was good (see the Table), and improved with a four- in place of a three-bladed propeller together with ejector exhausts; a Griffon 72SP gave a similar top speed. Handling was worse than earlier Marks, with a reduction in stability and a nose-over tendency on landing, yet retaining the excessive stick forces in dives.

Firefly Mark IV

In July 1945 trials started on Z2118, a Mk IV with a Griffon 72S, leading edge radiators, clipped wings and a larger fin. Initial flying was encouraging, the only complaint being rudder overbalance on the climb.

Firefly III Z1835 in August 1943, with a larger radiator to cool the Griffon 71, and showing the ejector exhausts. The effect of these three developments was to increase top speed and combine the worst features of handling of earlier Marks. The pilot's bead sight and early Mk II Hispano guns seen here were not tested. *A&AEE 1114*

Firefly IV Z2118 in July 1945, with five features not already illustrated: four-bladed propeller, wing root radiators, clipped wing, raised canopy for the pilot, and enlarged fin. *A&AEE 15171*

Seafire

Seafire Mark I

The first two Seafires at Boscombe were Spitfires with hooks, known as Mk IB, armed with two 20mm and four 0.303in guns, and powered by Merlin 45s; both made only short visits. BL676 did handling checks in two days early in April 1942 prior to carrier tests, and, at 6,880lb all-up weight, was very similar to the Spitfire V, the only major comment being the push force needed in dives to 450mph. The 30-gallon belly tank was satisfactory. AB376 had an improved and satisfactory radio (TR1196A) in June 1942.

Seafire Mark II

Retaining non-folding wings, but possessing a hook and catapult strong points, MA970 (Merlin 46) arrived in October 1942 for performance tests (see the Table). In October 1943 light stick forces on pull-out from dives continued to cause concern, and LR764 was flown for comparison with a folding-wing Mk III. LR764 was found to be considerably less prone to overstressing, and an aft limit of CG for all flying was fixed; the same limit, imposed on the later version, restricted flying to straight and level only. With a low-level Merlin 32, MB138 arrived in January 1943; performance is shown in the Table, and the range on 84 gallons of internal fuel was 582 miles, or 820 miles with a 30-gallon belly tank.

Seafire I BL676 in April 1942, with a faired arrester hook under the rear fuselage as the only evidence of its nautical connection. The minutiae are interesting: the 'intensifier' pipe from the exhaust to heat the gun bays, the tropical intake, 30-gallon belly tank and well-taped 20mm gun, with the IFF aerial behind. The good (or bad) 'BONDOWOSO' subscribed to the cost of the machine, and the fin (at least) was inspected and stamped at Castle Bromwich. Repair patches are visible on the fin, rudder and top of the fuselage. *A&AEE 9844*

With a four-bladed propeller, two F24 cameras and VHF, LR728 was designated FR Mk IIc, and was dangerous to fly as received in January 1944. A small inertia weight in the elevator circuit gave an improvement and a larger weight (6½lb) plus a larger horn balance produced acceptable characteristics at the same CG as the Mk I. MB261, built by Supermarine, was slightly worse in April 1944 than LR728 by Westland, and a standardised compromise aft limit for CG was recommended. MB293 (Merlin 46) reached only 420mph in dives with stores, such as 4½-inch flares, on light series bomb carriers under the wings. With a 200lb bomb under the fuselage, take-off and top speeds were noticeably affected, but the effect was acceptable. The intended tests of the braking propeller on MB178 from August 1944 were probably thwarted by unserviceability, and no report has been found.

Seafire Mark III

MA970, retaining the Merlin 46, but with folding, clipped wings and a four-bladed propeller, reappeared as a Mk III late in 1942. Handling at aft CG was again unacceptable, but take-off was improved (see the Table). The aircraft was destroyed while parked in January 1944, when a Welkin crashed into it on take-off. Trials on LR765 were abandoned on receipt in August 1943 due to unacceptable longitudinal characteristics. The next production aircraft, LR766, was acceptable with a small inertia weight, but restricted aft CG; with the same modifications LR765 returned and demonstrated better but still unacceptable handling in late 1943. A propeller cropped by 4 inches gave performance figures almost identical, with the full 10ft 9in propeller used earlier in LR874. Handling at extended aft CG was finally acceptable on NF545 in June 1944, fitted with metal-covered elevators; in this case the CG limit was set, not by the out-of-trim forces in a dive as previously, but by the tendency of the nose to rise on the approach if the speed was allowed to decay below the normal 80mph; a Merlin 55U was fitted.

Similarly powered and elevated, NN186 arrived in July 1944, and flew successfully with a centre-mounted 200lb smoke float. The following November PP975, with a 500lb smoke float, weighed 7,725lb and took an extra 43 yards (30%) to take off into a 20-knot wind. A slightly shorter run was measured on PR314 from March 1945 when carrying two 200lb floats plus a 45-gallon belly tank (8,010lb all-up weight); various combinations of stores were tried, many making the aircraft tiring to fly and again requiring the need to restrict the aft position of the CG. Eight 60lb RP on PX921 from April 1945 also aggravated the longitudinal handling and, landing at maximum weight, caused overheating of the brakes leading to a tyre bursting. Trials on PX921 with a modified Mk VIII RP installation were under way at the end of the war.

Seafire II MB138 in January 1943, still lacking wing-folding but having strengthening modifications for catapulting; the only visible evidence is the catapult spool just behind the wing trailing edge. Note the four-bladed propeller, two 20mm guns with four taped-over 0.303in guns, 30-gallon belly tank, ice guard and tubular oil cooler. Bulges on the wing roundel accommodate the bulky bits of the outboard gun. *A&AEE 11350*

Seafire III PR314 in mid-1945, carrying two 200lb smoke floats and a 45-gallon belly tank; several other stores were tested on this aircraft. *A&AEE 15200*

A close view of the 200lb smoke float on the starboard underwing rack on Seafire III PR314 during trials in mid-1945.

Seafire III PX921 in May 1945, with eight 60lb head rockets on an RP Mk VIII installation. The report refers to this aeroplane as an LFIII, ie low-altitude fighter with clipped wings. The picture clearly shows wing tips in place, but the line of the join of the tips can be seen. The hole on the port wing root is probably for a camera.

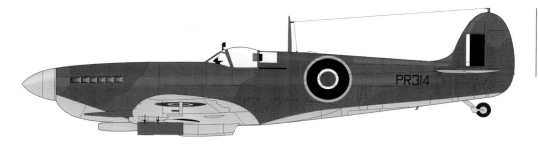

Supermarine Seafire PR314, March 1945, for performance/ armament trials. (Scale 1:72)

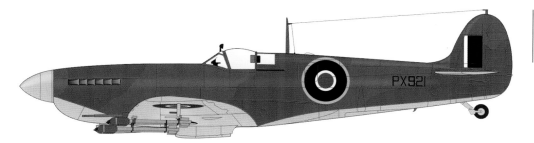

Supermarine Seafire PX921, April 1945, for rocket projectile trials. (Scale 1:72)

Seafire Mark XV

NS487, with a Griffon VI engine, was received in February 1944 and impressed the Establishment by its flush riveting, filled joints and polished surface. Handling was normal, but aft CG was limited to a more forward position than previously; a feature of the immaculate finish was the need for care in avoiding excess speed on the approach. With increased internal fuel, weight was 7,870lb; maintenance was easy. NS493 was representative of production aircraft and had a teardrop hood; the view was excellent and handling very good, with top speed as shown in the Table. NS490 had insufficient radiator cooling for the tropics on tests from July 1944; in 1945 it had a second arrester hook under the cut-away rudder, spun normally and had good directional behaviour. SR446, built by Westland, was criticised for left wing heaviness, starboard aileron upfloat (these observations seem contradictory) and aileron vibrations; reducing the fine pitch stops of the propeller did not cure the lack of drag on the approach. The

swing to the left on take-off was more manageable by reducing power from 15psi boost to 12psi; distances were little changed. Later, cooling and radios were satisfactory.

Returning in June 1945, SR446 had a metal elevator with the usual improvement in handling; a Mk XI depth charge, however, again reduced stability, making trimming very difficult. SR448 appears to have been improved before arrival in March 1945, and handling and spinning were acceptable. Shown in the Table is the limited performance, curtailed when the aircraft was damaged following disconnection of the rudder bolt. From March 1945 22-gallon wing drop tanks on PK245 were acceptable, but speed was limited to 440mph because of an increasing right-wing-down tendency. In January 1945 gunnery trials started on SR453 with two 22mm and four 0.303in guns; rearming was very difficult with the wings folded, as fourteen panels had to be removed. SW793 with American radio equipment arrived in July 1945.

Seafire XV NS493 in July 1944, with cut-down rear fuselage, bubble canopy, revised air intake and double radiators, one under each wing; the starboard radiator incorporates the oil cooler. The enlarged bulges on the cowling are for a Griffon VI motor. *A&AEE 11810*

Seafire 45 LA443 is seen in September 1945, having arrived a month earlier, but no trials had started before the end of the war. The five-bladed propeller, enlarged rudder with 'sting' arrester hook and a tail wheel guard can be seen. *A&AEE 15196*

Seafire Mark 45

TM379 underwent rapid assessment for deck landing on arrival in June 1945. The Griffon 45 with contra-rotating propellers eliminated swing on take-off and was generally well liked; aileron friction was excessive. LA443 arrived in August 1945 to start trials.

Kingfisher

Intended as an observation scout for ship use, the Vought-Sikorsky Kingfisher was supplied under Lend-Lease; two reached the A&AEE with fixed wheel-undercarriages.

FN651 (from July 1942) and FN656 (April 1942) shared testing; both had R-985-AN2 engines and weighed up to 5,435lb armed with anti-submarine bombs. With two 250lb depth charges, performance is as shown in the Table,

and the range on 83½ gallons of fuel without external stores was 730 miles. Handling was pleasant in all conditions, although elevator trim range was insufficient on the glide; stall occurred at 59mph (flaps down). Care was needed with depth charges fitted as initial climb was poor, and flaps required to be raised slowly. The ailerons drooped to give full-span flaps, then roll control was by spoilers only; roll response was satisfactory throughout the range. Criticism centred initially on the high concentration of carbon monoxide; careful sealing of all holes in the fuselage cured the problem. Also the US Navy bomb carriers had several poor features; the Establishment commented that the fixed forward 0.3in gun fired twice per propeller revolution – as typical in American aircraft.

The same aircraft in April 1942. The observer's 0.3in gun is stowed within his cockpit, and camouflage is standard US Navy non-specular Blue Grey and Light Grey. *A&AEE 9971*

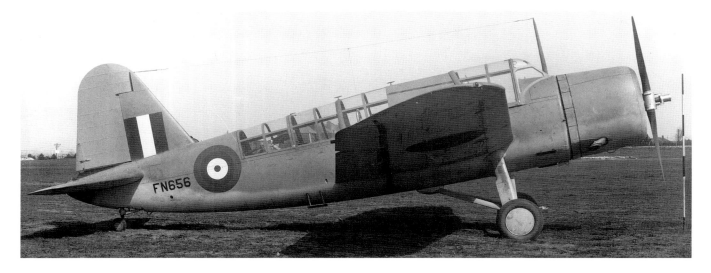

Kingfisher FN656 in May 1942 during trials at Boscombe Down. With a moderate armament load, performance was poor. *A&AEE recognition 93*

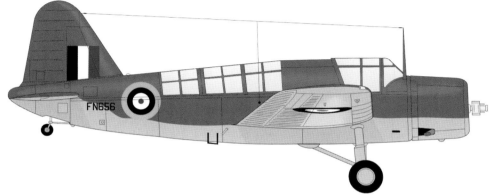

Vought Kingfisher FN856, April 1942, for handling trials. (Scale 1:72)

Gannet/Hellcat

Developed from the Wildcat, the Grumman Hellcat was delivered under Lend-Lease, the first of more than 1,000 for the Royal Navy arriving in the UK less than a year after the type's maiden flight.

Gannet/Hellcat Mark I

FN321, FN322 and FN323 arrived in June 1943, all powered by the Double Wasp R-2800-10, giving nearly twice the output of its predecessor. With 153 gallons of fuel, all-up weight was 11,400lb, and 12,130lb at overload; performance (as in the Table) was measured at the lower figure,

but altitude was restricted to 20,000 feet due to unsuitable magnetos. The normal contamination, flame damping, engine cooling, navigation and radio tests proceeded smoothly, although the Mk IIN IFF had to be replaced by the Mk III version, and the camera gun was subject to vibrations. FN331 and FN333 completed a total of 300 hours from July 1943; shortcomings were revealed in engine accessory drives. Changing an engine alone took 135 man-hours, but changing the whole power plant (engine change unit in later parlance) took a mere 15 man-hours. The gun installation (six 0.5in guns) was assessed as good, and rearming with wings folded, though awkward, was less difficult than other types. FN344 from January 1944 had a Mk I RP

Hellcat I FN344 in May 1944 displays its British RP Mk I installation with eight 60lb head rockets. It has the standard cockpit cover, HF masts and cranked pressure head. In the background a Sea Otter is being refuelled by the figure lying on top of the wing. *A&AEE 11773*

313

installation. Also from January 1944 all American aircraft in British service reverted to their US names. After weighing (12,248lb) and attitude measurements, handling was little affected but top speed was reduced initially by 40mph (true); fairings on the rails reduced the penalty to 27mph (true). The installation, including the Mk IIL sight, was satisfactory. With a 120-gallon drop tank FN360 weighed 13,260lb, stalled at 77mph (flaps and undercarriage down) and had a maximum range of 1,570 miles if the tank was dropped when empty; handling remained unaffected.

JV109 had a balloon hood in late 1944; an improved view with no handling effects resulted. JV127, received in June 1944, handled well up to 450mph with 500lb smoke, British 1,000lb bombs and 125-gallon drop tank separately, then with a 1,000lb bomb under the starboard wing and the drop tank on the centre line. In the latter case much buffeting and shaking ensued and a limit of 370mph was recommended. Without airbrakes the Hellcat needed drag for dive bombing; locking the undercarriage down was tried but induced shuddering. With the wheels trailing (ie out of their housing but not locked) dives up to 400mph were just acceptable but more drag was desirable. JV201 (Double Wasp R-2800-10W), used from February 1945, investigated the Avro bomb carrier.

Hellcat Mark II

JV224 flew to the A&AEE in August 1944 with water injection and spring tab ailerons. Low-level climb was improved by 650ft/min and top speed by 20mph (true) at 18,600 feet, while the ailerons could be applied fully at 360mph whereas previously only a very small displacement was possible. Dive recoveries at 460mph (Mach 0.77) required a 70lb pull initially, but this reduced rapidly as speed fell. JX822 handled well with two American 1,000lb ANM65 bombs, but the previous limit of 400mph was observed in late 1944. JX901, with zero-length rocket launchers, was investigating various undesirable features of the installation at the end of the war. JX998 arrived in July 1945 with a night-fighting radar scanner under the starboard wing.

Hellcat I JV109 faces into low January 1945 sun. Six wing guns and three aileron operating arms can be seen. The line between the two footsteps is not to indicate to the pilot the direction to the cockpit but to help on leaving when facing the aircraft. The canopy is a balloon type. The background has been edited behind the nose, and the lower gills have been cropped thereby; they are open. *A&AEE 15038*

Hellcat II JX822 in January 1945, carrying two American 1,000lb bombs. Their position close together and the tall carriers are noteworthy. The remains of the American-applied figure '822' can be seen on the lower cowling. *A&AEE recognition 244*

Hellcat II JX901 in May 1945, with an American Mk 5 RP installation of six rockets. Guns have been reduced to four 0.5in (patches cover the holes left by the two guns removed). *A&AEE 15230*

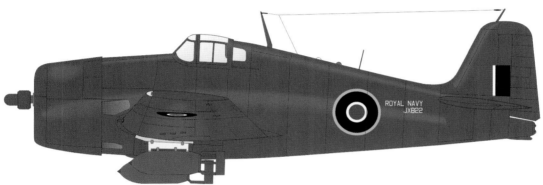

Grumman Hellcat JX822, November 1944, for bombing trials. (Scale 1:72)

Seamew

The Curtiss Seamew was intended for ship use in the observation role. FN475 arrived at Boscombe in May 1943 with a Ranger SGV-770-6 engine; the exhaust required lengthening and the rear fuselage sealing to eliminate contamination. Handling in the air was acceptable at normal CGs, but the controls became too heavy at forward CG. The aircraft, considered underpowered, had a mediocre climb made worse if the leading edge slats were open; locking the slats was recommended. No performance was reported, even after a 6% increase in power following carburettor change. Tests on JW627 were cancelled in April 1944, shortly after arrival.

Flying Officer W. G. Ross and Sergeant Loutit are aboard Seamew FN475 in May 1943. The aircraft was an underpowered reconnaissance machine; the large fin and rudder are justified by the alternative float undercarriage. An arrester hook can just be seen, and the upturned wing tips are novel. Fixed undercarriages were not de rigueur in 1943. *A&AEE recognition 158*

Curtiss Seamew
FN475, July 1943,
for handling trials.
(Scale 1:72)

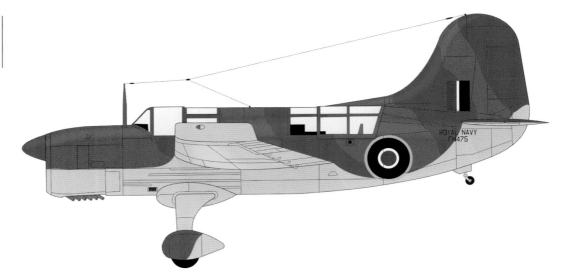

Corsair

More than 2,000 Chance Vought Corsairs were supplied to the Commonwealth naval services, a remarkable total in view of fact that deliveries started only in June 1943.

Corsair Mark I

JT113 (Double Wasp R-2800-8) needed lots of Bostik and a 9-inch exhaust extension to rid the cockpit of fumes, and the camera gun fitting leaked. Otherwise the armament of six 0.5in guns was liked, being well designed with good attention to detail, although heating required marginal improvement and barrel life was probably low (only 400 rounds). JT126 did little, if any, flying and left at end of 1943 after five months of unserviceability. JT118 was assessed for handling from airfields only, as the view was judged to be too poor for deck landing. Good flying qualities were spoiled by high elevator forces, in spite of a long but clumsy stick; poor ground handling resulted from bad design of the tail wheel. There was no standby compass.

Corsair I JT126, photographed in July 1943, posed well but flew little. The forward-mounted mast was necessary to give adequate length to the HF radio aerial. Rounded wing tips are fitted. *A&AEE 11494*

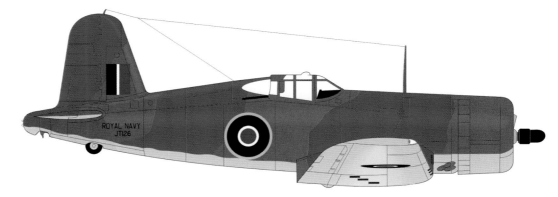

Chance Vought
Corsair JT126, July
1943-unserviceable.
(Scale 1:72)

Corsair Mark II

JT257 and JT259, with raised cockpit hood and seat and wings clipped by 1½ feet, shared handling and performance (see the Table) from November 1943. The latter gave a top speed well below that reported by the US Navy for its equivalent F4U-1D model. It was found that reducing the climb rpm increased high-level speeds and climb, caused, it was thought, by a high propeller tip speed of Mach 1.165 at 33,000 feet and low intake efficiency, particularly in the climb. The remarkable total of 287 gallons of fuel (internal) gave a range of 1,415 miles. The view was still considered bad for deck landing, in spite of the raised seat and a new windscreen. In three months from December 1943, JT218 and JT231 each completed successfully 150 hours, although minor engine faults became apparent.

JT406, intended for assessment of two types of control columns, departed shortly after arrival in June 1944. JT417 in June 1944 had a top speed slightly higher than the previous figure, attributed to individual aircraft variations. JT563 was used from September 1944 to assess the type's suitability as a dive-bomber. High stick forces imposed a limit of 400mph; however, a more comfortable speed of 330mph could be maintained in a dive with the undercarriage down. The figures were later confirmed on JT562 when carrying two 1,000lb bombs.

Corsair Mark III

JS843 (R-2800-8W engine) had unsatisfactory American modifications to cure contamination; the aircraft was wrecked in a forced landing following engine seizure shortly after arrival in

Corsair II JT259 in November 1943. Just visible is the clear canopy with raised top. The arrester hook evidently retracted with the tail wheel, but presumably needed selecting down separately. The gull wing is well shown, as are the square wing tips and wing root radiator intakes. The exhausts appear very close to the radiator intakes. *A&AEE recognition 192*

Corsair II JT562 in May 1945, carrying two American 1,000lb bombs (AN M65 type). It carries an additional HF mast behind the cockpit, probably to lower the aerial for easier stowage on aircraft carriers. Six 0.5in guns in the wings are taped over. The pilot's padded headrest looks comfortable. *A&AEE 12010*

July 1944. A heavy landing caused major damage to JS871 in February 1945, after five months' use during which the new standby compass proved satisfactory, but further changes to eliminate contamination were ineffective.

Corsair Mark IV

KD227, with the R-2800-8W engine plus the ability to carry bombs, arrived in November 1944 resplendent in the US Navy Gloss Blue overall. Top speed (see the Table) was the highest of the Corsairs, and range on 197 gallons of fuel was 1,010 miles. Buffeting limited KD835 from April 1945 to 420mph with an RP Mk V installation, while KD903 two months later revealed the need to separate by half a second release of two 1,000lb bombs to prevent jostling.

Tigercat

Trials of the single Grumman Tigercat, TT349, received at the A&AEE in December 1944,

appear to have been cancelled after a limited amount of flying; the first surviving report covers the pilot's poor plotting board, which had inadequate retention fittings. Cockpit features criticised included the lack of a rear view and the position of the ASI, on which the lower readings were hidden from view by the coaming. With two Double Wasp (R-2800-22W) engines, and an all-up weight with 355 gallons of fuel of 21,388lb, the hydraulic booster for the rudder was a welcome feature that worked well, although powered by only a single pump. Suitability for deck operation was aided by a good view, absence of take-off swing, low power-on stall (69mph flaps and undercarriage down) and good lateral stability. However, poor elevator response at approach speeds rendered the type unacceptable as tested, in the opinion of the A&AEE pilots, aggravated by a fierce draught with the hood open.

Corsair IV KD903 in mid-1945 carries two 1,000lb bombs and is powered by a Double Wasp (R-2800-8W) engine. *A&AEE 15214*

Tigercat TT349 (Bu Aer No 80293) in January 1944, still with American stars and stripes marking and resplendent in overall US Navy Sea Blue Gloss finish. The inscription on the fin reads 'NAVY 80293', and on the rudder 'F7F-1'. *A&AEE 15001*

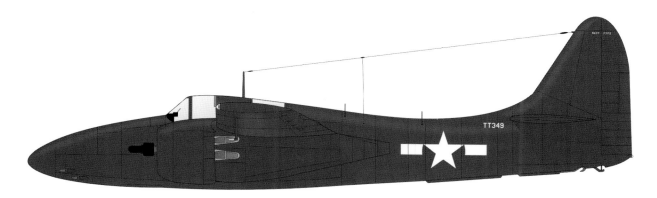

Grumman Tigercat
TT349, December
1944, for handling
trials. (Scale 1:72)

Sea Fury

The Hawker Sea Fury SR661 (Centaurus XII)
was flown in May 1945 to assess suitability for
deck landing. In the initial configuration an
unacceptable use of brake was needed to
prevent a swing to the right on take-off, and
engine response was slow and irregular with
extreme vibration over a large rpm range.
Modifications by the following July included a
five-bladed instead of a four-bladed propeller,
a larger fin and rudder, and changes to the
engine. Satisfactory results permitted deck
trials to be made; these were under way as the
Japanese surrendered.

Sea Fury SR661 in May 1945 is in initial configuration with a four-bladed propeller and an enlarged
fin and rudder. The test pilots were generally impressed with this aircraft's handling, despite early
reservations about swing on take-off and engine acceleration. Although an arrester hook is fitted,
the wings did not fold. *A&AEE 15125*

13 Wings for the Navy

Carrier attack aircraft

Cleveland

The requirement for trials on the Curtiss Cleveland AS467 were cancelled as soon as the aircraft arrived in August 1940, but not before it was photographed. The type survived from a French order for the Curtiss CW77 (Cyclone R-1830-34 engine) of a type named the Helldiver in the US Navy.

Cleveland I AS467 is seen during its stay of a few days in August 1940. Taken over from a French contract, the dive-bomber found no role in the Royal Navy, and the A&AEE trials were cancelled. Among features are the fuel tank, apparently mounted on a torpedo carrier, bomb racks under the wing, and a gunsight in front of the pilot for the pair of 7.7mm guns (not visible). The ailerons have fixed tabs (aft of the trailing edge) and moveable tabs (possibly balance type). *A&AEE 9651*

Curtiss Cleveland AS467, August 1940 – tests cancelled. (Scale 1:72)

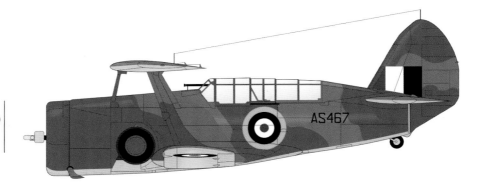

Chesapeake I AL909 in June 1941 was underpowered, had poor handling and was thus rejected for the Royal Navy. Of interest for A&AEE trials was the lack of loading and handling data usually supplied with the aircraft. The Establishment had to estimate even a mid-CG from which to explore the type's capabilities. No wing guns are fitted on this machine, but the U-shaped bracket extending from under the gills appears to be torpedo-shaped, and racks are fitted under the wings. Wing folding was a standard trial for aircraft so equipped. *A&AEE 9744*

Chesapeake

Intended for the French Navy, the Vought Sikorsky Chesapeake was modified for the Royal Navy before the first pair, AL909 and AL911, arrived in June 1941 (Twin Wasp Junior R-1535-SB4-G engine). AL909 was damaged following an engine failure in July 1941 and replaced by AL913, which embarrassed the delivery pilot by bursting both tyres on arrival. Handling was poor at high weight, and performance (see the Table) worse. To achieve even a modest take-off run, weight had to be restricted to 9,140lb, ie full fuel of 204 gallons and a single 500lb bomb of the three possible. The pilot's sight was of no use for dive-bombing. The blast tubes for the four wing guns were found to be flimsy and broke on removal, and the observer's gun could not be fired downwards. In its favour, the Chesapeake had a range of 1,170 miles and a maximum endurance of 7½ hours, but its long take-off condemned it for British carriers.

Another view of Chesapeake I AL909 in June 1941, this time with wings spread. Note the large intake on the engine cowling, which must have interfered with the pilot's view for landing. *A&AEE 9744*

Swordfish

Differences between the three versions of the Fairey Swordfish were small; the A&AEE did not distinguish between them, as most trials aircraft had features of all three. Testing of the Swordfish at the A&AEE was resumed after a break of more than eighteen months, when the first machine built by Blackburn, V4288, appeared in March 1941. The aft-most CG acceptable at 8,040lb was fixed by the available nose-down trim at full power of the Pegasus 30. In October 1941 V4645, fitted with anti-ship radar (ASV) and a new Mk VIII pitot head, had very small pressure errors. Similarly equipped, V4444 had an insufficiently rigid mounting for the rear Vickers 0.303in gun on receipt in September 1941; modifications by the Establishment reduced the 'jump' experienced at first on this aeroplane. However, in November 1941 V4523 continued to experience 'jump' due, it was found, to play in the swivel mounting; its special Fairey oil cooler was satisfactory.

Various trials on rockets lasting more than a year from April 1942 occupied three aircraft, starting with L7678/G, which eventually investigated the combination of RPs with depth charges. Provided the rockets were fired before the depth charges were dropped, the installation was satisfactory. Initial rocket trials had been carried out on DK747/G from July 1942, fitted with standard RP Mk I rails with a blast plate under the wings. The triple-bead foresight and the slow speed of the Swordfish gave inaccurate results. Accuracy was scarcely improved using an Aldis tube sight on L2840/G from February 1943, although greater attention to harmonisation of the sight with the rockets gave some benefit.

Structural failures in service involving Blackburn-built aircraft led to an investigation from June 1942 involving L2717 (Fairey), DK690 and HS192 (both Blackburn). The problems occurred on pulling out of dives, but the Establishment found no difference between the two manufacturers, commenting that stick forces were very low on all three machines (12lb pull gave 3.9g). HS192 then had a propeller of finer pitch in an attempt to reduce the take-off distance for use from smaller decks; results revealed little difference, the still air run being just under 300 yards in both cases. An even finer propeller on V4570 in March 1943 did give an improvement to 230 yards. HS553 from June 1943 handled normally, and without cockpit contamination, with an enclosed cockpit.

V4689/G, identified at the A&AEE in October 1943 as a Mk III, had a 'Pumpkin' searchlight under the starboard wing and could carry a range of loads, bringing the maximum weight to 9,250lb with corresponding reduction in performance (see the Table); handling was

Swordfish L2840/G in February 1943 shows off its eight 60lb RPs, and reveals its dated, but not ineffective, configuration. Slats on the top wing appear only partially retracted, and torpedo fittings stick out from under the fuselage between the wings. The crew entry ladder, arrester hook and tailplane bracing can be seen. Few other aircraft had elevators of greater span than the tailplane. *A&AEE recognition 129*

Swordfish HS553 in June 1943 was briefly assessed for cockpit contamination and handling with its enclosed cockpit. ASV radar aerials adorn the outer wing struts with a further aerial in front of the top centre section. The tie rods between upper and lower ailerons are well shown. Two (250lb?) bombs and light bomb carriers outboard are just visible. *A&AEE recognition*

acceptable. LS295 from January 1945 confirmed that the searchlight reduced top speed by 5mph. In August 1944 W5902 had special modifications enabling an American 1,000lb bomb (AN M65) to be carried and released without problems. LS364 was in use from November 1944 as a general-purpose bomber to check fuse functioning, and HS218 flew in for the armament demonstration in July 1945.

Skua

The Blackburn Skua completed trials before the war, and no formal wartime reports were written. L2867 and L2888 flew from Martlesham Heath, and left Boscombe very early in 1940, while L2868 spent a few days with the Bombing Flight in September 1939.

Swordfish III V4689/G in November 1943, with the 'Pumpkin' searchlight under the starboard wing and full ASV radar (dome under the nose and aerials on the wing struts). *A&AEE recognition 190*

Albacore

Brief pre-war trials of the Fairey Albacore were followed from February 1940 by L7079, joined by L7076 two months later, both powered by the Taurus II. Handling was marked by heavy elevator and ailerons in a dive, although its steadiness for target attacks received praise. For level bombing, the observer's view was restricted to the front and, in any case, was soon obscured by oil; diving and aiming by the pilot was recommended. Performance (see the Table) at maximum weight, 11,570lb, was achieved with four depth charges; a single torpedo was 470lb lighter. Later, L7079 handled well, although longitudinally unstable, at extended aft CG. Brief trials early in 1942 on L7125 with a cuffed (ie a sleeve near the hub) propeller indicated that engine cooling remained satisfactory, even for tropical conditions. L7142 in October 1941 retained the fundamental fault for its twin rear gun mounting experienced earlier on L7079. X9266 in February 1942 had an improved mounting, but lack of a lock for the moving arms on which the guns were mounted led to very poor shooting, and the design was condemned by the Establishment. BF617 joined for Porton in August 1944.

Barracuda

Sharing certain features, for example the Youngman flaps, with its stablemate the Firefly, the Fairey Barracuda also shared initially a major shortcoming – very large stick forces in a dive. In addition, the type had unusual behaviour in some configurations.

Prototypes and Mark I

P1767, with a low-set tailplane, suffered an undercarriage failure in the hands of an A&AEE pilot flying from Fairey's Heath Row aerodrome. The results of any trials he made are not known. After repair, and with the tailplane set on the fin, P1767 was delivered to Boscombe in October 1941 (Merlin 30), weighed 12,820lb with a 1,566lb torpedo, and completed handling during which it was found impossible to achieve more than 330mph in a dive without the use of dive flaps (425mph permitted) or 240mph (later 280) with the use of dive flaps (300mph permitted). These figures were obtained even with the use of nose-down trimming. The straightforward stall with torpedo occurred at 68mph (flaps and undercarriage down); with four underwing 250lb bombs, plus two bomb containers, the nose pitched down violently at 80mph. In the latter configuration, severe, sharp aileron buffeting appeared, cured by fitting 'boards' (large underwing fences). The aft-most acceptable CG was found to be limited by longitudinal instability, making flying very tiring and thus considered dangerous for night-flying.

Performance is given in the Table; the excessive take-off run at 13,800lb (achieved with four 500lb bombs) led to the recommendation to limit take-off to 13,400lb, although climb remained marginal. During further diving trials in April 1942 the propeller detached from the engine at 350mph, and the aircraft was seriously damaged. On return in late 1942, P1767 had a Merlin 32 engine (thus being near Mk II standard) and was used to compare four-bladed and three-bladed

Barracuda I P1767 is at Fairey's aerodrome (later Heathrow) in December 1940, where it was flown by the A&AEE. The Youngman flaps are in the neutral position and the undercarriage is locked down. The two items on the top fuselage appear to be an anti-spin parachute (rear) connected by rigging lines to an anchor point (front), with an operating line looped between them.

Barracuda I P1767 is at Boscombe Down in October 1941, with the braced tailplane set on the fin. Other changes since the earlier picture was taken (apart from the external finish) include the HF aerial mast, a post on top of the wing connected with wing folding, and the absence of fuselage fittings. In both views the arrester hook is just visible, and the ground handling bar is stowed outboard of the wing roundel. *A&AEE 9811*

Fairey Barracuda P1767, October 1941, for handling trials. (Scale 1:72)

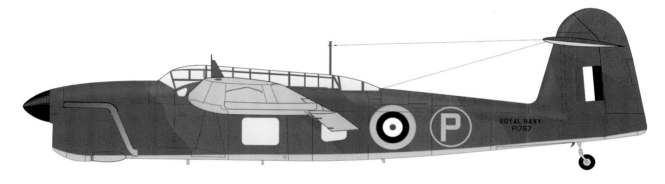

propellers; the former gave the better take-off and top speed. Faired undercarriage and wheel wells gave a marginal improvement in take-off distances, but were not considered a worthwhile complication for Service use. Earlier, the original Fairey mounting of two Vickers 0.303in guns on P1767 needed modification; loading the various external loads was straightforward, and a special mat was introduced to prevent slipping on wet wings.

Meanwhile, P1770 completed radio and IFF trials in March 1942. P9652 and P9653 flew intensively from October 1942, although P9652

managed only 86 hours due to engine failure; problems included exhaust damage, and cooling and hydraulic leaks, the latter due to the use of early synthetic seals in place of rubber. Six 250lb smoke containers proved too much for the Barracuda Mk I, making take-off a long and uncomfortable affair, and reducing top speed to 167mph (true). Fish-tail exhausts on P9653 did not meet damping requirements. P9644, also from October 1942, was able to achieve slightly increased diving speeds at aft CG, albeit with the need to increase port rudder and control twitching above 260 knots (300mph).

Barracuda I P9652 in April 1943, with SCI containers, 'boards' (the large fence under the wing), and a generally used appearance. Performance was only marginal with six Smoke Curtain Installations (gas-spraying tanks); two were the maximum for safe flying. Barracuda IIs, with greater power, could, it was considered, carry four. This view clearly shows the landing lamp, 'board' (fence), Youngman flap and catapult spools on the fuselage. *A&AEE 11410*

Barracuda Mark II

P9647 flew to Boscombe in October 1942, with the more powerful Merlin 32 giving adequate performance for take-off up to 14,250lb. Flaps at 8° proved to be a critical setting, but showed 15° on the pilot's gauge; it was recommended that a mark for 8° should be painted on the fuselage of each aircraft. Performance in tropical conditions was expected to be degraded by the need to keep the radiator shutter open. Trials stopped when the aircraft crashed following an engine failure in May 1943, after assessment of the cockpit for bombing identified the need for many modifications. P9667 spent a short time at the A&AEE in December 1942, before returning in the New Year with a Preston Green mounting for the rear pair of Vickers 0.303in guns; this was an improvement but needed eight modifications. Carriage of various bombs and mines was satisfactory, but in 1944 dive-bombing with four 500lb bombs needed full forward stick, and even then maximum speed could not be achieved. Considerable stretch of the elevator cables and an unexplained 'oddity' in the trim were blamed.

In September 1944 P9667 had a dorsal extension to the fin, thus reducing the tendency of the rudder to overbalance, and giving better dive stability. In the meantime, P9676 and P9677, on intensive flying, proved more reliable than the Mk I, although P9677 had achieved only 119 hours when it hit a ridge on take-off and failed to remain airborne from the ensuing bounce, causing extensive damage. P9651 had various flame damping exhausts from February 1943, finally meeting requirements with louvred ducts over Rolls Royce-designed fish-tails. P9715 had an unacceptable annular air-cooled fish-tail exhaust in February 1943; later it handled normally with six 250lb 'B' bombs, but with considerable loss in cruising speed. It had a modified oil system to prevent leaks and thus permit longer flights.

Barracuda II P9647 in October 1942 was the first of the type with the Merlin 32; the additional power was used to increase the weight and thus the stores that could be carried. The container (a 100-gallon drop tank) is ballast. Extensive minor modifications were made to reduce cockpit contamination; the visible change is an additional quarter-light on the side of the pilot's cockpit. Bomb carriers are fitted inboard of the 'boards'. The aircraft is seen at Fairey's airfield.

Barracuda II P1767 is seen again, now in November 1943 with a fixed undercarriage and openings faired over; the reduction in take-off run was negligible. The aircraft was written off in a forced landing in April 1944 following loss of the propeller; a similar but less catastrophic detachment had occurred in April 1942.
A&AEE 11328

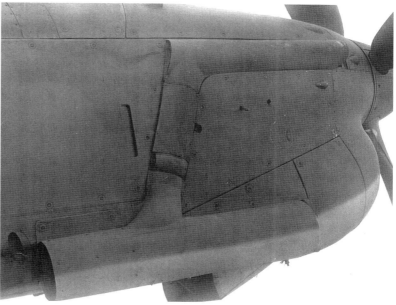

Two views of Barracuda P9715 in early 1943, both with and without the shroud fitted over the air-cooled fish-tail exhaust; it failed to meet requirements on P9715 in early 1943. *A&AEE 11317*

Entry of the Barracuda into service was followed by several accidents; A&AEE pilots visited the early squadrons, and returned with two reported rogue aircraft, P9833 and P9726, in July 1943. The former was alleged to turn after dives, and the latter to drop its nose in sideslips. No vice was found in P9833, but there was the usual large change of trim as the flaps operated (up and down) in the airbrake mode. Information from 827 NAS indicated that the abnormal behaviour in P9726 followed application of top rudder while sideslipping into a turn in all configurations. This cross-controlled manoeuvre had not been tested, but squadron reports were confirmed; it was

recommended that top rudder should not be used in sideslips. The apparently contradictory recommendation is discussed above in Part I.

P9816 from June 1943 investigated range and the effect of a torpedo (810 miles maximum, 650 miles practical) or alternatively six 250lb bombs (780 and 625 miles). ASV radar aerials cost 5% in range, and flying with hot air to the engine reduced range by 11%. Range on P9867 with single bombs up to 2,000lb on the centre line was similar to the torpedo figure. The SU carburettor for negative-g flying had no effect on range. Aerodynamic improvements to improve sensitivity to small rigging errors and asymmetric fuel usage included an effective aileron trimmer

Barracuda II P9726 in November 1943, during investigation of abnormal flying characteristics. It is in standard configuration, with the exception of the anchor points for the tufting being fitted on the fin and rudder. *A&AEE AC114*

Another view of P9726, which was borrowed from No 827 Squadron and fitted with tailplane tufts to investigate a puzzling handling problem, its unexpected diving on recovery from low-level attacks. A camera in the rear cockpit recorded results, while extensive instrumentation in the aircraft was also fitted. Note the ASV radar Yagi aerials, *A&AEE*

Barracuda II LS789 in July 1944, carrying a torpedo and ASV aerials. The flaps are down and the attachment points for the folded wings are on top of the rear fuselage. The purpose of the white line on the rear fuselage is not known, but may have been connected with the development of the Mk V, for which this aircraft was being used. *A&AEE 15156*

in P9819 early in 1944. To improve longitudinal trim changes, a more positive tailplane incidence and more negative angle on the flaps (dive brakes) were tried with encouraging results prior to a damaging landing in December 1944. P9806 from September 1943 could not cope safely with four 600lb anti-submarine bombs, and three were barely acceptable. A further sensitive item was the elevator shroud, which, if maladjusted by as little as 0.1 inch, severely affected handling; trials on P9806 pointed to an explanation of earlier problems. P9869 had the effective Rose mounting for the rear guns in a brief trial in October 1943. P9683, also briefly tested late in 1943, had a more robust Gallay radiator cooling system, but results in the cruise were disappointing.

Perhaps the most bizarre modification tested was that involving two 'Cuda' so-called floats under the wings, each designed to carry two men for later parachuting; the exhausts were suitably lengthened to pass under the fuselage. Apart from much vibrating above 250mph and erratic operation of the doors, handling was satisfactory and take-off at 13,650lb virtually unchanged. P9795/G was used for these trials from June 1944, and LS631/G briefly from March 1945. Handling of

MX613 early in 1945 with a lifeboat revealed marked directional oscillations above 180mph and increased directional trim changes with speed, but these shortcomings did not prevent a recommendation for Release to Service. The latter half of 1944 and early 1945 saw no fewer than five Barracudas (LS820, LS833, LS834, LS836 and LS837) at Boscombe in the IFDF, dedicated to intensive flying of new synthetic seals; a great improvement was reported. Compatibility of bombs and mines (of up to 1,800lb in the Mk IX version) with the latest aircraft modifications was checked on LS923 from October 1944.

Some aerodynamic modifications intended for the Mk V, tried on LS789 in July 1944, and again in March 1945, demonstrated improvements, among them an increase of 14mph (true) in speed when carrying 500lb bombs. A six-week investigation in the spring of 1943 of the braking (ie very fine pitch) propeller on LS708 included dives of up to 70° without the speed exceeding 250mph. It was concluded that the propeller was more effective and incurred less trim change than the earlier Youngman flaps. LS729 paid a fleeting visit to C Per T in July 1944 to assess minor drag reduction changes.

A view of Barracuda II MX613 during trials in early 1945 with a lifeboat, which considerably affected the type's already slightly eccentric handling – the boat did nothing for the Barracuda's aesthetics either.

362 Barracuda II P9795/C in June 1944 with the bizarre pair of 'Cuda' so-called floats designed to carry two men each. The exhausts point straight down, wing 'boards' are fitted and the photograph shows the HF aerial mast poking out of the rear observer's cockpit. Between the undercarriage legs is a stores container, which caused vibrations above 250mph. *A&AEE 11815*

Barracuda II MX613 is carrying a lifeboat in January 1945, which considerably affected directional stability. Above 180mph a continuous snaking (3°) occurred. *A&AEE 15017*

RK328 (Griffon VIII), with spring tab ailerons and various smoke containers, and P9833, with a sprung rudder trimmer, were being flown in August 1945.

Barracuda Mark III

The sole representative of this version with radar, including a dome under the rear fuselage, was DR318 (Merlin 32), appearing in April 1944 and weighing 13,900lb. Handling was at the aft CG, necessitated by the extra weight in the rear fuselage. At low speed instability was unacceptable – as speed reduced from 175 to 110 knots an 8lb push force was required. An aft limit for Service use well ahead of the trials position was recommended.

changed to torpedo and rocket; this change was compounded by an engine replacement. Over 3½ years twenty Firebrands in the basic versions reached the A&AEE before the type entered operational service.

Firebrand Prototypes, Marks I and II

Establishment flying of these Sabre III-engined aircraft started in April 1942 with DD804, but initial handling soon resulted in the aircraft's return to its makers. Back at Boscombe with a tailplane of increased span, longitudinal stability had improved. Serious faults, however, persisted, including rudder overbalance to the

Barracuda III DR318 in May 1944 retains the Merlin 32 but has stub exhausts. The main feature of this Mark, the large radome under the fuselage, caused an aft CG with resulting instability. The undercarriage door is well shown. *A&AEE 11753*

Barracuda Mark V

P9976 retained the original wings but, fitted with a Griffon VII, completed exhaust damping, contamination, cooling and engine maintenance and take-off trials from September 1944. The new fin and rudder (with dorsal fin and spring tab respectively) gave improved handling. Investigation of the representative production aircraft with increased wing span, spring tab ailerons and a Griffon VIII began in July 1945 on PM940 and PM941. Handling was pleasant, and trials continued after the war.

Firebrand

Blackburn's Firebrand was designed as a fighter, but initial tests revealed so many unsatisfactory features that its role was

left (ie it locked over), whereas right rudder caused the elevator and thus the nose to rise, and the ailerons also tended to overbalance; perhaps most serious was the poor response to all controls on the approach, becoming worse with reduction in power. A third visit with the original tailplane, but with tabs on all controls and other changes, showed no improvement to ailerons and rudder; the elevator ceased to hunt and trim changes with power and speed had been reduced, but flap operation still involved large changes in trim.

During the third visit, a larger fin and rudder were fitted; the swing to the right on take-off was reduced but forces remained too high. Changing the canopy shape did not reduce the exhaust fumes entering the cockpit. On the positive side, engine cooling and the compass were satisfactory, and the maintenance facilities praised. In February 1943 the armed prototype DD815 revealed further shortcomings in

Firebrand I DD804 is seen in May 1942, during initial trials that revealed many control deficiencies. This view emphasises the wide but short radiator under the fuselage and the wing roots, and the position of the tailplane set well back, a typical Blackburn feature. *A&AEE recognition 92*

handling at aft CG, and confirmed earlier observations that the elevator 'floated back' on take-off and landing. Many improvements by the Establishment and by the firm followed during the course of testing the four 20mm guns, to overcome, among other things, slack mountings and loss of pressure in the FMU. At the end of 1943 an acceptable handling standard was reached, but a further six modifications were needed. Ground trials of external stores were successful.

DK365 and DK366 started intensive flying in July 1943; the former suffered an engine control failure in September after 80 hours' flying. The trial was apparently cancelled, as by late 1943 DK366 on another trial had a cut-down rear fuselage in an attempt to further improve rudder forces; the control remained immovable at high speed.

Trials with rockets from October 1943 on DK367 were protracted due to two undercarriage failures and subsequent repairs. Weight with rockets was 14,775lb, and a buffeting stall (clean) was high at about 115mph; alteration in speed caused large lateral and directional trim changes. The aircraft was rejected on handling behaviour, and also because there was no downward view for launching an attack. Three weeks of gunnery occupied DK368 in May 1944, and the following September DK370 and DK371 had spring tab controls. The elevator was very sensitive, rudder authority critical with flaps down, and large trim changes following alteration in power, speed and flap position. With these shortcomings, the Establishment agreed to the Firebrand being used for airfield training only.

Firebrand I DK366 in November 1943, with the rear fuselage cut down in an attempt to improve rudder control forces; some benefit was found, but only at low speeds. Note an IFF aerial just behind the undercarriage door, the pilot's access ladder, the catapult spool just visible below the fuselage roundel and the static vent ahead of it. *A&AEE 11606*

Firebrand I DK367 in May 1944, with eight 25lb head rockets. The RP installation reintroduced some handling deficiencies previously cured and introduced others, and the view for rocket firing was also criticised. *A&AEE recognition 218*

Meanwhile, NV636 (the original second prototype renumbered) carrying a torpedo (and thus becoming a Mk II) had its trials stopped in July 1943, primarily because of shuddering above 200mph. A faired torpedo cradle cured the shuddering, but there remained the problem of poor longitudinal control exacerbated by the rear CG with a torpedo, and very heavy rudder and ailerons. Later DK377, with spring tab controls, was approved for airfield training in late 1944 despite poor handling identical to DK370; a maximum diving speed of 370mph with a torpedo was recommended. Cockpit contamination was also made just acceptable by sealing likely leaks in the fuselage. A C Squadron pilot flying DK379 from Gosport in February 1945 bailed out following loss of control due to a torpedo tail breaking away.

Firebrand Mark III

The Centaurus VII with a four-bladed propeller powered the Mk IIIs DK372 and DK373 on arrival in February and April 1944 respectively. The new powerplant gave few problems, apart from intake efficiency where the ram effect was far lower than predicted. Handling remained an area of great concern. DK372 had 'promising' interim standard spring tabs, but take-off swing was excessive and rudder heavy, while elevator forces were too light. DK373 had increased aerodynamic balances on the elevator and on the aileron spring tabs, together with a teardrop canopy and offset fin. The ailerons were better above 100mph, but poor on the approach, while the elevator remained too light at high speed but good on the approach; the view was good and the new fin effective on take-off but poor on the climb and approach.

Firebrand II NV636 in September 1943, with torpedo and showing the crutch fairing introduced after the Establishment experienced shuddering above 200mph. The rudder has two tabs: trim and balance. Four long 20mm guns protrude from the wings. *A&AEE recognition 183*

Firebrand III DK372 in March 1944, with a Centaurus VII engine and torpedo. The basic layout remains unaltered behind the engine, but subtle aerodynamic changes have been made, including enlarged fin and rudder and the control surfaces. The aircraft is in cruising configuration and, presumably, speed, yet the pilot has left rudder and down elevator applied. *A&AEE recognition 213*

Both aircraft returned in August with further modifications. Increasing rudder travel to starboard and enlarged tabs, also with greater range, improved control on take-off in DK373, but rudder trim range was still insufficient to cope with changes in speed and power. There remained the problem of large g forces on release from out-of-trim dives, among other criticisms. Performance (see the Table) was curtailed by a forced landing in September 1944 caused by the throttle linkage breaking. DK372 had a combined spring and trim tab on the rudder, giving foot loads on take-off acceptable for airfield operations when combined with reduced power and limited flap; take-off distances were thus increased by about 50 yards. A third visit in mid-1945 by DK373 with an enlarged rudder was to examine deck suitability. A high approach speed (98mph) was necessary for lateral control due to heavy and inefficient ailerons, and the elevator was barely effective; on overshoot the swing to starboard remained alarming. The Establishment found these characteristics unacceptable.

Firebrand III DK373 in September 1944, showing its four-bladed propeller, teardrop canopy and forward-sloping HF aerial mast, but hiding its new control surfaces and offset fin. *A&AEE 11928*

Following a fatal crash (with an RAE pilot) due to structural failure in DK386, the A&AEE received DK400 in May 1945 with fully mass-balanced elevators with a spring tab inertia weight; dives to 403mph were accompanied by heavy vibration sufficient to cause minor fatigue failures. A brave pilot later dived to 440mph, but it was still accompanied by vibrations. DK396 crashed shortly after arrival in April 1945, and gun firing of the four Hispano Mk V 20mm guns was completed on DK408; some flexing of the main spar occurred on recoil. A centrally mounted 100-gallon drop tank on DK394 in mid-1945 had little effect on handling, which remained unsatisfactory due to low-speed instability. Airbrakes on DK393 from June 1945 gave small trim changes on deployment, but buffeting led to rejection; the aircraft was written off in September following engine failure. DK392 was damaged when landing in July 1945, but after successful trials on cockpit contamination.

Firebrand Mark IV

Trials of EK602 (from June 1945) and EK605 (July 1945), with horn balanced and enlarged rudders together with a Centaurus IX engine with vibration damper mountings, were under way at the end of the war.

Bermuda

The US Navy's dive-bomber, made by Brewster, was supplied under Lease-Lend as the Bermuda, and a small number entered RAF service.

The first to arrive at the A&AEE was FF425 in January 1943 for gunnery trials (and possibly bombing – later cancelled). Eight 0.3in guns were carried – two above the engine, four in the wings and two in the rear cockpit. The pilot's ring and bead sight was described as useless and the forward armament as out of date. Restricted field of fire damned the rear installation. FF524 from February 1943 bore the brunt of handling and associated tests with its Cyclone (R-2600-A5B-5) engine. After weighing (14,773lb with 225 gallons of fuel and 3,000lb of stores), and determination of the best flap setting for take-off (75%), speed measurements (see the Table) and handling got under way. The view was badly obscured by the engine gills, the rudder and ailerons overbalanced in sideslips, and there was a large trim change with alterations in speed and power. Bombing, it was estimated, would require considerable practice to achieve accuracy. The dive brakes were good, once the very stiff lever could be operated. Altogether, the pilot needed to pay too much attention to flying at the expense of fighting. Extending the exhausts by 10 inches cured contamination, but cost 6mph (true) in top speed. Range was best at 5,000 feet, 225 gallons giving 950 miles (maximum). FF546 and FF510 appeared briefly in May 1943 to have variations in wing contour measured – the differences found were up to four times the permitted tolerances, but made no apparent difference to handling.

Bermuda I FF425 in February 1943, with the original short exhaust pipe that caused cockpit fumes, the externally mounted ring and bead sight and tube just ahead of the roundel, from which the trailing aerial(?) emerges. *A&AEE 11276*

Bermuda I FF557 is brought alongside in February 1944 by Flt Lt John Jarvis to reveal its Type B winch and undersurface stripes for the target towing role. *A&AEE recognition 201*

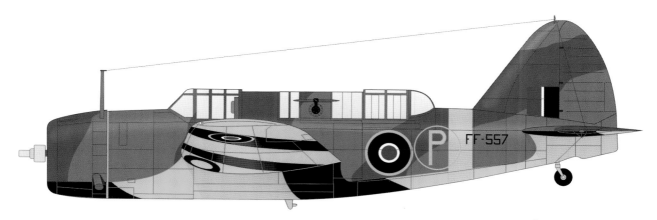

From November 1943 FF557, a target tug, had a Type B winch for an 8-foot flag at the end of 2,000 feet of cable. A smaller target flag was recommended, as results indicated that the winch motor would overheat in UK summer conditions.

Brewster Bermuda FF557, November 1943, for target towing trials. (Scale 1:72)

Avenger I (then known as a Tarpon) FN767 is seen in April 1943 with folding bomb doors taped over, prominent mast for the pressure head above the wing, and ASV aerial below it. The window ahead and below the roundel was fitted only to Lend-Lease Avengers. The arrester hook appears under the extreme aft fuselage and is fully stowed. *A&AEE 11368*

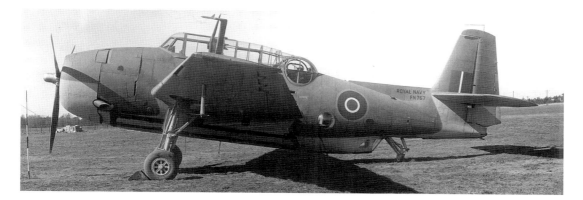

Tarpon/Avenger

The Grumman Avenger (Tarpon until January 1944) was supplied under Lend-Lease, and used mainly as a bomber in service aboard carriers.

Avenger Marks I and II

The use of two Mark numbers is puzzling as the only difference was in manufacturer (Grumman Mk I, and Eastern Motors Mk II) – the Establishment did not make the distinction. Both had the Double Wasp (R-2800-8) engines. FN767 spent nearly two years on trials from April 1943 after weighing – 15,965lb maximum including 475 gallons of fuel (225 external) – both capacities greater than the markings indicated. The interlink between the flap and undercarriage controls was considered dangerous – with the flap selector in neutral, raising the undercarriage also raised the flaps – otherwise the cockpit was well designed. All controls, particularly the elevator, were heavy; however, the stability about all three axes made the aircraft pleasant to fly. At night there were many reflections. The poor aerial for the IFF Mk IIN led to replacement by the satisfactory Mk III. Heating of the observer was negligible due to lack of sealing around his turret, and the American exhaust damping was initially inadequate and contaminated the cockpit in the climb. At 14,000lb (full fuel, no bombs), range was 1.890 miles (maximum), 1,512 miles (practical) – impressive figures.

Following fatal accidents in the Royal Navy due to wing failures, a trial on FN767 late in 1944 demonstrated stability at all CG, and a particularly high manoeuvring stick force (40lb per g at aft CG). Also, a hefty 50lb lateral force produced a rate of roll of only 30°/sec. Both control forces exceeded those acceptable in British aircraft and were thus unlikely to have been the cause of the accidents. FN844 from August 1943 tested the single 0.5in turret gun and the rearward 0.3in gun under the fuselage without problems. Minor comments, raised following bombing trials, included fusing and dropping 250lb depth charges Mk XI; the radio altimeter received fulsome praise. FN909 arrived in November 1943 for navigation investigation. The compasses were satisfactory, and the pilot (who did the navigating) had the benefit of a Plotting Board Mk V, which was pulled from its stowage under the instrument panel for use over the stick when clipped into position.

Next to arrive in February 1944 was JZ152, with American Mk 4 RP installation, the first such at the A&AEE; three essential modifications were required. The modifications were in JZ622 in June 1945, but assessment was incomplete when the aircraft was damaged later that month. JZ313 from April 1944 had its sights and turret examined. Two additional 48-gallon wing drop tanks raised the maximum weight of JZ570 in July 1944 to 17,250lb, but handling was unaffected. From January 1945 JZ462, with altered store carriers, cleared for service use all the weapons (mostly singly) contemplated for the Avenger. The list is instructive: Mines Type A Mks IV, V, VI, VII, VIII, IX and X, Type O Mk I, 1,900lb GP bomb, and 1,000lb bomb.

By chance, or with clerical humour, the new FN95 turret (the first made) arrived fitted in FN895 in January 1945. Initial results were disappointing: complete failure of the feed system, malfunction of the hydraulic cocking handle and inaccuracy between guns and sight – fourteen recommendations were made. JN625 arrived, possibly with the American Uncle Tom rocket installation, for the armament demonstration in July 1945.

Avenger Mark III

With a more powerful Double Wasp (R-2800-20), JZ635 started flying in November 1944. Various new armament trials were under way at the end of the war.

Avenger I JZ570 in September 1944, with two 48-gallon drop tanks The cooling gills are open. The air intake is visible above the cowling, as is the unusual (but common to Avengers) area of light grey paint up the cowling. On the leading edge, outboard of the starboard ASV aerial, can be seen the fixed slot. The serial number indicates that this aircraft was built by Eastern Motors and is thus a Mk II. *A&AEE 11945*

Avenger I FN895 in April 1945 with an FN95 turret intended for the Spearfish. It was in need of much further development, although the pair of 0.5in guns performed well. The background shows the stop butts. *A&AEE 15169*

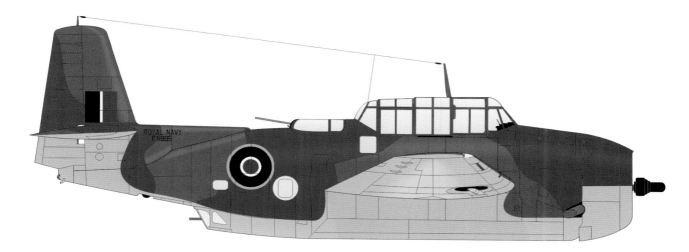

Grumman Avenger
FN895, March 1945,
for turret trials.
(Scale 1:72)

Avenger III JZ635, with a new version of the R-2600, the -20, has an additional air intake in the bottom of the cowling, and a slightly longer exhaust. The American Mk 5 installation has eight rockets in pairs. *A&AEE 15199*

Helldiver

The Canadian-built Curtiss Helldiver, with a Double Wasp (R-2800-8) engine supplied under Lend-Lease in small numbers, reached the A&AEE in the shape of JW115 (January 1945) and JW117 (April 1944); the latter bore the brunt of testing in the dive-bombing role. Cockpit layout was generally good, but nevertheless attracted sixteen recommendations for improvements; the armour plating could obstruct emergency controls and the Gosport tube intercom was antique (but standard in the US Navy). The transparent panel in the floor allowed the pilot to view the target before tip-in, but the magnesyn compass had large errors. At 13,700lb in the scouting role, handling was found unacceptable on account of directional oscillations (3° at speeds above 350mph), and very heavy ailerons above 280mph. The latter was partly due to excessive circuit friction, making lateral control difficult on the approach. The aft limit of CG was determined by marked instability in the climb; manoeuvring stick forces (11lb per g) were satisfactory. Flame damping and cockpit contamination did not meet current requirements. JW115 was scarcely serviceable, and left by road in May 1945.

Helldiver I JW117 in May 1944. Features include the 0.5in wing gun, open slat and completely stowed arrester hook; the observer's cockpit cover appears to be detached from its tracks. In the background behind the rudder can be seen contractor's plant, and in front of the fin the exposed chalk on the line of the runway together with some goods wagons. *A&AEE 11766*

Curtiss Helldiver JW117, April 1944, for armament trials. (Scale 1:72)

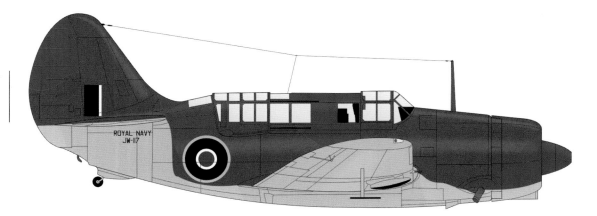

TABLE 1: HEAVY BOMBERS

Mark Serial	Engine	Weight (lb)	Run (yd)	To 50 ft (yd)	To Ht (ft)	(min)	Max rate (ft/min)	at Height (ft)	Service Ceiling (ft)	Max Speed (mph) [true]	(ft)	Remarks
HAMPDEN												
I L4033	Pegasus XVIII	18,750	425	710	10,000	10.1	1,100	5,000	24,300	254	13,800	1939 maximum weight
I P4293	Pegasus XVIII	21,000	500	805									
P4354	Pegasus XVIII	22,500	780	1,345	10,000	16.4	760	5,500	18,700	246	14,200	1940 maximum weight
					10,000	19.8	630	5,500	17,200	230	11,500	With Voke filters in operation
WHITLEY												
III K8936	Tiger VIII	26,500	470	755	10,000	27.1	450	4,000	17,100	192	14,300	Overload; grass take-off
V N1345	Merlin X	30,000	465	870	10,000	14.5	820	3,200	22,000	225	16,900	Overload; speed at 26,000 lb
N1349												
WELLINGTON												
I L4213	Pegasus XVIII	24,800	440	710	10,000	17.7	475	4,600	21,600	245	15,000	551 gal on trials pus 5,008 lb service load inc 2,000 lb bombs
IA N2865	Pegasus XVIII	26,640	435	865	10,000	19.3	670		18,530	234	15,100	750 gal petrol; 4,193 lb Service load inc bombs 15° flap for take-off (3,000/+9.5)
II R3221	Merlin X	30,000	575	1,065	10,000	13.1	670	7,700	21,500	245	17,000	
		32,000	750	1,300								
III P9238	Hercules XI	34,500	656	1,035	10,000	16.1	808	2,400	19,000	246.5	12,500	FS Superch (2,800 + 6)/Climb 2,500 + 3.5
IV Z1248	Twin Wasp	31,500	640	995	10,000	20.8	500	7,300	17,400			Take-off/12 ft dia propellers; climb 11.5 ft
V R3299	Hercules VIII	33,046			27,000	89.7	715	6,000	31,000	257	26,000	Auxilliary Supercharger above 18,000 ft; 4 crew in cabin 1 in tail turret
VI DR482	Merlin 60	32,200			30,000	75.1	830	10,000	31,000	271	31,000	Cruise ceiling 25,000
VI DR484	Merlin 62	28,400			30,000	35.2	1,300	MSL	34,000	300	32,000	Cruise ceiling 34,000 at 115 mph 2,380/-0.35 psi
X X3374	Hercules VI	34,500			10,600	12.5	1,030	4,100	19,300	253	13,300	Air cleaners in cruise 220 mph true at 18,000 ft in FS gear
XIII MP502	Hercules XVII	34,500			10,000	12.5	1,150	1,500		243	7,000	Climb @ increased IAS, full throttle height @ sea level
MANCHESTER												
I L7276	Vulture II	45,000	505	975	20,000	32.0	945	4,400	22,100	264	17,000	Flaps 30° for take-off; 3,000 rpm
I L7320	Vulture II	50,000	880	1,250								Flaps 25°; 3,200 rpm +9 psi
ALBEMARLE												
I P1360	Hercules XI	35,000	720	1,040	19,000	33.5	1,000	4,000	19,500	269	13,200	No aerials – glazed finish; Climb @ 33,500 lb
		32,500	545	880								
I P1361	Hercules XI	37,500	880	1,400								With aerials – plain finish; tapered cowlings
I P1362	Hercules XI	36,500	865	1,395	15,000	35.6	580	2,600	17,500	247	11,000	Take-off from concrete
IV P1406	R-2600-A5B1	33,500			17,000	32.5	880	2,200	(20,500)	255	11,000	Absolute ceiling; 769 gal
		36,026			14,000	28.2	700	5,200	16,400			769 gal; Type A Mk III turret
STIRLING												
I L7605	Hercules II	57,400	640	1,160	10,000	27.9			15,800	253	2,000	Early standard of engine
N3635												
I N6000	Hercules XI	70,000			10,000	19.4	655	1,000	16,650			Mock-up; standard air intakes, ventral, dorsal turrets
III R9309	Hercules VI	70,000			15,000	44.5	580	5,000	14,800			Marston oil coolers; oil shutters open barrage cutters fitted
III BK649	Hercules VI	70,000			15,000	28.2	740	5850	16,750	258	13,000	Ceiling 18,750 cooling gills closed
Conv EF143	Hercules VI	66,000			10,000	15.5	780	5,000			11,800	Transport conversion: max cruise speed 203 mph

Mark	Serial	Engine	Weight (lb)	Run (yd)	To 50 ft (yd)	To Ht (ft)	CLIMB (min)	Max rate (ft/min)	at Height (ft)	Service Ceiling (ft)	Max Speed (mph)[true]	Height (ft)	Remarks
HALIFAX													
I	L7244/L7245	Merlin X	55,000	580	1,015								40° flap for take-off 3,000 rpm +9.5 psi
I	L7245	Merlin X	50,000	570	1,000	20,000	27.4	1,230	2,900	22,800	270	18,000	1,392 gal max; speed 3,000 rpm +5.7psi
	L7245	Merlin X	58,000	930	1,300	15,000	28.1	750	3,200	18,000	260	18,400	No upper turret; climb 2,600 rpm +5.7psi
II	L9515	Merlin XX	60,000	780	1,150	20,000	39.0	770	9,500	20,700	256	18,500	3,000 rpm +11.5 psi for take-off. Rotol RFX 5/1propellers
II	W1008	Merlin XX	60,000			18,000	31.3	790	9,500	20,900	253	12,100	Rotol RS 5/17 propellers; dorsal turret
II	W7776	Merlin XX	60,000			20,000	35.5	730	1,000	21,750	232	12,000	Cleaned up: no nose/dorsal turret; shrouds off
II	DG221	Merlin 22	60,000			20,000	60.3	560	1,000	18,500	261	17,400	Squadron aircraft: large exhausts, shrouds, 2 x 4,000 lb bombs
II	HR679	Merlin 22	60,000			20,000	37.0	775	1,000	21,700	249	11,750	2 mph faster without dorsal turret
II	W7922	Merlin 22	60,000			20,000	42.0	680	1,000	21,100			Operational standard
II	HR845	Merlin 22	60,000			20,000	42.5	690	1,000	20,700			Original wings; speeds at 57,000 lb
II	HR845	Merlin 22	60,000			20,000	34.6	760		21,500			5 ft extended wings; cruise 1,700 ft higher 132 MF carburettors
III	HX226	Hercules XVI	63,000			20,000	49.5	800		21,000	263	13,000	
IV	LV838	Hercules 100	62,000			20,000	45.0	900		20,000	271	17,400	de Havilland flared propellers
LANCASTER													
	BT308	Merlin XX	38,800								310	21,100	No turrets – rich mixture
	DG595	Merlin XX	60,000	860	1,180	20,000	36.0	500	10,000	21,000	286	20,000	25° flap for take-off & 3,000 rpm + 12 psi
II	DT810	Hercules VI	62,300	620	970	18,000	50.0	800	5,000	18,600	273	14,000	Prototype
I	PB592	Merlin 24	72,000			15,000	26.0		10,000	17,500	245	16,200	with 22,000 lb bomb
II	DS602	Hercues XVI	62,300			20,000	35.6	710	9,200	23,000	273	14,000	Max speed 2,900/+7.8 climb 2,400/+6
III	W4114	Merlin 28	63,000	750	1,230	21,000	44.0	720	1,000	21,400	269	8,700	26° flap for take-off, max speed 3,000/+12 psi
I	W4963	Merlin 20	63,000			20,000	30.5	800	1,000	23,500	282	13,000	'Paddle' propellers; max speed 3,000/+18 psi
I	JB127	Merlin 24	65,000								280	10,000	
X	KB721	Merlin 38	63,000			20,000	46.0	780	2,000	22,200	270	12,600	Engines gave less than maximum rpm
VI	JB675	Merlin 85	65,000			28,000	44.7	1,080	1,000	28,500	313	18,300	Universal power plants
FORTRESS													
I	AN531	R-1820-73	49,360	535		20,000	17.4			34,000	286	20,000	Tare weight 2,760 lb more than Mk 1
II	FK187	R-1820-65	48,700			20,000	21.8						
LINCOLN													
I	PW925	Merlin 85	75,000			26,000	57.5	800	9,800	27,800	300	16,400	Max speed 3,000/+18 psi; climb 2,850/+12 psi

TABLE 2: MEDIUM & LIGHT BOMBERS

Mark	Serial	Engine	TAKE-OFF Weight (lb)	Run (yd)	To 50 ft (yd)	To Ht (ft)	CLIMB (min)	Max rate (ft/min)	at Height (ft)	Service Ceiling (ft)	Max Speed (mph) [true]	at Height (ft)	Remarks
BLENHEIM													
I	L1348	Mercury VIII	12,180	299	684	20,000	15.0	1,740	13,000	26,000	274	13,000	Rotol (standard) propellers. (2,750 rpm +5 psi); A/c cleaned up – speed 294
IV	L4835	Mercury XV	15,000	365	710	20,000	22.1	1,415	7,800	22,500	255	2,000	100 Octane fuel – boost +9 for take-off +5 for climb
V	DJ702	Mercury XV	16,300			10,000	12.8	785	10,100	17,800	243	5,900	Without air cleaner; cleaner lowered speed and ceiling
BOSTON													
I	AE458	R-1830-SC3-G	15,000	420	675	28,000	29.0	1,820	12,000	30,500	307	10,000	No armament fitted; range 880 miles endurance 4.9 hours
III	W8269	R-2600-A5B	21,550	585							312	13,000	318 gal fuel range 825 miles (max); with possible 438 gal – range 1,175 (max)
III (Int)	W8290	R-2600-A5B	21,813								291	13,400	Intruder 427 gal fuel
IIIA	BZ201	R-2600-23	20,500								329	11,500	Max with RP 288 mph at 9,800 ft; speed with air cleaners removed
MOSQUITO													
I	W4050	Merlin XXI	16,770					2,880	11,400	33,900	388	22,000	PR version; climb 2850/+12 max speed 3,000 +18
XVI	DZ540	Merlin 73	22,300			24,000	15.0	1,960	14,000	36,000	401	25,200	Trials curtailed by engines cutting at 23,750 ft
II	W4052	Merlin XXI	18,395								376	21,800	Extended wings, pressure cabin
XV	MP469	Merlin 61	17,465			43,000	32.7	2,940	14,000	43,000	408	27,800	616 gal fuel incl 2 x 50 gal underwing
30	MM748	Merlin 73	22,650								364	29,500	Speed with 3,000/+12; with 2 x 1,000 lb bomb
IV	DG290/G	Merlin 21	20,000								364	11,700	No external stores. Max speed 3,000/+18.2 x 500 lb reduced top speed 17 mph
IX	LR495	Merlin 72	21,910			26,700	15.5	2,060	14,000	37,000	405	25,700	Climb 2,850/+12, max speed 3,000/+18. Bomber version
XVI	ML937	Merlin 72/3	23,330			20,000	13.1	1,460	12,500	33,250	386	23,500	Max speed 3,000/+15
20	KB328	Merlin 31	21,430					1,780		29,700	364	12,500	Max speed 3,000/+18
VI	HJ679	Merlin 25	21,985			25,000	21.0	1,560	1,000	30,400	363	11,900	Intruder version: Mk IV W4057 at 18,980 lb took run of 445 yd/760 yd
VI	HJ662/G	Merlin 21	20,834	520	860								
MARYLAND													
I	AR703	R-1830-SC3G	17,890	395	605	15,000	12.7	1,260	10,000	24,600	282	8,800	Anson-type turret – Bristol BI Mk VI
			17,890	350	520	15,000	12.1	1,310	10,000	27,250	294	9,000	American turret – probably early Merlin 250-type
BALTIMORE													
III	AG837	R-1820-A585	21,340			20,000	19.6	1,560	4,700	23,500	301	10,400	Performance on other marks not measured
VENTURA													
I	AE748	R-2800-S1A4G	26,700			20,000	22.8	1,130	9,000	24,800	289	16,000	
V	FN957	R-2800-2SBG	31,000	960	1,645	10,000	13.0	830	7,000	17,200	286	3,000	Overload for maritime duties
MITCHELL													
II	FL671	R-2600-13	26,000			20,000	16.8	1,640	6,000	26,700	294	5,500	Speed 294 at 14,800 with full supercharging
MARAUDER													
	FKIII	R-2800-5	30,500			10,000	7.2	1,170	8,000	21,200			Climb only measured
BUCKINGHAM													
I	KV324	Centaurus VIII	38,900			16,000	14.6	1,570	5,000	21,600	337	14,400	Large tail unit with small elevators, with Bristol Type 12 turret

TABLE 3: SINGLE SEAT FIGHTERS

Mark	Serial	Engine	Weight (lb)	TAKE-OFF Run (yd)	To 50 ft (yd)	To Ht (ft)	CLIMB (min)	Max rate (ft/min)	at Height (ft)	Service Ceiling (ft)	Max Speed (mph true)	at Height (ft)	Remarks
HURRICANE													
I	L1750	Merlin II	6,169			20,000	11.0	2,200	10,200	30,500	302	16,800	Climb 2,530 rpm/+6.2 psi (two Hispano 20 mm guns)
I	L2026	Merlin III	6,750	280	465	20,000	9.8	2,380	11,600	32,500	310.5	17,200	Rotol constant speed propeller
I	P3157	Merlin 45	6,685	260	415	20,000	7.1	2,940	14,400	36,000	324	19,400	Trial installation of engine
IIB	Z3564	Merlin XX	7,397	235	440	20,000	8.5	2,710	8,300	35,900	330	20,800	All guns sealed
			8,050			20,000	10.4	2,160	10,600	33,400	310	19,800	With external tanks
IIC	Z3888	Merlin XX	8,275			20,000	10.8	2,060	10,500	34,400	306	20,250	With external tanks; range 980 miles maximum
IID	Z2326	Merlin XX	7,590			20,000	7.9	2,800	9,350	34,300	316	18,900	2 x 40 mm + 2 x 0.303 in guns
V	KZ193	Merlin 27	7,750			20,000	7.5	3,880	1,900	33,000	305	9,400	Four bladed propeller. Four mph slower with three blades. 2 x 40 mm guns
SPITFIRE													
I	N3171	Merlin III	6,050	225	370	20,000	7.7	2,905	11,000	34,700	354	18,900	Climb 3,000 rpm/+12.5 psi. K9793 with lower boost took 11.3 min to 20,000 ft
II	P8036	Merlin XII	6,513			20,000	9.8	2,240	12,800	33,900	328	16,500	Metal ailerons – one wing tank
V	K9788	Merlin 45	6,070			20,000	6.2	3,460	14,400	38,000	369	19,600	Oil froze in prop control
VA	X4922	Merlin 45	6,450	330	530	20,000	7.1	3,140	14,400	37,000	375	20,800	8 x 0.303 in guns
VB	W3134	Merlin 45	6,525			20,000	6.4	3,250	15,200	37,500	371	20,100	Fully equipped
VA	X4922	Merlin 46	7,420			20,000	10.1	2,050	16,000	35,000	355.5	21,600	With 90 gal drop tank and tropical intake
VC	AB320	Merlin 45	7,485	413		20,000	10.0	2,145	14,000	34,500	337.5	17,400	With 90 gal drop tank and tropical intake
VC	AA873	Merlin 45	6,917			20,000	7.4	2,900	13,400	36,400	374	19,000	Universal wing: 4 x 20 mm guns
VB	W3228	Merlin 50 (spec)	6,450			20,000	5.6	4,720	3,850	35,700	350	5,900	Low altitude engine
VI	AB200	Merlin 47	6,740			20,000	7.8	2,630	17,100	39,200	356	21,800	39,000 ft took 33.5 min
VI	N3297	Merlin 61	7,225			20,000	8.4	3,190	MSL	42,800 (absolute ceiling)	414	27,200	For Mk VIII; top speed 40,000 = 354 mph
VII	AB450	Merlin 61	8,000			20,000	8.2	2,880	MSL	39,600	390	16,200	Maximum speed in MS gear
HFVII	MD176	Merlin 112	7,990			20,000	5.4	4,060	MSL	45,100	424	29,400	Speed at 3,000 rpm/+18.5 psi
IX	BF274	Merlin 61	7,775			20,000	7.0	3,020	13,000	42,400	389	27,400	Speed at 3,000 rpm/+15 psi (combat rating; 30 gal drop tank)
IX	BS354	Merlin RM9SM	7,485			20,000	5.3	4,280	4,800	40,500	398	21,000	Low altitude engine
IX	BS543	Merlin 66	7,485			20,000	4.7	4,700	7,000	40,900	407	22,000	Low altitude engine ⎫ for
IX	BS551	Merlin 70	7,470			20,000	4.8	4,530	11,900	41,000	415.5	27,800	High altitude engine ⎭ comparison
LF IX	MA648	Merlin 66	7,000								411	21,000	Fuel injection by SU
XI	JL165	Merlin 66	7,400			20,000	4.5	5,080	500		389	13,800	Engine boost +25 psi 150 Octaine fuel
XI	MB789	Merlin 63	8,040								417	24,200	2,950 rpm/+18 psi
XII	DP845	Griffon IIB	7,415			20,000	6.7	3,760	2,600	39,000	397	17,800	Flown 3 Sep to 14 Oct 42
XII	DP845	Griffon VI	7,320			20,000	5.1	4,960	1,900	37,300	389	12,800	Without bomb
XIII	L1004	Merlin 32	6,355			20,000	5.8	4,920	3,000	37,000	349	5,400	3 cameras; low altitude version
XIV	JF319	Griffon RG5SM	8,400			20,000	5.1	5,040	2,100	44,000	446	25,900	Climb in MS gear; speed in FS gear 5-bladed propeller
21	PP319	Griffon 61	9,125								457	25,800	"Victor" model
21	LA187	Griffon 61	9,305			20,000	5.1	4,440	4,900	43,400	446	22,600	With 2nd engine
WHIRLWIND													
I	L6844	Peregrine I	10,071	375	710	20,000	8.2	2,715	12,200	30,300	354	15,800	With full fuel – 136 gal
I	P6997	Peregrine I	11,409			20,000	12.2	1,900	12,200	27,500	318	15,000	Two 500 lb bombs
MOHAWK													
I	AR645	R-1820-G205A	6,317	295	485	15,000	6.2	2,600	8,000	33,800	302	14,000	Ex French – contract – Model 75C
II	AR631	R 1830-SC3G	5,962	290	465	15,000	7.3	2,260	9,600	31,200	300	10,000	Ex Norwegian – 84 gal fuel
GLOSTER F.9/37													
	L7999	Taurus S(a) III	11,653			20,000	9.4	2,465	12,400	30,000	332	15,200	Gills half open; full open reduced climb by 540 ft/min

TYPHOON

Mark	Serial	Engine	Weight			Alt	Time	Climb	Alt	Ceiling	Speed	Alt	Notes
I	P5212	Sabre I	10,620	525	845	20,000	4.7	2,730	15,200	32,300	410	20,600	12 x 0.303 in guns taped over; trials at Langley
IB	R7700	Sabre I	11,070			15,000	6.2	2,790	6,300	32,200	394	20,200	4 x 20 mm guns; cruise speed 18 mph slower with 2 x 500 lb bombs
IB	R8762	Sabre IIA	11,090			15,000	4.9	3,840	1,700	34,500	390	17,200	Speed at 3,700 rpm/+9 psi ie increased limits

TOMAHAWK

| II | AK176 | V-1710-C.15 | 7,300 | 215 | 440 | 20,000 | 10.8 | 1,960 | up to 13,500 | 31,400 | 331 | 15,500 | Fully modified to British standards but no flame damper or air cleaner |

KITTYHAWK

I	AK572	V-1710-F.3.R	8,480			20,000	14.2	1,640	11,400	27,600	322	14,200	Climb trials only; Feb/Mar 1942
I	AL229	V-1710-F.3.R	8,840	385		20,000	15.0	1,530	12,000	34,300	354	20,400	With drop tank; speed 332 (without tank)
I	FL220	V-1650-1	8,910	465	785	20,000	10.9	2,020	10,200				Packard-built Merlin engine

BUFFALO

| I | AS430 | R-1820 G105A | 6,430 | 215 | 440 | 20,000 | 10.5 | 2,240 | up to 8,200 | 31,800 | 294 | 18,700 | 26° flap for take-off |

AIRACOBRA

| I | AH574 | V-1710-E.12 | 7,835 | | | 20,000 | 12.4 | 1,845 | 12,500 | 29,000 | 365 | 15,600 | Modified supercharger ratio |
| I | AH701 | V-1710-E.4 | 7,845 | | | 20,000 | 11.7 | 2,040 | 10,300 | 29,000 | 355 | 13,000 | AH573 also before crash |

TORNADO

| I | P5224 | Vulture V | 10,690 | | | 20,000 | 7.2 | 3,500 | 3,200 | 34,900 | 398 | 23,300 | Max boost obtained + 8 psi – + 9 psi designed |

MUSTANG

I	AG351	V-1710-39	8,622	335	640	20,000	11.7	1,980	11,300	30,000	370	15,000	Oil cored therefore blanking plates used
X	AM208	Merlin 65	9,100			20,000	6.3	3,560	7,500	38,500	433	22,000	Rolls Royce modified: 4-blade propeller; combat rating for performance
III	FR893	V-1710-81	8,200			20,000	6.9	3,800	6,000	34,000	409	10,000	Wing guns (4 x 0.5 in) taped over
III	FX953	V-1650-3	9,200			20,000	6.1	3,610	10,600	42,800	450	28,000	Maximum speed at reduced rpm (2,800) due compressibility
III	FX858	Merlin 100	9,260			20,000	5.2	4,500	1,600	39,800	455	17,800	Maximum rpm throughout; 130 octane fuel

TEMPEST

V	HM595	Sabre II	11,225			20,000	6.4	3,960	3,600	34,800	420	19,000	Initial results; climb and speed at combat – 3,900/+ 9 psi
V	JN731	Sabre IIA	11,480			20,000	6.5	4,380	MSL	38,200	432	18,400	Speed and climb at combat – 3,700/+9 psi
	LA602	Centaurus V	11,360			20,000	5.7	4,400	5,000		440	13,700	Engine max 2,700/+ 8 psi

WELKIN

| I | DG558 | Merlin 77 | 18,320 | | | 20,000 | 5.6 | 3,840 | 11,100 | 43,600 | 383 | 26,000 | DeHavilland propellers; Rotol gave 8 mph lower speed |

THUNDERBOLT (P-47D-1)

| | 27922 | R-2800-21 | 12,700 | | | 20,000 | 13.0 | 1,650 | MSL | 36,100 | 406 | 27,000 | Speed at 2,700/52.5 in Hg; climb 2,550/42.5 in |

METEOR

| I | EE212 | W2B-23C | 11,350 | | | | | 3,000 | MSL | | 434 | 12,000 | 2 seats; 300 gal fuel; Mk III (W2B/37) 465 at 16,000 ft |

VAMPIRE

| I | TG274 | Goblin I | 8,180 | | | | | | | | 526 | 25,500 | Critical Mach 0.76 |

TABLE 4: MULTI-SEAT FIGHTERS

Mark	Serial	Engine	Weight (lb)	Run (yd)	To 50 ft (yd)	To Ht (ft)	CLIMB (min)	Max rate (ft/min)	at Height (ft)	Service Ceiling (ft)	Max Speed (mph) [true]	Height (ft)	Remarks
DEFIANT													
I	K8620	Merlin III		315	560	20,000	15.1	1,610	10,000	28,100	312	10,000	Max speed 3,000/+12; 2 pitch propeller
I	L6954	Merlin III	7,562	340	520	20,000	11.9	1,500	15,000	30,000	303	16,500	104 gal fuel max speed 3,000/+6.5; constant speed propeller plus 8 x 25 lb bombs
II	N1551	Merlin XX	7,675	340	585	20,000	8.3	2,200	15,000	32,800	313	19,400	Without radar: 3,000 +9 for take-off, range 104 gal = 450 miles
II	AA370	Merlin XX	8,510			20,000	10.8	2,070	10,000	32,600	293	19,800	162 gal fuel 11ft 9 in propeller; with radar aerials
HAVOC													
II	AH450	GR-2600-A5B	17,500			20,000	10.2	2,520	5,800	31,200	311	11,800	Engine cooling holes uncovered; loaded to represent 12 x 0.303 in guns
BEAUFIGHTER													
I	R2054	Hercules III	19,550			20,000	13.4	1,885	4,000	27,900	309	15,600	Original windscreen, retracted tail wheel
I	T4623	Hercules X	19,190			20,000	13.5				335	15,800	'Shadow' built by Fairey
II	R2270	Merlin XX	15,750								298	19,000	With top filters and A1 Mk IV – but without aerials
											335	21,000	No flame damping, undercarriage doors removed
VI	X7542	Hercules VI	19,750			25,000	19	2,325	4,600	28,000	333	15,600	Without air filter;, Vokes filter cost 16 mph 2,900 rpm +8
VI	EL223	Hercules VI	24,300	440	760						312	8,200	Maximum fuel (679 gal) and torpedo; dihedral tailplane
X	EL290	Hercules XVII	24,000	440	760	20,000	27.9	1,460	2,600	24,000	308	9,200	With Mk XII torpedo, Hercules XVII 9 mph faster at low level

TABLE 5: MARITIME ROLES

Mark	Serial	Engine	Weight (lb)	Run (yd)	To 50 ft (yd)	To Ht (ft)	(min)	Max rate at Height (ft/min)	(ft)	Service Ceiling (ft)	Max Speed (mph) [true]	& Height (ft)	Remarks
HUDSON													
I	N7205	GR-1820-G120A	17,500	350	660	20,000	20.2	1,585	4,400	24,250	238	7,900	Dummy turret; N7206 with turret 15 mph slower
V	AM526	R-1830-S3C4G	18,500	415	775	20,000	18.3	1,070	14,000	28,000	258	14,000	Two-speed blower
BEAUFORT													
I	L4456	Taurus II	17,705	255	530	10,000	7.2	1,550	5,000	19,700	272	6,600	390 gal fuel; torpedo reduced speed by 9 mph; 3,300/+4.1 for speed
I	W6503	Taurus VI	21,000	425	830	10,000	15.5	800	5,000	13,600	247	7,880	538 gal fuel and 2,500 lb bombs
II	N1110	R-1830-S3C4G	21,000	440	790						261	14,400	Max speed 2,650/+5.4; engines overheated in climb
BOTHA													
I	L6105	Perseus X	16,850	380	720	10,000	10.8	985	13,100	26,100*	252	13,300	Take-offs by L6188 with 2,000 lb load and 301 gal
I	L6212	Perseus XA	16,600			10,000	10.5	1,030	5,000	18,400	235	6,250	
LIBERATOR													
I	AM912	R-1830-61(S3C4G)	56,000	760	1,065						262	5,000	Max speed at 45,000 lb; take-off with 2,500 gal and 6 depth charges
III	LV337	R-1830-43	56,000	895	1,295	20,000	63	430	MSL		269	20,000	Without ASV gear. Overload for take-off; speed and climb at 58,000 lb. No flame dampers
V	BZ791	R-1830-43	62,000	1,350	2,320						231	22,000	
VI	EW126	R-1830-65	65,000	1,550	2,630								Location of trial not known
SEA OTTER													
I	JM739	Mercury 30	9,150	253	532	10,000	15	870	2,000	16,200	150	5,000	Production aircraft; 144 mph max at overload 10,130 lb for take-off
I	JM739	Mercury 27	9,420	227	443	10,000	12.5	1,170	MSL	16,500	158	500	Boost increased from +4 psi (Merc 30) to +9.5 psi (Merc 27)
WARWICK													
I	BV255	R-2800-S1A-4G	44,630	870	1,210	10,000	14.1	720 up to 8,000			262	4,800	No turrets; medium supercharger used. G-AGFJ
ASRI	BV403	R-2800-S1A-4G	45,000	830	1,185			680			217	3,600	Mk II lifeboat; Mk I lifeboat = 2 mph faster
CIII	HG215	R-2800-2SBG	43,000			10,000	13.5	815	6,400		219	11,000	Increased weight to 45,000 ft increased time to 10,000 ft by 1.6 min
V	PN697	Centaurus VII	50,000			15,000	29.1	1,000	2,500	16,000			Climb at reduced power to cool engines

* Absolute ceiling

TABLE 6: TRANSPORTS, TUGS, CO-OPERATIVES

Mark Serial	Engine	Weight (lb)	TAKE-OFF Run (yd)	To 50 ft (yd)	To Ht (ft)	CLIMB (min)	Max rate (ft/min)	at Height (ft)	Service Ceiling (ft)	Max Speed (mph)[true]	at Height (ft)	Remarks
BOMBAY												
I L5809	Pegasus XXII	21,500	300	515	15,000	18.5	1,110	4,400	21,000	183	6,800	410 gal fuel plus 2,136 lb bombs, some trials pre war
LYSANDER												
III P1728	Mercury XX	6,645	200	360	15,000	29.1	1,515	2,000	21,400	212	5,000	2,550 rpm for take-off 95 gal fuel
III T1771	Mercury XX	7,850	285	470						200	3,000	With 150 gal external tank
FLYING WING												
OA.1 G-AFMB	Perseus XIVC	18,000	405	650			905	4,500	20,200*	218	6,700	14 passenger seats
PROCTOR												
I L6109	Gipsy Queen II	3,285	410	690	10,000	21.1	690	1,000	14,000	162	1,000	40 gal fuel – pilot plus 2 passengers
IV LA586	Gipsy Queen II	3,276			10,000	24.8	636	MSL	12,000	136	2,000	Pilot plus 3 passengers; aircraft known as "T.9/41"
VIGILANT												
I HL430	R-680-9	3,281	"Very short"		10,000	15.4	870	MSL	19,000	123	MSL	Army Co-operation role
AUSTER												
II MZ105	0-290-3	1,504	112	291	6,000	9.5	730	MSL		114	MSL	24 mph (indicated) at take-off
III LB319	Gipsy Major III	1,500	119	267	6,000	6.5	1,040	MSL		126	MSL	65 rpm overspeed at 126 mph
MARTINET												
I LR244	Mercury 30	6,555	275	500	10,000	8.9	1,420	3,400		240	5,800	Take-off on HN862; Type E winch; with ice guard
YORK												
I LV626	Merlin XX	60,000	780	1,230	10,000	11	860	10,400	21,100	280	13,000	Top speed measured at 13,000 ft maximum expected in service
II LV626	Hercules XVI	65,000	715	1,050	10,000	13.2	860	5,500				Maximum weak mixture cruise – 241 mph at 11,200 ft
MILES M38/28												
U-0223	Gipsy Major IIA	2,110	110	320	10,000	21.5	820	MSL	12,200	115	MSL	Triple fins and rudders – assessed for Army Co-operation

* Absolute ceiling

TABLE 7: TRAINERS

Mark Serial	Engine	Weight (lb)	TAKE-OFF Run (yd)	To 50 ft (yd)	CLIMB To Ht (ft)	(min)	Max rate at Height (ft/min)	(ft)	Service Ceiling (ft)	Max Speed & Height at which achieved (mph) [true]	(ft)	Remarks
MILES M-18												
U-0224	Gipsy Major	1,943	260	495	10,000	19.7	870	MSL	12,500	130	MSL	Strengthened second prototype, dives to 210 mph (in'ctd)
U-0224	Cirrus Major	1,944	240	420	10,000	22	780	MSL	12,500	130	MSL	Compare engines
HESTON T1/37												
L7709	Gipsy Queen I	3,250	285	450	10,000	23.9	690	MSL	12,800	159	MSL	Pre-war propeller replaced by 2 pitch
MILES T1/37												
P6326	Gipsy Queen I	2,555	236	451			785	MSL		138	MSL	New propeller since pre-war
ANSON												
I LT298	Cheetah IX	9,850	500	790	15,000	36.7	580	4,600	16,000	170	6,300	Bristol turret; Oxford-type intakes
XIX NL171	Cheetah XV	10,600					750	2,800		177	4,200	Cold air intake Max cruise speed 149 mph at 6,600 ft
ANSON												
I LT298	Cheetah IX	9,850	500	790	15,000	36.7	580	4,600	16,000	170	6,300	Bristol turret; Oxford-type intakes
XIX NL171	Cheetah XV	10,600					750	2,800		177	4,200	Cold air intake Max cruise speed 149 mph at 6,600 ft
OXFORD												
III P1864	Cheetah XV	8,100	206	428	10,000	9.1	1,270	4,000	21,700	197	4,600	DeHavilland constant speed propellers
III P1864	Cheetah XV	8,120	325	540	10,000	9.4	1,300	2,900	21,700	202	4,400	Seafox-type cropped propellers
MASTER												
I N7410	Kestrel XXX	5,380	240	475	10,000	8.8	1,140	11,000	26,800	226	14,400	70 gal Rotol variable pitch propellers
II N7447	Mercury XX	5,575	215	385	10,000	6.1	1,845	3,600	24,300	243	6,500	Damaged forced landing; some performance in AZ104
II AZ104	Mercury XX	5,570	190	350	10,000	5.6	2,120	2,000	25,100	244	5,800	Take-off on T8886 – Rotol propeller; performance with deHavilland propeller
III N7994	R-1535-SB4G	5,480	210	420	10,000	6.7	1,520	10,400	27,300	231	9,200	67 gal self sealing fuel tanks, engine near temp limits

TABLE 8: CARRIER FIGHTERS AND RECONNAISSANCE

Mark	Serial	Engine	Weight (lb)	TAKE-OFF Run (yd)	To 50 ft (yd) into 20 kt headwind	CLIMB To Ht (ft)	(min)	Max rate at Height (ft/min)	(ft)	Service Ceiling (ft)	Max Speed & Height at which achieved (mph) [true]	(ft)	Remarks
ROC													
I	L3059	Perseus XII	7,819	260		15,000	25.6	840	5,700	18,200	224	7,500	Standard propeller; 50° flap take-off
I	L3057	Perseus XII	7,820	365		15,000	20.5	1,000	6,000	20,100	221	7,800	Skua-type propeller
I	L3058	Perseus XII	7,815	295		15,000	19.4	1,090	5,800	19,000	227	7,300	Whitley (Tiger) type propeller
FULMAR													
I	N1854	Merlin III	9,800	320	170	20,000	26.6	1,200	7,000	22,400	255	2,400	N1855 and N1858 also used
II	N4021	Merlin 30	9,980	300		20,000	20.3	1,440	7,200	24,200	264	9,600	Tropical cowling gave 7 mph lower top speed
MARTLET/WILDCAT													
II	AM991	R-1820-S3C4-G	7,790	320	165	20,000	12.5	1,940	7,600	31,000	293	13,800	Same maximum speed at 5,400 ft in medium supercharger
IV	FN111	R-1830-86	7,350	(390	265)	20,000	14.6	1,580	6,200	30,100	298	14,600	Take-off in FN202 – 8,100 lb with 6 rockets
VI	JV642	R-1820-56	6,750								322	16,800	Without external tanks
MILES M-20													
	DR616	Merlin XX	7,566	270	450	20,000	9.5	2,300	9,400	32,800	333	20,400	Fixed undercarriage; take-off with 30° flap
FIREFLY													
I	Z1826/8	Griffon II	11,830	(235	125)	20,000	12.4	2,140	3,800	30,100	315	16,800	Three aircraft used Z1826, Z1828, Z1888
III	Z1835	Griffon 71	12,153								347	18,300	4 blade propeller; 3 blade gave 334 mph
SEAFIRE													
IIC	MA970	Merlin 46	7,145	(265	130)	20,000	8.5	2,380	16,000	37,500	342	20,700	Clean; with 30 gal tank top speed 332 mph; take-offs by MB293
IIC	MB138	Merlin 32	6,995	190	160	20,000	6.4	4,680	2,700	34,600	339	5,100	18° flap used for take-off
III	MA970	Merlin 46	7,026	229	125								1st production by Westland
III	LR765	Merlin 50	7,100			20,000	8.1	2,600	14,200	35,600	351	10,500	Curved windscreen and tear-drop hood; level speeds only
XV	NS493	Griffon VI	7,955									395	12,800	
XV	SR448	Griffon VI	7,845	(240	129)			4,340	2,000	35,800	378	13,000	Take-off in SR446 using reduced boost (+12 psi)
KINGFISHER													
I	FN656	R-985-AN2	5,435	310	105	10,000	29.2	440	4,800	11,600	163	3,900	With 2 x 250 lb depth charges; without charges – maximum 171 mph
HELLCAT													
I	FN322	R-2800-10	12,130	300	155	20,000	10	2,260	5,400		(375)	23,600)	Speed in FN360
CORSAIR													
II	JT259	R-2800-9	11,865	185	95			2,470	2,000	33,200	382	22,600	Propeller reduced by 2 in diameter; only speed measured
IV	KD227	R-2800-8W	12,080									400	18,400	

TABLE 9: CARRIER BOMBER/TORPEDO DROPPER

Mark Serial	Engine	TAKE-OFF				CLIMB			Service Ceiling (ft)	Max Speed & Height at which achieved (mph) [true]		Remarks
		Weight (lb)	Run (yd)	To 50 ft (yd)	To Ht (ft)	(min)	Max rate (ft/min)	at Height (ft)		(mph)[true]	(ft)	
CHESAPEAKE												
I AL913	R-1535-SB4G	9,150	600		10,000	10	500	10,000	16,000	222	9,900	One 500 lb bomb on centre rack
SWORDFISH												
III V4689	Pegasus 30	9,250	440	205			400±	3,500		(128	3,800)	Speed in LS295 at 8,660 lb
ALBACORE												
I L7079	Taurus II	11,570	380		10,000	24.4	555	4,600	12,300	160	4,800	Maximum speed 12 mph higher without 4 depth charges
BARRACUDA												
I P1767	Merlin 30	12,820	420	200	15,000	19.5	925	8,400	19,100	250	10,900	At 13,800 lb take-off 335 yd into 20 kn headwind; full flap for take-off
II P9647	Merlin 32	14,250	425	225	10,000	13.6	(840	5,200	15,000)			Take-off 8° flap; climb by P9816 with 6 x 250 lb bombs (same weight)
V P9976	Griffon VII	15,000	340	185								With 2,000 lb mine and 2 x 250 lb depth charges; take-off trials only
V PM940	Griffon VIII	14,690								243	10,300	Speed trials only
FIREBRAND												
I DD804	Sabre III	13,715	315	170	20,000	10.3	2,435	4,300	33,800	353	17,700	30° flap take-off; maximum speed 4,000/+9; performance at 13,175 lb for take-off
III DK373	Centaurus VII	13,860								313	11,000	Speed only measured
BERMUDA												
I FF524	R-2600-A5B5	13,745	420							270	9,700	Take-off and speed only
AVENGER												
I FN767	R-2800-8	15,965	335	180	13,200	13.7	1,140	5,000	23,600	252	4,200	10° flap take-off; top speed in medium supercharger, full gave slower

Appendix 1

Senior staff

Commanding Officers

1939	Group Captain B. McEntegart CB CBE
23 Feb 40	Group Captain/Air Commodore R.S. Sorley OBE DSC DFC
30 May 41	Air Commodore R.B. Mansell OBE
25 Feb 43	Air CommodoreD.D.A.Greig DFC AFC
5 Jul 44	Air Commodore J.N.Boothman CB DFC AFC
23 Jun 45	Air Commodore H.P. Fraser CBE AFC

Senior Technical Officer
(from 1 Oct 1944: Chief Superintendent)
Mr E.T. Jones

Superintendent of Performance
(from 1 Oct 1944)
Oct 44   Mr Scott Hall

Officer Commanding Performance Testing Squadron
(from 1 Oct 1944: Officer Commanding Flying)

1939	Squadron Leader/Wing Commander J.F.X. McKenna AFC
21 Jul 40	Wing Commander J.A. Gray DFC
8 Nov 40	Wing Commander J.A.P. Harrison
30 Jan 41	Wing Commander A.H. Wheeler
25 Feb 42	Wing Commander J.W. McGuire AFC
18 May 42	Wing Commander/Group Captain H.A. Purvis
26 Apr 45	Group Captain S. Wroath AFC

Senior Armament Technical Officer
(from 1 Oct 1944: Superintendent of Armament)

1939	Wing Commander C.N.H. Bilney
10 Dec 40	Wing Commander E.S.D. Drury
28 May 41	Wing Commander/Group Captain A.E. Dark
4 Feb 44	Group Captain J.G. Franks
27 Jan 45	Group Captain E.S.D. Drury AFC

Chief Engineer
(from 1 Oct 1944: Superintendent of Engineering)

1939	Mr F. Rowarth
24 Mar 42	Mr L.E. Caygill
30 Nov 44	Mr B.D. Clark

Appendix 2

Roll of honour

Killed while flying A&AEE aircraft 1939-1945

22 Oct 40	Mr E.L. Oxley Photographer Mr J.W. Parsons Photographer Hampden P4354		Pilot Squadron Leader J.D. Harris Crew	23 Oct 42	Wing Commander H.R. Allen Pilot Hurricane Z4993/G
16 Nov 40	Pilot Officer E. Stansbury Pilot Blenheim L4893		Flight Lieutenant N.G. Wilson Crew Flying Officer P.F. Wakelin	23 Dec 42	Flight Lieutenant G.L. Campbell Pilot Spitfire BS139
21 Feb 41	Flying Officer L.G.H. Kells Pilot Hurricane Z2398		Crew Sergeant K.J. Jones Crew Lancaster R5539	4 Feb 43	Flight Lieutenant S.F. Reiss Pilot Sergeant J. Fielding
1 Mar 41	Squadron leader J.E. Dutton Pilot Mohawk BK877	6 May 42	Aircraftman F.E. Bartlett Crew Master T8852		Crew Mr J.J. Unwin Crew Halifax W7917
3 Jul 41	Flight Lieutenant S.A. Ellaby Pilot Spitfire P8273	12 Jul 42	Squadron Leader C.L.F. Colmore Pilot Pilot Officer K. Radford Crew	10 Sep 43	Flight Lieutenant F.J. Robinson Pilot Flight Sergeant J.W. Bamber
3 Nov 41	Flying Officer F.N. Heapey Pilot Leading Aircraftman V.Hinks Crew Blenheim V5797		Sergeant A.J. Smith Crew Sergeant R.P. Gillott Crew Mr C.V. Abbott Crew		Crew Mr R. Stevenson Crew Lancaster JA894
11 Feb 42	Wing Commander S. Jenkins Pilot Airacobra AH573	26 Aug 42	Wellington W5795 Squadron Leader W.J. Carr Pilot Corporal R. Leigh	29 Jan 44	Squadron Leader E.M. Metcalfe Pilot Mosquito LR495
28 Feb 42	Pilot Officer T.W. Caston Pilot Pilot Officer J.C. Fisher Pilot Flight Sergeant D.L. Mullins Crew Albemarle P1368		Crew Corporal F.W. Shenton Crew Mr E.R. Staniland Crew Warwick BV214	1 Mar 44	Wing Commander P.F. Webster Pilot Firefly Z1839
24 Mar 42	Wing Commmander J.W. McGuire Pilot Liberator AL546	24 Sep 42	Squadron Leader V.M. Bright Pilot Leading Aircraftman R.F. Brown Crew Beaufighter EL329/G	24 Mar 44	Flying Officer D. Grundy Pilot Typhoon JR448
18 Apr 42	Wing Commander P.S. Salter			26 Mar 44	Squadron Leader H.N. Fowler Pilot Typhoon JR307
				8 Aug 44	Mr M.E. Ainsbury Crew Monitor NF900

9 Aug 44	Flight Lieutenant H.J. Camps Pilot Flying Officr T.G. Thomas Crew Mosquito KB209
24 Aug 44	Squadron Leader J.F. Pettigrew Pilot Hurricane HW187
19 Jan 45	Group Captain J.F.X. McKenna Pilot Mustang KH648
12 Apr 45	Flight Lieutenant J.R.Smith Pilot Mr G. Douglas Crew Mosquito NS586
25 Jul 45	Squadron Leader L. Gregory Pilot Tempest NV946
31 Aug 45	Sub-Lieutenant K.W.A. Fehler Pilot Lieutenant Habgood Crew Monitor NP409

Appendix 3

A&AEE flying organisation 1939-1945

SQUADRON/FLIGHT	SHORT TITLE	FORMATION DATE	REORGANISATION SEPT 1944	REMARKS
Performance Testing Squadron				
A Flight	A Per T	Pre-war	No. 1 Flight A Sqn	Sept 1944 naval aircraft to C Sqdn
B Flight	B Per T	Pre-war	No. 1 Flight B Sqn	As above
C Flight	C Per T	Pre-war	C Squadron	
D Flight	D Per T	Formed March 42	D Squadron	Jan 45 split into No 1 and No 2 Flights
Armament Testing Squadron				
A Flight	Gunnery Flight	Pre-war. June 40, part to Exeter, part to B Flt. Jan 42 re-formed	No 2 Flight A Sqdn	Sept 1944 naval aircraft to C Sqdn
B Flight	Bombing Flight	Pre-war	No 2 Flight B Sqdn	Sept 1944 naval aircraft to C Sqdn
C Flight	Special Duty Flight	Pre-war. Jan 40– May 41 into Arm Sqdn	SD Flt of Comms & SD Sqdn	
High Altitude Flight	HAF	30 Dec 41	Absorbed into A Sqdn	Incorporated Wellington Flight, June 41 (no aircraft)
Intensive Flying Development Unit	IFDF	Dec 41	IFDF	
Gun Proofing Flight	GPF	Sept 42	Absorbed into No 2 Flt, A Sqdn	

A&AEE war establishment also included:

BATDU/WIDU/109 Squadron   Sept 39-Jan 42

ETPS   Jun 43-end 45

Lodger and attached units:

58 Squadron	Sept 39-Feb 40	Handling Flight CFS	Nov 40-Aug 42
56 Squadron	Sept 40-Nov 40	Bomber Development Unit Nov 40-May 41	
249 Squadron	Aug 40-Sept 40		

Appendix 4

A&AEE flying hours 1939-1945

Flying hours for C Flight Performance Testing only shown in brackets [ ]

	1939	1940		1941	1942		1943	1944	1945
JAN	–	[62]		[74]	[74]	561	866	798	481
FEB	–	[25]		[123]	[89]	1002	1142	1031	731
MAR	–	[102]		[130]	[124]	894	1233	1489	1221
APR	–	[97]		[124]	[111]	1454	1182	1270	1072
MAY	–	[112]		[117]	[108]	1042	1436	1391	809
JUN	–			[171]	[203]	1440	1013	1222	946
JUL	–			[159]	[117]	1352	1584	1415	932
AUG	–	[121]		[196]	[128]	1357	1624	1632	864
SEP	[42]	[71]	288	[136]	[161]	1235	1626	997	669
OCT	[65]	[105]	279	[170]		1048	1198	1051	–
NOV	[55]	[100]	359	[101]		880	857	742	–
DEC	[58]	[101]		[72]		894	784	579	–

Appendix 5
Production aircraft tests

NO	DATE/S OF FLIGHTS	A/C TYPE	A/C NO	MANUFACTURER	RAF STATION	REMARKS
1	26 Jan & 2 Feb 43	Lancaster III	ED453	Avro Woodford	Scampton	Normal
2	11 & 18 Feb 43	Lancaster I	ED574	Avro Woodford	Scampton	Normal
3	31 May & 17 Jun 43	Lancaster III	W5008	Metro Vick	Scampton	Normal
4	4 Feb 43	Halifax II	DT744	English Electric	Linton-on-Ouse	Normal
5	21 Mar 43	Halifax II	JB857	English Electric	Linton-on-Ouse	Low performance
6	15 May 43	Halifax II	JD145	English Electric	Linton-on-Ouse	Stbd wing heavy at 320mph
7	4 Mar 43	Halifax II	BB324	London Group	Linton-on-Ouse	Normal
8	18 Mar 43	Halifax II	HR748	Handley Page	Linton-on-Ouse	Normal
9	28 Feb 43	Halifax V	DK128	Fairey	Linton-on-Ouse	Normal
10	11 May 43	Halifax II	EB138	Rootes Security	Linton-on-Ouse	Normal
11	11 Jun 43	Halifax II	HR874	Handley Page	Linton-on-Ouse	Low cruise performance
12	15 Apr & 17 Jun 43	Stirling I	EF386	Shorts Swindon	Oakington	Low performance: A&AEE mods– OK
13	24 Jun 43	Lancaster III	JA684	Avro Woodford	Scampton	Normal
14	3 Apr 43	Stirling III	BK761	Austin Birmingham	Oakington	Normal (hot SI engine)
15	Apr 43	Stirling III	EH945(sic)	Austin Birmingham	Stradishall	Normal
16	4 Apr 43	Stirling III	BF501	Shorts Belfast	Oakington	Normal
17	19 Jul 43	Stirling III	EE945	Shorts Belfast	Stradishall	Normal
18	16 May 43	Stirling III	EF401/G	Shorts Rochester	Oakington	Normal
19	2 Jul 43	Lancaster III	JA914	Avro Woodford	Scampton	Normal
20	22 Mar 43	Lancaster III	ED726	Avro Woodford	Scampton	Normal
21	2 Sep 43	Lancaster III	JB178	Avro Woodford	Scampton	Normal
22	25 Jul 43	Halifax V	LK892	Rootes	Pocklington	Normal
23	25 Jul 43	Halifax II	JN891	London Group	Pocklington	Normal
24	27 Aug 43	Halifax II	JD471	English Electric	Pocklington	Normal
25	17 May 43	Lancaster II	DS659	Armstrong Whitely	E Wreatham	Normal
26	23 Sep 43	Lancaster I	DV297	Metro Vick Woodford	Syerston	Normal
27	13 & 18 Sep 43	Lancaster II	DS777	Armstrong Whitworth	Little Snoring	Normal
28	15 Sep 43	Halifax II	HX180	Handley Page	Pocklington	Normal
29	16 Apr 43	Lancaster III	ED361	Avro Woodford	Scampton	Normal
30	2 Oct 43	Stirling III	EF182	Shorts Belfast	Stradishall	Normal
31	3 Oct 43	Lancaster III	JB373	Avro Woodford	Syerston	Normal
32	19 Oct 43	Halifax II	LW341	English Electric	Pocklington	Normal
33	18 May 43	Lancaster III	ED989	Avro Woodford	Scampton	Normal
34	19 Apr 43	Lancaster III	LM322	Avro Yeadon	Scampton	Normal
35	24 Jul – 9 Sep 43	Halifax V	DK256	Fairey Stockport	Pocklington	Very low performance; to A&AEE
36	3 Nov 43	Lancaster III	JB565	Avro Woodford	Scampton	Normal
37	24 Nov 43	Halifax V	LL127	Rootes Speke	Pocklington	Normal
38	25 Nov 43	Halifax V	LK729	Fairey Stockport	Pocklington	Low performance due shrouds
39	26 Nov 43	Halifax II	JP128	London Group	Pocklington	Below average performance
40	2 Dec 43	Lancaster I	LL740	Armstrong Whitworth	Waddington	Normal
41	12 Dec 43	Lancaster I	HK535	Vickers Castle Brown	Waddington	Normal
42	4 Dec 43	Lancaster III	JB710	Avro Woodford	Waddington	Low performance due H2S
43	16 Dec 43	Stirling III	LJ483	Shorts Belfast	Stradishall	Normal
44	10 Jan 44	Lancaster III	LM436	Avro Yeadon	Waddington	Cruise: 2 div stbd rudder
45	17 Dec 43	Stirling III	LK450	Austin Birmingham	Stradishall	Normal
46	2 Jan 44	Lancaster III	ND405	Avro Yeadon	Waddington	Normal
47	4 & 9 Jan 44	Halifax III	HX339	Handley Page Radlett	Pocklington	Normal
48	28 Dec 43	Lancaster I	ME563	Metro Vick Woodford	Waddington	Poor climb
49	7 Jan 44	Halifax III	LW498	English Electric	Pocklington	Normal

NO	DATE/S OF FLIGHTS	A/C TYPE	A/C NO	MANUFACTURER	RAF STATION	REMARKS
50	30 Dec 43	Stirling III	EF299	Shorts Belfast	Stradishall	Low cruise ceiling
51	5 Feb 44	Lancaster III	ND537	Avro Woodford	Waddington	Normal
52	3 Feb 44	Halifax V	LL253	Rootes Speke	Pocklington	Normal
53	6 Feb 44	Lancaster II	LL729	Armstrong Whitworth	Waterbeach	Heavy controls
54		Lancaster – compare production from Avro at Yeadon with Woodford				
55	29 Feb 44	Halifax III	LW650	English Electric	Leconfield	Normal
56	2 Mar 44	Halifax III	LV907	Handley Page	Leconfield	Normal
57	3 Mar 44	Lancaster III	ND656	Avro Woodford	Binbrook	Normal
58	Jul – Dec 43	Halifax II	JD304*	English Electric	Pocklington	Speeds low; to A&AEE
59	27 & 28 Mar 44	Halifax II	JP288	London Group	Pocklington	Good performance: close exhausts
60	25 Mar 44	Lancaster I	ME698	Metro Vick Woodford	Binbrook	Normal
61	6 Apr 44	Halifax III	MZ541	English Electric	Leconfield	Normal
62	22 Mar 44	Lancaster III	ND792	Avro Woodford	Waddington	Normal
63	8 Apr & 14 May 44	Lancaster I	LL905	Armstrong Whitworth	Binbrook	Normal

*On 7 Jul 43, Halifax JD304, ASI leaked causing limiting speed to be exceeded; wing doors fell off, windscreen cracked and rear turret loose.

Appendix6

Rogue aircraft known to have been tested by A&AEE

DATE	AIRCRAFT	SERIAL NO	SQUADRON	ALLEGED DEFECT	A&AEE COMMENTS/ACTION
May 44	Albemarle I	P1367	297 Brize Norton	Very nose heavy	Within tolerance
Sep 43	Barracuda II	P9806	847 Macrihanish	Cannot reach high speed	Agree; to go to Fairey's
Sep 43	Barracuda II	P9835	847 Macrihanish	Asymmetric fuel flow	Agree; but acceptable
Jul 45	Barracuda II	BV726	767 Easthaven	Handling	Loose articles in aircraft?
Jul 44	Harvard III	FT958	ECFS	High rate spin	Agree; but little faster than Mk II
Jun 44	Hudson IIIA	FK747	269 Azores	Aileron snatch on T/O	Agree; not dangerous
Aug 44	Hudson IIIA	FK803	161 Tempsford	Aileron snatch	Agree; to Boscombe: bad patches
Apr 45	Lancaster I	PB731	227 Balderton	Bad handling	Not rogue; CG near aft limit
Aug 43	Lancaster II	DS670	115 Little Snoring	Shakes	Normal
Mar 44	Mosquito XVI	ML932	Marham	Vibrations	Agree; but slight only
Jul 43	Oxford I	DF448	1515 BAT Pershore	Nose heavy	Not rogue
Dec 43	Seafire IIC	LR367	899 Ballyherbert	High speed stall	Very poor condition
Aug 45	Seafire LIII	NN263 +2	St Merryn	Contamination	None found
Dec 40	Spitfire II	P7525	66	Handling; max 320	Bad rigging
Jul 43	Spitfire LFVB	BL712	602 Kingsworth	Flicks out of turns	Seal camera gun port
Dec 43	Spitfire LFVB	BM257	118 Castleton	Very left wing down	Match ailerons then OK
Feb 44	Spitfire LFV	AA973	3037 Echelon Hawkinge	Excess aileron up float	Aileron hinge points
Aug 43	Spitfire VII	BR302	616 Ibsley	Shudder in turns	Agree; sealing gap needed
Aug 43	Spitfire IX	BS317	222 Hornchurch	Crabs	Ailerons needed freeing
Aug 43	Spitfire XII	EN624	91 Tangmere	Very heavy ailerons	Agree; to A&AEE
Oct 44	Spitfire 21	RM709	Kirton-in-Lindsey	Handling	Ailerons transposed; OK
Mar 42	Stirling I	N6040		Low performance	Due extra drag but still poor
Nov 42	Stirling I	BK597 +2	149 Lakenheath	Bad climb	Austin-built; agree; 597 to A&AEE
Jan 43	Stirling I	BF380 +2	Bourn	Low performance	Shorts-built; BF382 re-rigged
Feb 44	Stirling I	BF394	(3 Group)	Bad asymmetric	Power down one engine
Apr 44	Typhoon IB	TR210 +3	Redhill	Excessive vibration	Agree; all 4 to RAE/Hawkers
Apr 45	Traveller I	FT520	Lee-on-Solent	CO in cabin	Fumes not CO
Sep 43	Wellington XII	HF116/G	407 Chivenor	Poor handling	OK; but at limit of tolerance
Jul 41	Whirlwind I	P7057		Unintentional spin	Slats sealed; OK

Appendix 7

Tempest V, JN798 and EJ891

Results of Bomb loading trials
September 1944 to March 1945 (excludes rockets)

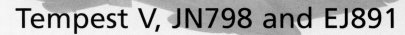

Index	Store	Tail	No	Time (min)	Loading Crew	Ground Clearance	Flap Clearance	Remarks
1	1000 lb MC	No 37	2	15	3	24	10	Medium Capacity
2	1000 lb AN-M65	No 65	2	15	3	26	11	
3	1000 lb AN-M59	USA	2	15	3	33	25	
4	500 lb AN-M64	No 54 USA	2	15	3	26	20	
5	500 lb MC Mk IV	No 77	2	15	3	27	5	
6	65 lb Nickel	None	2	10	3	34	23	Leaflets
7	500 lb AN-M76	No 54 USA	2	15	3	26	20	
8	500 lb GP	No 77	2	15	3	27	5	General Purpose
9	500 lb SAP	No 11	2	15	3	25	11	Semi-Armour Piercing
10	250 lb GP or MC	No 2 Mk II	2	15	3	31	15	Crutches bear on tail unit positioning stud
11	500 lb MC Mk III	No 25 Mk III	2	15	3	27	6	
12	1000 lb LC	Experimental	2	15	3	24	9	Filler cap under fusing box rear
13	M10 Tank	None	2	20	3	15	10	Smoke curtain installation
14	Cluster No 24	No 66	2	15	3	23	6	
15	Cluster No 7	No 46	2	15	3	22	8	
16	Cluster No 17	No 63	2	15	3	21	12	
17	250 lb T1	No 75	2	15	3	31	19	Target indicator
18	1000 lb T1	Experimental	2	15	3	23	12	Tail unsuitable for external stowage
19	200 lb Smoke Float No 2 Mk II	Fairings	2	15	3	28	12	Rear crutches almost fully contracted
20	120 lb Smoke	No 41	2	10	3	35	29	
21	Mine A Mk VIII	No 11Parachute	2	15	3	31	19	
22	500 lb Smoke Mk II	No 81 Mk I	2	15	3	28	11	
23	1000 lb Incendiary	None	2	10	3	23	5	Tanks loaded empty for filling on a/c

Appendix 8

Other wartime units at Boscombe Down

In addition to A&AEE, Boscombe Down was home during the war to various units on a long or short-term basis, whose functions were either unconnected with the work of the Establishment or related to, but separate from it. These units are noted here:

Royal Air Force Squadrons
Nos 88 and 218 Squadrons, with Fairey Battles, left on 11 and 2 September 1939 respectively.

No 58 Squadron with 16 Armstrong Whitworth Whitley IIIs, on loan to Coastal Command from Bomber Command patrolled the SW Approaches from Boscombe between 13 September 1939 and 14 February 1940, and operated frequently in appalling weather, including the period of severe frost in January 1940.

Frequently in print, this photograph of an ice-covered Whitley of No 58 Squadron illustrates the appalling conditions experienced in early 1940. The protective cover of the nose has slipped off, and the turret is glazed with ice.

No 249 Squadron, Hawker Hurricane I, were attached from 14 August to 1 September 1940 at the height of the Battle of Britain. Two days after arrival, a section of the Squadron engaged in a combat with German Bf 109s and Bf 110s; the leader, Flight Lieutenant N.B. Nicholson was later awarded the Victoria Cross for his gallantry that day the only VC awarded to Fighter Command.

No 56 Squadron, Hawker Hurricane I replaced No 249 until 29 November 1940, and flew under the control of the Middle Wallop Sector.

Bomber Development Unit

This unit formed on 20 November 1940 and disbanded on 1 May 1941. It used two Blenheims, three Wellingtons and two Hampdens under the control of No 6 Bomber Group to undertake trials from an operational point of view of bombing equipment to assist Bomber Command in evaluating bombing problems. The reasons for disbandment are unclear but may be concerned with duplication; for example, a major trial on a bombsight in a BDU aircraft was reported by A&AEE.

The Handling Flight (Squadron from June 1941) of the Central Flying School wrote Pilots' Notes at Boscombe from 8 November 1940; by July 1942, the number of aircraft held had reached 13, of 12 types. Pressure on space led to the Squadron's departure on 22 August 1942.

Blind Approach Training and Development Unit

This unit formed at Boscombe on 29 September 1939 to train pilots using Ansons for bad weather approaches using the newly introduced Lorenz equipment.

Unlike the units mentioned above, BATDU was part of the A&AEE in that the aircraft were serviced under Establishment arrangements; the function, however, was unconnected. Two week courses began in October 1939, and ceased in June 1940 when it was decided to use the Unit to investigate and later counter the German use of radio beams for bombing the UK. The Unit's title changed to the Wireless Intelligence Development Unit on 30 September 1940, by which time Whitleys had been added to the Ansons, and to No 109 Squadron on 10 December 1940 as the unsatisfactory Whitleys were replaced by Wellingtons. The Squadron grew in size, and increasingly operated from other airfields; on 19 January 1942 the Squadron split, and moved to Tempsford and Upper Heyford. One particularly bad crash of an Anson in September 1940 resulted in the award of the George Medal to Sergeant D.F. Allen for rescuing the crew.

Test Pilots' School

The School was established on 21 June 1943 in response to the situation described in the second chapter. It was part of A&AEE with its own staff, accommodation and aircraft; its role of training test pilots was, however, distinct from the rest of the Establishment. The School, shortly renamed the Empire Test Pilots' School, left for Cranfield after the war.

Index of Aircraft